DISCOVERING
the
OLD
TESTAMENT

Contributors

Robert D. Branson, Ph.D.
Professor of Biblical Literature
Chair of the Division of Religion
  and Philosophy
Olivet Nazarene University
Bourbonnais, Illinois

Jim Edlin, Ph.D.
Professor of Biblical Literature and
  Languages
Chair of the Division of Religion
  and Philosophy
MidAmerica Nazarene University
Olathe, Kansas

Tim M. Green, Ph.D.
Professor of Old Testament
Dean of the School of Religion
Trevecca Nazarene University
Nashville, Tennessee

Alex Varughese, Ph.D.
Professor of Religion
Chair of the Division of Religion
  and Philosophy
Mount Vernon Nazarene University
Mount Vernon, Ohio

Advisory Committee for
Discovering the Old Testament

Rev. Kendall Franklin
Pastor
Hutchinson First Church of the
  Nazarene
Hutchinson, Kansas

Ray Hendrix
Director of World Mission
  Literature
Church of the Nazarene
Kansas City, Missouri

Tom King, Ph.D. (Alternate)
Chairman of Biblical/Theological
  Studies
Nazarene Bible College
Colorado Springs, Colorado

Rev. David Roland
District Superintendent
Northeastern Indiana District
Church of the Nazarene
Marion, Indiana

John Wright, Ph.D.
Associate Professor of Theology
Point Loma Nazarene University
San Diego, California

DISCOVERING
the
OLD
TESTAMENT
*S*TORY AND *F*AITH

ALEX VARUGHESE, EDITOR
*R*OBERT *D. B*RANSON ❖ *J*IM *E*DLIN ❖ *T*IM *M. G*REEN

Copyright 2003
Beacon Hill Press of Kansas City

ISBN 978-0-8341-1994-9

Printed in the United States of
America

Cover Design: Paul Franitza
Cover Art: Frederic Edwin Church,
American (1826-1900). *Jerusalem
from the Mount of Olives,* 1870. Oil
on canvas, 54¼ x 84⅜ inches (137.79
x 214.30 cm). The Nelson-Atkins
Museum of Art, Kansas City, Mis-
souri. Gift of the Enid and Crosby
Kemper Foundation, F77-40/1.
Interior Design: Sharon Page

10 9 8 7 6 5 4 3

Picture Credits

Illustrations
Keith Alexander: 287
Gustave Doré: 235, 240, 251 (top), 283, 288, 312, 326, 329, 334
Gary Mowry: 65, 73
Sharon Page: 106

Photographs
Steven Allan: 21, 36, 61, 67, 119 (top), 127, 163, 173, 174, 209, 269, 276
Bill Aron: 98, 129, 271, 278
Díamar Interactive: 16, 18, 46, 92, 212, 234, 246, 268, 280, 282, 338
Digital Stock: 217
Sonia Halliday Photographs: 307, 367
HIP/Art Resource, NY: 207
Reed Holmes/Holmes Photography: 181 (top), 264, 309, 320
Illustrated Bible Life/Brad Elsberg: 1, 3 (l.), 11, 13, 17, 24, 25, 28, 35, 42, 47,
    52, 57, 60, 80 (top), 85, 86, 94, 95, 97, 101, 106, 107, 123, 126, 133,
    141 (top), 142, 148, 157, 160, 164, 165 (both), 167, 169, 171 (bot.),
    181 (bot.), 183, 257, 260, 266, 281, 285, 291, 300, 352, 360, 363,
    366, 372, 381, 396
Illustrated Bible Life/Richard Houseal: 3 (c. & r.), 9, 15, 20, 56 (bot.), 59, 102,
    111, 116, 119 (bot.), 130, 141 (bot.), 147, 151, 225, 236, 303, 305,
    317, 324, 349, 378
Illustrated Bible Life/Greg Schneider: 134, 135, 140, 213, 218, 237, 241, 327,
    351, 357
Index Stock Imagery/Photo by Stephen G. Maka: 346
Erich Lessing/Art Resource, NY: 204, 226, 265, 375
Susan Meiselas/Magnum Photos: 251 (bot.)
Nazarene Publishing House: 31, 132
Sharon Page: 335
PhotoDisc: 261
Z. Radovan, Jerusalem: 27, 34, 81, 82, 89, 112, 122, 149, 154, 171 (top),
    191 (both), 195 (both), 197, 232, 242, 286, 293, 294, 297, 370, 371
Alex Varughese: 19, 56 (top), 75, 80 (bot.), 84, 87, 93, 177, 180, 182, 186,
    187, 189, 192, 202, 203, 208, 222, 223, 227, 339, 345, 356
William Youngman: 247, 255

Library of Congress Cataloging-in-Publication Data

Branson, Robert, 1941-
    Discovering the Old Testament : story and faith / Robert Branson, Jim Edlin, Tim Green ; Alex Varughese,
editor.
        p. cm.
Includes bibliographical references and index.
    ISBN 0-8341-1994-3 (hardcover)
    1. Bible. O.T.—Textbooks. I. Edlin, Jim, 1950- II. Green, Timothy Mark, 1961- III. Title.

    BS1194 .B73 2003

    221.6'1—dc21

                                                                                    2002013256

Contents

UNIT III
DISCOVERING THE HISTORICAL BOOKS
133

Preface

The Old Testament plays an important role in the Christian faith and in Christian education. Virtually all Christians affirm the Old Testament to be inspired Scripture as part of the Word of God. Yet the Old Testament is a closed book for the majority of Christians. The stories of Noah, Abraham, Joseph, and David are taught in children's Sunday School, but rarely do Christian adults engage in serious study of the Old Testament. The ancient customs, the strange geography, and Israel's occasional violent deeds and words confuse many readers. The result is that while we claim the Old Testament to be the inspired Word of God, in practice we ignore it.

Clearly we need a better understanding of the Old Testament if it is truly to function as God's Word to us. This book, *Discovering the Old Testament: Story and Faith,* can help us understand the Old Testament better. It is designed as a clear, concise, easy-to-read, and pedagogically sound textbook for introductory Old Testament survey courses. However, this volume will also become an important resource for general readers and adult students of the Old Testament. The pictures, maps, and color-coded sidebars appeal to readers who are visually oriented. Younger readers accustomed to textbooks using the technology of modern visual aids will find themselves at home in this volume.

Many introductory Old Testament textbooks are on the market. A special feature of *Discovering the Old Testament* is the historical, cultural, archaeological, hermeneutical, and theological sidebars. These sidebars offer concise insights into the information that takes the reader into a deeper understanding of the Old Testament as the Word of God. Historical sidebars address the background of significant historical events and the development of significant concepts of the ancient world. Cultural sidebars illustrate the customs and religious practices of Israel and the other cultures of the ancient Near East. Archaeological sidebars provide windows into significant archaeological discoveries illuminating the biblical text. Hermeneutical sidebars provide guiding principles for interpreting the various kinds of Old Testament literature, such as narrative, law, wisdom, poetry, and prophecy. The theological sidebars address significant Old Testament theological issues.

Students and teachers will find helpful pedagogical aids. Each chapter features learning objectives, vocabulary lists, guiding questions, summary statements, questions for further reflection, applications, and key resources for further study. The four authors all teach freshman level Old Testament courses at Christian liberal arts colleges and universities. Each author is qualified as a specialist at the doctoral level in the area of his writing. I can attest that these authors' students come to seminary with a clear understanding of Scripture and a lively, informed faith.

Most Old Testament survey texts focus on introducing the content of the Old Testament books with little attention to the important theological issues. It is precisely those theological issues that lie at the heart of the Christian claim that the Old Testament is the inspired Word of God. While *Discovering the Old Testament* is not an Old Testament theology, every chapter demonstrates the conviction of the authors that God was at work in the people and events of the Old Testament. Wesleyan perspectives on sin, salvation, grace, faith, holiness, and the hope of the believer undergird each chapter and are summarized in the theological sidebars.

Both students and teachers will find *Discovering the Old Testament* inviting them into the message of the Old Testament. Clear and concise explanations, easy-to-read summaries, and attractive visual aids answer the questions and remove the misunderstandings that keep people from reading and enjoying the study of the Old Testament. It is my prayer that your love for Scripture and your relationship with God will deepen through your study in this book.

—Roger L. Hahn
General Textbook Editor
Beacon Hill Press of Kansas City

Editor's Note to the Student

Welcome to a journey that will lead you to discover the Old Testament in new and refreshing ways. As a reader and student of the Old Testament scriptures, you will find this journey a challenging as well as an exciting adventure. The purpose of this book is to provide you with a clear and strategically designed road map that will make this journey an incredible learning experience.

In this journey you will come across various major crossroads in the story and faith development of the Old Testament people of God—Israel. The various chapters in this book are designed to help you understand the significance of these historical events and religious traditions that shaped the course of Israel's history. Each chapter is carefully laid out not only with descriptions of these events and religious ideas but also with "markers and signposts" that will help you to navigate through the chapter without much difficulty. We invite you to take some time at the outset to get acquainted with these "markers and signposts" before you embark on your adventure of discovering the Old Testament.

Objectives

At the beginning of each chapter, you will find a list of objectives. These objectives explain what you should be able to do as a result of your study of each chapter. As you read and study each chapter, we suggest you keep these objectives in mind. Underline or highlight the sections in the chapter where you find descriptions of topics that would help you accomplish the objectives.

Key Words to Understand

Each chapter contains explanations or definitions of terms and identifications of key people and places. These terms are placed at the beginning of each chapter and identified in boldface type where they appear in the chapter text. Your understanding of these terms and ability to identify or describe them are essential to your successful journey through the Old Testament.

Questions to Consider as You Read

At the beginning of each chapter, you will also find two or three questions. These questions are aimed at setting the stage for your reading and study of the subject matter in the chapter. Before you start reading, write down your answers to these questions. This exercise will help you to think ahead and be prepared for the historical and theological issues to be presented.

Summary Statements

It is natural for every reader of a book or a chapter in a book to ask the question, "What's the main point?" We have provided you with some significant statements at the end of each chapter that summarize the main points in the chapter. Use these summary statements to review what you have learned and return to the sections you may have overlooked.

Questions for Reflection

Each chapter also ends with some questions. These questions will help you to think further about the issues, events, and religious ideas you have learned. The goal of these questions is not only to guide you to process what you have learned but also to challenge you to apply the lessons in your own life situation.

Resources for Further Study

We do not presume that this textbook will answer all the questions you have about the Old Testament. Though much work has gone into the production of this book, we also acknowledge the providence of God's grace through other scholars who contribute to our understanding of His Word. Each chapter ends with a list of three or four Bible commentaries or resources that we hope would help you in your continued study of the Old Testament.

Sidebars

Throughout each chapter we have included color-coded sidebars with brief but useful information on topics related to biblical interpretation, theology, history, ancient Near Eastern culture, and archaeology. The symbols and color coding of these sidebars are given below.

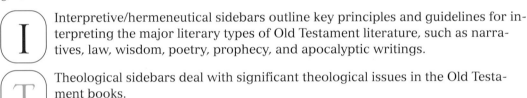

I — Interpretive/hermeneutical sidebars outline key principles and guidelines for interpreting the major literary types of Old Testament literature, such as narratives, law, wisdom, poetry, prophecy, and apocalyptic writings.

T — Theological sidebars deal with significant theological issues in the Old Testament books.

H — Historical sidebars give insight into the development of religious concepts, ideas, or other historically relevant matters related to particular topics.

C — Cultural sidebars illustrate cultural customs and religious ideas of Israel and the ancient Near East.

A — Archaeological sidebars explain significant archaeological discoveries that shed light on selected biblical texts.

Visual Aids

We have provided in this book pictures, maps, and illustrations that will be of help to you as you study this book. It is our hope that a "picture is worth a thousand words!" We also encourage you to study the maps and attempt to bridge the geographical distance between you and the actual location of the biblical events.

Finally, our prayer is that you will find these "markers and signposts" immensely useful as you begin your adventure of discovering the Old Testament.

Editor's Note
to the Instructor

The primary purpose of this volume is to present a clear, concise, easy-to-read, and pedagogically sound textbook for introductory level Old Testament survey courses that are an important part of the general education curriculum at Christian colleges and universities. Each chapter of the book addresses pedagogical concerns that are crucial to the mastery of the content as well as its evaluation and application. The pedagogical method includes learning objectives, vocabulary lists, questions for the students to get them oriented to the materials in each chapter, surveys of the contents of the Old Testament books, summary statements, questions for further reflection, evaluation and application of lessons learned, and three or four key resources for further reading and study.

We have also included in each chapter numerous sidebars that address a variety of topics and issues. These color-coded sidebars—categorized as interpretive, theological, historical, cultural, and archaeological—are placed at strategic places throughout the chapter. Interpretive sidebars provide the reader with proper hermeneutical guidelines for interpreting the Old Testament materials. Theological sidebars focus on in-depth analysis of key theological issues and their relevance and application to the Christian reader of the Old Testament. Historical, cultural, and archaeological sidebars give supplemental information that will help the reader to place the Old Testament in its proper context. It is our hope that you would find these sidebars as a valuable resource for your students' deeper understanding of God's Word.

The contributors of this book bring with them unique perspectives and specialized training in different parts of the Old Testament. Chapter assignments were made on the basis of each writer's specialized area of interest and study at the doctoral level. Each chapter thus reflects the writer's scholarly interest, academic preparation, and teaching expertise. The book contains materials and methods of instruction we have tested and tried in our Old Testament survey classes. Our long years of experience in teaching Old Testament courses have guided us in making decisions about the structure, format, and content of this book. We present this book as a scholarly work, yet written at the level of college freshmen, in an easy to understand language. We have attempted to deal with critical issues with profound clarity without short-changing scholarship with a superficial treatment of the subject matter.

Finally, we have dealt with the Old Testament as Christian Scriptures, keeping in mind the profound truth that the Church inherited this part of God's enduring Word from Israel's story and faith. So wherever it is appropriate, the writers have sought to make points of contact between the story and faith of Israel and that of the Church. Unity of the Bible, the continuity between the two testaments, and God's redemptive plan for all humanity that He accomplished through the death and resurrection of Jesus Christ are primary convictions of the writers of this volume. New Testament passages are often used in this volume to explain, clarify, and interpret the Old Testament message in light of the central message of the New Testament.

May you find this book an important tool in your hands as you teach your students God's eternal and faithful Word and minister His grace to them in the classroom!

 # Acknowledgments

We wish to acknowledge a number of people who have contributed to this book either through their direct participation or through their enthusiastic support and encouragement. The writers worked together on a number of key issues related to the formatting and organization of the book. Alex Varughese wrote the introductory materials (chaps. 1—4) and the chapters on various books of the Pentateuch (5—11) and Israel's prophets (25—28, 30—31, and part of 32). Robert Branson wrote the chapters that cover Israel's wisdom and poetic literature (21—24). Jim Edlin wrote the chapters on the Exile and Restoration, and the books that belong to the postexilic period (18—20, 29, most of 32, and the Appendix). Tim Green wrote the chapters that deal with Israel's history from the Conquest of Canaan to the Babylonian Exile (12—17).

Roger Hahn, the Centennial Initiative editor for the Church of the Nazarene, and Bonnie Perry, managing editor of Beacon Hill Press of Kansas City, have given us their faithful support at various stages of the writing of this book. We are profoundly grateful for their help and constant encouragement. We also extend our special thanks to Judi King for her help in securing the photographs and Sharon Page for her skillful design and layout of this book.

No words are adequate to show our appreciation to our teachers (some of whom have entered into their eternal reward), who have helped us and directed us in the study of God's Word in our undergraduate, seminary, and graduate school years. We are also in debt to the countless number of students who have patiently sat through our introductory courses in the Old Testament, where we have tried out the content of this book. Our families and friends who have given us their loving support during the course of the writing of this book deserve special recognition. With profound gratitude, we dedicate this book to all who have taught us the eternal truth, "the fear of the Lord—that is wisdom" (Job 28:28).

Robert D. Branson
Jim Edlin
Tim M. Green
Alex Varughese, Editor

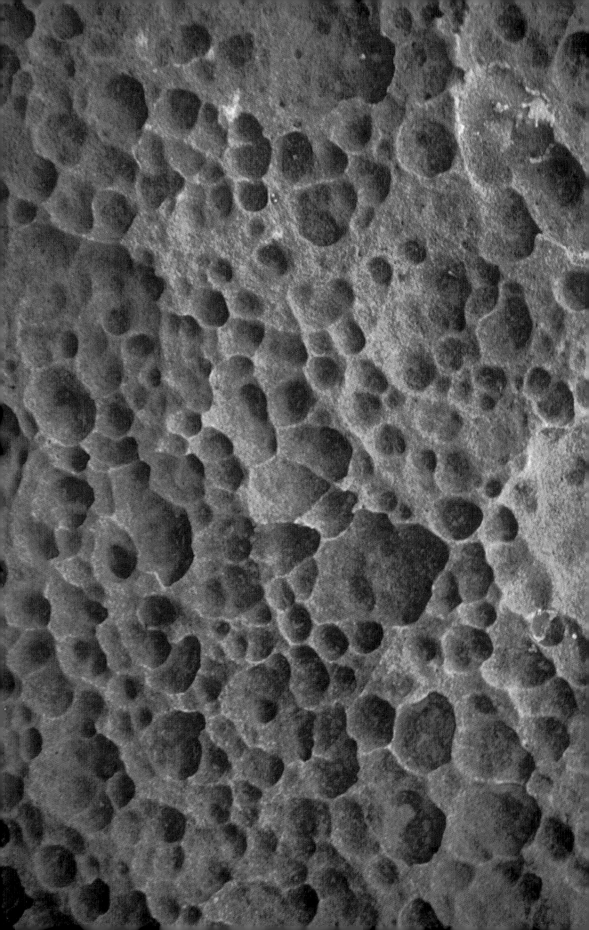

UNIT I

GETTING READY TO DISCOVER THE OLD TESTAMENT

This unit introduces the reader to:

- An overview of the Bible as the authentic record of God's revelation, and biblical history as theological interpretation of historical events
- The story of the making of the Old Testament as Scripture and the history of Bible translation
- Various principles and guidelines for interpreting the Old Testament
- The geographical and cultural setting of the Old Testament stories

■ Biblical History: An Introduction

■ The Old Testament as Scripture

■ Interpreting the Old Testament

■ The World of the Old Testament

1 Biblical History: An Introduction

 **bjectives:**

Your study of this chapter should help you to:
- Recognize the unique nature of biblical history and its distinction from secular history.
- Define biblical history.
- Define revelation and inspiration.
- Discuss the biblical view of the relationship between God and history.
- Relate your own story in the framework of the story of the Bible.

Questions to consider as you read:

1. Reflect on your personal life story and identify those times you consider as the "great moments" of your relationship with God.
2. What does it mean for you to say that your life is a journey with God?

 ey Words to Understand

Revelation
Special revelation
General revelation
Incarnation
Inspiration
Dictation theory of inspiration
Dynamical theory of inspiration
Canon
Authority
Theological history
Theology
Kairos
Salvation history

God reveals himself to us through His creation; a sunset over the sea of Galilee.

The story of the Bible is often called "the greatest story ever told." This is an appropriate way to characterize the Bible because it is the story of a relationship in which God reveals and expresses His love toward humanity. This story reveals to the reader who God is. It is the story of divine **revelation,** the account of God's self-disclosure to humanity through His words and actions. Thus, this story is more than a mere "story"; rather it is history, because historical events serve as the setting of divine revelation recorded in the Bible.

Historical events, beginning with God's creation of the universe and humanity, the rise of human civilization, and the emergence of world political powers, are all part of the story of the Bible. The focal point of the biblical story is the revelation of God in and through the person of Jesus of Nazareth. God took the flesh-and-blood form of a human being in the person of Jesus **(incarnation)** and thus He revealed himself totally and completely to the world. Historical events in the Old Testament constitute the setting of this ultimate reality of God's self-disclosure. History continues to serve as the arena of God's actions through Christ and His Holy Spirit. We need to consider this essential relationship between revelation and history as we embark upon a journey with the community of faith in the Old Testament.

Various biblical stories relate to us what God has done in the past, what God is doing in the present, and what God will do in the future. Biblical writers have not only collected and arranged historical materials but also interpreted events to show the meaning and purpose of God's activities in human history. Biblical history is thus **theological history,** some-

Revelation

T The Bible is the most reliable and authentic record of God's self-disclosure to humanity (revelation). Revelation comes not only through God's spoken words but also through His actions. The Bible, however, does not make a distinction between the two, because what God speaks is indeed the same as what He does. The term ***special revelation*** is often used to describe God's self-disclosure in history through His words and actions. The purpose of this revelation is to encounter humanity with God's love and His will for our lives, and to elicit our response to Him through faith and obedience. The ultimate expression of divine love is the coming of Jesus Christ into the world. Special revelation helps us understand God's plan of salvation. This view of revelation complements and supports the understanding that God also reveals himself to us through His creation, which is the world and everything we see around us. We may use the term ***general revelation*** to describe this revelation of God's majesty, power, and glory, which is visible to us in the beauty of the natural world.

thing quite distinct from secular history in content and orientation (**theology** properly is the "science" or the study of God and His attributes). It is distinct from secular history because it focuses on the activities of God and assumes a direct relationship between God and various historical events.

Biblical writers view events that happened in their faith history as divinely planned events to bring about the salvation of all humanity. In Christian thinking, God fulfilled the salvation plan through Christ, who came into our world "according to the definite plan and foreknowledge of God" (Acts 2:23, NRSV). The apostle Paul speaks of the Incarnation as God sending forth His Son "when the fullness of time had come" (Galatians 4:4, NRSV). This "fullness of time" (***kairos*** in Greek) is the time or the season set by God to fulfill His plans and purposes.[1] Scholars often describe biblical history as **salvation history** (*heilsgeschichte* in German) because of its emphasis on humanity's redemption from sin.

Biblical history has continuity

A *sofer* (Jewish scribe) prepares a scroll for use in the synagogue.

Inspiration

Divine **inspiration** in the source for the receiving and recording of revelation by the ancient biblical writers. Though we cannot adequately explain the method and process of inspiration, the Scriptures testify that God played an active part in the writing of the Bible (2 Timothy 3:16-17; 2 Peter 1:20-21). Some Christians view inspiration as God's dictation of His words to the writers of the Bible **(dictation theory of inspiration).** Another approach, that of Wesleyan Evangelical theologians, recognizes the active involvement of the Holy Spirit in the writing of the Scriptures **(dynamical theory of inspiration).**[2] The Holy Spirit prepared the biblical writers to receive and communicate revelation. These writers received special understanding of God's activities in history, which they interpreted through the eye of their faith traditions, and communicated through the activity of writing. Dynamical theory focuses on the actual involvement of God's Spirit in the life and work of the biblical writers. Since the Holy Spirit is the active Agent in communicating revelation through the Scriptures, we need to submit ourselves to the authority and guidance of the Spirit for our correct understanding of the Word of God.

and unity. This is evident in the stories of both the Old and New Testaments. The Old Testament, which is the focus of this book, is the story and faith traditions of the nation Israel. The following major events constitute the framework of the Old Testament story:

Creation and Humanity's Sin (Genesis 1—11)

The Bible as Canon

Revelation and inspiration give the Bible the distinctive place in the Christian Church as its **canon.** In a popular sense, the term *canon* refers to a collection of writings accepted by a religious body as authoritative and normative for faith and practice. The Bible as canon reflects the authority of the Scriptures in the Christian tradition. The Bible has **authority** because it is the record of God's self-disclosure. The Bible sets the standard (literally, the word *canon* in Greek means a rod, standard, or something straight) for faith and practice.

God's covenant with Abraham and his descendants (Genesis 12—50)

Israel's exodus from Egypt and the Sinai (Exodus 1—40)

Israel's wilderness journey and the conquest of Canaan (Books of Numbers, Deuteronomy, Joshua)

Israel under the leadership of charismatic leaders (Book of Judges and 1 Samuel 1—9)

The beginning of monarchy (1 Samuel 10—1 Kings 11)

The divided kingdoms of Israel (1 Kings 12—2 Kings 25)

The exile and restoration (Books of Ezra and Nehemiah)

The later story of Israel (the Jews), though not recorded in the Old Testament, is well known. After the Persians, the Greek rulers controlled Palestine for nearly 170 years. Following the Greek rule, the Jews established an independent Jewish kingdom that lasted for about 100 years. Jewish independence came to an end when Rome gained political control of Palestine. The story of the New Testament is set in this larger historical context of the story of Israel.

We know God primarily through the historical events recorded in the Bible. Since these historical events are part of our own faith traditions, biblical history in a real sense is our history. We cannot remain on the sidelines of biblical history as spectators, but we must enter into this "story" and thus experience a living and dynamic relationship with God. Our journey through this "story" would take us from the Garden of Eden to Jesus' death and resurrection. We will encounter in that journey the God who comes to us with words of judgment against our sinfulness. More importantly, we will find in that journey the God who comes to us through His Son Jesus Christ with the offer of His grace, forgiveness, salvation, and eternal life.

Summary Statements

- Revelation is God's self-disclosure to humanity.
- The Bible is a record of revelation, written by individuals inspired by the Holy Spirit.
- The Bible is the canon of the Christian church.
- God's self-disclosure through Jesus Christ is the focal point of biblical history.
- Biblical history is a theological interpretation of historical events.
- Historical events in the Bible show continuity and purpose.
- Biblical history challenges us to enter into a personal relationship with God.

Questions for Reflection

1. Read the following passages and discuss "what is God doing?" in these passages: Genesis 1:1—2:4; 15:7-21; 45:4-8; Jeremiah 29:1-14.
2. What is being said about God and His activities in Job 38:1—39:30; Isaiah 40:12-24; 41:1-4; 43:1-28?
3. Read Psalm 107. Give a list of the characteristics of God that you find in this psalm.
4. Biblical faith holds the conviction that our history is a history with God. If this is true, what are the implications of this belief to your personal life?

Resources for Further Study

Cullman, Oscar. *Christ and Time*. Trans. Floyd V. Filson. Philadelphia: Westminster Press, 1964. Read Part 1: "The Continuous Redemptive Line."

Dunning, H. Ray. *Grace, Faith, and Holiness*. Kansas City: Beacon Hill Press of Kansas City, 1988. Read Chapter 4: "Revelation: Its Meaning and Necessity."

2 The Old Testament as Scripture

O bjectives:

Your study of the chapter should help you to:
- List the various divisions and books of the Old Testament.
- Summarize the history of the formation of the Old Testament in the Hebrew language.
- Describe the various stages of the canonization of the Old Testament.
- Identify the major phases in the history of Bible translation.

Q uestions to consider as you read:

1. What are some of the popular teachings about the Word of God that have influenced your understanding of "how we got the Bible"?
2. Why is it necessary to have a proper understanding of the character and makeup of the Bible?
3. We often hear people say: "It says in *my* Bible . . ." What do people imply when they refer to the Bible in such a way?

K ey Words to Understand

Torah
Nebiim
Former Prophets
Latter Prophets
Kethubim (the Writings)
Oral tradition
Autographs
Scribes
Qumran
Dead Sea Scrolls
Codex
Masoretic Text
Biblia Hebraica
Canonization
Targums
Septuagint
Apocrypha
Deuterocanon
Jerome
Vulgate
Wycliffe
Tyndale
King James I
Formal equivalence
Dynamic equivalence

What is the Old Testament all about? Who wrote the Old Testament? When did the writing of the books of the Old Testament take place? How did the books of the Old Testament become part of the Bible? How did we get the English Bible? In this chapter we will deal with these important questions and discuss some of the basic facts about the Old Testament.

What Is the Old Testament All About?

The Old Testament (also known as the Hebrew Scriptures) is the Bible of Judaism and part of the Bible of Christianity. Except for a few passages in the Aramaic language (such as Ezra 4:8—6:18; 7:12-26; Daniel 2:4b—7:28), the books of the Old Testament were written in the Hebrew language. The Protestant edition of the Old Testament and the Jewish Bible are alike in that they both have the same 39 books. The Roman Catholic Old Testament has 7 additional books (a total of 46 books). In addition, the Books of Esther and Daniel in the Roman Catholic Old Testament have additions or supplements (see the sidebar on the Apocrypha later in this chapter).

The Jewish tradition divides the Hebrew Scriptures into three sections: Torah (the Law), Nebiim (the Prophets), and Kethubim (the Writings). The term *TaNaK* refers to this threefold division of the Hebrew Scriptures. The following classification of the Old Testament books is based on the Jewish tradition.

The books that belong to **Torah** or the Law (Genesis, Exodus, Leviticus, Numbers, and Deuteronomy) contain the earliest records of human history and the earliest history of Israel. The stories of Israel include the stories of the ancestors of that nation, their establishment as a people by God, the rules and regulations established by God for Israel's faith and life in the world, and the story of their journey into the land of Canaan. Except for Genesis 1—11, these books cover the history of Israel from about 1800 B.C. to 1240 B.C.

The section **Nebiim** (the Prophets) has two subdivisions. The first section, also known as the **Former Prophets** (Joshua, Judges, 1 and 2 Samuel, and 1 and 2 Kings), deals with the history of the people of Israel, from their entrance into the land of Canaan to the beginning of their captivity in Babylon (1240 B.C. to 587 B.C.). These books are known as the historical books in the Christian tradition. The second section, the **Latter Prophets,** contains the books of Israel's great prophets Isaiah, Jeremiah, and Ezekiel, and the Twelve (Hosea, Joel, Amos, Obadiah, Jonah, Micah, Nahum, Habakkuk, Zephaniah, Haggai, Zechariah, and Malachi).

The section **Kethubim (the Writings)** contains the following books: Psalms, Job, Proverbs, Ruth, Song of Songs, Ecclesiastes, Lamentations, Esther, Daniel, Ezra, Nehemiah, 1 Chronicles, and 2 Chronicles.

The Jewish, Protestant, and Roman Catholic editions of the Bible differ in the arrangement of the books of the Old Testament. In the Jewish tradition, the Latter Prophets are placed after the Former Prophets and the Writings are placed after the Book of Malachi. In the Protestant Bible the writings are scattered throughout the Former and Latter Prophets. The Roman Catholic arrangement of the books of the Old Testament

The Temple scroll from Qumran.

has no consistent pattern. For a more accepted order of arrangement in the Roman Catholic tradition, see the recent editions of the *Jerusalem Bible* or the *New American Bible*.

The Making of the Old Testament

It is difficult to establish the precise date for the shaping of the Old Testament in its present form. We think that it is the result of a long and complex process that included the writing and development of manuscripts and the acceptance of selected manuscripts as recognized Scriptures by Judaism. References in the Book of Exodus seem to indicate that writing was an activity during the days of Moses. Some biblical texts make reference to the "Book of the Law" (see Deuteronomy 31:24-26; 2 Kings 22:8-10) as the "scriptures" of ancient Israel. In addition, we also find references to ancient documents such as "the Book of the Wars of the LORD" (Numbers 21:14), "the Book of Jashar" (Joshua 10:13), and "the annals of the kings of Israel" (2 Chronicles 33:18). Jeremiah 36 gives us the story of Jeremiah dictating his words to Baruch, who wrote down the words of the prophet on a scroll. However, these few references do not adequately explain the complex process by which the books of the Old Testament came to have their present form.

We think that the stories in the Book of Genesis were part of Israel's faith traditions during the days of Moses (13th century B.C.). Beginning with the Book of Exodus, the biblical events focus on the life and ministry of Moses.

Qumran Cave IV, which contained a nearly complete copy of the Greek translation of the 12 minor prophets.

The stories of Exodus, Leviticus, Numbers, and Deuteronomy belong to the Mosaic period. Perhaps a substantial part of these stories remained as Israel's **oral tradition** (orally transmitted stories from one generation to another) for another 3 or more centuries before they were fixed in a written form. It is also possible that large portions of the Books of Joshua, Judges, 1 and 2 Samuel, and 1 and 2 Kings existed in the form of oral tradition for a considerable period of time. We assume that most of the Old Testament books received their final form between 800 B.C. and 400 B.C.

The locations where the writing of the books of the Old Testament took place are not clearly known

to us. Palestine and Babylon are the likely locations of the writing activity. We do not have the original manuscripts **(autographs)** of the Old Testament books. Later copies or manuscripts of the Old Testament books are the products of **scribes** who made careful and accurate copies of existing manuscripts. The wear and tear and the decay of the scrolls would have prompted the making of new copies of older manuscripts.

After the destruction of Jerusalem in 587 B.C., Jewish communities flourished in Babylon and Egypt, in addition to those who remained in Palestine. Many scholars believe that these communities in Palestine, Babylon, and Egypt continued the task of copying and preserving the biblical text. However, we do not have manuscripts that attest to this copying activity. One reason for this lack of ancient manuscripts is that when new copies were made, the Jewish rabbis carefully and with reverence disposed of the old and worn-out manuscripts.

The oldest Hebrew manuscripts we have today come from a period around 100 B.C. These manuscripts, found at **Qumran** in the northwest area of the Dead Sea, shed some light into our understanding of the history of the manuscripts of the Old Testament. The **Dead Sea Scrolls,** discovered between A.D. 1947 and 1956, include two copies of the Book of Isaiah (one in its complete form), a commentary on the Book of Habakkuk, a number of psalms, and fragments of all the books of the Old Testament, except Esther. In addition, the caves at Qumran also yielded a large number of nonbiblical materials.[1]

Qumran discoveries confirmed the scholarly opinion that a variety of manuscript traditions existed during pre-Christian times. Though not much is known about the history and growth of Old Testament manuscripts, we believe that around 100 B.C. Jewish authorities in Palestine began the process of examining the various manuscript traditions in order to establish the standard and official Scriptures of Judaism. This meant that a large number of manuscripts did not receive recognition as Scriptures. This process was completed by A.D. 100.[2]

Once they had established a standard and authoritative manuscript tradition, Judaism took special care in copying and preserving the manuscripts of the Old Testament books. The scribes followed specific rules, including the counting of words and letters in each line, when they made new copies of the Scriptures. Generations of scribes faithfully carried out the task of copying the manuscripts in the first four centuries of the Christian era. The text of the Hebrew Old Testament prior to the Christian era was made up of consonants only, without any word division. Introduction of word divisions was one of the significant contributions of the scribes during the early Christian period. The manuscripts were originally written on scrolls made of leather or papyrus. Beginning in the third century A.D., the **codex** form (book with pages) replaced the scroll form, though Jewish communities continued to read from the latter during worship.

By about A.D. 500, a family of Jewish scribes in Tiberius on the western shore of the Sea of Galilee became the leading copyists of the Old Testament manuscripts. This family of scribes contributed significantly to the present shape of the Hebrew Bible. They introduced a system of vowels to the consonantal text of the Old Testament. These scribes are known as the Masoretes because of their contribution of marginal notes and explanations of the biblical texts (the Masora). The work of the Masoretes was completed around A.D. 900. The manuscript tradition established by these scribes is known as the **Masoretic Text** (MT). Kittel's third edition of ***Biblia Hebraica*** (Hebrew Bible) is based on a copy of the Ben Asher manuscript, produced by the Masoretic scribes around A.D. 900.

Canonization of the Old Testament

At various stages in the history of the growth and transmission of the books of the Old Testament, Judaism took steps to recognize these books as authoritative and normative for faith and practice. The precise history of this process **(canonization)** is not known.[3]

Scholars believe that the books of the Law (Torah) were the authoritative Scriptures (canon) of Judaism by about 400 B.C. It is possible that these books became authoritative under the influence of Ezra, the priest who influenced the Jewish life in the fifth century B.C. Judaism accepted the Former and Latter Prophets as canon around 200 B.C. Some of the Kethubim (the Writings) were part of the sacred Scriptures of Judaism early in the first century A.D. The references to the Law and the Prophets and the Psalms in the New Testament (see for example Luke 24:44) indicate the nature of the Jewish canon in the first century A.D. Official acceptance of the Kethubim as canon took place during the Council of Jamnia around A.D. 95. During this council, the rabbis gave their official endorsement to all the 39 Old Testament books.

Translation of the Bible

By about the sixth century B.C., Aramaic, a language closely related to Hebrew, became the spoken language of the ancient Near East. For the benefit of the Aramaic-speaking Jews, synagogues began the custom of giving an extemporaneous rendering of the Hebrew Scriptures in the Aramaic language. This custom existed during the days of Ezra and Nehemiah in the middle of the fifth century B.C. (see Nehemiah 8:8) and continued through the first 400 years of the Christian era. The Jewish scribes began to put these oral paraphrases into writing before the time of Christ. These writings are known as **Targums** (which means

The Apocrypha

The Septuagint translators included in their work other religious writings that did not receive official recognition as inspired and authoritative Scriptures of Judaism. These writings are known to the Protestant tradition as the **Apocrypha,** which means books that are "hidden." The following 15 books make up the traditional list of the apocryphal books: 1 and 2 Esdras, the Prayer of Manasseh, Wisdom of Solomon, Ecclesiasticus, Judith, Tobit, Additions to Esther, Baruch, Epistle of Jeremiah, the Song of the Three Children, Susanna, Bel and the Dragon, and 1 and 2 Maccabees. The Septuagint in the first century A.D. contained all the apocryphal books, except 2 Esdras. Later these books became part of the Bible in the Latin language, and they received canonical status during the Middle Ages in the Roman Catholic Church. During the Protestant Reformation, the reformers questioned the authority of the apocryphal books. Martin Luther expressed the view that these books lacked inspiration, though they have value as historical or devotional writings. The Roman Catholic tradition continues to view these books as inspired and refers to them as **deutero-canon** (canon of a lesser authority). Protestant churches in general follow Luther's view. Bibles produced by ecumenical scholars include the Apocrypha in their work.

"translation"). The Targums attained their final written form in the fifth or sixth century A.D.

Translation of a portion of the Old Testament from Hebrew into Greek was the first actual event in the history of Bible translation. This was done in Alexandria, Egypt, for the benefit of the Greek-speaking Jews who lived in Egypt. According to a legendary writing *(Letter of Aristeas),* the work was done at the initiative of the Greek ruler Ptolemy Philadelphus (285-246 B.C.). Some scholars think that the initiative for this translation came not from the Greek ruler but rather from the Greek-speaking Jews in that city. By about 250 B.C., the translators produced the Torah in the Greek language. Within the next 200 years the entire Old Testament was available in Greek and was the Scriptures used by the Early Church. This translation is known as the **Septuagint** or LXX, which refers to the tradition that 70 or 72 Jewish elders translated it.

The Bible in the Latin language was the second major attempt in the history of Bible translation. Scholars believe that a version of the Bible in the Latin language existed as early as A.D. 180. In the fourth century A.D., Bishop **Jerome** began the task of translating the Bible into Latin, using existing Latin versions and the Septuagint. In A.D. 385 he moved to Bethlehem, where he spent the next 14 years translating the Hebrew Bible into Latin. During the sixth and seventh centuries, the church fathers gave priority to Jerome's work over other existing Latin versions. Though the word *vulgata* (meaning "common") was previously a term applied to the earlier Latin versions, eventually Jerome's translation came to be

Page from 1611 edition of the King James Version.

known as the **Vulgate.** Gradually, the Latin Vulgate became the official Bible of Western Europe during the Middle Ages.

John **Wycliffe** (1330-84) made the first systematic attempt to translate the Bible from the Latin into the English language. The goal of Wycliffe's work was to fight against the corruption in the Church by making the Bible available to the common people. His complete New Testament appeared in 1380. Two years later, he and his friends completed the whole Bible. After his death in 1384, his friends revised the first

I Modern Translations of the Bible

Two theories of translation guide the work of translators who aim to produce English translations of the Bible in our day. The first theory calls for a word-for-word (literal) translation that preserves as much as possible the original word order and sentence structure. This **formal equivalence** method, though it is the more desirable way for the average reader to get closer to the original texts of the Bible, is often difficult to accomplish. Since thought forms and sentence structure vary from language to language, it is very difficult to maintain a strict adherence to this theory. Even the most faithful literal translations to a certain extent must modify sentence structure and arrive at meanings of words that seem most appropriate to the context. The *New American Standard Bible* (NASB) is the closest example of a literal translation. The second method calls for **dynamic equivalence** or thought-for-thought translation, which requires the use of modern idioms and thought forms to convey the message most authentically and accurately to the modern readers. The *New International Version* (NIV), the *New Revised Standard Version* (NRSV), and the *New King James Version* (NKJV) represent translations that utilize elements of both word-for-word and thought-for-thought methods of translation.

edition. The church authorities condemned Wycliffe's writings and ordered his bones to be dug out of his grave and burned.

William **Tyndale** (1494—1536) was the first scholar to translate a portion of the Bible into English from the original languages. Fearing reprisals from the Church authorities, Tyndale moved to Germany in 1524 and published the first edition of the New Testament in 1526. This was the first printed edition of the English Bible. The Church authorities condemned his work, charged him with heresy, and in 1536 he was condemned to death.

Since the work of Tyndale, the following translations appeared in English in the 16th century:

Miles Coverdale, an associate of Tyndale, published the first complete Bible in English in 1535. John Rogers, under the pen name Thomas Matthew, published Matthew's Bible in 1537. Sir Thomas Cromwell, secretary to King Henry VIII, commissioned the production of the Great Bible in 1539, which was the first authorized English version. The Geneva Bible, produced in 1560, was the first English Bible to use numbered verses. In 1568, the Bishops' Bible appeared as a revision of the Great Bible.

In 1604 **King James I** commissioned a translation of the whole Bible into English, which would stay as close as it could to the original languages, to be used in all churches of England during worship. About 54 scholars worked in six groups. The translation work was started in 1607 and was completed in 1611. The New Testament portion of this new version was mostly an adaptation of Tyndale's work. The King James Version remained as the most popular Bible in English for nearly two and a half centuries since its original publication.

Now, we add this word about the trustworthiness of English translations. The best translations are those that work directly with the original texts in Hebrew and Greek with the aid of all the resources available to modern biblical scholarship. Translation should be guided by a commitment to preserve the integrity of the biblical text by maintaining the historical, theological, cultural, and literary character of the original text. Translation should include footnote explanations to the reader on matters such as variant readings, possible meanings of difficult readings in the original texts, and reference to ancient versions such as the Septuagint and the Vulgate. Contemporary idioms and thought forms should be used only to bring clarity to the ancient thought forms and ideas. Translators should avoid free renderings, paraphrases, and expansions. If these translation guidelines are followed, God's Word will not remain obscure behind archaic words and phrases. Neither will it be lost in the flood of words that may mean different things to different people.

Summary Statements

- The Old Testament has a total of 39 books grouped under three major divisions.
- The textual source of our Old Testament is a manuscript tradition recognized by Judaism as the official Scriptures by about A.D. 100.
- The canonization of the Old Testament Scriptures was completed in various stages in the history of Judaism.
- The Greek translation of the Old Testament was the Scriptures of the Early Church.
- The Latin Bible was the Bible of the Middle Ages.
- Wycliffe carried out the pioneer work of translating the Bible into English from the Latin Vulgate.
- Tyndale's New Testament was the first English translation from the original Greek New Testament.
- The King James Version was produced in A.D. 1611.
- Modern translators adhere to the principles of formal equivalence and/or dynamic equivalence theory of translation.

Questions for Reflection

1. Why do you think it was necessary for Judaism to take action to "close" the canon (to limit the list of books as authoritative scriptures)?
2. Why is it important for a Christian to consult two or three translations during a serious Bible study time?
3. "Every translation is an interpretation." How do you evaluate the modern Bible translations using this maxim?

Resources for Further Study

Cross, Frank Moore, and Shemaryahu Talmon, eds. *Qumran and the History of the Biblical Text.* Cambridge, Mass.: Harvard University Press, 1975. Read the article "The Old Testament Text" by Shemaryahu Talmon.

Ewert, David. *From Ancient Tablets to Modern Translations.* Grand Rapids: Zondervan Publishing House, 1983. Read chapter 7, "The Text of the Old Testament," and chapters 15—20 on the history of English Bible.

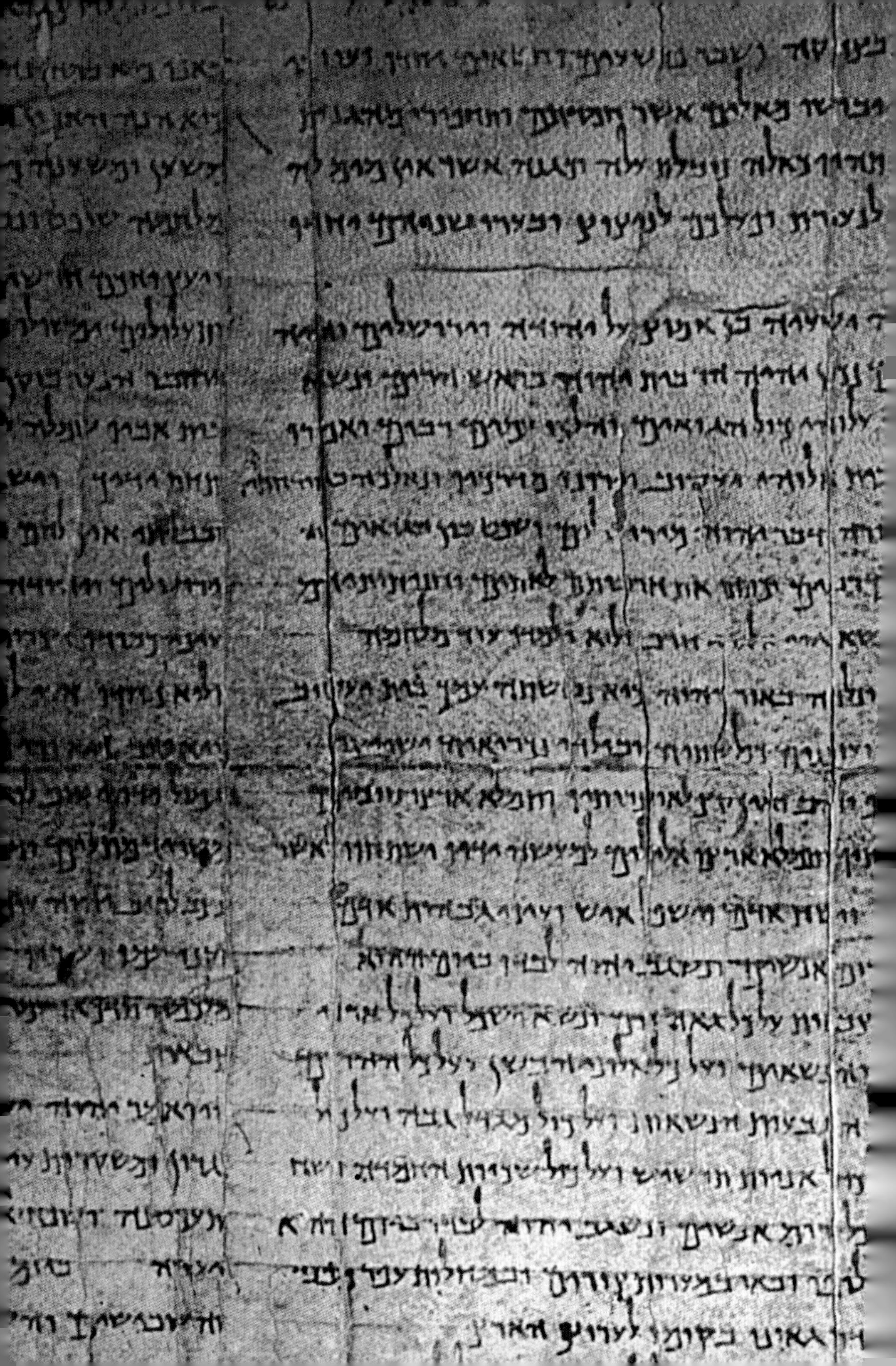

3 Interpreting the Old Testament

bjectives:

Your study of the chapter should help you to:
- Define and describe hermeneutics and exegesis as these terms relate to biblical interpretation.
- Briefly describe the various ancient methods of biblical interpretation.
- Define the various historical-critical methods of interpreting the Bible.
- List the steps of an inductive Bible study.
- Study the biblical text using a proper method of biblical interpretation.

ey Words to Understand

Hermeneutics
Targum
Essenes
Pesher
Mishna
Talmud
Midrash
Literal interpretation
Typological
Allegorical
Christocentric
Apologetic
Scholasticism
Pietism
Historical criticism
Literary criticism
Source criticism
Documentary hypothesis
Form criticism
Redaction criticism
Canon criticism
Exegesis

Questions to consider as you read:

1. What is the outcome of an incorrect reading and interpretation of the Bible?
2. What is your approach to the study of the Bible?
3. How do you determine if a certain teaching or practice is "biblical"?

Every reader of the Bible is engaged in the task of interpreting the Word of God. Interpretation is an ongoing activity in the life of the Church. This chapter is an attempt to establish the necessity of proper biblical interpretation and the need for a proper method that allows us to understand God's Word today. What methods have both Judaism and Christianity utilized in the past to interpret the Scriptures? What are some of the modern methods of biblical interpretation? What is a method that allows us to preserve the integrity and authenticity of the Old Testament as God's Word to us today? We will now deal with these questions.

ents of the Bible. This is a distance not only of time but also of language, thought forms, culture, and geography. We need to journey into the ancient world and understand the linguistic, cultural, and geographical context in which God first revealed himself through His words and actions. This journey will lead to the discovery of what the author intended to communicate through the text. This step is necessary for our understanding of the relevance of God's Word to us today.

The Task of Biblical Interpretation

Biblical interpretation is both a science and an art that utilizes principles, rules, and specific methods. **Hermeneutics** refers to the rules and principles that govern the practice of interpretation. Biblical interpretation (biblical hermeneutics) is necessary because of the distance that separates the modern reader from the authors and the original recipi-

An Overview of Various Ancient and Modern Methods of Biblical Interpretation

Ancient Jewish Interpretation

Scholars regard the ancient practice of translating and interpreting the Hebrew Scriptures into Aramaic (such a translation is called a *Targum*) for the Aramaic-speaking Jews as the first systematic attempt in the history of Jew-

Jewish students study the Scripture at rabbinical schools.

ish biblical interpretation. The origin of this practice perhaps goes back to the fifth century B.C. (see Nehemiah 8:7-8). By the second century A.D., the Jewish scribes took the step to commit the oral translation and interpretation into writing. The **Targum** in its written form was completed around the fourth century A.D. Even today the Jewish rabbis refer to the Targum in their explanation of the Hebrew Scriptures.

The Dead Sea Scrolls reveal evidence of active interpretation of the Scriptures by the **Essenes** in the century that preceded the beginning of the Christian era. They followed an interpretive method known as **pesher,** in which the interpreter may suggest a change in the text or introduce an alternate reading to support a particular interpretation. Their study of the text often included atomizing the text into words and phrases without regard for the context, in order to give biblical support for their religious system. The Essenes related many of the Old Testament prophecies to various contemporary events, including their own history.

The Mishna (the written work of the oral teachings of the great rabbis of early Judaism) and the **Talmud** (commentary on the Mishna by later rabbis) provide us with illustrations of various features of the rabbinic Jewish interpretation of the Scriptures. Rabbinic interpretation depended on the interpretive traditions established by previous rabbis. Rabbis often applied to the text its literal meaning or the plain sense of the text. Rabbis also followed **midrash,** the practice of uncovering the meaning hidden in the text by the use of various

I	**Quotes from the Mishna on the Sabbath Rules and Regulations**

A vessel may not be put under the lamp [on the Sabbath] to collect the [dripping] oil; but if it was put there before the nightfall it is permitted. But no use may be made of that oil [on the Sabbath] since it is not a thing already prepared [for the Sabbath]. . . . R. Eliezer says: He is culpable that weaves three threads [on the Sabbath] at the beginning [of the web], or a single thread onto a piece already woven. But the Sags say: Whether at the beginning or end [of the web] the forbidden quantity is two threads.[1]

techniques including atomizing the text into words and phrases and cross-referencing the text without regard for its context.

Christian Interpretation—First 1,800 Years

The New Testament writers interpreted the Old Testament based on their conviction that God fulfilled His promises concerning the coming of the messianic king through the person of Jesus of Nazareth. In the Gospels we find a large number of quotations from the Old Testament prophetic books that are aimed to show that Jesus literally fulfilled the prophecies about the Messiah **(literal interpretation).** Occasionally we find in the New Testament the use of the contemporary Jewish methods such as midrash and pesher to relate some of the Old Testament passage to the life and ministry of Jesus. Some New Testament writers also utilized the **typological** and **allegorical** methods. Typology assumes that certain Old Testament events, persons, and religious concepts foreshadowed the realities presented in the New Testament. The allegorical method assumes that the text has a spiritual meaning underneath the literal details and that the spiritual meaning is more important than the literal meaning of the text.

In the patristic period of the Christian Church (A.D. 100—590), the church fathers utilized both typological and allegorical methods of interpretation. Again, biblical interpretation during this period was **Christocentric** (centered on the person and ministry of Jesus Christ) and **apologetic** (defending the Christian faith against heresies and opposition against Christian teachings) in nature. The allegorical method was very popular in Alexandria where Clement of Alexandria (ca. A.D. 150—215) and Origen (ca. A.D. 185—254) were the great teachers. At Antioch in Syria, the church fathers promoted the literal interpretation method through historical and grammatical study of the Scriptures.

Later, during the Middle Ages (A.D. 500—1500), a great deal of emphasis was given to the traditions handed down by previous generations of scholars and lead-

ers of the Church. Some scholars of **scholasticism** (a pre-Renaissance intellectual movement that began in monasteries and later spread to universities) continued to use the literal method during this period through the historical study of the text.

During the Reformation period (A.D. 1500—1650), the Protestant movement placed more emphasis on the authority of the Scriptures than on the traditions perpetuated by the Roman Catholic Church. The Reformers for the most part utilized the literal method of interpretation, although we find in Martin Luther's commentaries occasional use of allegorical interpretation. Martin Luther and John Calvin, the great leaders during the Reformation, were Christocentric in their interpretation of the Bible. Luther thought that Christ was to be found everywhere in Scripture, whereas Calvin was more cautious and applied the Old Testament to Christ only where a legitimate connection could be made.

Pietism (a movement that emerged in reaction to the lack of spirituality in the Church created by the intellectual and scholastic approach to the Christian faith) during the post-Reformation period emphasized the literal method. Under the pietistic influence, the Bible became a source of personal piety and devotional life. We see this influence in the life of John Wesley, who emphasized personal piety through Bible study and prayer.

Biblical Interpretation— Modern Period

The modern period in the history of biblical interpretation (early 19th century to the present) saw

---

I

An Example of Typological Interpretation

In the First Epistle of Clement, the writer deals with the story of the spies whom Joshua sent to spy out Jericho and Rahab the prostitute who saved their lives (Joshua 2). The writer narrates the story and gives an exposition of the instruction and the promise the spies gave to Rahab before they returned to Joshua. "Moreover, they gave her a sign . . . that she should hang forth from her house a scarlet thread. And thus they made it manifest that redemption should flow through the blood of the Lord to all them that believe and hope in God."[2]

the rise of **historical criticism** as a new method in the study of the Bible.[3] This method emerged under the influence of Rationalism and Enlightenment of the 17th and the 18th centuries. This approach to the study of the Bible aims to explain Scripture in terms of human reason and one's understanding of natural laws. The emphasis of this method is on uncovering the historical, religious, and literary environment that produced the biblical text, rather than on the meaning of the text in its present form. This method as a whole raises questions about the historical reliability of the biblical text and its authority as God's Word. From an evangelical perspective of the Bible, we hold the conviction that the Bible speaks with divine authority to human issues and concerns. However, we also hold that questions concerning the literary and historical context of the text and the theological climate that produced the text will lead us to a more objective understanding of Scripture and its meaning for both its ancient and modern listeners. Historical-critical method challenges us to investigate these complex aspects of the biblical text. In that regard, we have benefited from the contributions of modern historical-critical approach to the study of the Bible. The following is a brief description of some of the significant developments within the historical-critical method of modern biblical interpretation.

Literary criticism is an umbrella term that covers a variety of methods that in some way seek to explain the meaning of the text by evaluating the literary structure and features, date of writing, authorship, original audience, lit-

I — An Example of Allegorical Interpretation

The following is an excerpt from The Epistle of Barnabas, written by an Alexandrian Jewish Christian around A.D. 100. Here we see the writer applying New Testament spiritual lessons to the various aspects of the story of the offering of a heifer in Numbers 19.

"Now what do you suppose this to be a type of, that a command was given to Israel, that men of the greatest wickedness should offer a heifer, and slay and burn it, and then boys should take the ashes and put these into vessels, and bind round a stick purple wool along with hyssop, and that thus the boys should sprinkle the people, one by one, in order that they might be purified from their sins? Consider how He speaks to you with simplicity. The calf is Jesus: the sinful men offering it are those who led Him to the slaughter. . . . And the boys that sprinkle are those that have proclaimed to us the remission of sins and purification of heart. . . . And why was the wool [placed] upon the wood? Because by wood Jesus holds His kingdom, so that [through the cross] those believing on Him shall live for ever."[4]

erary sources, and so forth.[5] The historical and literary environment that produced the text is a primary concern of literary criticism. Literary criticism in recent years has branched off into more specific areas of study, such as source criticism, genre criticism, rhetorical criticism, structuralism, narrative criticism, and so forth. Among these various branches of literary criticism, source criticism has been an important method in biblical study.

Source criticism aims to understand the various sources that contributed to the development of a biblical book. For example, this methodology led to the argument by Julius Wellhausen (*Prolegomena* to the History of Israel, 1878) that the Pentateuch was composed of four different literary and theological documents **(documentary hypothesis)**. He labeled these documents as J (Yahwistic), E (Elohistic), P (Priestly), and D (Deuteronomic). Wellhausen postulated the theory that these four sources originated at various times, ranging from the middle of the ninth century B.C. to the middle of the fifth century B.C. Modern historical-critical scholars continue to view the Pentateuch as a composite of various sources. In recent years, many scholars have expanded and revised the four sources introduced by Wellhausen.

Form criticism is another discipline of the historical-critical method.[6] This critical approach to the study of the Bible focuses on the various literary types (genres) found in the biblical books. The underlying assumption is that the biblical books are composed of clearly identifiable literary units, which in their original forms were preserved through memory (oral tradition). Also, form criticism assumes that these literary units originated and were circulated in a specific cultural and religious life setting or life situation (Sitz im Leben). In Israel, the life setting may have been the Temple or other religious setting, family or other social setting, the royal court or other political institutions, and so forth. Recovering such a life situation is a goal of form criticism. Form criticism also seeks to discover the intention or the purpose of the particular genre. The purpose that a particular genre aimed to fulfill is important to the interpretation of the text (e.g., instruction, edification, explanation, warning, hope). Hermann Gunkel's study of the

various types of psalms is the pioneering work in Old Testament form criticism.[7] Gunkel grouped the psalms as hymns, community laments, songs of the individual, thanksgiving songs, laments of the individual, entrance liturgies, and royal psalms, and he placed most of the psalms in the setting of Israel's worship. Martin Dibelius and Rudolph Bultmann have made significant impact on New Testament form criticism with their studies on the Gospels.[8]

Redaction criticism is a relatively late discipline developed in the mid-20th century.[9] This method first appeared with an investigation of the Gospels. Redaction-critical scholars saw the Gospel writers as theologians in their own right who arranged and modified the narratives to convey their particular theological understanding or the theology of the Church of their time. Thus the aim of redaction criticism is to reconstruct the theological themes or motifs reflected in the present form of the text that may be different from its original theological purpose. This method assumes that the book has its final form as a result of an editorial process or design. This process included arrangement, revisions, and reworking of the older materials. Virtually all the books of the Bible have been subjected to the scrutiny of redaction criticism.

There have been several other recent developments in biblical scholarship. Most of these developments fall within the literary approach to the study of the Bible (see discussion on literary criticism). We will conclude this section with a brief look at **canon criticism,** another recent approach that is theological in its orientation.[10] The aim of this method is to treat the Bible in its present canonical form. The underlying conviction is that the Bible contains traditions that have been accepted as authoritative by the Jewish and the Christian faith communities. Therefore, proponents of this method seek to uncover the theological convictions that influenced the writers and editors of the biblical books. Though canon criticism does not reject the basic findings of historical criticism, this method gives emphasis to the theological message of various biblical books and that of the Bible.

An Inductive Method of Studying an Old Testament Text

Evangelical scholars support an inductive approach to the study of the Bible that attempts to draw out the meaning of the text by making observations and conclusions about the details presented in the text. The inductive method presupposes a methodical and systematic study of the text. **Exegesis** is the actual process of bringing the meaning out of a biblical text by its modern reader. We recommend the following as steps to be followed in an inductive approach to the exegesis of an Old Testament passage.

Step 1. The study of an Old Testament passage should begin with an *investigation of the book in which the passage is located.* What section of the Old Testament does the book belong to? What is the relationship of the book to other Old Testament

Major Literary Forms (Genre) in the Old Testament

Some of the more common literary forms (genre) of the Old Testament are listed below:

Narratives: Substantial sections of Genesis, Exodus, Numbers, Joshua, Judges, 1 and 2 Samuel, 1 and 2 Kings, Ruth, Esther, 1 and 2 Chronicles, Ezra, and Nehemiah in the Old Testament contain narratives. Narratives may be simple accounts that deal with historical events (historical narratives), or biographical accounts, or autobiographical accounts, or accounts that explain the origin of the name of a place or a custom (etiological narratives), or family or tribal history.

Law: The Books of Exodus, Leviticus, Numbers, and Deuteronomy contain large amounts of legal materials. These may be in the form of prohibitions, prescriptions, instructions, or commands.

Poetry: Approximately one-third of the Old Testament is poetry. Psalms, Proverbs, Song of Songs, and Lamentations are some of the Old Testament books that are completely poetry.

Prophecy: The books of the prophets contain prophetic speeches given by Israel's prophets. A prophecy, also called an oracle, is a message from God that the prophet was under constraint to speak. Usually the prophet gave his prophecy through messenger style speeches (speeches that begin with "thus says the LORD" [NRSV]).

Wisdom: Wisdom teachings that utilize discourses or dialogues and proverbial statements are found in the Books of Job, Proverbs, and Ecclesiastes.

Apocalyptic: The Book of Daniel is known as apocalyptic literature because it contains visions about the sudden and catastrophic end of history and the establishment of God's kingdom through His direct intervention in human affairs.

Jewish reader wearing tefillin containing Scripture on his forehead.

aries of various literary units in a biblical book.

Step 3. *Identify the literary form (genre) and its purpose or intention.* The Old Testament books contain a variety of literary types. Each literary type or genre reveals a certain distinctive style and pattern. Each genre has its own particular function that it seeks to accomplish. For example, a narrative may seek to explain the origin of a custom or a religious tradition, or it may be instructional in purpose. Law sets the nonnegotiable requirements of God in the form of prescriptions, prohibitions, and instructions. Prophecy gives hope and encouragement or warning, and even threat of judgment. Psalms as a whole provides the reader with the language of worship and prayer. Wisdom instructions set the moral and ethical guidelines for human conduct and relationship. Apocalyptic writings reveal future events and visions of God's sovereign rule in the world. The identification of the genre of the text thus helps the interpreter to focus on the intended purpose of the text.

Step 4. *Discover the immediate setting of the biblical passage.* The goal of this step is to place the text in its actual historical, social, cultural, and religious setting. Each book of the Old Testament belongs to a particular historical-cultural setting. Who was the author? Who were the recipients? When did the message of the book first originate? What is the particular historical situation of that period (political leadership and political developments of that time)? Does the text contain references to particular cultural customs of that period? What were

books? What period in Israel's history does the book belong to? What are the major theological themes of the book? What is the major literary type form in the book? What is literary structure of the book? The student will find answers to these basic questions in an Old Testament survey such as this textbook.

Step 2. *Identify the literary unit that is the focus of exegesis.* A literary unit is a passage of Scripture that has a clearly defined theme or central idea. For the most part, books of the Old Testament are made up of a large number of individual passages or literary units, each with a key idea or theme. Changes in theme, characters, speakers, addressees, location, literary form, and so forth, help us identify the bound-the religious practices or beliefs of the people being addressed? What spiritual need prompted the writing of the message contained in the text? Reconstruction of the setting will allow the reader to engage the text and enter into the world in which the text originated. This is essential to one's understanding of the meaning of the text intended by the writer.

Step 5. *Establish the relationship of the text to the passages that precede and follow the text.* Biblical passages also have a literary setting. That means the text belongs to a literary context marked by preceding and following passages. These preceding and following passages may be related to the text being studied by a common theme and/or literary arrangement. Some passages may be chronologically arranged; others may be arranged by a common literary type or genre. Often, the meaning of the preceding and following passages may determine the meaning of the text being studied. Recognizing the literary and theological continuity of the text to the surrounding texts (or lack thereof) is important for a proper understanding of its meaning.

Step 6. The next step of exegesis involves the identification of *literary structure of the text* that the writer has utilized to expand the main idea. Here we must analyze the text as a literary work and look for subthemes and the development of the plot or the main idea. How does the text begin? Does the text address specific people? Does the text introduce a speaker? Does the speaker utilize subthemes to expand the main idea? Are there transitions within the passage? How does

the text end? A careful reading of the text will show the literary structure or different verse units within the text that outline the development of the main theme of the text being studied.

Step 7. *Study the grammatical structure, relationship of words and phrases, and meaning of words and phrases.* When dealing with prose materials, we need to identify the sentence structure (the main clause and subordinate clauses). It is important to note how the subordinate clauses (dependent clauses) are related to the main clause (independent clause). This task should also include asking questions about the nature of the independent clause (is it a command or a declaration or assertion?) and dependent clause (does it answer questions of when, where, why, how?). The main objective is to discover the flow of thought that clarifies our understanding of the message of the text. When dealing with poetic passages, we must look for various types of parallelism and poetic devises such as similes and metaphors (see chap. 21 on Hebrew poetry).

The next part of this step is the investigation of the meaning of words in their original ancient setting. It is important to determine what the author intended by his words and phrases and how his original audience might have understood the text in its original historical and cultural context. Often a word may have a range of meanings. Some words may have particular theological meaning. It is important to select the meaning that is appropriate to the context. Our attempt here is to connect words and phrases to each other and to understand the meaning of the text in its original setting. This task involves the use of Bible commentaries, Bible dictionaries, study Bibles, and other resources that contain Hebrew word studies.

Step 8. *Make conclusions about the theological truth or lessons that the writer of the text intended to communicate to his ancient listeners.* Our attempt here is to discover how God speaks or acts in response to human needs. In the context of human sin, the text may contain a word of warning, a call to repentance, or even a threat of judgment. In the context of despair and hopelessness, His word may be a word of hope, an assurance, a comfort, or a promise of help or salvation. In the context of doubt, His word may be a revelation of His majesty and glory or a miracle to create faith. God's word may be one of instruction, guidance, counsel, or admonition. Since God's word or action is an event of revelation, we must ask, "What response did the revelation elicit from its recipients?" The human response may be praise and worship, obedience and submission, humility and gratitude—all characteristics of those who are faithful to God. Where the human response had been disobedience and rejection of God's word—rebellion and stubbornness—the text instructs us to model our lives after those who have been faithful to God. The theological lessons of the text give us the proper basis for determining the biblical principles that are relevant to contemporary Christian life.

Step 9. *Relate the text and its theology to the overall message of the Bible.* The following questions will help us here: Does the theology of the text before us deal with a particular culture or specific situations in the life of ancient Israel or the early Christian church? Do we find parallel expressions elsewhere in the book in which the text is located? Do we find parallel expressions elsewhere in other books of the Bible? Is the theology of the text consistent with the overall theological teachings of the Bible? Do we find clarifications or expansions of the theology of the text elsewhere in the Old Testament? Does the New Testament interpret the Old Testament text or clarify it or modify it? These questions will help us establish the biblical authority of the text. Further, this step will help us distinguish between religious practices that are culturally conditioned and time-bound, and theological truths that are timeless and unchanging in character and application.

Step 10. *Apply the message of the text to contemporary Christian life.* Exegesis cannot remain in a vacuum. The theological lessons of the text contain the message of God to us today. That is a message that we need to listen to and obey. Some texts may suggest lessons that may be constrained by the limits of time and culture. Theological lessons that have universal application are those that promote the divine characteristics and attributes, God's plan of redemption for all humanity, proper moral and ethical conduct, and those that enable all human beings to become truly the image of God. In general, a theological principle that may lend itself to various forms of practical expression consistent with the intent of the biblical text can be considered a timeless principle. Specific lessons, on the other hand, relate to a particular context with limited application. In most cases, proper exegesis of the text will guide us in this evaluation process.

We add here a final word about inductive Bible study. Throughout this process, the interpreter must prayerfully seek divine guidance and the assistance of the Holy Spirit, who alone can illuminate our feeble minds to discern the mystery of God's revelation, and enable us to respond to God's Word in faithfulness and obedience.

Summary Statements

- The goal of interpretation is to understand the meaning of the biblical text and to relate that meaning to our day.
- Jewish and Christian interpretation of the Bible includes different methods and practices.
- Modern critical methods of reading the Bible focus on the environment that produced the text.
- Biblical interpretation requires a systematic study of the biblical text by paying attention to its historical and cultural context.
- Proper biblical interpretation should conclude with the application of the message of the text to our day.

Questions for Reflection

1. What are some of the advantages of utilizing the historical-critical methodology when we study the Bible?
2. What are some of the limitations of the historical-critical methodology?
3. How does your understanding of the history of biblical interpretation inform you about the whole enterprise of biblical interpretation?

Resources for Further Study

Fee, Gordon D., and Douglas Stuart. *How to Read the Bible for All Its Worth*. 2nd ed. Grand Rapids: Zondervan, 1993.
Klein, William W., Craig L. Blomberg, and Robert L. Hubbard, Jr. *Introduction to Biblical Interpretation*. Dallas: Word Publishing, 1993.

4

The World of the Old Testament

bjectives:

Your study of the chapter should help you to:

- Describe the general geographical setting of the Old Testament.
- Identify the various cultures of the ancient Near East.
- Recognize and locate key Old Testament sites on a map of Palestine.

ey Words to Understand

Fertile Crescent
Cuneiform
Sumerians
Akkadians
Amorites
Semitic
Hittites
Hurrians
Assyrians
Babylonians
Persians
Pharaohs
Hyksos
Philistines
Palestine
Canaanites
Phoenicians
Arameans
Ammonites
Moabites
Edomites
Midianites
Amalekites
Coastal plain
Central hill country
Jordan valley
Transjordan

Questions to consider as you read:

1. Discuss how your particular geographical origin and culture may have shaped or influenced your religious perceptions.
2. What is the end result of studying history without the knowledge of geography?

Israel's story took place in a world that is known to us as the Middle East. Though the land called Canaan in the Old Testament became the home of Israel, her people also lived in Egypt and Babylon at various times in her history. We will now look at this larger world in which Israel came into existence as a nation. Our goal is to briefly survey the geographical, cultural, religious, and political conditions that constitute the setting of the Old Testament story.

The Ancient Near East

The world of the Old Testament is called the ancient Near East (ANE) or the ancient Semitic world. This area extends east to west from the northern part of the Persian Gulf to the northern part of the Nile delta in Egypt, and north to south from the mountains of eastern Turkey to the northern part of the Red Sea. This vast region is made up of dry and barren desert, with some fertile river valleys and numerous high and rugged mountains. Modern countries such as Israel, Jordan, Lebanon, Syria, and Iraq are located within this region.

Civilizations and cultural groups emerged in this region near the fertile valleys and river systems. Conflict and struggle for power was a way of life in this an-

Ancient Near East—the Fertile Crescent.

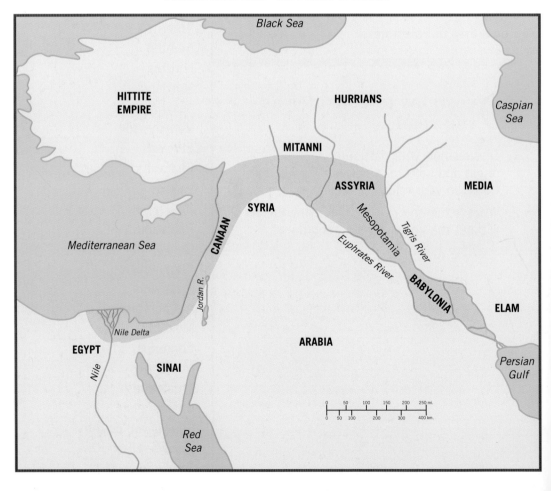

cient world. Various powerful ethnic groups dominated this region at different times and controlled its fertile land and trade routes. It was also frequently the setting for drought, famine, flood, locust attack, and other natural disasters. Life in this region, in short, was far from safe and secure.

The fertile and watered land area within the ancient Near East is made up of the Mesopotamian valley, the Nile delta, and Syria-Palestine. These three regions together form roughly the shape of a crescent (the **Fertile Crescent**). The Syria-Palestine region is the land bridge between the continents of Africa and Asia. At different times in ancient history, various political powers have made attempts to control this region because of its strategic location and significance to transportation and trade in the ancient world.

The Mesopotamian Valley

Mesopotamia, the land between the Euphrates and the Tigris rivers, had been the home of many different cultural groups in ancient times. In biblical times it was made up of Assyria in the north and Babylon in the south. We will summarize here a few of the significant groups of people that inhabited Mesopotamia from 3000 B.C. to 330 B.C.

The **Sumerians** established their culture and civilization in the southern part of the Mesopotamian valley in the early part of the third millennium B.C. Scholars regard the Sumerian civilization as the first significant civilization in the history of humanity. Sumerians invented wedge-shaped

The *Enuma Elish*

An excerpt from the *Enuma Elish* that depicts the creation of man by the god Marduk who fought and defeated Tiamat and her forces.

When Marduk hears the words of the gods,
his heart prompts (him) to fashion artful works.
Opening his mouth, he addresses Ea
To impart the plan he had conceived in his heart:
"Blood I will mass and cause bones to be.
I will establish a savage, 'man' shall be his name.
Verily, savage-man I will create.
He shall be charged with the service of the gods
That they might be at ease!"[1]

writing **(cuneiform)** and built cities such as Sumer, Eridu, Ur, Larsa, and Nippur. The creation story *Enuma Elish* is an important product of Sumerian religious thinking.

The **Akkadians,** a seminomadic Semitic group, gained control of the southern part of the Mesopotamian valley around 2300 B.C. and built an empire under the leadership of Sargon the Great. Though the Sumerian control of this area came to an end, their culture continued to have influence over this region. The Akkadians borrowed or adapted various elements of the Sumerian culture and religion. The Akkadian myth of creation is an expansion of the Sumerian story *(Enuma Elish)*.

The **Amorites** dominated virtually all parts of Mesopotamia and Syria-Palestine by the 18th century B.C. They were a Semitic group who established the cities of Mari and Babylon as centers of their political power. Mari discoveries include thousands of inscriptions

Who Are the Semitic People?

The term **Semitic** has different connotations. Some scholars apply this term to those racial groups that have descended from Shem, one of the three sons of Noah. More broadly, this term applies to all who speak languages that belong to the Semitic family of languages (ancient languages such as Akkadian, Ugaritic, Canaanite, Phoenician, Hebrew, Aramaic, Ethiopic, Arabic, etc.). More narrowly, this term has been applied in modern times to the people of the Jewish ancestry. We use the term *Semitic* here in the broader sense to include all the ancient people that were related to each other by common cultural and linguistic characteristics.

that deal with legal, domestic, and business matters. Scholars believe that Israel's ancestors belonged to the Amorites.

The **Hittites** occupied the central part of Asia Minor between 2000 and 1700 B.C. The Hittite laws and treaty texts are important sources of our understanding of the ancient Near Eastern legal and political customs.

The **Hurrians,** or Horites, originally lived in the mountains of Armenia. In the 17th and 16th centuries B.C. there was a tremendous influx of Hurrians into all parts of the Fertile Crescent. In Mitanni, the Hurrians established a dynasty and an empire that controlled Syria and Upper Mesopotamia. This empire was later taken over by the Assyrians. Nuzi, in the East Tigris region, was a center of the Hurrian civilization. Nuzi tablets (dated to the 15th century B.C.) contain several parallels to the customs and culture of Israel's ancestors.

The **Assyrians** played a key role in the destiny of the nation of Israel in the eighth and seventh centuries B.C. The northern part of Mesopotamia was the home of the Assyrians. Asshur and Nineveh were the chief cities of Assyria. The Assyrians launched an empire-building program in the eighth century B.C. under the leadership of Tiglath-pileser III and gained political control over Syria, Israel, and even Egypt. In the middle of the seventh century B.C., Assyria began to decline in power and lost control of its empire under the joint attack of Medes, Babylonians, and Scythians. The Babylonians destroyed Nineveh in 612 B.C. and with that the Assyrians ceased to exist as a nation.

The **Babylonians** became a major political power in the seventh century B.C. The southern part of Mesopotamia came to be known as Babylonia. The city of Babylon located on the Euphrates was the most influential city of the Babylonians. In 587 B.C. the Babylonians captured Jerusalem and forced the Jews to go into exile in Babylon. The Jewish exile lasted until 539 B.C., when Babylon was taken over by the Persian Empire. Cyrus the Persian king gave freedom to the Jews in exile, and he allowed them to return to their homeland. However, Jewish communities continued to exist in Babylon even after the Exile came to an end.

The **Persians** became a major political power in the sixth century B.C. under the leadership of Cyrus. Their home was in what is modern Iran. Cyrus incorporated the once powerful Medes and later the Babylonians into his empire. The empire extended westward to include Asia Minor, Syria, Palestine, and Egypt. The expansion eastward reached as far as India. Eventually the Persians declined in strength and their empire later became part of the world that Alexander the Great conquered around 330 B.C.

The Nile Delta Region (Lower Egypt)

The Old Testament mentions Egypt as the home of the people of Israel in the early part of her existence. The Egypt of the Old Testament is the northern part (also known as Lower Egypt or the Delta region) of the modern land of Egypt. Israel, in her later history, remembered Egypt as the land of her bondage. Egypt continued to exert political power over Israel at various times. Israel's kings often made alliances with Egypt, though the prophets condemned such actions as returning to bondage and slavery. A substantial number of the Jews made Egypt their home during the Babylonian invasion of Judah in 587 B.C. Later Alexandria became a center of the Jewish life in Egypt.

Egyptian history is divided into the Old Kingdom period (2900—2300 B.C.), the Middle Kingdom period (2100—1710 B.C.), and the New Kingdom period (1550—330 B.C.). The two intermediate periods (2300—2100 B.C. and 1710—1550 B.C.) were marked by political and economic instability and struggle for power among rival rulers known as **pharaohs.** It is likely that Abraham made his journey to Egypt during the latter part of the Middle Kingdom period. During the second intermediate period, Egypt's rulers were **Hyksos,** a Semitic people who ruled Egypt for over 100 years. Joseph and the rest of Jacob's family settled down in Egypt during the early part of the Hyksos domination. The stories of Moses, Israel's bondage, and the exodus from Egypt belong to the early part of the New Kingdom period. By about 1000 B.C., Egypt lost its political strength, and it continued to deteriorate, as the world saw the rise of new emerging powers such as Assyria, Babylon, Persia, and Greece in the next several centuries.

Syria-Palestine Region

Syria-Palestine is the most frequently mentioned region in the Old Testament. This region is made up of countries such as Israel, Lebanon, Syria, and Jordan on the political map today. On the eastern coastal area of the Mediterranean Sea were the lands of the Philistines (Philistia), the Canaanites (Canaan), and the Phoenicians (Phoenicia). Other ancient countries in this region included Syria (northeast), Ammon, Moab, Edom, and Midian (east and southeast). The southern Negev area was the home of the ancient Amalekites.

The **Philistines** were the primary inhabitants on the coastal plain southwest of Canaan, on the eastern shore of the Mediterranean Sea. They came to this region from Crete or some other islands in the Mediterranean Sea around 1200 B.C. Ashkelon, Ashdod, Gaza, Ekron, and Gath are among the key cities the Philistines established in this area (the Philistine Pentapolis). We know from biblical records that they were a constant threat to the Israelites. In the early years of Israel's history in **Palestine,** the Philistines exercised control over

Late Bronze Age
Gate at Megiddo.

much of the coastal region and the lower hill country of Judah. The Philistine threat against Israel came to an end when David became king over Israel (1000 B.C.).

Prior to Israel's coming into the land of Canaan (Palestine), the primary inhabitants of this region were the **Canaanites,** a mixture of various ethnic and cultural groups, most of which descended from Canaan, grandson of Noah. Cities like Jericho, Megiddo, Beth-Shan, Ai, Shechem, Gezer, and Lachish were centers of the Canaanite culture in the third millennium B.C. Toward the end of the third millennium B.C., the Amorites from the Mesopotamian valley invaded Canaan and destroyed many of the Canaanite cities. The Amorite invasion continued through the early part of the second millennium B.C. Various Amorite groups settled down in Canaan and rebuilt the cities they destroyed. Abraham, who left his home Ur in southern Mesopotamia to settle in Canaan, was most likely a part of the Amorite settlers (see Genesis 11:27—12:4). The inhabitants of this area include Girgashites, Perizzites, Jebusites, Hivites, and Hittites (see 15:19-20). It is likely that

all of these people were subgroups within the Amorites.

The **Phoenicians,** who inhabited the northwest area on the eastern shores of the Mediterranean, were traders and seagoing people who spread into Palestine and influenced the culture and religion of the Canaanites. Tyre was an important center of their trade and culture. They made alliances with David and Solomon, kings of Israel, and helped design and build the Temple in Jerusalem during the days of Solomon.

The **Arameans** probably descended from the Amorite group and made Aram or Syria their home sometime during the second millennium B.C. The Bible makes several connections between the Israelites and the Arameans. The home of Abraham for a while was Haran, also known as Padan-Aram, the city of Nahor, and Aram Naharaim. The ancestors of Israel (Abraham, Isaac, and Jacob) maintained contact with this region. The earliest confessional creed of Israel (see Deuteronomy 26:5-10) refers to the father of Israel (most likely Jacob) as "a wandering Aramean" (v. 5). The center of the state of the Arameans was Damascus, which still remains the capital of Syria. The people of Israel had frequent border struggles with the Syrians/Arameans from the 10th through the 8th centuries B.C.

The **Ammonites,** the **Moabites,** and the **Edomites** were the three primary groups of people who inhabited the area east of the river Jordan. The Book of Genesis describes the Ammonites and the Moabites as the descendants of Lot (19:30-38), and the Edomites as the descendants of Esau, Jacob's brother (chap. 36). The Am-

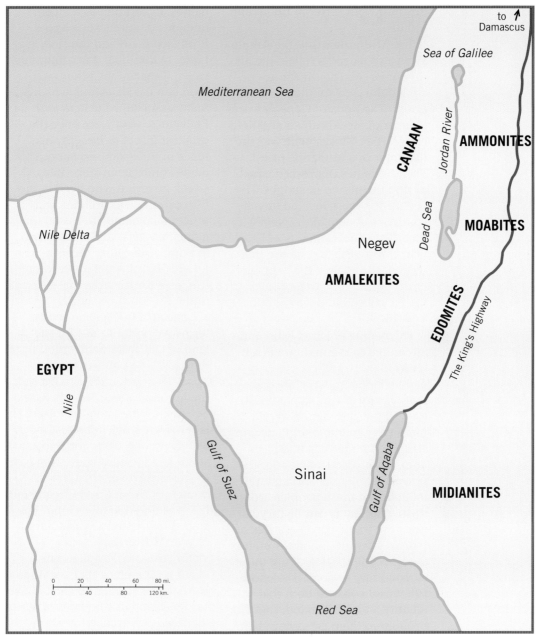

Israel's neighboring kingdoms in 13th cent. B.C.

monites lived directly east of the Jordan valley, with Rabbath-Ammon (modern Amman) as their capital. The Moabites, located south of the Ammonite territory, and the Ammonites maintained social and religious contact, including marriage relationships with the Israelite population. The Edomites, also related to the ancestors of Israel, kept a more hostile attitude toward the Israelites. They were located directly south of Moab. The most important trade route of the ancient times—the King's Highway—going north to south went through Edom and Moab.

The **Midianites** and the **Amalekites** also played a role in the history of Israel. The Midianites occupied the land southeast of Edom. The Book of Genesis traces their origin to Abraham and Keturah (25:1-2). Moses' wife was the daughter of a Midianite priest. The Midianites oppressed Israel during the period of Judges. The Amalekites were located directly south of Canaan, in the Negev area. These descendants of Esau (36:12) were the first nation that waged war against the people of Israel during Israel's journey to the Promised Land (see Exodus 17:8-16).

The people of Israel lived and attempted to maintain their religious identity as God's chosen people in the midst of a world that was for the most part hostile toward their existence. While there were military conflicts and struggle for survival and freedom, Israel also came under the powerful religious and cultural influence of these peoples around them. Old Testament history narrates the tragic consequences of Israel's attempt to borrow cultural and religious ideas from these surrounding nations. The end result was the loss of both their identity and the freedom that God brought to them by saving them from their bondage to the Egyptians. To this story, we shall return later.

The Land of Palestine

The land God promised to give to the descendants of Abraham is described in Exodus as "a land flowing with milk and honey" (3:8). This land has various names, in addition to the common designations such as the Promised Land and the Holy Land. In the Bible it is commonly called Canaan. The other common name is Palestine, which actually associates the land with the Philistines, who were once the greatest threat to Israel's existence in the Promised Land. This name comes from Herodotus, a Greek historian who lived in the fifth century B.C. Romans and others who came after used the name *Palestine,* and it remained in popular use until recently. The *Land of Israel* is the modern political term for the area that belongs to the Jewish state today.

Canaan and *Palestine* are the terms we prefer to use for the land of Old Testament Israel, since they carry no political connotations. This land is located between the Mediterranean Sea (the Great Sea in the Bible) and the desert. It is relatively small in area, about 350 miles long from north to south and 60 miles wide from east to west. However, the biblical boundary "from Dan to Beersheba" was only 150 miles long. This land shows extreme variations in physical features and climate. Within this small region, one could be at a place such as Mount Hermon, which is 9,100 feet above sea level, and in a few hours reach the Dead Sea area, which is nearly 1,300 feet below sea level, the lowest spot on earth.

Palestine has four distinct geographical regions. The **coastal plain** along the Mediterranean Sea stretches from Gaza in the south to Lebanon in the north. This area is a narrow strip of land with hills on the east and the sea on the west. The Mount Carmel range, which almost reaches the

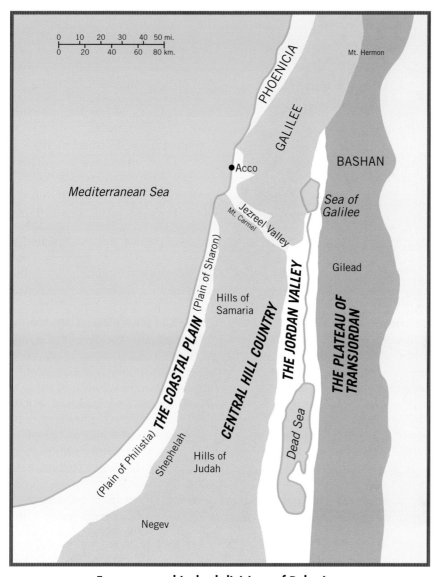

Four geographical subdivisions of Palestine.

sea in the northern part of the land, divides the coastal plain into a northern and southern section. Acco, in the northern part of the plain, was an important harbor city in ancient times. The southern section includes the plain of Sharon, a fertile area with a natural harbor called Joppa (modern Jaffa). The Philistines controlled the southern part of the plain of Sharon, the area south of Joppa, and hence this region is sometimes called the plain of Philistia.

The **central hill country** is the second main geographical subdivision of the land of Palestine. This strip of land extends from Galilee in the north to the Negev in the south. It has three parts: the hills of Galilee, the hills of Samaria, and the hills of Judah. A valley that runs from east to west divides the hills of Galilee into upper Galilee

Jerusalem is located in the northwest region of the Judean Desert.

A view of the Sea of Galilee.

and lower Galilee. The mountains of upper Galilee are higher in elevation than those of lower Galilee. The lower Galilee region has isolated mountains such as Mount Tabor and broad valleys. The plain of Jezreel (also known as the valley of Jezreel), which is about 50 miles long, connects the coastal region with the Jordan valley. It is about 20 miles wide from north to south and separates the Galilee region from the hills of Samaria. Important trade and military routes went through this region in ancient times. Megiddo was an important fortified city located on the western edge of the Jezreel valley. Samaria includes many hills and broad, fertile valleys that are well known for agriculture. Mount Gerizim and Mount Ebal are located in this region. Two primary cities of this region in ancient times were Samaria and Shechem. The hills of Judah are a continuation of the hills of Samaria. Jerusalem, located in this region, has an altitude of 2,600 feet above sea level. Hebron and Bethlehem also belong to this region.

The third distinctive geographical subdivision of Palestine is the **Jordan valley,** which is part of a geological depression that extends from the foothills of Mount Hermon in the north to the Red Sea in the south. The Jordan River, which originates in the north in the area of Dan, runs through this valley. Between the Sea of Galilee and the Dead Sea, the Jordan River takes a twisting and winding path. The Sea of Galilee (also known as Chinnereth and the Lake of Tiberius), a freshwater lake about 13 miles long and 8 miles wide, is well known for its plentiful fish and sudden storms. The Dead Sea (also known as the Salt Sea, at 1,296 feet below sea level), about 65 miles south of the Sea of Galilee, is approximately 50 miles long and 10 miles wide. Though the freshwaters of the Jordan River run into this sea, it has a high salt and mineral content because of constant water evaporation. The salt content (about 30 to 33 percent) makes it impossible to support any plant or animal life. The most important city in the Jordan valley, and perhaps the oldest city in Palestine, is Jericho, located 7 miles north of the Dead Sea.

We now turn to the last major geographical subdivision of Palestine. The plateau of **Transjordan** is located east of the Jordan River and makes up the modern country of Jordan. In the north is the region of Bashan, a fertile plateau well known for its pastureland and cows and bulls. The Yarmuk River separates Bashan from the hills of Gilead in the south. The region of Gilead is also known for its fertile soil and agricultural products. The river Jabbok runs east to west through this region. The ancient kingdoms of Ammon, Moab, and Edom were located south of Gilead.

We need to include two other areas in our study of the geographical regions of Palestine.

The Negev area, which makes up the southern border of Palestine (see Genesis 12:9; 20:1), is a dry, hot, and barren region that did not have any economic significance in biblical times. Beersheba is an important place in the Negev region because of its association with the patriarchs of Israel (see Genesis 21:31-32; 26:17-33). Kadesh-barnea, where the people of Israel encamped during their wilderness journey, is about 50 miles south of Beersheba. The next area, the Shephelah region (the lowlands) separates the southern part of the coastal plain (the area of the Philistines) from the hill country of Judah. This region was the scene of many encounters between the Israelites and the Philistines. Lachish was

One of the sources of the Jordan River near the Lebanon-Israel border.

an important fortified center in the Shephelah region.

This ancient world is where God brought into existence a people called Israel. The Israelites developed their unique belief system within this general geographical region. Perhaps the most important element of Israel's faith is the belief that one true God, who is sovereign and majestic, created the universe. This belief stands in sharp contrast to the polytheistic beliefs of creation we find among Israel's neighboring cultures.

We shall now turn to the creation stories in the Book of Genesis. This is where our journey as the people of God begins, a journey that will take us beyond the Garden of Eden to where we are today.

Summary Statements

- Our knowledge of the geographical setting is essential to our understanding of the message of the Old Testament.
- The land of the Old Testament is a part of the ancient Near East.
- Palestine is the land bridge between Asia and Africa.
- Israel's ancestors belonged to the Amorite ethnic group.
- God brought Israel into existence as a nation in a world once dominated by the cultural, political, and religious influences of various polytheistic peoples.
- Egypt's history helps place some of the biblical stories in historical perspective.
- Palestine is a land characterized by distinct geographical regions, which include plains, hills, mountains, deserts, and valleys.

Question for Reflection

Read Genesis 11:27—13:18 and locate all the places mentioned in this text on a map of the ancient Near East during the time of the patriarchs. Consult a Bible atlas that provides you with different maps of the ancient Near East and Palestine.

Resources for Further Study

May, Herbert G., ed. *Oxford Bible Atlas.* New York: Oxford University Press, 1984.
Page, Charles R., II, and Carl A. Volz. *The Land and the Book: An Introduction to the World of the Bible.* Nashville: Abingdon, 1993.

UNIT II

DISCOVERING THE PENTATEUCH

This unit introduces the reader to:
- Israel's understanding of the universe and humanity
- Israel's ancestors and their stories
- Israel's bondage and deliverance from Egypt
- Israel's journey toward the Promised Land
- The laws and instructions that Moses gave to Israel

5 Israel's View of the World: Genesis 1—11

Objectives:

Your study of the chapter should help you to:

- Explain the title, authorship, and main content of the Book of Genesis.
- Evaluate the key theological truths found in the creation stories.
- Identify the main stories found in Genesis 3—11.
- Evaluate the theological lessons of the main stories found in Genesis 3—11.
- Make assessment of the present condition of humanity.
- Develop a theological framework for personal faith and life in the world today.

Questions to consider as you read:

1. Give a list of your perceptions and beliefs about God. From this list, choose the most basic and most essential belief about God. Explain why.

2. Why is it important to have faith in God as the Creator of the universe?

3. Why do we resist authority?

4. What are the various areas of human relationship where resistance to authority is found?

Key Words to Understand

Torah
Pentateuch
Genesis
Septuagint
Primeval narratives/
    traditions
Patriarchal narratives/
    traditions
Theocentric
Anthropocentric
Enuma Elish
Creatio ex nihilo
Sabbath
Image of God
Tree of life
Tree of the knowledge of
    good and evil
Protevangelium
Garden of Eden
Heart
Covenant with Noah
Gilgamesh epic
Ziggurats
Babel

The opening statement of the Bible establishes God as the supreme Creator. This confession of faith is the beginning point of Israel's story. The Christian confession through the Apostles' Creed, "I believe in God the Father Almighty, Maker of heaven and earth," also sums up this foundational belief about God. The people of Israel also understood their own particular history in the context of God's creation of the universe and humanity. In this chapter, we will deal with the Genesis narratives on God, creation, and humanity that serve as a preamble to the story of Israel's origins.

Title and Authorship

The Book of Genesis is the first book of the Bible. It is also the first book of the **Torah** (or **Pentateuch**). The title **Genesis** (meaning "beginning" or "origin") comes from the Greek translation of the Bible (the **Septuagint**). Who wrote this book and the other four books of the Pentateuch? We do not know. The composition of the entire Pentateuch in its final form continues to be a subject of debate among biblical scholars.

We think that a substantial part of the traditions, stories, and laws in the Pentateuch originated during the period of Moses (13th century B.C.). It is difficult to say how much of these materials existed in written form during Moses' time. Perhaps most remained as oral traditions for a long period. We also think that at a much later period, Israel's scribes collected the literary sources and oral traditions of the previous generations and fixed them into writing. This process must have gone through different stages and different generations of scribal activity. It is difficult to assign a specific time for the final form of the Pentateuch. Modern critical scholars think that at least four major literary and theological sources make up the Pentateuch. They label these sources as a Yahwistic (J), Elohistic (E), Priestly (P), and Deuteronomic (D). They also regard the Yahwistic source as the oldest (9th century B.C.) and the Priestly source as the latest (5th century B.C.) and assign 400 B.C. for the final shaping of the Pentateuch.

Content

The story of the Book of Genesis is told in 50 chapters. The book can be divided into two parts:
1. Primeval traditions (1:1—11:32)
2. Patriarchal traditions (12:1—50:26)

The first 11 chapters contain stories about creation and the earliest history of humanity. These stories focus on events that took place long before humanity began to document its history and civilization. Therefore we designate the content of these chapters as **primeval narratives/traditions.** These chapters contain narratives about the world out of which Israel's ancestor Abraham came to follow God's call. In that respect, these chapters look back at the universal setting of the birth of the nation Israel. Chapters 12—50 deal with the stories of Israel's great ancestors—the patriarchs Abraham, Isaac, and Jacob. Scholars label these chapters as Israel's **patriarchal narratives/ traditions.** Taken as a whole, the Book of Genesis contains several family stories that connect one generation with the next. Where there are gaps in these family stories, we find extended genealo-

Narratives—Principles of Interpretation

The following are some general principles that we need to keep in mind when we attempt to interpret narratives in the Old Testament.

- Narratives in Genesis 1—11 presuppose historical realities. However, they do not offer to us sufficient data to establish the specific date of any event in these chapters. Some Christians view these stories as literary accounts of religious themes. Others find in these chapters literal accounts of actual historical events. A more balanced view is that these chapters contain both oral and literary traditions that convey Israel's religious beliefs about the earliest history of humanity.
- Narratives convey the reality of divine revelation. Often, we may find details lacking in the narratives. Also, historical gaps are very much a part of the biblical narratives. We must avoid the temptation to fill the gaps with fictional or imaginary events.
- Revelation presupposes supernatural events. Some may be easily explained; others we may not be able to explain.
- Attempt to identify the particular focus of the narrative and its intention or purpose by the storyteller (a family story, an explanation of the origin of a custom, the naming of a place, a heroic story, a report of family conflict, a report of divine revelation, etc.).
- Attempt to place the narratives in their historical, cultural, social, and religious setting. Placing a story in its actual setting would allow us to see its relationship to the larger Old Testament story and its impact on subsequent events.
- Attempt to identify particular theological concepts or religious ideas underlying the narrative (such as election, covenant, divine promises, and fulfillment).
- Attempt to evaluate biographical narratives in light of the entire biography of the main character. A single story may serve only as a link in a chain of events. The reader should focus on the total assessment of the character by the biblical writers.
- In all the narratives, attempt to discover the role played by God. Even when some narratives may lack any reference to God, the story may imply the mysterious activity of God.

gies or family trees that trace groups of people or individuals to particular ancestors (see chaps. 5; 10; 11:10-32; 25:12-18; and 36). These genealogies seem to show the interrelationships and familial connections of various social and ethnic groups that existed in the ancient world.

■ Israel's Primeval Traditions (1:1—11:32)

Two Creation Accounts

Genesis 1 and 2 contain the most precise and systematic treatment of God as the Creator of the universe. These chapters contain two separate creation accounts or traditions. The first account (1:1—2:4*a*) is a summary description of the creation of the world and everything in it. This account may be called a **theocentric** account (in Greek, *theos* means "God") because God and His majestic work of creation is its primary focus. The second account (2:4*b*-25) is a more specific treatment of the making of the man, the animals, the woman, and the divine assignment of work to the man in the garden. It is an **anthropocentric** account (in Greek, *anthrōpos* means "man") in which the emphasis is on humanity's nature, destiny, and vocation. The rest of the story of humanity, including the story of Israel in the Old Testament, is a continuation of the second creation account.

We will now study these creation accounts to gain an overall understanding of what the Bible says about God and His work of creation.

The First Creation Story (1:1—2:4a)

Careful reading of Genesis 1:1—2:4a shows that the focus of the text is on the Creator and what He made. The subject of the action (God) is prominent (see the repeated phrase "And God said . . ."). The result of the action, namely, what God made, is also clear.

Genesis 1:1 is a summary statement that affirms faith in God as the sovereign Creator. The Creator "created" the universe ("the heavens and the earth"). The Hebrew verb (*bara'*, meaning "created") used here to describe God's activity denotes God's power to bring into existence things that do not exist. In the Old Testament *bara'* is never used as a verb to describe human activities. This faith statement alone makes the biblical account distinctive and unlike any pagan myth of creation such as the Mesopotamian account of creation known as the ***Enuma Elish***. The universe was a "formless void" (NRSV) covered with darkness when it was brought into existence by God (v. 2). However, even this original condition of chaos was under the control and power of the Spirit of God (v. 3).

The rest of the first account focuses on six days of God's creative activities that brought the light, life, and beauty that we see in the world today.[2] The recurring

C   The *Enuma Elish*

The *Enuma Elish,* the Mesopotamian story of creation, begins with the account of two deities, Apsu (a male god) and Tiamat (Apsu's female counterpart). Subsequent generations of gods were born, which resulted in a struggle for order and authority between the older generations and the younger generations of gods. Apsu was killed in this struggle, and Tiamat gathered up her forces to retaliate. Other frightened gods chose Marduk —a younger, energetic god—to confront the forces of Tiamat. Marduk fought and killed Tiamat. Using her corpse, Marduk laid out the cosmos. The pantheon of gods proclaimed Marduk as their king. Marduk created humanity with the blood of a slain god, and he built Babylon for him to reside. The story ends with a praise of Marduk.[1]

T   Creation Out of Nothing

Genesis 1:1 maintains the truth that the world was created out of nothing **(creatio ex nihilo).** The world in which we live is God's world, conceived by the wisdom of God, fashioned, designed, and brought into being by the powerful speech of God. The Bible affirms the faith that God's creative power has been at work since the beginning of history. God continues to speak His powerful and authoritative word to His creation and causes things to come into existence. The apostle Paul speaks of this power at work in the life of Abraham, who believed in the God "who gives life to the dead and calls into existence the things that do not exist" (Romans 4:17, NRSV). It is this faith that enables us today to hope in God "against hope" as Abraham did, "being fully convinced that God was able to do what he had promised" (vv. 18, 21).

phrase, "And God said," describes creation by the power of God's word or command. There is no satisfactory explanation of the "day" in the first account of creation. The Hebrew word for a day (*yom*) is used in the Old Testament in different ways, including measured time as well as an indefinite duration of time. The recurring phrase in this narrative, "And there was evening, and there was morning" (1:5, 8, 13, 19, 23, 31), shows that Israel's faith placed the creation narrative within the framework of the Jewish understanding of the day. This narrative structure further anticipates the culmination of God's creative work and His rest on the "seventh" day (the **Sabbath**).

During the first three days of creation God focused on the activity of separation or setting boundaries to what He created. On the first day of creation, God created the light and separated it from the darkness that existed over the universe (vv. 3-5). He made the sky and separated the waters above the sky from the waters below on the second day (vv. 6-8). He separated the waters below into seas that led to the formation of the land (vv. 9-10). This natural order and boundary that God established at the time of creation gave Israel confidence in the dependability and authority of God as the Creator (see Psalms 46:1-3; 75:3; Isaiah 40:21-26).

After the land was formed on the third day, God commanded the earth to produce various plants and fruit-bearing trees (1:11-13). The creation of the sun, the moon, and the stars took place on the fourth day (vv. 14-19). This activity parallels the creation of light on the first day. God

Israel's Understanding of the Universe

The first account of creation reflects Israel's understanding of the structure of the universe (cosmology). Israel viewed the earth as flat and circular. Above the earth is a dome-shaped sky or the firmament that rests on the mountains around the edge of the earth. Water above the sky is the source of rain. The earth rests on pillars that float in the waters below the earth (Psalm 46:2). These waters supply the springs, streams, and rivers (Job 38:16).

Diagram showing the Hebrew understanding of the universe (see sidebar above).

filled the sky with birds and the sea with various kinds of living creatures on the fifth day (vv. 20-23). This activity parallels the establishment of the firmament (the sky) on the second day. On the sixth day He made the land animals and humanity as male and female (vv. 24-26). Again, the sixth day's creative work parallels God's activity of forming the land on the third day.

522

2222232333

2222

333

33333333333333333

God's final activity on the sixth day was the creation of humanity. He created both male and female in His image and commanded them to subdue the earth and have dominion over every living thing that He created (vv. 27-28). For humanity and animals, God established a vegetarian way of life (vv. 29-30). After completing His work of creation in six days, God "rested" (in Hebrew, *shabat*, meaning "to cease") from all His work on the seventh day. He blessed and made the seventh day "holy" or set it apart from the six days of creation (2:2-3).

Sexuality and the gender distinction of humanity are part of God's creation plan. The phrase "he created him; male and female he created them" (1:27) expresses the divine plan for the solidarity of human beings, their gender distinction, and community existence. The biblical view that both male and female are created in the image of God also highlights the equality of both genders. Exploitation, devaluation, and manipulation of the opposite gender deny that individual the rightful place in human society.

The Second Creation Story (2:4b-25)

This text also deals with the work of God as the Creator. How-

Humanity in the Image of God

The image of God is a significant biblical idea. The words *image* and *likeness* mean the same. In the context of the Genesis account of creation, these words refer to humanity's function, place, and responsibility in the created world (1:26). God created humanity to be the **image of God,** to rule over His creation as His earthly representatives. Humanness in a biblical sense is our God-given capacity to love and care for God and His creation. Human individuals and the community reflect God's image when they love God with their whole being—heart, soul, and strength (Deuteronomy 6:4), and love each other with unselfish love (Leviticus 19:18; Mark 12:29-31). The New Testament portrays Jesus as the "image" of the invisible God (Colossians 1:15), who for the sake of the salvation of the world, took the "very nature of a servant" and "became obedient to death, even death on a cross" (Philippians 2:7-8). Loving God with unreserved obedience and loving others in an unselfish manner are thus essential marks of being the "image of God."[3]

The Sabbath

The Sabbath teaches the following lessons: First, God's rest (in Hebrew, *shabat*) on the seventh day means that the creation is a completed act. All that He intended to create, He brought into existence during the six days of creation. The world that He created for humanity is therefore a finished work—a dependable world fashioned and created by a dependable Creator God. We do not need to be anxious about the stability of the world in which we live. Second, God "rested" from the work He did in six days. The rhythm of work and rest in the first creation story models for us a divine pattern for an orderly and wholesome life in God's world. Both work and rest are part of God's plan for His creation. The Sabbath offers us freedom from the bondage of excessive work, self-sufficiency, and materialism. Third, the Sabbath is a time for retrospection and reflective living. Retrospection and reflection would lead us to gratitude and dependence on God's gracious provisions for our daily existence. Finally, Jesus models for us the lesson that the Sabbath is for all humanity—a time to bring healing and rest to all who are weary and tired (Matthew 11:28; Mark 2:23—3:6).

ever, in this second account, the emphasis is on the nature of the human individual and the divinely set agenda for human existence. Who are we as human beings? What is the nature and makeup of human beings? What is the divinely intended purpose for human existence? What is the nature and the proper basis of our relationship with God? What is the essential foundation for harmony in family and societal life? These are the questions the text seeks to answer.

The second creation story begins with an observation about the uncultivated condition of the earth (v. 5). This serves as the reason for God's decision to make the man. In most instances, the reference to the man in Genesis 1—4 (in Hebrew, `adam) has the definite article, which conveys the idea of the man in a generic sense (humanity). God "formed" the man (`adam) from the ground (in Hebrew, `adamah) and the man became a living being (in Hebrew, *nephesh*) when God breathed into his nostrils the breath of life.

God made a garden, a place for the dwelling of humanity (vv. 8-10, 15). The **tree of life** and the **tree of the knowledge of good and evil** were located in the middle of the garden. A river that branched out into four rivers watered the garden.

Scholars think that the word *Eden* means "luxury," "abundance," "delight." The common reference of Eden as paradise comes from the meaning implied in the Septuagint translation. In Genesis 2 and 3, Eden is a large geographical region in which God made a garden for the existence of humanity. The phrase "in the east" (2:8) has led some schol-

ars to think that Eden was located in the Mesopotamian region.

God placed Adam in the garden to work and to take care of it. Along with the vocation, God also granted to the man permission to eat from "any tree in the garden" except "the tree of the knowledge of good and evil" (2:16-17). The prohibition included the warning that death would be the consequence of the violation of the divine command. The tree of the knowledge of good and evil appears again in chapter 3 as the focus of temptation. Scholarly opinions regarding the meaning and significance of the tree of the

Jewish mother and child pronounce blessing over the Sabbath candles.

Permission and Prohibition

The issue of human freedom and divine prohibition in the second creation story clearly conveys the truth that obedience is the key to a meaningful and harmonious relationship with God. On the one hand, God granted to the man freedom or permission to enjoy the garden. Yet, on the other hand, this permission also came with a prohibition and a warning (2:16-17). The text makes it clear that the freedom God granted to the man was not absolute freedom. Human beings are not autonomous creatures. There are divinely established limits to our freedom, and we must keep the boundary of our freedom. Freedom calls for expressions of our gratitude to God's graciousness. Prohibition calls for acts of obedience. Obedience to God's command is the most appropriate way to acknowledge God's sovereignty as our Creator.

knowledge of good and evil include humanity's moral values and judgment, omniscient knowledge, and sexual awakening. In Genesis 2 this tree is a symbol of the limit of human freedom in the **Garden of Eden.**

The tree of life that was also located in the middle of the garden receives mention elsewhere in the Bible and seems to represent the possibility of human immortality (Genesis 3:22). In other biblical texts, the tree of life is associated with wisdom, righteousness, hope, healing of relationships, and eternal reward for one's faithfulness (see Proverbs 3:18; 11:30; 13:12; 15:4; Revelation 2:7; 22:2, 14, 19).

The second account of creation concludes with a report about the actions that God undertook to make for the man "a helper as his partner" (2:18). God made first the beasts of the field and birds of the air. The man gave the animals and the birds their names and thus assigned them their particular task under his authority. However, the suitable helper for the man was a woman whom God made from the "ribs" of the man. The Hebrew word for helper (`ezer`) does not imply a subservient, servant role, but rather a strong, upholding, strengthening, and sustaining function of the woman in the life of the man. The man recognized the woman as a part of his own being, of his own kind, the one with whom he was destined to become "one flesh" (vv. 23-24). Here we find a divinely established pattern for marriage and the establishment of family (vv. 18-24). Mutual strengthening and helping is the biblical pattern for a healthy and wholesome relationship between a husband and a wife. Paul illustrates this biblical concept by drawing an analogy to the relationship between Christ and His Church and the sacrificial love Christ demonstrated through His death (Ephesians 5:21-33). The narrative ends with the final statement that the man and the woman were "naked," but they were not ashamed. This reflects the state of innocence, truthfulness, and integrity of relationship that characterized the existence of the first human couple.

The next chapter in the Book of Genesis tells us that the first man and the first woman failed to uphold God's image in the garden. We shall now turn to this story.

Humanity's Sin (3:1-24)

The story of Genesis 3 is a continuation of the story that begins in 2:4b. The narrative begins with a conversation between the woman and the serpent, a creature "the LORD God had made" (3:1).

The text does not give any further significance to the creature except that it was cunning ("crafty") and untamable ("wild").

The serpent began the conversation with the question, "Did God say, 'You must not eat from any tree in the garden'?" (v. 1). The conversation was between the serpent and the woman; however, the man was also on the scene as a silent partner (see v. 6). The serpent's question was a deliberate attempt to divert the focus from freedom to the prohibition. The woman's response also focused on the prohibition and the warning of death (vv. 2-3). The serpent forcefully claimed that death would not happen. On the contrary, he asserted that they will become "like God, knowing good and evil" (v. 5).

Humanity trusted the word of the serpent and ate the fruit of the tree prohibited by God (3:6-7). The result was the opening of the eyes of the man and the woman and the recognition that they were "naked." Guilt and shame of their act prompted them to make a covering to hide their nakedness. Moreover, they attempted to hide from the presence of God. God, nonetheless, encountered them (v. 9). In the trial that followed, the man accused the woman, the woman accused the serpent, and both claimed innocence (vv. 9-13). The power of sin broke up not only the divine-human relationships but also interpersonal relationships (vv. 10-13). The man and the woman were no longer "one flesh" bound together by a harmonious, faithful, and loving relationship. Each one saw the other as responsible for their predicament. Before God they stood, not in corporate solidarity

T Definition of Sin

Though the word *sin* is not found in Genesis 3:1-7, various aspects of this narrative help us describe and define sin. The narrative makes it clear that sin cannot be explained with a simple definition. However, the narrative reveals various facets of sin. The man and the woman trusted the serpent's word against the word of God. Sin in this narrative is thus lack of trust in God and His word. The narrative shows that lack of trust in God has damaging consequences. Their mistrust of God led them to the act of disobedience (v. 6). Moreover, the eating of the fruit from the tree of prohibition was a voluntary and deliberate act on the part of the man and the woman, who were under the divine command to live in faithful obedience to God in the garden (see 2:15-17). Rather than trusting God and recognizing God's authority as the Creator, the first couple became victims of the seductive power of the tempter. Doubt and lack of trust led them to the false claim that they have the potential to become "like God" (3:5). In the final analysis, the eating of the fruit from the forbidden tree was a display of lack of trust, self-sovereignty, pride, and rebellion against God's sovereign authority over them.

and accountability, but blaming each other and trying to justify their individual actions.

God's judgment came upon the serpent, the woman, and the man (vv. 14-19). He destined the serpent to be humanity's enemy. He made childbearing a painful experience for the woman. The consequence of her sin would be her domination by her husband (v. 16). God's punishment of the man was no less severe (vv. 17-19). He made the ground a difficult place for the man to cultivate. Humanity will exist in toil and hardship. God pronounced death as punishment for humanity's sin.

The narrative concludes with

the naming of the woman by the man. The man called the woman Eve (the Hebrew word is similar to the word for "living"). The name anticipates that life would continue to come forth through her, though they were under the curse of death (v. 20). God also clothed the sinful and guilty couple with garments of skin (v. 21). The final outcome of sin was the expulsion of the sinners from the garden. God placed cherubim to guard the entrance of the garden, so that the sinful humanity may not forcefully reenter the home from which they were driven out.

The instruction we find in this narrative is that we must live in the experience of freedom that God graciously offers to us, but with the discernment and recognition that our freedom has limits. God calls us to trust Him and His words when we are faced with the anxieties of life. When we are tempted, our model is Jesus, who resisted the power of the tempter and his attempts to exploit the human anxieties and desires of life (see Matthew 4:1-11).

Cain and Abel: Humanity Outside the Garden (4:1-16)

The world outside of the garden is the context of the story that follows in Genesis 4. The story moves from the report about the birth of Cain and Abel, to a brief reference to their respective vocations. Both brothers came to worship God with their offerings. This is the first act of worship reported in the Bible. God accepted Abel and his offering. We do not know why God did not accept Cain and his offering (vv. 4-5). One thing we do know: God rejected Cain but also offered him an alternative way to seek His approval. However, Cain remained angry and rejected God's instruction as well as warning about the power of sin. What follows in the narrative is actually the story of Cain (vv. 8-16). Cain murdered his brother, and this bloodshed of an innocent human being further alienated humanity from God. Following the trial, God pronounced His judgment that Cain would be a fugitive and wanderer on the earth. Cain was horrified at the prospect of living life as a homeless fugitive. When love is not expressed and practiced as the axiom of relationships, the outcome is alienation and fear. However, in the midst of his death-filled existence, he heard the gracious word of God's protection of his life (v. 15). God placed a mark of protection on Cain. Cain went out from the presence of God to live his life in the land of Nod (which means "wandering"), east of Eden.

T Sin and Grace

Throughout this story, we also find God acting toward the sinful human beings with compassion and grace. Even His visitation of the man and the woman after their disobedience was an act of grace. Most evangelical scholars see Genesis 3:15 as a word about God's final victory over the power of sin through the Messiah **(protevangelium).** Though death was the punishment for disobedience, God granted continued existence for human life through childbirth. God dealt with the issue of humanity's shame and guilt by providing for them garments that He made out of skin (3:21). The narrative thus powerfully illustrates the life-giving grace of God at work, even in the midst of sin and death. The God of this narrative is a God who insists on offering life to those who are dead through their sin (Ephesians 2:1-7).

The Grieving God (4:17—9:29)

The next segment in the primeval stories shows that the power of sin continued to exploit and dominate the human society. Violence became a way of life for the descendants of Cain (4:17-24). Adam and Eve became parents of a third son, named Seth, who was born in the "likeness" and "image" of Adam (vv. 25-26; 5:3). Chapter 5 is a genealogy that traces the ancestry of Noah to Seth. In this genealogical record, we find long life spans for humanity. Two names in this genealogy deserve special mention— Enoch, who did not suffer death because he walked with God (vv. 21-24), and Methuselah, with the longest recorded life of 969 years. Genesis 6:1-8 shows that sin continued to dominate humanity. The story of the marriage between the "sons of God" and "daughters of men" (vv. 1-4) perhaps reflects the view of Israel that in the primeval period sin affected even the divine realm. Divine beings broke the boundaries of their conduct and entered into unholy alliance with the sinful humanity. This story also sets the stage for the story of the universal flood.

The biblical story of the Flood (Genesis 6—9) begins with the report that the widespread and malignant growth of sin brought grief and pain to God. Human beings became corrupt to the point that every thought of their hearts was evil.

God decided to bring an end to human history that was filled with evil. In the midst of sin and judgment, Noah, a righteous and blameless person, "found favor in the eyes of the LORD" (6:8). God's decision was to destroy the earth

Heart

Heart (in Hebrew, *leb*) is the seat of human emotions, understanding, and will. The human heart represents the whole human being. A corrupt heart is a heart that has lost all sensitivity to pure thoughts and motives, because it is evil through and through. Ezekiel describes such a heart as a "heart of stone" (36:26). This heart cannot grieve, because it is stubborn and rebellious. In contrast to this human heart, the Genesis account describes the heart of God as a grieving heart (6:6). Sin, though it may bring joy to a sinner, breaks the heart of God.

with a flood. At the command of God, Noah built an ark to save himself and his family. He also took into the ark male and female specimens of all types of animals. The rain and the flood that lasted for a period of 150 days destroyed all living creatures. When the floodwaters receded, the ark came to rest on the mountains of Ararat. The narrative ends with an account of God making a **covenant with Noah** (8:21—9:17). This is the first covenant mentioned in the Bible. The covenant contained the promise that God would never again destroy the earth with a flood. God promised a predictable and dependable world with seasons and cycles of nature. He blessed Noah and his family and gave them permission to eat meat without blood in it. God also established the value and sacredness of human life on the basis of the fact that He made humanity in His image. The narrative concludes with the report that God set the rainbow as a sign of His covenant with His creation.

Other ancient cultures also maintained their own traditions

of a universal flood that destroyed the earth in the ancient past. The most notable one is the Mesopotamian account preserved in the **Gilgamesh epic.**

Even though the Mesopotamian flood story has some external parallels to the Old Testament account, there are significant differences between the two in content and theology. Perhaps the most important difference is the lack of any moral or ethical reason for the acts of the deities in the Mesopotamian accounts.

The concluding statement of the Flood narrative establishes the three sons of Noah (Shem, Ham, and Japheth) as the ancestors of all the people who inhabited the world (9:18-19). The genealogical record in chapter 10 gives the list of nations that descended from Shem, Ham, and Japheth. Of the three sons, Ham (the ancestor of Canaan) received a curse from his father because of his disrespectful attitude and conduct toward his father (vv. 20-27).

His sin was that when he saw the nakedness of his drunken father, he did not do anything to cover it and thereby prevent his father from becoming an object of public ridicule and disgrace. His brothers received the blessing from Noah for their respectful action to preserve the honor of their father. The blessing statements show the preeminence Noah gave to Shem, who was the ancestor of the Semitic people.

God made provision for a new beginning for humanity. In the midst of grief and judgment, God remained gracious and offered the world a new beginning. The covenant God made with Noah was the basis for a new relationship between God and the world. God promised to sustain the world in spite of human wickedness and rebellion. This covenant is eternal in nature. It is a solemn promise by the sovereign Creator who understands the frailties and sinfulness of humanity and treats us with patience, love, and compassion. The keeping of this covenant is God's responsibility. The Flood account thus ends with a note of hope for post-Flood humanity. This graciousness of God toward us, in the final analysis, is our hope and salvation.

A Scattered and Confused Humanity (11:1-9)

In this new beginning for humanity, the whole world had one language (vv. 1-2). A common language is the key to unity, understanding, cooperation, and harmony. Humanity moved eastward and settled down at Shinar (Babylon). It is possible that the story places the origin of human civilization and sedentary life in the southern part of ancient Meso-

C The Gilgamesh Epic

The Epic of Gilgamesh contains the Mesopotamian version of the flood account. This epic is the story of Gilgamesh, king of Erech, two-thirds god and one-third man, and his search for immortality. The fear of death drove the hero Gilgamesh to go on a journey to meet Utnapishtim, who long ago survived a great flood and attained immortality. When the great gods planned to destroy humanity with a flood for no apparent reason, the god Ea warned Utnapishtim and instructed him to build a boat to escape the catastrophe. The story also includes reference to the sending of birds to see if the water was subsiding. In another version of the flood story, the Atrahasis epic, the hero is called Atrahasis, who also received warning about the flood and built a boat to escape it.[4]

Ziggurat; the altar was located on the top of this towerlike structure. The Tower of Babel may have been a similar structure.

potamia. Some scholars also see in this story Israel's indictment of the city of Babylon, and its temple-towers known as **ziggurats.**

The first goal of this new humanity was to build a city with bricks and tar, as well as a tower to reach the heavens, so that they may make a name for themselves (vv. 3-4). Their fear of being "scattered abroad upon the face of the whole earth" (v. 4, NRSV) shows that they were resisting God's mandate to multiply and fill the earth (see Genesis 1:28; 9:1), so He came down and disrupted the human plans (11:5-9). God confused (in Hebrew, *balal*) their language, which was the source of their pride, strength, and false security (the city's name, **Babel,** which literally means "gate of god," sounds like the word *balal* in Hebrew). The result was the scattering of humanity abroad over the face of the earth.

In this narrative the city and its citizens stand as the earliest examples of human pride and arrogance. The world continues to witness prideful attempts by human beings to immortalize their name. Some do it with bricks, concrete, steel, and marble. Some do it by their restless effort to move upward in our upwardly mobile society. We often forget the truth that "unless the LORD builds the house, its builders labor in vain (Psalm 127:1).

Where there is pride and rebellion, God steps in as the heavenly Judge. God's decision to confuse humanity's language and scatter the people was His judgment upon their rebellion. However, we also find here God fulfilling His will for His creation that they multiply and fill the earth. The divine act of scattering separated humanity into distinctive ethnic and language groups (see the Table of Nations in Genesis 10, NIV).

The rest of the biblical story informs us that the God who divides and scatters in judgment is also the God who gathers humanity to salvation. The next chapter in the Book of Genesis (12) focuses on the beginning of the gathering activity of God. God encountered and called Abraham, a member of this scattered humanity, to obedience so that through him God may unite and bless all the families of the earth (vv. 1-3). We shall now turn to this story.

Summary Statements

- The first creation story focuses on the universe and its creation by the sovereign Creator God.
- The second creation story focuses on humanity's purpose for existence.
- God created humanity in His image.
- Obedience is essential to our relationship with God.
- Humanity yielded to the temptation to mistrust God's word and His authority.
- In the midst of judgment, God showed grace to humanity.
- Noah lived a blameless life in the midst of a sinful world.
- Though God judged the world with the Flood, He also provided for it a new beginning.
- God scattered the descendants of Noah, who were united in their plan to resist God's will for them.

Questions for Reflection

1. What hope do you find in the truth that God has the power to bring into existence things that do not exist?
2. What are the practical implications of our understanding of God as the God who sets boundaries to His creation?
3. What should be the proper Christian response to gender inequality and sex discrimination, based on the biblical concept of both male and female in the image of God?
4. How do we express self-sovereignty (cite examples)?
5. What are some of the negative outcomes of blaming others for our actions?
6. What are the things we do that cause grief to God's heart?
7. What are the things we do to make a name for ourselves?

Resources for Further Study

Blocher, Henri. *In the Beginning: The Opening Chapters of Genesis.* Downers Grove, III.: InterVarsity Press, 1984.

Brueggemann, Walter. *Interpretation: A Bible Commentary for Teaching and Preaching: Genesis.* Atlanta: John Knox Press, 1982. Pages 1-104.

Hamilton, Victor. *The Book of Genesis: Chapters 1—17. New International Commentary on the Old Testament.* Grand Rapids: Eerdmans, 1990. Pages 103-368.

Fretheim, Terence E. *The Book of Genesis: Introduction, Commentary, and Reflections.* Vol. 1 of *The New Interpreter's Bible.* Nashville: Abingdon Press, 1994. Pages 321-416.

6 God's Covenant with Abraham: Genesis 12—25

 bjectives:

Your study of this chapter should help you to:
- Recognize the continuity and relationship between Israel's primeval and patriarchal traditions.
- Identify the major segments within the patriarchal traditions.
- Describe the historical setting of the patriarchal traditions.
- Evaluate the theological significance of God's call of Abraham to the overall scheme of biblical history.
- Analyze the journey of faith, using illustrations from the life events of Abraham.

 ey Words to Understand

Abraham
Ur
Amorite
Hebrews
Habiru
Terah
Sarah
Lot
Haran
Patriarchs
Melchizedek
El Elyon
Covenant
Hagar
El Roi
Ishmael
El Shaddai
Circumcision
El Olam
Isaac
Moriah
Jehovah-jireh
Binding of Isaac
Rebekah

Questions to consider as you read:

1. Why is it important for an individual to have a clear understanding of the past history and traditions of his or her religious faith (regardless of one's religious background)?
2. If you were asked to explain your religious faith, what particular event will you describe as its beginning point?

The biblical accounts that follow the Tower of Babel story focus on God's encounter with **Abraham**. The Old Testament story of Israel begins with the traditions about Abraham and his family with whom God entered into a special relationship. We shall now turn to this story of Israel's beginning.

The Setting

The patriarchal stories belong to the early part of the second millennium, when the Amorites controlled most of Mesopotamia and Syria-Palestine (1950—1700 B.C.). We may assign 1900—1800 B.C. as the approximate date for Abraham. Abraham was a descendant of Shem, one of the three sons of Noah (Genesis 10:1). He was a native of **Ur,** an urban center in the southern part of Mesopotamia (11:31). He belonged to the **Amorite**/Aramean ethnic group (see Deuteronomy 26:5), among whom **Hebrews** perhaps existed as a subculture (Genesis 14:13). Some scholars think that the Hebrews were part of a lower socioeconomic group in the ancient Near East known as **Habiru.**

Terah, Abraham's father, took his family out of Ur, and traveled toward Canaan (11:31). The family included Abraham and his wife, **Sarah,** and **Lot,** his nephew. They stopped their journey at **Haran** in the northwestern part of Mesopotamia, where they settled down and established their home.

Content

Israel's patriarchal traditions (Genesis 12—50) contain the summary accounts of the life events of Abraham, Isaac, and Jacob, the three great ancient ancestors (**patriarchs)** of the nation Israel. The

following is a brief outline of this section of the Book of Genesis:
1. Abraham traditions (12:1—25:18)
2. Jacob traditions (25:19—50:26)

The Jacob traditions include the stories of Isaac, Jacob's father (chap. 26), and the stories of Joseph, Jacob's son (chaps. 37—50).

■ Abraham: From Haran to Canaan (12:1—14:24)

The Abraham stories begin with God's command (known as the call of Abraham) that came to him while he was living at Haran (12:1-4). God commanded Abram (who later became known as Abraham [see 17:5]) to leave his home and set out on a journey to a destination that God would show him later. The command was followed by the divine promises that God would make Abraham a great nation and a blessing to all the families of the earth. Abraham obeyed this command and departed Haran when he was 75 years of age. He took with him his wife, Sarah, his nephew Lot, and all his possessions. The journey took Abraham to Shechem in Canaan. God appeared to Abraham there and promised to give his descendants the land of Canaan. From there, Abraham journeyed southward and pitched his tent near Bethel and later in the Negev region. Abraham set up altars at the places of his journey to worship God, who frequently appeared to him.

A famine in the land of Canaan prompted Abraham and his family to go down to Egypt (12:10-20). When they entered Egypt, Abraham disguised himself as Sarah's brother. Pharaoh took Sarah into his court and gave Abraham a generous dowry of animals and servants. However, God intervened and afflicted Pharaoh and his house because of Sarah. Pharaoh learned the truth about Sarah and asked them to leave Egypt with the wealth they acquired there.

After Abraham returned to Canaan, he made an agreement with Lot that each would go his separate way (13:1-18). He permitted his nephew to choose the fertile and watered plain of the Jordan. Lot settled down near the city of Sodom. Abraham lived in the land of Canaan and made Hebron his home. Later, in a heroic effort, he led a team of his servants and rescued Lot from a

T "The Gospel in Advance"

God promised to make Abraham a blessing to "all peoples on earth" (12:3). This divine promise meant that Abraham's obedience and trust in God would usher in a new reality of life for all the people of the world. The blessing of Abraham would inspire the nations to seek God's blessings for their own lives through their own exercise of faith and obedience to God. The apostle Paul finds in this divine program "the gospel in advance," which invites all nations to share in the blessings of Abraham by following his example of faith (Galatians 3:8-9). From the perspective of the biblical faith, this element of God's promise to Abraham is most crucial because of its universal implication.

Abraham's journey from Ur to Canaan and his sojourn in Egypt.

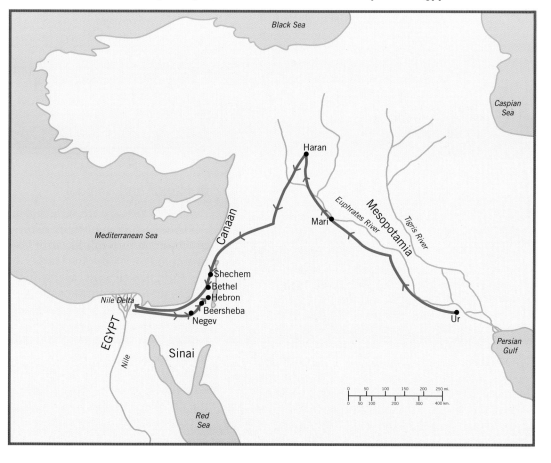

group of foreign kings who raided Sodom (14:1-24). On his return from this victory, he met with **Melchizedek,** priest-king of Salem (14:18-20). Melchizedek blessed Abraham in the name of God Most High, Creator of heaven and earth **(El Elyon).**

■ God's Covenant with Abraham (15:1-21)

God made a **covenant** with Abraham and promised to give him a son and to multiply his descendants to be as countless as the stars of the sky. Abraham believed the Lord, and God "credited it [his faith] to him as righteousness" (v. 6). God affirmed His promise through a covenant-making ritual (vv. 7-17). The covenant making was concluded by an oath from God that He would give the land between the Nile and the Euphrates to Abraham's descendants.

C   Covenant

A covenant is a formal and legally binding contract between two parties. A covenant ceremony consisted of oath taking by both parties, sacrificial rituals, and eating a meal together to seal the terms of the covenant. The sacrificial ritual in some instances also included cutting animals into two halves. Biblical examples show different types of covenants. A covenant between two people of the same socioeconomic status is called a parity covenant (see Genesis 21:22-34; 26:17-33; 31:43-54). God's covenants that focus on the divine promises (God's covenants with Noah, Abraham, and David) may be called promissory covenants. God's covenant with Israel at Mount Sinai focused on the conditions He set forth for His relationship with that nation. Conditional covenants require the beneficiaries of the covenant to show loyalty and allegiance to the covenant maker.

T   Righteousness Through Faith

"Abraham believed the Lord, and he credited to him as righteousness" (Genesis 15:6). This statement serves as the guiding principle for life that is lived between divine promise and its fulfillment.

God granted righteousness to Abraham because he believed God. Faith leads to righteousness before God. Righteousness here is more than being a good person, but it involves maintaining a right relationship with God. A righteous life is a life lived on God's terms, in submission to His will, and according to His plans for one's future. Abraham not only heard the word of promise but also embraced it as a reality for himself and for his future generations. He believed that the Promise Maker was also the Promise Keeper.

■ Hagar and Ishmael (16:1-16)

The delay in the birth of a son to Abraham through Sarah prompted Sarah to give **Hagar,** her Egyptian servant, as a wife to Abraham for the purpose of having a son. Hagar's conception resulted in jealousy and strife that led to Sarah's mistreatment of her maid. Subsequently, Hagar ran away from the house; however, God met with her and gave her the promise that her son would become a great nation. She worshiped God by calling Him "the

God who sees" **(El Roi)**. Hagar returned home and gave birth to her son, **Ishmael**, when Abraham was 86 years old.

■ Circumcision (17:1-27)

Again God appeared to Abraham and affirmed himself as "God Almighty" **(El Shaddai)**. God commanded Abraham to be blameless in his life. Blamelessness means total allegiance to God and living life in the conscious awareness of God's presence in all aspects of one's life. God changed Abram's identity to Abraham and Sarai's to Sarah. This was not only a change of their names but also the beginning of a new relationship between God and this couple. He promised that Abraham would become a "father of many nations" and that Sarah herself would bear a son for Abraham.

In response to God's covenant promise, He required Abraham to establish the ritual of **circumcision** as a sign of the covenant for all the future generations. Abraham circumcised all the male members of his household, including himself and Ishmael. On the part of Abraham, the act of circumcision was an act of obedience to God as well as faith in action through an external, visible, and ineradicable sign. This mark established Abraham as the faithful and trusting recipient of God's covenant promises. Later in the biblical tradition, circumcision became a metaphor for the true commitment of faith that originates within one's heart.

■ Sodom and Gomorrah (18:1—19:38)

God visited Abraham again when he was 99 years old and reiterated the promise that Sarah would bear a son a year later (18:1-15). During this visit, God informed Abraham of His plan to destroy the wicked cities of Sodom and Gomorrah. Though Abraham interceded with God to spare these cities, the absence of even 10 righteous individuals left God with no choice but to carry out His judgment (18:16—19:29). Lot and his family escaped the

---

T Circumcision

The ritual act of circumcision, which once marked the external sign of the covenant, receives a spiritual meaning in later biblical texts. Moses challenged the people of Israel to circumcise their "hearts" (Deuteronomy 10:16) and later promised that God will circumcise their "hearts" and the "hearts" of their descendants (Deuteronomy 30:6; see also Jeremiah 4:4; 9:26). The cleansing of one's heart and commitment to live on God's terms are implied by these passages.[1] The Wesleyan doctrine of entire sanctification finds its Old Testament pattern and promise in these passages.

In the New Testament, Paul also equates true circumcision with the "circumcision of the heart" evident through faithful and obedient living (Romans 2:29; Colossians 2:11-12; 3:11). Spiritual circumcision is thus the means through which we receive deliverance and cleansing from our rebellious and disobedient nature. God's gracious work of cleansing our sinful hearts gives us a new disposition and a new commitment to live a life of wholehearted love for God and humanity.

fiery destruction of Sodom. Lot's wife, however, disregarded the divine command not to look back at the destruction while they were fleeing, and she became a pillar of salt. The narrative concludes with the origin of the Moabites and the Ammonites through the incestuous acts of Lot's daughters.

■ Abraham and Abimelech (20:1-18)

Abraham, while living in the Negev region, spoke again of Sarah as his sister because of his fear for his life. Abimelech, the king of Gerar, subsequently took her into his harem. The king returned Sarah to Abraham because God revealed to him the truth about Abraham and Sarah. Later, Abimelech and Abraham made a covenant to live in peace with each other with loyalty and faithfulness in their conduct toward each other (see 21:22-34). After this covenant was made at Beersheba, Abraham worshiped

Salt covered rocks are common in the southern part of the Dead Sea, near the ancient cities of Sodom and Gomorrah.

Dome of the Rock on the Temple Mount—the traditional site of Mount Moriah.

The Binding of Isaac

God's command to offer Isaac as a sacrifice is known as the **binding of Isaac** (the *Akedah* in the Jewish tradition).

God's command to Abraham was a test, a test through which God would know if Abraham truly *feared* God. It was also a test through which Abraham would come to know the trustworthiness of God. In the biblical tradition, *the fear of the Lord* is one's submission to the sovereign authority of God. There was obedience on the part of Abraham without hesitation or questions about God's promises. This kind of obedience does not require evidence or proof or even promises, because it is founded on faith. Here we have a biblical illustration of genuine faith—believing in God simply because He is God. The story ends with the report that God remained faithful to His promises and Abraham received the promises again because he obeyed God's voice (22:17-19). God proved to Abraham that He was a trustworthy God. Both Abraham and God passed the test.

the Lord by calling Him the name "the Eternal God" **(El Olam)**.

■ Isaac' Birth and the Expulsion of Ishmael (21:1-34)

A son was born to Abraham and Sarah when Abraham was 100 years old, and they named him **Isaac** (which means "he laughs"). The name implies God's laughter in the end because Abraham and Sarah responded to the divine promise with laughter (17:17-19; 18:12-15). The birth of the promised son prompted Sarah to take action against Hagar and Ishmael. At the insistence of Sarah, Abraham sent them away into the wilderness. However, God came to the help of Hagar and Ishmael, provided for their lives, and promised to make Ishmael a great nation (21:1-21).

■ The Offering of Isaac (22:1-24)

The story of God's command to Abraham to offer Isaac as a burnt offering is the climactic event in the Abraham narratives (vv. 1-19).

Abraham took his son to one of the mountains of **Moriah** (which according to tradition is the place where Solomon built the Temple in Jerusalem, known today as the Temple Mount) and nearly fulfilled the divine demand. God intervened and stopped him from carrying out the sacrifice of Isaac and provided instead a ram as a substitute offering. That mountain became a reminder of the truth that "The LORD Will Provide"—**Jehovah-jireh**—another name for God in the patriarchal narratives.

Machpelah is the burial site of the patriarchs of Israel.

C Patriarchal Customs and Religion

Israel's patriarchal traditions give us a glimpse of the way of life and worship in ancient times. The patriarchs lived a seminomadic life, wandering from place to place, seeking pasture and water supply. They lived in tents, raising sheep and other animals. They often entered into covenant relationships with their neighbors and lived in peace in the land that God had promised to give them (21:22-34; 26:26-31).

The patriarchal family included extended members and household servants. The head of the household was the leader of the family. Abraham's rescue of Lot shows that the servants of the house constituted an "army" that protected, defended, and even rescued the family in trouble (chap. 14). Marriage was arranged by the groom or by the family. Marriage custom included the payment of dowry by the groom or the family in the form of gold and silver or through labor (24:52-53; 29:16-30). A wife had the right to choose her maidservants as surrogates to conceive children for her husband. In the absence of progeny, couples designated an adopted slave as their heir (15:2-3).

The patriarchs worshiped God by erecting an altar at the places where God appeared to them (Shechem, Bethel, Beersheba, and Hebron). They revisited these places to remember God's appearance. There was no priesthood or elaborate rituals. The patriarchs called God by various names. These names convey their understanding of the manifestation of the power of God in various ways. In Israel's later history, the places of patriarchal worship became important religious centers and places of spiritual pilgrimage.

Bedouin tents in modern Israel. Abraham lived in tents while he sojourned in the land of Canaan.

■ Sarah's Death and Isaac's Marriage (23:1 — 24:67)

At the age of 127, Sarah died while Abraham was still living in the land of promise as "an alien and a stranger" (23:4). He purchased the cave of Machpelah in Hebron from the Hittites to bury his wife (vv. 1-20). This act shows his hope and trust that the Promised Land would indeed become the resting place for the covenant family. Later, this cave became the burial site of Abraham, Isaac, Isaac's wife, **Rebekah**, Isaac's son Jacob, and Jacob's wife, Leah. The patriarchs were thus joined in death to the Promised Land, and in death they became heirs to the land.

Abraham sent a faithful servant to his homeland in Mesopotamia to seek a wife for Isaac. The servant brought back with him Rebekah, who was the granddaughter of Abraham's brother Nahor, to be a wife for Isaac (Genesis 24). The servant was a man of prayer, who models before us piety in the patriarchal times. His prayer for divine guidance (vv. 12-14) and his praise and thanksgiving for God's guidance (vv. 26-27) illustrate for us the personal nature of a believer's relationship with God in the Bible.

■ Abraham's Final Years (25:1-18)

The concluding segment of the Abraham narratives includes a report about the patriarch's marriage to Keturah, who gave birth to a number of sons to him. Midian, who became the ancestor of the Midianites, was among the sons of Abraham (vv. 1-6).

The story of Abraham ends with the account of his death at the age of 175 (vv. 7-11). His death united the promised son Isaac with Ish-mael, the son who stood outside of the covenant promises. They buried their father in the cave of Mach-pelah. The Abraham narratives end with a summary description of Ish-mael's descendants who occupied the Arabian Desert.

The rest of the patriarchal stories focus on the family history of Abraham's covenant children and God's work in their lives to shape them to be the instruments of justice and righteousness in the world. We will now turn to this story.

Summary Statements

- Israel's patriarchal traditions contain the stories of Abraham, Isaac, and Jacob.
- Israel's patriarchal traditions belong to the early part of the second millennium B.C.
- God called Abraham to become a source of blessing to all the families of the earth.
- God promised Abraham a land and a great nation.
- Abraham responded to God's call and the covenant through obedience and trust.
- Abraham is a model of faith and righteousness because his life events show how to remain in submission to God's sovereign authority even in the midst of the difficult circumstances of life.

Questions for Reflection

1. What are some of the obstacles to spiritual growth and maturity, as evident in the stories of Abraham?
2. What lessons do we learn about overcoming obstacles from the stories of Abraham?
3. Make a list of the spiritual qualities that you find illustrated in the various life events of Abraham in which faith and obedience are evident.
4. Discuss how we can live a life that is a source of blessing to others in the world in which we live today (using illustrations from the life events of Abraham).

Resources for Further Study

Brueggemann, Walter. *Interpretation: A Bible Commentary for Teaching and Preaching: Genesis*. Atlanta: John Knox Press, 1982. Pages 105-203.
Hamilton, Victor. *The Book of Genesis: Chapters 1—17*. New International Commentary on the Old Testament. Grand Rapids: Eerdmans, 1990. Pages 369-483.
———. *The Book of Genesis: Chapters 18—50*. New International Commentary on the Old Testament. Grand Rapids: Eerdmans, 1995. Pages 3-169.
Fretheim, Terence E. *The Book of Genesis: Introduction, Commentary, and Reflections*. Vol. 1 of *The New Interpreter's Bible*. Nashville: Abingdon Press, 1994. Pages 417-515.

7

The Covenant Family: Genesis 26—50

bjectives:

Your study of this chapter should help you to:
- Define the biblical concept of election.
- Describe the key events in the life of Jacob.
- Compare and contrast Jacob's Bethel and Peniel experiences with Christian religious experiences today.
- Summarize the story of Joseph and discuss his place in the patriarchal history.
- Evaluate biblical concepts such as promise and fulfillment, God's sovereignty, and divine providence as they are illustrated in the life events of Jacob's children.

ey Words to Understand

Esau
Jacob
Birthright
Election
Edom
Beersheba
Haran
Luz
Bethel
Laban
Rachel
Leah
Dinah
Mizpah
Israel
Penu'el/Peniel
Shechem
Hyksos
Manasseh
Ephraim
Goshen

Questions to consider as you read:

1. What role do parents play in creating sibling rivalry? What are some of the negative consequences of sibling rivalry?

2. What are some ways to overcome the negative impact of family crises and conflicts?

3. What are some of your life dreams? How would you respond to unfulfilled dreams?

The second part of the patriarchal traditions (Genesis 25:19—50:26) contains the story of God's continued involvement in directing the destiny of the family of Abraham. Here we find the stories of Abraham's son Isaac, Isaac's son Jacob, and Jacob's 12 sons. In these stories the narrator portrays history with remarkable honesty and with very little attempt to hide the negative characteristics and traits of the covenant family. These stories also show how God worked out His plans and purposes through the children of Abraham, though conflict and crisis was an everyday event in their lives.

■ Jacob-Esau Stories (25:19—28:22)

The patriarchal narratives continue with the story of the birth of

T　Election of Jacob

Theologians describe God's choice of Jacob over Esau as the **election** of Jacob. Election is not the operative principle by which God works out our salvation. This divine action simply shows that the promise belongs to God and does not have any human ownership. As the second-born son Jacob simply received the promise of something that was not a natural right to him by his birth order. The election of Jacob is an excellent example of the mystery of God's grace at work in our lives.

two sons to Isaac and Rebekah (25:19-26). God answered Isaac's prayer on behalf of Rebekah, who was barren. She conceived and gave birth to **Esau** (later called Edom, meaning "red" in Hebrew; 25:30; 36:9), and **Jacob** (in Hebrew, the name means "he supplants" or "he takes by the heel"). Before the birth of her sons, God's word came to Rebekah: "Two nations are in your womb . . . and the older will serve the younger" (25:23). Esau, the natural heir to the **birthright** privileges (a double portion of the family inheritance and leadership privileges), will take a second place in the family.

Perhaps the most well known story in this section of the patriarchal narratives is Esau's sale of his birthright to Jacob for a bowl of stew that Jacob made (25:22-33). Red stew in Hebrew is `adom, which contains the same letters of the name **Edom,** the land situated

Abraham, Isaac, and Jacob dug out wells to claim ownership of water in the places where they sojourned in Canaan.

southeast of Israel and occupied by the Edomites, who were the descendants of Esau.

Genesis 26 is the only chapter devoted to Isaac's story. While living at Gerar, Isaac spoke about Rebekah as his sister, fearing that he might be killed. King Abimelech discovered the truth and chastised Isaac for creating the context for bringing evil and guilt upon his people. After moving from place to place, Isaac finally came and pitched his tent at **Beersheba,** where God appeared to him and reaffirmed the covenant promises.

The familiar story of Isaac bestowing the birthright blessing upon Jacob the younger son is a classic example of deception in the Bible (chap. 27). The central issue in this story is the ritual of blessing. Through deception, Jacob received from his father the blessing that rightfully belonged to Esau. When Isaac later learned the truth, he could not revoke the word of the first blessing because it was a solemn and powerful word.

Esau threatened to kill Jacob when their father died (27:41—28:9). Rebekah, who heard about the threat, persuaded Isaac to send Jacob away to marry a girl from her people at **Haran.** On the way to Haran, Jacob spent a night at a place called **Luz.** In a dream, he saw a stairway that connected the earth with heaven and angels ascending and descending on it. God gave him the covenant promises and the blessings of Abraham, and safety during his journey. Jacob gave the name **Bethel** (which means "house of God") to that location, made a pledge to God, and went on his journey toward Haran.

The Dream of Jacob at Bethel

The dream of Jacob at Bethel (Genesis 28:10-22) was an important turning point in Jacob's life. The dream introduced Jacob to an alternative way of life, trusting in a future that was hidden in the promise of God. God bound himself to a deceiver, the one who was far away from home, with unconditional promises. God continues to come into our sinful world. The Gospel writer John speaks of this coming of God: "The Word became flesh and lived among us" so that we all may receive "grace upon grace" (John 1:14, 16, NRSV). God's coming into our lives is a moment of grace; it is also the moment that initiates us into faith in the One who comes with the promise of His gracious presence.

■ Jacob at Haran (29:1—31:55)

Jacob came to Haran where he spent the next 20 years of his life at the home of **Laban,** his uncle (29:1—31:21). There he became the victim of his uncle's deception. He served Laban for 14 years to marry **Rachel. Leah,** his first wife, gave birth to six sons and a daughter (Reuben, Simeon, Levi, Judah, Issachar, Zebulun, and **Dinah**). She also had two sons (Gad and Asher) through her maidser-

An ancient mudbrick gate dated to the middle Bronze Age (the period of Abraham) at Dan in northern Israel.

Jacob's Wrestling with God

The story of Jacob at Peniel/Penu'el is a remarkably powerful narrative in the Bible. The story clearly suggests that God initiated the struggle so that Jacob could have a "face to face" encounter with the God who elected him. This encounter led Jacob to acknowledge before God his name, which conveyed his sinful and deceptive nature. God renamed him *Israel*, meaning "God protects" or "God preserves." Confession resulted in the transformation from a sinful being to a person dependent on the strength that comes from God. Paul writes, "If anyone is in Christ, he is a new creation; the old has gone, the new has come!" (2 Corinthians 5:17).

vant Zilpah. Rachel gave birth to Joseph and she had two other sons (Dan and Naphtali) through her maidservant Bilhah. (Later, Rachel died while giving birth to Jacob's youngest son, Benjamin, after the family arrived back in Canaan; see 35:16-18.)

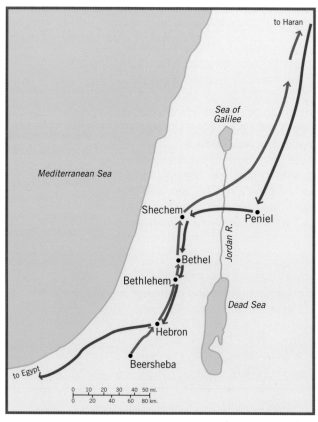

Jacob's journey to Haran and return to Canaan, and later to Egypt.

■ Jacob's Return to Canaan (32:1—36:42)

Twenty years later, Jacob decided to return to Canaan. His homecoming is the subject of the narratives in Genesis 31:22—33:20. He left Haran with all his family and possessions when Laban was away. Laban pursued him to reclaim his property. The two tricksters finally resolved to go their separate ways by making peace with each other through a covenant at **Mizpah.**

Genesis 32 powerfully portrays the difficulty of homecoming for Jacob, who had left his home in conflict, fear, and broken relationship. God gave Jacob a vision of His angels (God's army), which assured him safe passage into Canaan. In addition, Jacob sent his messengers and gifts to Esau to appease his brother.

When Jacob realized that neither his prayer nor his gifts worked, he sent his family and possessions across the Jabbok River. He remained on the other side where he engaged in a struggle with God. When Jacob begged for God's blessing, He gave him the name **Israel.** Jacob called the place of that encounter **Penu'el** or **Peniel** (meaning "the face of God"). He continued his journey and met with his brother Esau.

Jacob journeyed on and finally arrived in the land of Canaan and settled down at Shechem (33:18). He purchased property for himself from the local inhabitants. Though Jacob wanted to live in peace among the local inhabitants, his sons massacred them in retaliation for the rape of their sister Dinah by a member of the royal family of **Shechem** (chap. 34). Jacob was grieved over this dishonor and disgrace his sons brought to him through their treacherous conduct.

Jacob returned to Bethel where God met with him (chap. 35). The narratives include the accounts of the death of Rachel, Jacob's beloved wife, and of Isaac, Jacob's beloved father. Rachel died while giving birth to Jacob's youngest son, Benjamin, at a location in the vicinity of modern Bethlehem. Chapter 36 is a list of the descendants of Esau.

■ Joseph Stories (Genesis 37—50)

The last major segment of the patriarchal stories is the story of Jacob's children, in which Joseph, the 11th son, plays a prominent role. Scholars place the accounts of Joseph in Egypt during the early part of the **Hyksos** rule in Egypt (about 1700 B.C.).

Jacob's special love for Joseph caused resentment and hatred among the rest of his sons toward their younger brother. This crisis was intensified by the dreams of Joseph that alluded to his royal status over the rest of his family. The brothers responded to the dream with a plot to kill the dreamer and his dream. Later they sold him to Ishmaelite caravan traders, who in turn sold him as a slave to the Egyptians. They

The traditional site of Rachel's tomb in Bethlehem.

told their father that his beloved son had been killed by wild animals (chap. 37).

Joseph's life in Egypt took him from an Egyptian official's house to jail, and from there to the presence of Pharaoh. His ability to interpret the dreams of Pharaoh brought him success and a high-level position in the kingdom of Egypt. Pharaoh also gave Joseph an Egyptian name and gave him an Egyptian wife, who gave birth to his two sons **Manasseh** and **Ephraim.** These two sons later became two of the 12 tribes of Israel (chaps. 39—41).

A famine in Canaan prompted Jacob to send his sons to go down to Egypt to buy grain (chap. 42). Joseph, who recognized his brothers, sent them back with grain but with the demand that they return with their youngest brother. Jacob was strongly opposed to sending Benjamin to Egypt. When the famine continued in the land, Jacob had no choice but to send Benjamin with his brothers (chap. 43).

When they returned, Joseph, through a ploy, planned to keep Benjamin in Egypt (chap. 44). Judah begged Joseph to let Benjamin

"The LORD was with him"

The Lord was with Joseph in all the circumstances of his life. This is the theme of Genesis 39—50. "The LORD was with him"—that is no easy statement of faith. In this powerful theological summation of Joseph's life experiences, we find a challenge to live life in a faithful manner, with integrity, courage, and hope through difficult and uncertain times. Such times will provide the context to experience the inexplicable and gracious presence of God. The apostle Paul echoes this theme in his words, "Neither death nor life, . . . neither the present nor the future, . . . neither height nor depth, nor anything else in all creation, will be able to separate us from the love of God" (Romans 8:38-39).

go back to his father. He told Joseph that the loss of Benjamin would be too much for his father to bear. Judah's emotional speech and his willingness to take the place of Benjamin moved Joseph to tears. He finally revealed his identity to his brothers. He also comforted his brothers by saying that God sent him to Egypt to preserve the life of his family. He sent them back to Canaan to bring Jacob to Egypt. Jacob came down to Egypt to meet his son and the two

were reunited in the region of **Goshen** in the Nile delta region. At the request of Joseph, Pharaoh gave permission to Jacob and his sons to settle down in Goshen (chaps. 45—47).

Prior to his death, Jacob made Joseph take an oath that he would not bury him in Egypt. Jacob gave Joseph's sons a place equal to that of his own sons. He blessed Joseph and his sons and gave preeminence to Ephraim over his older brother Manasseh. He also called his other sons and gave each one his final blessings, and gave Judah a royal position among his brothers (see 49:10). Jacob died after the pronouncement of blessings, and his sons took his body to Canaan to bury him in the cave of Machpelah. After the burial the whole family returned to Egypt.

The final segment of the Genesis story focuses on the reconciliation between Joseph and his brothers (50:15-26). Joseph's brothers were afraid that he might retaliate since their father was now dead. They came to him seeking his forgiveness for the wrong they had committed against him. He comforted them again with the assurance that their harmful actions were in-

The God of Joseph

We recognize two key theological affirmations in Joseph's words to his brothers (45:4-13; 50:19-21). First, *God's sovereignty is at work in our lives.* God seldom cancels His plans because of negative human response to His will. We, too, live in a world that plots evil schemes against the faithful. But the plans that God has for His people are not evil plans, rather plans for their welfare to give them "a future with hope" (Jeremiah 29:11, NRSV). Indeed, "In all things God works for the good of those who love him" (Romans 8:28), even through human actions that may stand in direct conflict with His will and purposes for us. Second, *God remains faithful and gracious to us through His providence.* He preserved Joseph's life so that Jacob's family would have a future. In His own strange and mysterious ways He provided for His people. That is good news for us who "worry about . . . what [we] will eat or drink" (Matthew 6:25).

deed part of God's good plan to bring about the benefits they were enjoying in Egypt. At his request, they promised to take his bones with them when God would visit them and take them out of Egypt. Joseph would thus be buried in the Promised Land. Joseph died at the age of 110, and his embalmed body was placed in a coffin for his future journey back to the Promised Land.

The remainder of the Pentateuch (Exodus, Leviticus, Numbers, and Deuteronomy) is in a real sense the story of God's visitation of Israel to fulfill His promises to the patriarchs. In the Book of Exodus we encounter the events that set in motion the homeward journey of Israel from Egypt.

We will turn now turn to this segment in the story of Israel that we find in the Book of Exodus.

Summary Statements

- God in His gracious freedom chose Jacob to receive the covenant blessings.
- Jacob encountered God at Bethel and received the covenant promises.
- Jacob struggled with God at Peniel and received a blessing and the name Israel.
- Joseph's early life was filled with trouble, but the Lord was with him.
- God demonstrated His sovereignty and providence in and through the various life events of Joseph.
- The entire family of Jacob left Canaan and settled down in Egypt.

Questions for Reflection

1. Cite some examples of the activity of God's freedom and grace in our lives today, which may seem to upset human standards and cultural/religious expectations. How would you respond to these divine actions?
2. What is the outcome of a life that is lived partly trusting God and partly trusting our own resources?
3. Relate Jacob's Peniel experience to your religious experience today.
4. What evidence is there in your life that "God is with you" in all of life's circumstances?
5. "In all things, God works for the good of those who love him"—what are some of the challenges this biblical promise presents to our lives that are filled with brokenness, disappointments, pain, and tragedy?

Resources for Further Study

Brueggemann, Walter. *Interpretation: A Bible Commentary for Teaching and Preaching: Genesis.* Atlanta: John Knox Press, 1982. Pages 204-380.

Hamilton, Victor. *The Book of Genesis: Chapters 18—50. New International Commentary on the Old Testament.* Grand Rapids: Eerdmans, 1995. Pages 169-715.

Fretheim, Terence E. *The Book of Genesis: Introduction, Commentary, and Reflections.* Vol. 1 of *The New Interpreter's Bible.* Nashville: Abingdon Press, 1994. Pages 516-673.

8

The Birth of a Nation: Exodus 1—18

O bjectives:

Your study of this chapter should help you to:
- Identify the content and organization of the Book of Exodus.
- Describe the historical and social setting of the exodus story.
- Explain the theme of promise and fulfillment as it relates to the early history of Israel.
- Discuss the significance of the call of Moses.
- Describe the significance of the name Yahweh.
- Describe the Passover and its theological significance to the Christian Church.

K ey Words to Understand

Exodus
Hyksos
Seti I
Avaris
Rameses II
Hebrews
Pithom
Rameses
Moses
Midian
Jethro
Horeb
Yahweh
Adonai
Plagues
Passover
Pesach
Amalekites

Q uestions to consider as you read:

1. What is the difference between personal faith and ancestral religion?

2. What do you think was the religious belief of the children of Israel (their attitude to God and the covenant promises He had made to their ancestors) while they lived in Egypt for 430 years? What were some of the questions they might have asked about their faith?

God's visitation of His people to bring salvation to them is a prominent theme in the Bible. God came to visit the children of Israel in Egypt. He set them free from their bondage in Egypt. This redemption story is not an isolated event in biblical history. It is directly linked to God's call and covenant with Abraham, Isaac, and Jacob. Moreover, the **Exodus** story of redemption is also connected to Israel's creation faith. In biblical theology, redemption is the goal of creation. Redemption attests to the truth that God the Creator is also the Redeemer. In this chapter, we will deal with the great drama of God's creative-redemptive work that He performed in the history of Israel.

Title and Authorship

The Book of Exodus is the second book of the Torah (or, the Second Book of Moses). The title *Exodus* comes from the Greek word *exodos* (meaning "going out" or "departure") in the Septuagint translation. Scholars who maintain the documentary hypothesis trace the materials in this book to three literary sources (Yahwist, Elohist, and Priestly). We see the book as a theological document that draws heavily on the traditions that belong to the Mosaic period and on Moses' authority as Israel's greatest lawgiver. It is likely that the book reached its final form prior to 700 B.C.

Setting

The stories of the Book of Exodus belong to the New Kingdom period in Egypt. By the middle of the 15th century B.C., the Egyptians expelled the **Hyksos** and regained control of their land. Most likely the Israelites lived in relative freedom in Egypt from the time they settled down there (around 1700 B.C.) to the time of the New Kingdom Pharaoh **Seti I** (1309—1290 B.C.). Seti I established **Avaris** in the Nile Delta as his capital, perhaps to keep political control over Canaan and Syria. He began the construction of a palace city in Avaris, which was continued by his son **Rameses II** (1290-1224 B.C.). This city is known as Rameses (see Exodus 1:11). It is likely that events described in Exodus 1:8-22 (Israel's bondage and slavery) belong to the period of Seti I. Thus there is a gap of approximately 400 years between the last event in the Book of Genesis and the beginning of the Book of Exodus (from 1700 to 1300 B.C.). Israel's escape from Egypt (the Exodus event) took place during the reign of Rameses II. We regard 1280 B.C. as the approximate date of this event. Biblical tradition maintains that Israel was in Egypt for 430 years (see Exodus 12:40; Gal. 3:17).

Content

The Book of Exodus has two main parts:
1. Bondage and Deliverance (1:1—18:27)
2. Israel at Mount Sinai (19:1—40:38)

Sphinx near the Pyramids of Giza.

In this chapter, we will focus on the events narrated in the first part of this book.

■ Israel's Bondage in Egypt (1:1-22)

The story of the Book of Exodus begins with a summary statement about the settlement of Jacob and his 12 sons in Egypt and their growth in population. The early chapters of the Book of Exodus at times refer to the Israelites as **Hebrews,** the descendants of Abraham the Hebrew (see Genesis 14:13). When the Israelites became too numerous, the Egyptians saw them as a potential threat to their national security. An unnamed Pharaoh (most likely Seti I) oppressed them with forced labor and gave them the task of building **Pithom** and **Rameses,** two store cities. Slavery did not control the population growth. So Pharaoh ordered the Hebrew midwives to kill the Hebrew male children when they were born. The midwives who feared God disobeyed the royal command and let the infants live. Pharaoh subsequently

ordered the Israelites to throw their newborn male children into the Nile.

■ Moses' Birth and His Call (2:1—4:31)

Chapter 2 briefly summarizes the early years of Moses. His rescue by Pharaoh's daughter illustrates the mysterious way God decreed life for the infant who was destined to die by the royal powers. The name **Moses** *(mosheh)* was most likely a royal Egyptian name, and it sounds similar to the Hebrew word *mashah,* which means "to draw out" (see 2:10). He grew up as the son of Pharaoh's daughter. However, he recognized his heritage

The Nile Valley is well-known for its rich soil.

T God's Response to Oppression in the World

The bondage and slavery of Israel is central to the story of the Old Testament. An oppressive ruler issued the decree of death against a people who belonged to the lowest social and economic structure of the society. However, we find here also the story of God's care and concern for the poor and the oppressed in the world. In the midst of the royal decree of death, He came to a marginalized community with His offer of freedom and life.

These stories convey to us truths about humanity's spiritual bondage under the power of Satan. But more than that, they also challenge us to become sensitive to the political and social realities of our society. Genocide, ethnic cleansing, and racial violence are tragedies that we witness all too often in our world. These stories speak about and speak for the economically disadvantaged, socially ostracized, and ethnically and racially segregated people in our society. These stories also speak against those who rule with self-serving political ideologies and oppressive economic and social policies. The good news, however, is that God continues to be the source of strength and life to the poor and afflicted in the world.

and identified himself with his suffering people. His passion for justice for his people prompted him to take matters into his own hands, and he killed an Egyptian who mistreated a Hebrew. Becoming a fugitive, he escaped to **Midian,** where he lived in the home of Reuel (also known as **Jethro**) and married Reuel's daughter Zipporah.

Meanwhile, in Egypt the slavery of the Israelites continued. God heard their cry for help and remembered His promises to Abraham, Isaac, and Jacob. He encountered Moses who was with his flock at **Horeb,** in the southern region of the Sinai Peninsula. In the midst of a bush that was burning but not being consumed by the fire, God called to Moses to go and rescue the Israelites from Egyptian oppression. Moses attempted to resist this divine demand by expressing his lack of credibility (3:11), asking questions about God's identity (v. 13), and expressing his fear that Israel will not believe him (4:1). He raised a final objection citing his inability to speak eloquently (v. 10). God responded each time with the assurance of His presence with Moses. He revealed His identity as **Yahweh,**

The God Who Calls

In the story of God's call of Moses, we encounter the God who summons us to walk out of our daily, mundane, and self-seeking ways of life to pursue a life that may take us into a new awareness of His sovereign work in the world. The call of God is not simply a call to commitment and obedience but also a call to live our lives by our full participation in all the difficult realities of life. Moses "chose to be mistreated along with the people of God rather than to enjoy the pleasures of sin . . . ; he persevered because he saw him who is invisible" (Hebrews 11:25, 27). Our limited abilities to carry out the awesome divine task should not hinder us from being obedient to the One who calls us. The encounter with the Holy God and obedience to His holy call will open up for us new possibilities to experience His grace. The One who calls us is the One who promises to be with us to bring to completion the good work He initiates in us (Philippians 1:5-6).

God's Personal Name

The origin of God's personal name Yahweh is a much-debated issue. The divine name contains four Hebrew consonants transliterated as YHWH. We do not know the exact pronunciation of the name. The later Jewish tradition supplied the vowels of **Adonai,** another epithet for God, to the four letters YHWH. In the old English tradition, this name was known as Jehovah. Yahweh is a popular pronunciation adopted by modern biblical scholars. However, Jews do not pronounce the divine name because of its sacredness. Most English Bibles translate the divine name as "the LORD."

The four letters of the divine name come from the root form of a Hebrew verb *hayah,* which means "to be." God's eternal existence, His continuing presence in His creation, and His power to cause things to happen are all ideas conveyed by this root verb form of the divine name. Yahweh is the God who was, who is, and who will be with His people in all of their history. The name signifies His *being there with us* in all of life's circumstances. He is *Immanuel*—God with us (Isaiah 8:10). The phrase "I AM" essentially conveys this understanding of God (Exodus 3:14).

which is God's personal name in the Israelite tradition.

■ Moses Confronts Pharaoh (5:1—11:10)

God sent Moses and his brother, Aaron, to Pharaoh with the demand to let Israel go from Egypt for a three-day journey into the desert to worship God. Pharaoh rejected the appeal and ordered his men to make life more difficult for the Israelite slaves. Moses, having been ridiculed by Pharaoh and despised by the Israelites, turned to God with frustration and complaint. God reassured him with the promise that with His mighty hand of deliverance and judgment, He would lead Israel out of Egypt and bring them into the Promised Land.

God reminded Moses that his assignment would be difficult. He said he would "harden Pharaoh's heart" (7:3) through a series of miraculous signs. This divine plan included sending upon Egypt a series of calamities or **plagues.** These calamities included turning the water of the Nile into blood, the plagues of frogs, gnats, flies, death of the livestock, boils, hail, locusts, darkness, and finally the death of the firstborn male children of the Egyptians and their animals (chaps.

7—11). It is possible that the plagues were directed not only against the political powers that controlled Egypt but also against the gods of that nation (see 12:12).[1]

Horus, an Egyptian god, with Pharaoh, king of Egypt.

T The Hardening of Pharaoh's Heart

Pharaoh refused to acknowledge God's sovereign power (he "hardened" his heart) and continued to do so from the beginning to the end. God also "hardened" the heart of Pharaoh (9:12; cf. 4:21) by sending more "signs" to him who consciously and repeatedly chose to resist His sovereign rule. God's hardening of Pharaoh began after the sixth plague (9:12). At that point, the divine judgment began to take its force upon a person who has not given heed to repeated calls for repentance (see similar divine judgment actions in Psalm 81:11-12; Romans 1:24-27).

A traditional Jewish Passover Seder includes parsley, a boiled egg, a roasted shank bone, bitter herbs, and haroseth (a walnuts and wine mixture).

The 10th plague prompted Pharaoh to let Moses and Aaron take Israel out of Egypt for their journey into the wilderness to worship God. Though there was a direct route to Canaan along the Mediterranean Sea, God led Israel in a different direction because of the prospect that a war with the Philistines in the coastal

■ The Passover and the Crossing of the Sea of Reeds (12:1—15:21)

Though the plagues came as a sign of God's power, Pharaoh himself remained stubborn. During the last plague, God spared the children of Israel by giving them instruction to observe the **Passover** ritual. The ritual included smearing the blood of a lamb on the doorframes of their houses and eating its roasted meat in a hurried manner.

The Passover

In Israel's religious traditions, the Passover *(Pesach)* is a seven-day springtime celebration that commemorates Israel's deliverance from Egypt. The ritual is called the Passover *(Pesach)* because on the day God passed through Egypt in judgment, He passed over (the verb *pasach* in Hebrew means "to have compassion," "protect," "skip over") the children of Israel (see 12:11-13). We find specific instructions in Exodus 12 and 13 to keep the ritual of *Pesach* and the Feast of Unleavened Bread as annual events to evoke the memory of God's gracious protection. These festivals also aimed to instill faith in each new generation. Through the reenactment and retelling of the Passover story, the people of Israel even today enter into their past history and find an identity with their ancestors who held on to the hope of entering the Promised Land in the midst of their struggle for life.

The Passover and the Church

The crucial element in the Passover ritual was the blood of the sacrificial lamb, which provided protection for the Israelites. In the New Testament, the sacrifice of Christ receives significance as the sacrifice of the Passover lamb (1 Corinthians 5:6-8), and Jesus as the Lamb slain to ransom men and women for God (Revelation 5). The Passover, both in the Old and the New Testaments, deals with God's redemptive work that culminates in giving hope to the community of faith. The Old Testament Passover provides us with an initial contact and entry point into the redemptive work of God that is fully realized through our redemption in Jesus. The New Testament redemption is first and foremost freedom from sin and evil, which leads to a new life in Christ. The Passover meal for the Church is the Lord's Supper, which links and identifies the Christian life with the suffering, death, and resurrection of Jesus. This sacred fellowship also energizes us with the hope for our future life with Christ.

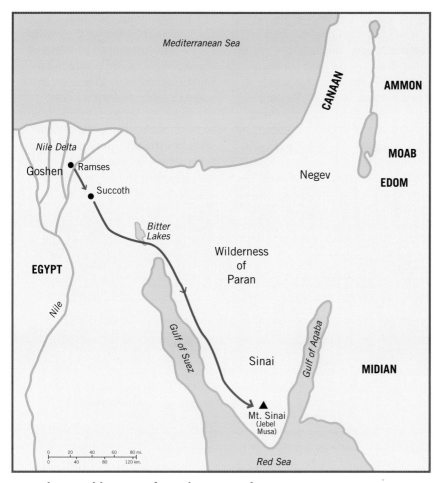

The possible route of Israel's journey from Egypt to Mount Sinai.

region might prompt Israel to return to Egypt.

Israel's exodus began from Rameses and the journey took them down toward the Sea of Reeds. Scholars find it difficult to give a precise identification of the sea (in Hebrew, *yam suph* is not the Red Sea, rather the Sea of Reeds, probably a lake located in that vicinity). God went before Israel to lead them in this journey by manifesting His presence in a "pillar of cloud by day" and a "pillar of fire by night" (13:21). Pharaoh made one last-minute attempt to retake the Israelites under his control by pursuing them with his army. At the Sea of Reeds, God delivered His people by dividing the sea and by drowning the Egyptian army in the sea. Israel saw and witnessed the power of Yahweh, her God. "The LORD saved Israel," and they "believed" in Him (14:30-31, NRSV). Moses sang a song of praise to the God who saved Israel from the power of Pharaoh (15:1-18).[2]

■ Israel's Journey to Mount Sinai (15:22—18:27)

The crossing of the Sea of Reeds took Israel right into the wilderness, and there was no return to Egypt. Moses led Israel to

Mount Sinai/Horeb. On the way at Marah, Israel complained against Moses because the water was bitter. In the wilderness of Sin, they complained because there was no food. At Rephidim, they complained because there was no water. Israel's complaints on the way to Mount Sinai seem incomprehensible in light of the great and mighty acts of God on their behalf. These stories reveal the truth that Israel soon forgot the redemptive power of God and His providential care and concern for His people. When they were faced with the harsh realities of the wilderness, they refused to trust God as their Provider. In spite of their repeated complaints, God gave them meat and manna, water from a rock, and victory against the **Amalekites,** who attempted to stop their journey through the wilderness. On the third month after they left Egypt, they arrived at Mount Sinai (19:1-2).

Summary Statements

- After the death of Jacob, his descendants (Israel) stayed in Egypt for over 400 years.
- Even in a foreign land, Israel multiplied and became great in number according to the covenant promises of God.
- The Egyptians oppressed the Israelites and enslaved them.
- The early story of Moses reveals the miraculous way in which God intervened in his life.
- God heard the cry of the people of Israel and appointed Moses to lead them out of Egypt.
- God revealed himself to Moses and Israel by His personal name Yahweh.
- God revealed himself to the Egyptians and to Israel as the sovereign God of the universe.
- God redeemed Israel from the Egyptians and led them out of Egypt under the leadership of Moses.

Questions for Reflection

1. What are some of the lessons we learn about promises in the Bible based on the story of Israel in Egypt?
2. What are some of the attitudes and temptations that might develop among us when we wait for God's promises to be realized in our lives?
3. Describe your experience of God as a God who is "there being with us."
4. How does God perform His act of deliverance today? Give illustrations from your personal life or the life of someone very close to you.

Resources for Further Study

Brueggemann, Walter. *The Book of Exodus: Introduction, Commentary, and Reflections.* Vol. 1 of *The New Interpreter's Bible.* Nashville: Abingdon Press, 1994. Pages 690-829.
Childs, Brevard S. *The Book of Exodus: A Critical, Theological Commentary.* The Old Testament Library. Philadelphia: Westminster Press, 1974. Pages 4-339.
Fretheim, Terrence E. *Interpretation: A Bible Commentary for Teaching and Preaching: Exodus.* Louisville: John Knox Press, 1991. Pages 23-200.

9 The Covenant Community: Exodus 19—40

 bjectives:

Your study of this chapter should help you to:
- Describe the goal and purpose of the Mount Sinai covenant.
- Discuss Israel's understanding of God, based on the Exodus-Sinai stories.
- Describe the contemporary relevance of the Ten Commandments.
- Relate the Exodus themes of the covenant and the Tabernacle with corresponding themes in the New Testament.

ey Words to Understand

Mount Sinai
Jebel Musa
Covenant
Sinai covenant
Theophany
Ten Commandments
Covenant code
Code of Hammurabi
Casuistic laws
Apodictic laws
Tabernacle
Court
Holy place
Holy of holies
Ark of the covenant
Mercy seat
Altar of burnt offering
Eleazar
Ithmar
Golden calf

Questions to consider as you read:

1. What is the most important factor that determines stability in human relationships?
2. What are the reasons people worship God today?
3. Why do people call marriage a "covenant"?

In the previous chapter, we traced the story of Israel's exodus from Egypt and their journey to Mount Sinai. The second part of the Book of Exodus (chaps. 19—40) deals with the story of God's meeting with Israel at Mount Sinai.

■ The Covenant Making at Sinai (19:1—24:18)

Israel arrived at **Mount Sinai** on the third month after they left Egypt. We do not know the exact location of Mount Sinai. The tra-

Mountains in the vicinity of Sinai. St. Catherine's monastery is in the valley.

Israel's Election

At Mount Sinai, Israel became an elect and holy nation by entering into a covenant relationship with God (19:3-8). His election of Israel brought that nation to a specially privileged place in the world. Election also meant for Israel the responsibility to bear witness to God's redemptive work in the world. Through election, Israel became God's "treasured possession" (in Hebrew, *segullah*). God promised to give Israel the status of nationhood, not of a ruling political kingdom, but of a servant kingdom with a priestly vocation. Israel's destiny in the world was to promote the knowledge of God and mediate His blessings to the nations in the world. Likewise, God called her to be a holy nation, a nation "set apart" (in Hebrew, *qadash*) for His service. Holiness was thus to be the hallmark of this covenant people. The "if . . . then" formula (v. 5) clearly shows the conditional nature of this covenant and election. The holy character of the nation depended on their covenant commitment to listen and obey God in their daily walk with Him. In biblical theology, the pursuit of holiness means a moment-by-moment relationship of obedience and listening to God, who calls His people to be holy.

ditional site is **Jebel Musa** ("Mountain of Moses") in the southern part of the Sinai Peninsula where St. Catherine's monastery is located. At Mount Sinai, God met with Moses and revealed to him His purpose for the people whom He redeemed from Egypt (19:3-6). God saved Israel from Egypt to bring them to a new relationship with himself (v. 4). The relationship is called a **covenant** *(berith),* and the future of the God-Israel relationship depended on Israel's willingness to "obey" their God (literally, "listen to my voice") and to "keep" the covenant with Him (v. 5). This covenant (known as the **Sinai covenant**) was a further develop-

ment of God's covenant with Abraham. The people whom God addressed at Sinai were the children of Abraham and the recipients of the promises God made to him. In return for Israel's faithfulness, God promised to treat them as a specially prized possession, a kingdom of priests, and a holy nation (vv. 5b-6).

Moses told the people the covenant offer from God, and the people made the commitment to enter in to the covenant with God (vv. 7-8). God commanded Moses to consecrate the people so that they may be ready to meet God when He appeared on the mountain. God appeared on the mountain in the midst of smoke, fire,

T The Ten Commandments

The first commandment (20:3) calls for Israel's exclusive relation to Yahweh as her only God. Genuine love for God demands from us our complete loyalty and devotion to God. The second commandment (vv. 4-6) prohibits any attempt to give God a visible representation in any form. This commandment invites us to contemplate with wonder and amazement the awesome holiness of the Creator who fills the whole earth with His glory (Isaiah 6:3). The third commandment (Exodus 20:7) prohibits the misuse of God's holy name for self-serving and illegitimate purposes. The commandment calls us to carefully scrutinize our words and actions in the name of God, to see whether we are glorifying God or profaning His name. The fourth commandment (v. 8) calls for the experience of "rest" after the six days of labor. The Sabbath is holy—a time for rest *set apart* from the ordinary times of the day or the week.

The fifth commandment (v. 12) is the only commandment with a promise attached to it. The way we love God is best reflected in the way we treat our parents, who are our most immediate neighbor. The sixth commandment (v. 13) is a prohibition against violating human life, which is sacred. This commandment upholds the dignity and worth of every human being. The seventh commandment (v. 14) calls for faithfulness in the marital relationship. Fidelity in marriage reflects fidelity to the covenant with God.

The eighth commandment (v. 15) prohibits the violation of the rights of others to hold and enjoy property. This commandment speaks against economic inequities, profit making at the expense of the poor and the disadvantaged, and all other forms of exploitations in our society. The ninth commandment (v. 16) prohibits lying in the court that would lead to the miscarriage of justice in the society. Our community life depends on our commitment to speak truthfully about our neighbor. The tenth commandment (v. 17) prohibits lustful ambition and desire to acquire what is not legitimately one's own. Our covenant with God calls us to treat others and their property with love and care.

thunder, lightning, and earthquake. The people stood at the foot of the mountain and saw the awesome glory of God (vv. 10-25). **Theophany** is the theological term that describes such manifestations of God in supernatural ways to human beings.

Israel received from God the **Ten Commandments** at Mount Sinai as the 10 primary conditions of the Sinai covenant (Exodus 20:1-17). The commands are generally divided into two groups or "two tablets" (see Exodus 24:12; 31:18; 34:1). The first 4 com-

mandments deal with relations to God (20:3-11), and the last 6 commandments deal with relations to other individuals (vv. 12-17). Of the 10, 8 are stated as negative commandments but with positive implications. When an action or behavior is prohibited, the opposite of that action or behavior is elicited by these negative commandments.

The Ten Commandments are rooted in the theophany at Mount Sinai, and they belong to the context of the Sinai covenant. The Ten Commandments, or the Decalogue ("ten words"), revealed the holy character of God. At the outset of the giving of these commands, God identified himself as the God who redeemed Israel out of the bondage in Egypt, thus implying His legitimate claim over Israel and His authority to express His will for them (20:2).[2] The overall purpose of the commandments was to instill unreserved and unqualified love for God and love for others (see Deuteronomy 6:5; Leviticus 19:18; Mark 12:29, 32). However, it is important for us to understand that love for God and love for others are not mutually exclusive. We cannot truly love our neighbor without truly loving God; indeed, it is our love for God (or more appropriately the way we love God) that determines and defines our love for others.

Exodus 20:22—23:33 contains the specific laws related to the Sinai covenant. This section is often called the Book of the Covenant or the **covenant code**. This collection of laws has several parallels to the laws of the ancient Near East, particularly to the **Code of Hammurabi** (1792-1750 B.C.) and the Hittite laws of the 16th century B.C.[3] This section be-

C

Excerpts from the Code of Hammurabi (numbers show the number of each law)

120. If a seignior deposited his grain in a(nother) seignior's house for storage and a loss has then occurred at the granary or the owner of the house opened the storage-room and took grain or he has denied completely (the receipt of) the grain which was stored in his house, the owner of the grain shall set forth the particulars regarding his grain in the presence of god and the owner of the house shall give to the owner of the grain double the grain that he took [see Israel's law in Exodus 22:7-9].

196. If a seignior has destroyed the eye of a member of the aristocracy, they shall destroy his eye.

197. If he has broken a(nother) seignior's bone, they shall break his bone.

198. If he has destroyed the eye of a commoner or broken the bone of a commoner, he shall pay one mina of silver.

199. If he has destroyed the eye of a seignior's slave or broken the bone of a seignior's slave, he shall pay one-half his value.

200. If a seignior has knocked out a tooth of a seignior of his own rank, they shall knock out his tooth.

201. If he has knocked out a commoner's tooth, he shall pay one-third mina of silver [see Israel's personal injury laws in Exodus 21:12-27].[1]

Law/Legal Materials—Principles of Interpretation

- The interpreter must understand the specific historical context and the character of the legal statements in the Old Testament. The covenant God made with Israel at Mount Sinai is the historical context of the Law.
- Biblical laws fall into three categories: **casuistic laws** (laws with an "if . . . then" clause) contain specific case illustrations and penalty statements; **apodictic laws** are absolute prohibitions; instructions are rules for worship and rituals.
- The Law also deals with different dimensions of human life and relationships including worship, sacrifice, morality, social conduct, social order, family life, and hygiene. The Law as a whole aims to preserve the distinctiveness of Israel as a holy people.
- The Old Testament laws presuppose certain spiritual and theological principles. These laws provide a model for ethical and moral conduct.
- Personal responsibility in all areas of human relationships is a significant emphasis of the Old Testament laws.
- The Ten Commandments are the nonnegotiable standards of spirituality, morality, and ethical conduct for all humanity.
- When we deal with specific Old Testament laws, which may seem contrary to the spirit of the New Testament teachings, we must give emphasis to the supreme law of love in the Sermon on the Mount and God's grace and righteousness that come to us through Jesus Christ.

gins and ends with a call to loyalty demonstrated through proper worship and God's promise of blessings and protection (20:21-26; 23:20-33). The main body of the covenant code contains specific laws dealing with slaves, capital crimes, noncapital crimes, damage to property, social and religious duties, ethical duties, and religious festivals (21:1—23:19). Following is a list of some of the larger issues that receive attention in the covenant code: humane treatment of each other; punishment for crime that is equitable and sanctioned by the society; protection of the property rights of others; restitution for damages done to others; care, concern, and compassion for the economically disadvantaged; commitment to honesty and justice; and setting aside specific time to give thanks to God.

Exodus 24 describes the Sinai covenant making between God and Israel. The ritual of covenant making included making an altar, the sacrifice of peace offering, the reading of the Book of the Covenant, the people's oath to obey all the words of the Lord, the sprinkling of the blood on the people, and the eating of a meal by the elders of Israel in the presence of God (24:3-11). The narrative ends with the report about Moses going up on the mountain, and the cloud covering the mountain. He remained there for 40 days and 40 nights (v. 18).

■ Instructions About the Tabernacle (25:1—31:18)

At Mount Sinai, God instructed Israel to build a tentlike structure, following the specific pattern and plan provided by him (chaps. 25—31; 35—40). This structure, known

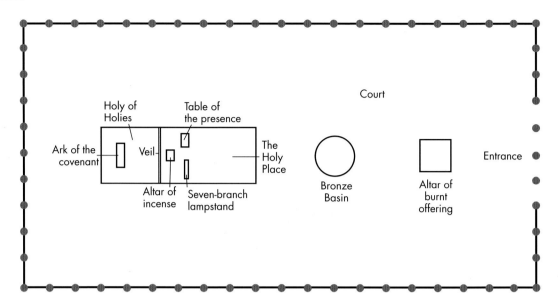

Court

Holy of Holies

Table of the presence

Ark of the covenant

Veil

The Holy Place

Entrance

Altar of incense

Seven-branch lampstand

Bronze Basin

Altar of burnt offering

A diagram of the Tabernacle.

as the **Tabernacle,** or the Tent of Meeting, was the visible dwelling of God in the midst of the people of Israel. Though God gave the plan and pattern of the Tabernacle, the building of the Tabernacle rested entirely on the freewill offering of the people and the labor of skilled workers who were gifted by the Spirit of God (25:1-7; 31:1-11).

Exodus 25:8 is crucial to our understanding of the purpose of the Tabernacle, which was to be a "sanctuary" (in Hebrew, *miqdash;* from *qadash,* which means "to set apart" or "consecrate"; the adjective *qadosh* means "holy") for God. The holiness of God required this tent to be a holy place, set apart from the tents in which Israel lived. The divinely given specifications of its furnishings, measurements, and materials further

The innermost sanctuary (Holy of Holies) at an Israelite temple at Arad in the southern part of Israel. Solomon may have built this temple for the soldiers stationed here during his reign.

An altar for sacrifice at the Israelite temple at Arad.

attest to the holy character of the tent. The Tabernacle was not a place for God to dwell but rather a place that conveyed to the people that God dwelt (from *shakan,* meaning "to dwell") among them (see 25:8). (The word *shekhinah,* which means "indwelling" or "divine presence," is a derivation of *shakan.*) The function of the Tabernacle (in Hebrew, *mishkan*) was to give Israel the visible and tangible evidence of the reality of God's abiding presence with His people in their daily journey.

The Tabernacle was comprised of three areas: the **court,** the **holy place,** and the **holy of holies.** The holy place and the holy of holies constituted the sacred and restricted space in the Tabernacle. The holy of holies, the innermost area of the Tabernacle, was the most holy place and was separated from the holy place with a veil (Exodus 26:31-33). No one except the high priest in Israel had access to the holy of holies. He was allowed to enter into that innermost sacred chamber only on the

The Tabernacle and Worship

In the Tabernacle narratives, we find not only the place of worship but also a proper pattern of worship. Doing God's work, giving to God, and receiving from God—all were done in faithfulness to the One who was present with Israel in their daily life. In the Tabernacle, every object and material, from the least sacred to the most sacred, from the least valuable to the most valuable, had its properly assigned place and function. Everything in the Tabernacle reflected the holiness of God. Everything in the Tabernacle invited the people of God to reflect on the mystery of His presence among them. Everything in the Tabernacle pointed to the possibility that Israel could meet with God. We may be tempted to skip over this long and rather cumbersome material because we do not worship in this prescribed, ritualistic, and archaic way. But hidden in the details of this narrative is the promise that a meeting with God who is holy, majestic, and mysterious is a possibility for those who seek Him. The Tabernacle invites us to reflect on the mystery of God's holy presence among us and to find meaningful and disciplined ways to worship Him "in the splendor of his holiness" (Psalm 29:2).

The Tabernacle in the New Testament

A number of New Testament writers have adopted the terminology of the Tabernacle in their writings. The Gospel writer John speaks of the ultimate reality of the presence of God with His people through Jesus of Nazareth in the Incarnation. "And the Word became flesh and dwelt [or *tabernacled*] among us" (John 1:14, RSV). John thus connects the place of the divine presence with the incarnate Christ. Perhaps the most detailed Christian interpretation of the Tabernacle is found in the Letter to the Hebrews. The writer of this letter refers to the earthly Tabernacle as a "copy and shadow of what is in heaven" (8:5). The writer further conveys that the furnishings and the rituals in the earthly Tabernacle reflected the truth that "the way into the Most Holy Place [i.e., the real presence of God] had not yet been disclosed" (9:8). However, Christ who appeared as "high priest" "entered the Most Holy Place once for all by his own blood" not only for the "eternal redemption" but also to "cleanse our consciences from acts that lead to death" and to enable us to "serve the living God" (9:11-14). The Tabernacle in the Old Testament thus reminds us of the pledge and guarantee of God's promise to dwell with us through our Lord Jesus Christ. The apostle Paul further describes the Christian believer as "God's temple," the dwelling place of the Holy Spirit (1 Corinthians 3:16-17; 6:19-20).

Day of Atonement (see Leviticus 16). The **ark of the covenant,** a wooden chest overlaid with pure gold, was located in this sacred space. The ark housed the testimonies or the two tablets of stone on which the Ten Commandments were written. In Israel's later history, the ark became the visible symbol of God's power and presence. The lid of the ark, or the "atonement cover" (the Hebrew noun *kapporet* literally means "a cover"), was a solid slab of gold. This cover is popularly known as the **mercy seat** (in Greek, *hilasterion;* see Romans 3:26; Hebrews 9:5). On each end of the mercy seat was a cherub, with its wings overshadowing the mercy seat.

The holy place was the outer chamber of the Tabernacle. Only members of the priesthood had access to this place. This sacred space contained the table for "the bread of presence," a seven branched lampstand (menorah),

and an altar of incense for the offering of fragrance.

The court was part of the enclosure of the Tabernacle that defined the boundary of the sacred area. The altar and the basin for washing were placed in the court. The altar (also known as the **altar of burnt offering** or the altar of bronze) was for offering sacrifices on behalf of the worshiping community (see Leviticus 1—7). Exodus 29:38-39 stipulates a morning and evening burnt offering at this altar. The basin for washing provided the water for the ritual cleansing of the priesthood. The priests were required to be clean before they entered the holy place to perform the daily rituals.

The Tabernacle narrative includes two chapters on the garments for the priesthood and the ordination ritual of the priests (Exodus 28—29). Though Israel as a nation received the status as a kingdom of priests at Mount Sinai, the special privilege of serving

God in the Tabernacle as priests went to Moses' brother Aaron and his sons, who belonged to the tribe of Levi. Of the four sons of Aaron, **Eleazar** and **Ithmar** became the ancestors of the priests in Israel (see 1 Chronicles 24:1-6). Exodus 28 deals with the elaborate and colorful priestly garments. Instructions for ordination of the priests are given in chapter 29. The holiness of the priests is reflected in their vestments. The ritual of ordination set them apart from the laity. Israel's access to the holy presence of God and their meeting with God required the mediating presence of the priesthood. Those who serve God in this capacity must reflect God's holiness in all spheres of their life. This seems to be a central concern in Exodus 28—29.

■ **Israel's Sin and Restoration (32:1—34:35)**

In the midst of the description of the Tabernacle, its furnishing, and the appointment of workers to build it, we find the story of Israel's apostasy and breaking of the covenant with God (chaps. 32—34). While Moses was on the mountain, the people approached Aaron and coerced him to make a calf made out of gold. Aaron presented the **golden calf** to Israel as their god and they worshiped the idol with offerings and other merry-making activities (32:1-6). When Moses came down from the mountain with the tablets that contained the commandments written by God, he saw celebration and dancing before the golden calf. In his anger he broke the tablets, burned the calf, and made the people drink the water that was mixed with the powder of their idol. Aaron attempted to excuse himself from his responsibility for this idolatry. By Moses' command the Levites slaughtered about 3,000 men that day as punishment for their sin (vv. 7-29).

Moses interceded with God to show mercy and forgiveness to the sinful people (vv. 11-14, 30-34). He pleaded with God to continue to lead and guide the people to their destination (33:12-16). God responded favorably to Moses and once again showed His glory to him as a sign of His favor toward His faithful servant (vv. 17-23). At the command of God, Moses made two tablets of stone and went up on the mountain again where he once again received the covenant stipulations from God. Moses was on the mountain for another 40 days and 40 nights, and he wrote the Ten Commandments on the tablets he took with him. He returned and gave the commandments to the people of Israel (34:1-35).

■ **The Construction of the Tabernacle (35:1—40:38)**

The concluding section of Exodus (chaps. 35—40) carefully narrates in detail the making of the Tabernacle, its furnishings, and the priestly garments. "The glory of the LORD filled the tabernacle" when Moses and Israel did all that the Lord commanded them to do concerning the building of the Tabernacle (40:34).

The story of the Exodus ends with a postscript—a remembrance by a later faithful community that the God who came to dwell among His covenant people at a designated place guided them by "the cloud . . . by day, and fire . . . in the cloud by night *during all their travels*" (v. 38, emphasis added). Israel's "going out" (exodus) from Egypt thus turned out to be a *going out with* the God who saved them from their bondage. The community of faith in the New Testament found in Jesus of Nazareth, the Word Incarnate, the real presence of God with them (John 1:14). We, too, can have confidence and joy in the reality of the presence of the Holy Spirit, who gives us guidance and comfort in our daily journey.

As for Israel at Mount Sinai, this was only the beginning of their journey with God.

Summary Statements

- God brought Israel to Mount Sinai and entered into a covenant relationship with them.
- God gave Israel the Ten Commandments as the basic guidelines for their life as God's people in the world.
- Israel sinned against God through idolatry, but God restored them through the intercessory prayers of Moses.
- God promised Israel His indwelling presence among them through the plan and pattern for the construction of the Tabernacle.

Questions for Reflection

1. What does it mean to say that our relationship with God is a covenant relationship?
2. What are the responsibilities and obligations of a Christian who claims to have a covenant relationship with God through Jesus Christ?
3. What suggestions do you have to carry out our worship of God today in the beauty of His holiness?
4. How do we make worship a way of life today?

Resources for Further Study

Brueggemann, Walter. *The Book of Exodus: Introduction, Commentary, and Reflections.* Vol. 1 of *The New Interpreter's Bible.* Nashville: Abingdon Press, 1994. Pages 830-981.

Childs, Brevard S. *The Book of Exodus: A Critical, Theological Commentary.* The Old Testament Library. Philadelphia: Westminster Press, 1974. Pages 340-638.

Fretheim, Terrence E. *Interpretation: A Bible Commentary for Teaching and Preaching: Exodus.* Louisville: John Knox Press, 1991. Pages 201-312.

10 Israel in the Wilderness: Leviticus and Numbers

O bjectives:

Your study of this chapter should help you to:

- Describe the content of the Book of Leviticus.
- Discuss the significance of sacrifice and offerings to the faith of Israel.
- Relate the holiness rituals in Leviticus to the Christian emphasis on holy living.
- Describe the content of the Book of Numbers.
- Identify the major events that took place during Israel's journey from Sinai to the plains of Moab.
- Discuss the issues of doubt and trust as they relate to one's spiritual pilgrimage, using the story of the Book of Numbers.

Q uestions to consider as you read:

1. Why is it necessary to have rules and regulations for worship?
2. How do you maintain purity in life today?
3. What are some of the obstacles to faith in our religious life?
4. Why is it difficult to trust God in the midst of difficult situations in life?

K ey Words to Understand

Burnt offering
Grain offering
Peace offering
Sin offering
Guilt offering
Yom Kippur
Azazel
Holiness code
Kadesh
Moab
Levites
Purity
Nazirite
Miriam
Joshua
Caleb
Meribah
Edom
King's Highway
Balaam
Balak
Plains of Moab
Cities of refuge

So far we have followed the story of the people of Israel from the days of the patriarchs to their deliverance from Egypt and God's covenant with them at Mount Sinai. At Mount Sinai, God set forth the laws that were designed to order Israel's existence as a holy people. We now turn to the Book of Leviticus, which contains guidelines for Israel's holy living and fellowship with the God who redeemed her from Egypt.

The Book of Leviticus

Title and Authorship

Samaritan Passover ceremony; the fire on which the unclean parts of the lamb are burned.

The English title *Leviticus* comes from the Greek and Latin translations of the Old Testament. The title implies that this book was an instruction manual for Israel's priests. We cannot give a precise date for its writing. The laws promulgated at Sinai were most likely expanded during Israel's later history. It is likely that most of these complex laws existed in a written form around 700 B.C.[1] However, the consensus among most critical scholars is that the laws and regulations found in this book are the work of Israel's priestly writers (P), dated approximately to 400 B.C.

Setting

The book belongs to the setting of the covenant making at Mount Sinai (see Leviticus 27:34). In its canonical setting, the book seeks to address the covenant community with God's requirements for their holy pilgrimage with Him.

Content

Though the content of the book is often addressed as God's

Sin and Guilt Offerings

Sin and guilt offerings were God's way of dealing with sin. Through these offerings, the grace of God's forgiveness came to the faithful community of Israel. That divine grace now comes to us through Christ and His atonement. Enjoying that grace means that we must give grace to others "who trespass against us" (see Matthew 6:12). But more than that, God's people today must practice restoration and restitution, and thereby bring healing and reconciliation in a world that does not know how to make things right.

speeches to Moses, and occasionally to Aaron, it is clear that the people were to be the ultimate recipients of these words (see the recurring formula, "The LORD said to Moses, 'Speak to the Israelites'" throughout this book). In that sense, we think of this book not as a manual for the priesthood but rather as God's instructions to the people who have made a covenant with Him. The content of the book may be outlined as follows:

1. Sacrifices and Rituals (1:1—16:34)

2. Holy Living (17:1—27:34)

■ Various Offerings and Sacrifices (1:1—7:38)

Chapters 1—7 describe the laws of five different offerings to God. An offering (in Hebrew, *qorban;* from a verb stem meaning "to approach" or "to bring near") is a gift that brings a person to the holy presence of God.

The whole **burnt offering** was the sacrifice of unblemished male animals from cattle or flock or certain birds; the whole animal was burned on the altar. The Hebrew term means "that which goes up," perhaps implying the going up of the flame and smoke of the sacrifice. The sacrifice yielded "an aroma pleasing to the LORD" (1:9, 13, 17). In the **grain**

offering, a small portion of the dough made from the flour of the inner kernel of the wheat grain mixed with olive oil and frankincense was burnt on the altar. The **peace offering** included a sacred meal participated in by the priest and the worshiper. As a rule, only those who stood in a right relationship with God were allowed to bring these three offerings.

The **sin offering** brought forgiveness through the sacrifice of an animal. The **guilt offering** required the payment of restitution to correct the wrong committed by a sinner.

■ The Ordination of the Priests (8:1—10:20)

The consecration and ordination of Aaron and his sons as priests to minister in the Tabernacle is the subject of Leviticus 8—10. These chapters, like the rest of the Book of Leviticus, contain complex rituals and ceremonies that call for precision in their enactment. Two sons of Aaron (Nadab and Abihu) kindled fire in the censer and put incense on it without divine sanction. They were consumed by fire for their illegitimate and unholy action.

■ Cleanness and Uncleanness (11:1—15:33)

Chapters 11—15 deal with various types of uncleanness and prescriptions to remove them. The dietary laws distinguish between the clean and unclean animals, and the procedure to remove uncleanness caused by one's contact with a carcass.[2] The law of purification includes specific actions a new mother should take to restore her cleanness after childbirth. The law of cleanness also stipulates the procedure for purification from the uncleanness caused by infectious skin diseases, mildew, and bodily discharges. All of these laws show that God was intensely concerned with the health and well-being of the covenant community.

■ The Day of Atonement (16:1-34)

Leviticus 16 focuses on the complex procedure by which the nation as a whole was cleansed from sin and its consequences on a designated day known as the Day of Atonement **(Yom Kippur)**. This was the only day in which the high priest entered the holy of holies. The ritual included the offering of a bull as a sin offering to make atonement for the high priest and for his house, the offering of a goat as a sin offering to make atonement for the nation Israel, and sending away a goat **(Azazel)** into the wilderness. The high priest entered the holy of holies once with the blood of the bull and a second time with the blood of the goat and sprinkled it in front of and on the mercy seat ("atonement cover" in the NIV). God instituted this day as an annual day for Israel to seek the divine cleansing of sin from the na-

Blood Sacrifice and Atonement

The shedding of the blood of an animal was God's gracious provision to sinners (see Leviticus 17:11). The blood made "atonement" for one's sins (17:11). The word *atonement* conveys the idea of "covering" something; in this case, the covering of sin by the blood. But it also involved the cleansing from sin. In the Old Testament, the blood cleansed a sinner from all sins (16:30). The animal sacrifice was a substitute act with which a sinner received from God both His justice and mercy. Blood sacrifice was thus effective in gaining forgiveness, restoration, and cleansing from God.

New Testament writers describe the death of Jesus as God's provision of atonement for all humanity. The writer of Hebrews states that "the blood of Christ . . . cleanse[s] our consciences from acts that lead to death, so that we may serve the living God" (9:14).

The Day of Atonement

The rituals on the Day of Atonement focused on the cleansing of sin from the holy community of Israel, so that they might experience the reality of God's presence in the Tabernacle. An important purpose of this day was to remove sin and its effects from the community. Israel accomplished this by sending the scapegoat into the wilderness (16:20-22). John the Baptist's testimony of Jesus, "Look, the Lamb of God, who takes away the sin of the world!" is a remarkable way of expressing the cleansing and removing of sin connected with the sacrificial death of Jesus (John 1:29). The added dimension of Christ's atonement is that He is also the High Priest who entered the heavenly holy of holies with his own blood "to do away with sin . . . ; to take away the sins of many people" (Hebrews 9:26, 28). The death of Jesus in that sense stands in direct continuity with the purpose of the Day of Atonement.

tion (16:29-31). This day was for Israel a day of Sabbath, rest not only from work but also from the power of sin.

■ The Holiness Code (17:1 — 26:46)

Leviticus 17—26 contains miscellaneous laws, connected by the theme of holiness. This section is popularly known as the **holiness code.** The holiness code addresses areas such as proper worship, eating, sexual activities, social conduct, conduct of the priesthood, religious calendar, blasphemy, fair and equitable justice, restoration of the land and property ownership, and reward and punishment from God.

The instructions in the Book of Leviticus end with detailed regulations concerning making special vows to God (chap. 27).

The Book of Numbers

The Book of Numbers continues the theme of holiness set forth in the Book of Leviticus by its emphasis on the centrality of the Tabernacle and the guidance of God in the journey of Israel through the wilderness. The book contains narratives about Israel's murmuring and rebellion against God when they were faced with the difficult realities of life in the wilderness. The story of this book takes Israel from Sinai to the plains of Moab.

Title and Authorship

The English title derives from the Greek and Latin translations (*arithmoi* in Greek and *Numeri* in Latin). This title reflects the census accounts in chapters 1 and 26.

Holiness in Leviticus

The call to holiness ("be holy") is an important theme in the holiness code (see 19:2; 20:7, 26; 21:6, 8). The holiness code describes the arena of daily life as the most appropriate context to practice holy living. Holiness in Leviticus is not a private affair for the enjoyment of the individual. It is the community's business to be holy so that it would be the mediating agency of God's holiness in the world. The Law insists on "love your neighbor as yourself" as the operative principle for achieving this goal (19:18). The New Testament emphasis on "love your neighbor as yourself" (Matthew 22:39; Romans 13:9; James 2:8) also reiterates the centrality of the law of love in Christian conduct.

The Hebrew title *bemidbar* ("in the wilderness") fits well with the geographical setting of the book.

As in the case of the other books of the Pentateuch, we think that the stories and the legal materials in Numbers have their origin during the period of Moses. The book in its canonical form presents the wilderness context in the 13th century B.C. However, we also recognize the fact that the book in its present form and arrangement may have been the work of later generations. Critical scholars find in this book a mixture of J, E, and P materials.[3]

Setting

Various events described in Numbers 1:1—10:10 took place in the vicinity of Mount Sinai in the 2nd year of Israel's departure from Egypt. Israel departed from Mount Sinai on the 14th month after they left Egypt. Their immediate destination was the wilderness of Paran, directly north of Mount Sinai. They arrived at **Kadesh,** probably an oa-

The Plains of Moab where the Israelites camped at the end of their wilderness journey.

look over the land of Canaan and the strength of its inhabitants (12:16; 13:26). In the 40th year of their journey, Israel arrived at **Moab,** the region directly east of Jericho beyond the river Jordan (20:22; 22:1).

We do not know for sure where Israel spent the time during the intervening years (approximately 38 years). It is possible that Israel, after the initial arrival at Kadesh, stayed there for a few months and left that region, wandering aimlessly in the wilderness for 38 years. They eventually returned to Kadesh to begin the final phase of

sis located just south of the border of the Promised Land. From Kadesh, Moses sent out 12 spies to

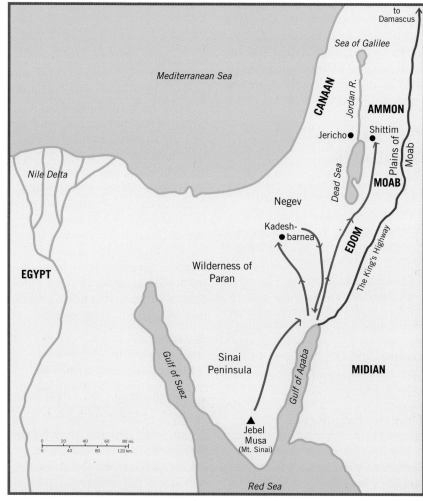

The possible route of Israel's journey from Mount Sinai to the Plains of Moab.

the journey that took them to Moab. The narratives do not cover the entire history of Israel in the wilderness. The focus is on the 2nd year and the 40th year of Israel's journey. The book, as it stands in the Bible, covers Israel's history between 1280 and 1240 B.C.

Content

The narratives in Numbers can be assigned to the following three sections:

1. Preparations for Departure from Sinai (1:1—10:10)
2. Journey from Sinai to Moab (10:11—21:35)
3. Israel in the Plains of Moab (22:1—36:13)

■ The Preparation for Departure (1:1 — 10:10)

Israel's preparation to leave Mount Sinai began with the organization of the nation as an army. At the instruction of God, Moses took a census of the people (all the tribes, except the tribe of Levi) who were "able to serve in the army" (1:3). At the outset, Israel anticipated opposition and the possibility of war with her enemies on the way to occupy the Promised Land.

The preparation to leave Sinai also included an organized positioning of Israel's tribes around the Tabernacle. The **Levites** encamped around the Tabernacle to preserve the sanctity of the sacred space. Moses enlisted all the Levites who were between 30 and 50 years of age to attend the duties of the Tabernacle.

The preparation for the journey included steps taken to eliminate impurity from the camp of Israel (chap. 5). God made the provision to all who wished to take a vow of

---

T A God-Centered Community

The positioning of the tents of Israel with the tent of God's dwelling at the center conveys the theme of a God-centered life for the people of God (2:1-2). On every side, the tents of Israel faced the Tabernacle. This theme of God-centered community and family existence speaks powerfully against our tendency to give God only a marginal place in our life. When God is no longer the center of our life, life becomes empty and void of holiness. The result is a life dominated by materialism, self-sufficiency, and pride.

---

separation to demonstrate their **purity** in life. The person who took such a vow was known as a **Nazirite.** Samson, Samuel, and John the Baptist were among those who were Nazirites at one time in their lives (Judges 13:5; 1 Samuel 1:11; Luke 1:15). Prior to their departure from Mount Sinai, God bestowed upon the priesthood the duty to pronounce His blessing upon His people who were ready to embark on a life-long journey with Him.

Numbers 7:1—10:10 describes the final stage in the preparations to depart Mount Sinai. The leaders of the tribes of Israel brought the offerings for the Tabernacle. Moses consecrated the Levites for their service. Both the laity and the priesthood were involved in the final preparations for their journey to the Promised Land.

■ Murmuring and Rebellion (10:11 — 14:45; 16:1 — 17:13)

Numbers 10:11-28 describes Israel's journey from Sinai under the guidance of the cloud of God's presence. Each tribe had an assigned place in the marching order, with the tribe of Judah in the front and Naphtali in the rear. The Levites who carried the sacred objects were at the middle of the marching line. Those who carried the ark of the covenant were at the front line to give Israel a visible sign of God's leadership during their journey (see v. 33; see also Joshua 3:14).

The narratives in the next few chapters give us a glimpse of Israel's rebellious life in the wilderness. At Taberah, the people complained about their hardship. They also craved meat and murmured that they were better off in Egypt. God responded by sending quail for meat, but along with meat also came God's judgment. Even Moses was exhausted with weariness and with the weight of his responsibility as the leader. God instructed Moses to appoint 70 elders to share the responsibility of leadership. **Miriam** and Aaron, the siblings of Moses, complained against Moses' leadership. They claimed that they, too, were the recipients of God's word. God revealed to them that Moses indeed was His chosen servant with whom He spoke directly, and not through visions and dreams.

Numbers 13—14 contains the story of Israel's spying out the land of Canaan, and the subsequent events of rebellion and God's judgment. From Kadesh, close to the southern border of Canaan, Moses sent out 12 men to spy out the land. They traveled throughout the land for 40 days and made assessment of the strength and productivity of the land. The spies came back with samples of the fruits of the land. The good news they brought was that the land was indeed a land of

"milk and honey." Caleb encouraged the people to go up and occupy the land (13:30).

The majority report, however, concluded that the inhabitants of the land were giants, before whom Israel was like "grasshoppers" (v. 33). This bad news caused panic, and rebellion. They misconstrued God's good intentions and promises as His evil plans and attempted to find a leader who would take them back to Egypt. **Joshua** and **Caleb** pleaded with the nation not to rebel against God. God punished the people with the judgment of their wandering in the wilderness for 40 years and the eventual death of everyone who left Egypt, except Joshua and Caleb.

Korah, Dathan and Abiram, and other lay leaders challenged the priestly authority of Moses and Aaron and claimed that the whole congregation was holy and therefore had the priestly rights and privileges (chap. 16). Through a miraculous sign of the budding of Aaron's rod, God authenticated the house of Aaron as the legitimate priestly family (17:1-13).

■ Miscellaneous Laws (15:1-41; 18:1—19:22)

Various miscellaneous laws interrupt the narrative of Israel's journey in the wilderness. These include laws concerning grain offerings, offerings for sins committed unwittingly, Sabbath breaking, and tassels on the garments (chap. 15). Chapter 18 deals with laws concerning the priests and Levites. Moses assigned the Levites the task of attending the duties of the Tabernacle. The offerings of the people belonged to the priests. The tithe of the people belonged to the

Levites. The tithe of the Levites belonged to the high priest. Chapter 19 contains laws of purification from uncleanness.

■ Journey from Kadesh to Moab (20:1 — 21:35)

Numbers 20—21 describes the last segment of Israel's journey in the wilderness. At **Meribah,** the people once again rebelled against Moses because there was no water. God commanded Moses to take his rod and speak to the rock that was before them to yield water. Moses in a moment of rage struck the rock twice with his rod. Though water came out of the rock, this was an act of disobedience on the part of Moses. God pronounced upon Moses the judgment that he would not be permitted to lead Israel into the Promised Land.

The king of **Edom** refused to allow Israel to travel on the **King's Highway,** which was the most important trade route of ancient times, going from the Gulf of Aqaba region in the south to Damascus in the north through Edom, Moab, Ammon, Gilead, and Bashan. Israel traveled around Edom and arrived at

Mount Hor. Aaron died and was buried at Hor. On the way to the plains of Moab, Israel encountered and gained military victory over the king of Arad; Sihon, king of the Amorites; and Og, king of Bashan.

The King's Highway, a commercial route that went through the lands of Edom, Moab, and Ammon.

■ Balaam Oracles (22:1 — 24:25)

Israel reached the plains of Moab and camped there. The story of **Balaam** and his donkey provides a humorous interlude to the wilderness episodes in Numbers. **Balak,** the king of Moab, sent his messengers to hire Balaam, a magician and seer from northern Mesopotamia, to pronounce a curse on Israel so that his army

Mount Hor, Aaron's burial place.

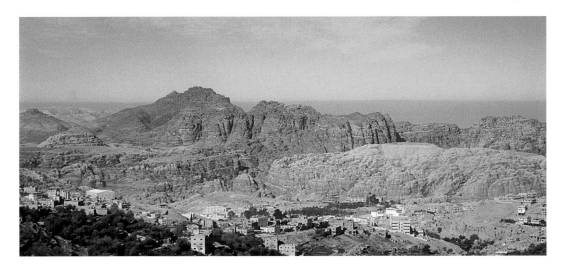

Life in the Wilderness

The Christian life is often compared to the wilderness journey of Israel. We learn three theological lessons from Israel's wilderness journey. First, *in our daily walk with God, we must depend on His mysterious and gracious provisions.* In the land of nothingness, God provided Israel with an "all you can eat" menu of manna and meat. God's provision of "daily bread" is God's graciousness toward us. And for that, we must be grateful. The gospel also invites us to "seek first his kingdom and his righteousness" and to trust in the gracious provisions of God (Matthew 6:33; see vv. 25-34).

Second, *we must trust in the unseen yet powerful reality of God's presence with us.* Israel rebelled against God because they lost the vision of God who saved them from Egypt. They saw only the giants in the land of Canaan. The visible and life-threatening forces of life often have the capacity to distract us from the invisible reality of God's presence with us. The apostle Paul said, "If God is for us, who can be against us?" (Romans 8:31). Real faith is "being sure of what we hope for and certain of what we do not see" (Hebrews 11:1).

Third, *we must be submissive to God's faithful leadership.* In the wilderness, Israel rejected both human and divine leadership. The tragic outcome of this was an aimless and misguided journey that resulted in many lost years and the judgment of death and destruction. Israel's story cautions us about the peril of individualism and autonomy. Submission to the authority of responsible and God-directed leadership is a mark of holy living.

would be able to defeat and drive them out of his land. This story is filled with puzzling issues and questions. Was Balaam a believer in Yahweh (LORD)? Why did God permit Balaam to go with Balak's messengers and then try to stop him? The most amazing part of this story is the capacity of the donkey to speak to her master. Though we cannot answer these

questions, one thing is clear. God used a donkey and a pagan person to bring blessings upon Israel, instead of curses. This story upholds Israel's conviction that no magical powers in the world can curse or bless Israel. Only God can bring a curse or a blessing to His people. They do not need to worry about being destroyed by the evil powers around them.

■ Israel in the Plains of Moab (25:1—36:13)

Chapters 25—36 relate various incidents that took place in the **plains of Moab.** While camped there, Israel worshiped Baal and engaged in the Canaanite fertility cult. Later records show that Balaam was responsible for this corrupt influence on Israel (31:16; Revelation 2:14). God's judgment came upon the nation because of idolatry and immoral sexual practices (Numbers 25).

Moses took another census of Israel to determine the number of people able to go to war (chap. 26). He also established the Law to safeguard the inheritance rights of women where there were no male children, and to prevent the transfer of inheritance through marriage (27:1-11; 36:1-12). Joshua was designated as Moses' successor (27:12-23). Chapters 28—30 contain various laws concerning special offerings and religious vows. The destruction of the Midianites is the theme of chapter 31. Moses permitted the tribes of Reuben, Gad, and the half-tribe of Manasseh to settle east of Jordan, and established the boundaries of the land of Canaan (chaps. 32, 34). He also designated 48 cities for the settlement of the Levites and 6 cities as **cities of refuge** for those who were guilty of unintentional murder (chap. 35).

We have traveled with Israel from Mount Sinai to the plains of Moab. Here Israel, a new generation, mostly children born in the wilderness, the second generation of those who have left Egypt, wait for instructions to enter the Promised Land. We will now turn to the Book of Deuteronomy to examine Moses' final instructions to Israel on how life should be lived in the Promised Land.

Summary Statements

- Leviticus is an instruction manual for Israel's priests.
- Leviticus makes a distinction between voluntary offerings to please God and offerings for the forgiveness of sin and removal of guilt.
- Holiness is separation from the secular influences of the world and consecration to God.
- Maintaining holiness in all areas of life and in all relationships is a necessary component of holy living.
- God guided and provided for Israel in the wilderness.
- Israel rebelled against God in the wilderness because they failed to trust Him for their provisions.
- The wilderness became a place of judgment because of Israel's rebellion and complaint.
- Moses brought Israel into the plains of Moab and appointed Joshua to lead the nation into the Promised Land.

Questions for Reflection

1. Discuss ways to maintain holiness in our everyday Christian life.
2. What are some of the areas where we tend to erase the boundary between the sacred and the profane?
3. What are some practical ways to atone for our sins, other than repentance and prayer for forgiveness?
4. What are the things that tend to bring anxiety, doubt, and fear for existence today?
5. In what ways do we rebel against God's love and care for us?

Resources for Further Study

Kaiser, Walter C., Jr. *The Book of Leviticus: Introduction, Commentary, and Reflections.* Vol. 1 of *The New Interpreter's Bible.* Nashville: Abingdon Press, 1994. Pages 985-1191.

Wenham, Gordon J. *The Book of Leviticus: New International Commentary on the Old Testament.* Grand Rapids: Eerdmans, 1979.

———. *Numbers: An Introduction and Commentary. Tyndale Old Testament Commentary.* Downers Grove, Ill.: InterVarsity Press, 1981.

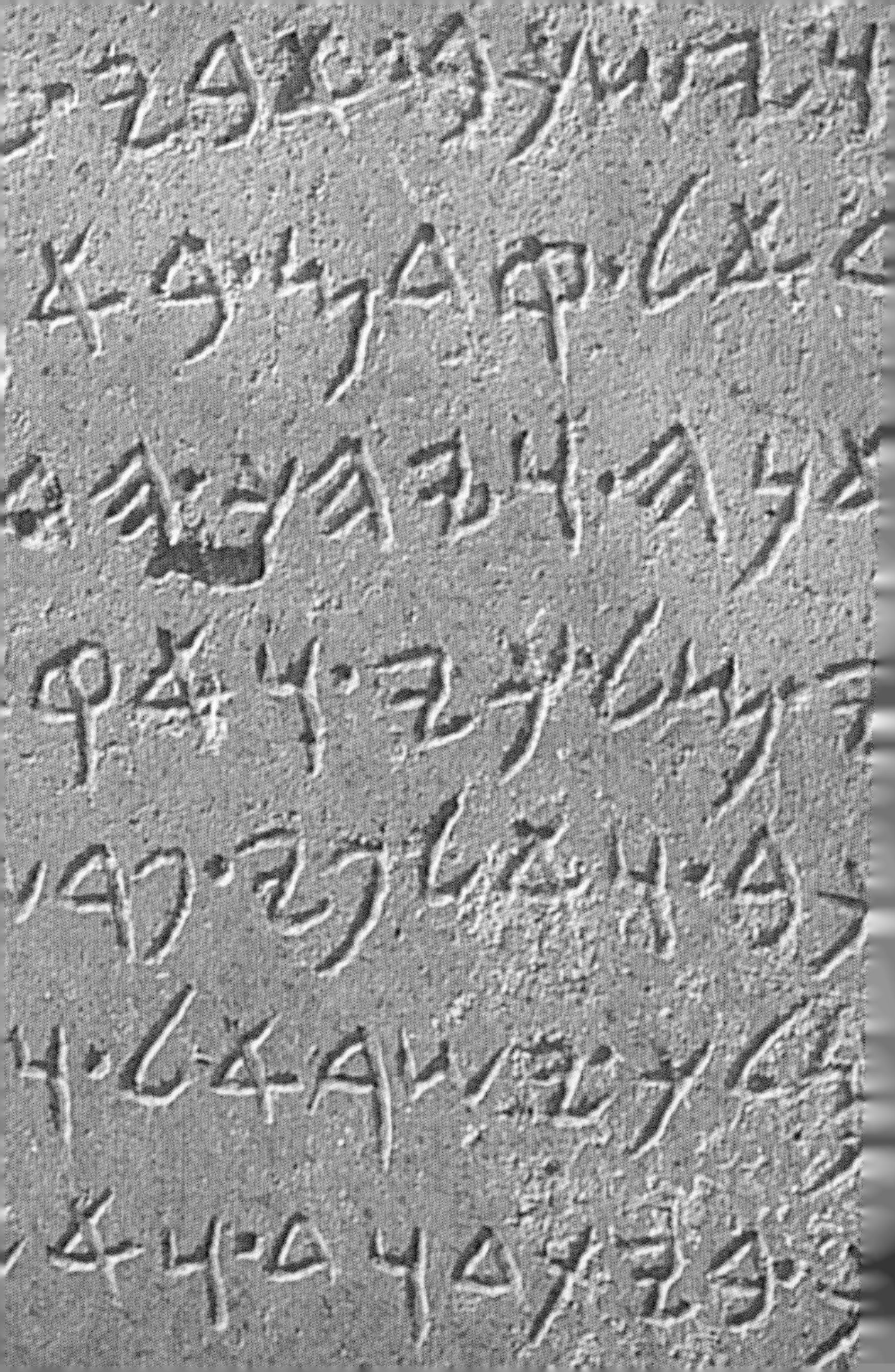

11 Instructions for Life in the Land: Deuteronomy

Objectives:

Your study of this chapter should help you to:
- Describe the content of the Book of Deuteronomy.
- Discuss the historical and geographical setting of Deuteronomy.
- Identify the Shema and the theological principles promoted by the Shema.
- Discuss the various religious festivals of ancient Israel.
- Discuss the significance of the covenant renewal and the theology of blessings and curses.
- Evaluate the theological teachings of Deuteronomy, and show how these teachings are helpful in shaping our present-day life as the people of God.

Questions to consider as you read:

1. What are the guiding principles of your religious life?
2. What does "you shall love the LORD your God with all your heart" (Deuteronomy 6:5, NRSV) mean to you?

Key Words to Understand

Deuteronomion
Torah
Shema
Cherem
Passover
Feast of Unleavened Bread
Feast of Weeks
Pentecost
Feast of Booths
Feast of Tabernacles
Feast of Ingathering
Mount Ebal
Mount Gerizim
Deuteronomic theology
Mount Nebo
Pisgah

The Book of Deuteronomy contains Moses' farewell speeches to the nation that was ready to occupy the Promised Land. Those who composed the historical books (Joshua, Judges, 1 and 2 Samuel, and 1 and 2 Kings) found this book as the theological source for their interpretation and evaluation of Israel's history. This book is one of the most frequently quoted Old Testament books by New Testament writers. Jesus overcame the temptation in the wilderness by claiming the theological truths conveyed in Deuteronomy 6:13, 16, and 8:3 (see Matthew 4:1-11). Also, Jesus' teaching, "Love the Lord your God with all your heart and with all your soul and with all your mind" is a direct quote from Deuteronomy 6:5 (Matthew 22:37).

Title and Authorship

The English title comes from the Greek title **Deuteronomion** ("the second law"). Deuteronomy is "the second law" in the sense that it is the Law given or repeated a second time. Deuteronomy sums up the essence of the law that God gave to Israel at Mount Sinai.

There is no consensus on the date and authorship of Deuteronomy. Critical scholars think of the book as a document produced in the late 7th century B.C. in the context of King Josiah's religious reforms. However, since the book in its present canonical form contains Moses' exhortations to the Israelites who were preparing to enter the Promised Land, that would presuppose a 13th century B.C. context for the content of the book. For this reason it is very likely that the basic core of instructions in the Book of Deuteronomy belong to the Mosaic period, and the book may very well have existed in written form long before the Josianic reform in the

7th century B.C. (see 2 Kings 22:8-13).[1] It is also possible, though, that later inspired writers expanded the Mosaic instructions to address specific theological challenges of their particular religious contexts. In any regard, it is difficult to determine a precise date for the final shaping and arrangement of the content of this book.

Setting

The opening verses (1:1-5) identify the plains of Moab as the setting of Moses' farewell speeches. Moses brought Israel from Egypt to the plains of Moab. Israel was camped in the Transjordan region, on the eastern side of the Jordan River. The wilderness was behind, and the Promised Land was ahead. The nation would soon witness a momentous event in their history. They would enter the land that God had promised to give Abraham as an inheritance for his descendants. God's promise to make Abraham a great nation was already fulfilled. Their entry into Canaan would set the stage for Israel to become a blessing to "all peoples on earth" (Genesis 12:3).

Content

The introduction to the book presents its content as Moses' explanation of the Law **(Torah)** that God gave to Israel at Horeb (1:5). Torah, usually translated as "law," receives in this book a new meaning. Here the Law is more than what God prohibits or permits; rather it is God's gracious will, His *instructions* for one's conduct and life. We may appropriately call this book God's guiding principles for Israel's faithful and obedient living in the Promised Land. The book has the following major sections:

Moses' First Sermon (1:6—4:43)

Moses' Second Sermon (5:1—28:68)

Moses' Third Sermon (29:1—30:20)

The Epilogue (31:1—34:12)

■ Moses' First Sermon (1:6—4:43)

Moses began his sermon with a summary account of Israel's journey from Mount Sinai to the plains of Moab, and concluded with a call to obedience and faithfulness to God. In this sermon Moses brought to the memory of the people significant events during their wilderness journey. Moses reminded the Israelites that their redemption from Egypt was evidence of God's love and faithfulness to the patriarchs. Israel must live by the truth that their God is the only God. The sermon ended with the establishment of three cities of refuge for the tribes of Reuben, Gad, and Manasseh in the land east of the river Jordan.

■ Moses' Second Sermon (5:1—28:68)

This section is for the most part a collection of instructions on various matters. In its present form, it is a lengthy sermon.

Moses addressed his audience as those with whom God made a covenant at Mount Sinai (5:1-5). He spoke as if his listeners were at Mount Sinai, where they saw the glory of God. He also gave the new generation the Ten Commandments (vv. 6-21). He reminded his audience that at Mount Sinai they committed themselves to live their lives in obedience to God's words (vv. 22-27). The future of God's people in the Prom-ised Land depended on their commitment to the covenant they had made with God (5:32—6:3).

Moses challenged his audience to shape their life in the Promised Land on the theological claim that the LORD (Yahweh) alone is God (6:4). They were to live their lives by loving their God with all their heart, soul, and strength (v. 5). Each generation must teach the

The Shema

Deuteronomy 6:4-9 is part of the morning and evening prayer of Judaism. In the Jewish daily worship, this text is recited along with Deuteronomy 11:13-21 and Numbers 15:37-41 as "Recitation of the Shema." The name **Shema** comes from the opening word "Hear" in 6:4 (in Hebrew, *shema*).

The Shema begins with the confession that "the LORD our God, the LORD is one" (6:4). This confession explicitly calls for a life of relationship with God in which there is no room for other gods. The covenant calls for absolute loyalty to God. This confession invites us to reflect on the words of Jesus, "No one can serve two masters" (Matthew 6:24).

Moses also invited the people of God to demonstrate their exclusive loyalty to God through their wholehearted, exclusive, and energetic expression of love for Him (Deuteronomy 6:5). The call to love God is without doubt the most central challenge of the Book of Deuteronomy. Jesus called this command to love as "the first and the greatest commandment" (Matthew 22:38). Here we find the summons to model love in the most intimate way, involving the heart, soul, and strength of the believer.

The Shema is God's gracious invitation to holy living. The call to love God is first and foremost a call to live in the experience of His faithful and unfailing devotion to us. Only then can we truly love Him. John states, "God is love. Whoever lives in love lives in God, and God in him. . . . We love because he first loved us" (1 John 4:16, 19).

The Torah-Centered Life

Moses challenged the people of Israel to order their life with constant attentiveness to the instructions of God. He instructed the Israelites to let God's Torah permeate and influence their thinking, feeling, desires, and actions. Moreover, Moses laid the Torah as the foundation and the guiding truth for the Israelites' existence at home or outside the home. Even today, tefillin on the arm and forehead, and mezuzah on the doorpost remind the Jews of the power of the Torah to order life in a world of oppressive forces. The psalmist reminds us that happiness (or blessedness) is the experience of those who live the Torah-centered life day and night (Psalm 1:1-2). We are challenged by this ancient text to shape our lives by the Word and not by the world.

Mezuza on the doorpost of a Jewish house. Moses instructed Israel to write the law on the doorposts of their house.

Law to the children. The Law should be the constant preoccupation of the people at all times. They were to make signs and reminders of the centrality of the Law in their lives.

Moses also challenged Israel to categorically reject the temptation to go after other gods (Deuteronomy 6:10-19). He charged the parents with the responsibility to explain to their children the meaning of a Torah-centered life. Future generations may ask, "What is the meaning of the stipulations, decrees and laws the LORD our God has commanded?" In response, parents should tell their children the story of redemption, acknowledge God's ongoing faithfulness, and challenge them to remain faithful to the Lord (vv. 20-25). Parents' recital of their journey of faith was aimed to give children the oppor-

tunity to order their lives in the living memory of the past, in faithful gratitude for the present, and in hopeful anticipation for the future. In Israel, the home was the first place of religious training. The apostle Paul found in young Timothy a living and vibrant faith that he inherited from his grandmother, Lois, and his mother, Eunice (2 Timothy 1:5).

Moses charged the nation with the responsibility to remove from the Promised Land its native inhabitants, who were a threat to Israel's faith and loyalty to God (Deuteronomy 7:1-5). These people and their gods would turn Israel away from their commitment to serve God. God chose Israel because of His love for her and because of His covenant with her ancestors (vv. 6-11). In the Promised Land, God would prosper His people and remove from their midst all their diseases and afflictions (vv. 12-16). Moreover, He would manifest His mighty power among the Canaanites and remove them and their idols from the land. Israel must not covet the gold and the silver of the Canaanites, but rather destroy everything because whatever belonged to them was under the divine curse (the Hebrew term **cherem** means things devoted to God for destruction).

Moses portrayed the wilderness as a place where God tested Israel and humbled His people so that they would learn the truth that He is the sole provider for all their needs (8:1-10). God's people must not think that they occupied the land by their power and the strength of their hands (vv. 11-18). The consequence of forgetting God and going after the Canaanite gods would be the destruction of Israel (vv. 19-20).

Chapter 9 focuses on the theme of God's righteousness and covenant loyalty in spite of the unrighteousness and rebelliousness of Israel. God's action of removing the wicked nations from the Promised Land did not mean that Israel was a righteous nation. God's actions only served to prove His covenant commitment to Israel's patriarchal ancestors. Moses recalled his own intercession with God to remember the covenant in the midst of Israel's sin and rebellion at various places during her wilderness journey (9:1-29).

God's great requirement is the central theme of chapter 10. Moses challenged the nation to fear

the Lord, walk in all His ways, love Him, serve Him with their whole being (heart and soul), and keep the covenant commandments (10:12-22). In order for this relationship to become a reality, the people must circumcise their hearts—submit themselves to God's will. Meeting this requirement also meant an intense commitment to care for the widow, the fatherless, and the sojourner in the land. The call to obedience

An Orthodox Jew with tefillin, small black boxes containing scripture passages; Jewish men are required to place one box on their head and tie the other one on their arm each weekday morning.

Israel's Social Responsibility

Moses challenged the covenant community to be a compassionate people who love and care for the widow and the alien in the land—the oppressed and the marginal in society. They represented a group that seldom received protection from the powerful and oppressive social and political systems in the ancient world. The emphasis on Israel's social responsibility is found in references like Deuteronomy 14:29; 15:7-11; 24:19-22; 26:12-15. We are reminded here to be "imitators of God" by doing righteousness, by promoting justice, and by giving food and clothing to the poor among us. At the heart of the Christian gospel is the call to live the compassionate life of Jesus, the One who was moved with compassion when He saw the oppressed, harassed, and the marginal in His own day (Matthew 9:36; James 1:27).

in chapter 11 ends with a solemn announcement of a blessing and a curse—a blessing upon Israel for her obedience to God's great requirement and a curse for disobedience.

Among the various and miscellaneous rules and regulations in Deuteronomy 12—26, we find repetitions and adaptations of laws from other legal collections in the Pentateuch, along with some new laws and regulations. These instructions serve as guidelines for the establishment of an orderly life in the Promised Land. Israel must not follow after the pagan model of worship, but rather follow the legitimate and authorized ways of worship at the place chosen by God to establish His sanctuary (12:1-32). Destruction of idolaters and idolatrous cities is the theme of chapter 13. Chapter 14 deals with the laws of clean and unclean animals, and tithing of the produce of the field and the firstlings of herd and flock. The beneficiaries of the tithing included the Levites, the sojourner, the widow, and the fatherless. The concern for the poor is also reflected in the laws that deal with the release of debt and the freeing of slaves in the seventh year (15:1-18). Israel must observe the great saving events of God and His bountiful harvest blessings upon her through the observation of the Passover, the Feast of Weeks, and the Feast of Tabernacles (16:1-17).

Concern for maintaining the court system and judicial process, qualifications for future kings who would rule Israel, and guidelines for their conduct are themes in chapter 17. The priests and the Levites were to depend upon the offerings of the people for their livelihood (18:1-8). Moses' instruction prohibited all forms of divination and established prophets and prophecy as the legitimate means of seeking God's word (vv. 9-22). Proper judicial process, protection of those who have unintentionally committed murder, and the requirement of two or three witnesses to establish guilt are themes found in chapter 19. The Law granted exemption from compulsory military service to new homeowners and newly married men and stipulated guidelines for Israel's conduct during war and siege of enemy cities (20:1-20).

Chapters 21—25 contain a number of miscellaneous laws. Chapter

H Israel's Pilgrim Festivals

Israel remembered and celebrated God's saving actions and His blessings through various annual festivals. The **Passover** celebrated Israel's redemption from Egypt. The **Feast of Unleavened Bread** commemorated the removal of leaven from the Israelite household and the eating of unleavened bread for 7 days. During the **Feast of Weeks** the Israelites presented the firstfruits of their wheat harvest to the Lord. Weeks refer to the seven-week period of harvest that began with the cutting of barley and concluded with the wheat harvest. The celebration happened on the 50th day following the Passover (so the name **Pentecost,** from the Greek meaning "fiftieth"). Later in Israel, the Pentecost festival became a commemoration of the giving of the Law at Mount Sinai. The **Feast of Booths** marked the completion of the agricultural year. This festival also reminded Israel of her wandering days in the wilderness. This feast is also known as the **Feast of Tabernacles** and the **Feast of Ingathering.** The people set up booths and dwelt in them for 7 days to remind themselves of their tent dwelling days in the wilderness. These festivals were pilgrim festivals that required every Israelite male to appear before God in Jerusalem with appropriate offering to express gratitude to God (Deuteronomy 16:16-17).

26 outlines the guidelines for bringing offerings of thanksgiving for the bountiful harvest of crops and produce in the Promised Land. The worshiper must not only bring some of the firstfruits in a basket at the appointed place of worship but also recite the story of redemption from Egypt and the gift of the land "flowing with milk and honey" as a thanksgiving response to God. Again, God's gracious actions on behalf of Israel in the past constituted the theological basis of these guidelines for her life in the Promised Land. What was at stake was the future of Israel as God's people. And that future rested on their commitment to live in obedience to God's instructions.

The second sermon concludes with the call to renew the covenant (chaps. 27—28). Moses called Israel to enter into a covenant of obedience and faithfulness (see 26:16-19; 27:9-10). He further challenged the nation to reaffirm this covenant when they entered the Promised Land through specific rituals performed at **Mount Ebal** and **Mount Gerizim,** near Shechem. The ceremonies included inscribing the covenant laws on stones, building an altar, and offering sacrifices at Mount Ebal. The tribes were then to proclaim the blessings and curses—six tribes standing on Mount Gerizim to pronounce the blessings of obedience, and the other six tribes standing on Mount Ebal to pronounce the curses of disobedience. Scholars label this theology of blessings and curses as **Deuteronomic theology.**

■ Moses' Third Sermon (29:1—30:20)

Covenant making is the theme of the third sermon of Moses.

Moses began this sermon with a rehearsal of the history of God's gracious redemptive actions on behalf of Israel. He then challenged Israel to enter into a covenant with God that was necessary for her establishment as a people in the Promised Land. This covenant was binding for the present as well as the future generations. The covenant called for loyalty and single-minded allegiance to God. Chapter 29 ends with a detailed description of the consequence of stubbornness and the breaking of the covenant (vv. 16-29). Moses emphasized repentance as the key to the restoration of God's people when they suffer the consequence of disobedience (chap. 30). He promised that the Lord would circumcise the heart of His people so that they would love Him with all their heart, soul, and strength (vv. 1-10). God's word is very near to His people; He has placed His words in their mouth and in their heart (vv. 11-14). Moses ended the sermon with the choice of life or death. Obedience means life and blessings; disobedience means death and destruction. Israel's life in the Land depended on her decision to choose life (vv. 15-20).

Bar Mitzvah ("son of the commandment") ritual near the Western Wall in Jerusalem. At the age of 13 (12 for girls, who have bas mitzvahs), children become obligated to observe the commandments.

The Choice of Life and Death

Moses included in his sermon the choice of life and death (Deuteronomy 30:15-20). The Bible presents to its readers an alternative, a reality other than death as their destiny. Choosing God means life. This choice, however, means renouncing all other gods who have made claims on one's life. Choosing other gods means death and destruction. Joshua's challenge, "Choose for yourselves this day whom you will serve" also echoes this invitation. Life is the gift to those who say with Joshua, "As for me and my household, we will serve the LORD" (Joshua 24:15). In our death-filled society, the choice of life is the only real alternative reality that offers hope. The gospel presents that alternative in the words of Jesus, "I am the way and the truth and the life" (John 14:6).

■ The Epilogue (31:1—34:12)

The final chapters of the Book of Deuteronomy (31—34) make up the epilogue, the conclusion of the book as well as of the entire Pentateuch. These chapters contain Moses' final preparations to send Israel across the river Jordan into the Promised Land. He appointed Joshua to lead the people (31:1-8). He gave the Torah to the priesthood with the instruction that every seven years they should read it before the hearing of the people (vv. 9-13). Chapter 32 records his farewell song, a reminder of God's faithfulness in spite of Israel's unfaithfulness. After giving his final blessing to the tribes of Israel (chap. 33), he went to the top of **Mount Nebo,** to **Pisgah,** from where he saw the Promised Land (34:1-9). There he died and God buried him in the valley below in the land of Moab. The book ends with a fitting eulogy that "since

Mount Nebo. Moses saw the Promised Land from this site before his death.

then, no prophet has risen in Israel like Moses, whom the LORD knew face to face" (v. 10).

The challenge underlying the concluding words of the Torah is clear. It is an invitation to Israel to rise up as a people who live in the experience of seeing God and knowing Him "face to face" as Moses did. Only Israel can fill the void left by the death of Moses. Moses was dead, but Israel lives on.

We have followed the story of Israel from Egypt to the plains of Moab. The dream of the Promised Land will soon be fulfilled in the history of God's people. We will now see what kind of destiny Israel has chosen for herself when she entered the Promised Land. To this, we will turn to the historical books, beginning with the Book of Joshua.

Summary Statements

- Moses gave his final instructions to Israel prior to their entrance into the Promised Land.
- Remembering God is an important theme in Deuteronomy.
- Moses repeated the Ten Commandments to Israel.
- Moses challenged Israel to obey, love, and serve God with all their heart and all their soul.
- Social responsibility to the widows, orphans, and aliens in the land is an important part of Israel's covenant life.
- Israel's future in the Promised Land depended on her commitment to live by the requirements of God.
- Blessings for obedience and curses for disobedience is the underlying principle of Deuteronomic theology.
- Moses challenged Israel to renew their covenant with God.

Questions for Reflection

1. What are some of the practical implications of our acknowledgment of God as the only God?
2. What are some outward expressions of our commitment to love God with all of our heart, soul, and strength?
3. Using the Book of Deuteronomy as a guide, make a list of the guiding principles that would give us directions to live a faithful life in the secular world in which we live today.

Resources for Further Study

Craigie, Peter C. *The Book of Deuteronomy: New International Commentary on the Old Testament.* Grand Rapids: Eerdmans, 1976.

Miller, Patrick D. *Interpretation: A Bible Commentary for Teaching and Preaching: Deuteronomy.* Louisville, Ky.: John Knox Press, 1990.

Thompson, J. A. *Deuteronomy: An Introduction and Commentary. Tyndale Old Testament Commentary.* Downers Grove, Ill.: InterVarsity Press, 1974.

nd had obtained part of this
ery.
18 * Now this man purchaſed a
ith the reward of iniquity, and fa
eadlong, he burſt aſunder in the m
nd all his bowels guſhed out.
19 And it was knowen vnto a
wellers at Jeruſalem, inſomuc
hat field is called in their p
ongue, Aceldama, that is to ſay,
eld of blood.
20 * For it is written in the boo
ſalmes, Let his habitation b
olate, and let no man dwell the
And his ‖ Biſhopricke let an
ake.
21 Wherefore of theſe men w
aue companied with vs all the
hat the Lord Jeſus went in an
mong vs,
Beginning from the Baptiſ

UNIT III

DISCOVERING THE HISTORICAL BOOKS

This unit introduces the reader to:

- Authorship and content of the Deuteronomistic history
- The story of Israel's occupation of the Promised Land
- The beginning of the monarchy in Israel
- The establishment of the house of David
- The division of the Davidic kingdom
- The events that led to the destruction of the divided kingdom
- Israel's history after the Babylonian exile

■ Israel in the Promised Land: Joshua

■ Israel's Moral and Spiritual Crises:
Judges and Ruth

■ Transition to Monarchy: 1 Samuel

■ A Kingdom with a Royal House: 2 Samuel

■ The Kingdom Divided (Part 1): 1 Kings

■ The Kingdom Divided (Part 2): 2 Kings

■ The Exile and Restoration

■ History Revisited: 1 and 2 Chronicles

■ The Building of Community Life:
Ezra, Nehemiah, and Esther

12 Israel in the Promised Land: Joshua

Objectives:

Your study of this chapter should help you to:
- Describe the relationship of Deuteronomistic history to the Book of Deuteronomy.
- Understand the significance of the generations in the Deuteronomistic history as it is portrayed in Joshua.
- Describe the role and meaning of holy war.
- Discuss the manner in which the people entered, possessed, and distributed the land of promise.

Questions to consider as you read:

1. What factors might influence modern historians when writing the history of a nation?
2. What is a "holy war" today?
3. What have you learned about God and Israel from the story up to this point?

Key Words to Understand

Nebiim
Former Prophets
Historical Books
Deuteronomistic history
Deuteronomistic
Prophetic history
Josianic reform
Rahab
Commander of the army of the LORD
Holy war
Cherem
Achan
Gibeonites
Cities of refuge
Shechem
Covenant renewal

The second major portion of the Old Testament, known as the Prophets or the **Nebiim**, is concerned to tell "the rest of the story" of the people of God. As the people settled in the land of promise, would they be faithful to live in wholeness of heart, soul, and strength, as Moses instructed them? Would the people ultimately place their trust in other gods, in idols, or even in their own schemes? If so, what would happen to them? These questions reflect the primary concerns of the Prophets (Nebiim). The first part of the Nebiim is commonly known as the **Former Prophets,** a collection of books that contain Israel's history from the nation's settlement in Canaan to its exile to Babylon. In this section, Israel's historians and writers evaluate and interpret the life and destiny of God's people in the Promised Land on the basis of Moses' instructions in Deuteronomy.

We will now turn to the story of Israel recorded in the Former Prophets, also known as the **Historical Books.** We will deal with the rest of the Nebiim (also called the Latter Prophets) in Unit V. We include in our study of the Former Prophets the other historical books of Chronicles, Ezra, Nehemiah, and Esther, which come from the postexilic part of Israel's history. In the Hebrew canon, Chronicles, Ezra, Nehemiah, and Esther belong to the Writings (Kethubim) section.

The Deuteronomistic History

In biblical studies, the Former Prophets has often been referred to as the **Deuteronomistic history.** (For the sake of convenience, biblical students make the following distinctions in terminology: Deuteronomy is the fifth book of the Torah;

Deuteronomic refers to the language and theology of the Book of Deuteronomy; **Deuteronomistic** refers to the story of Israel told in Joshua, Judges, Samuel, and Kings.) This designation recognizes that the story of Israel told in its final shape in Joshua, Judges, Samuel, and Kings is a single work written with the concerns and theological convictions of Deuteronomy in mind. These books view and evaluate the various events of Israel's life in the Promised Land with Deuteronomy serving as the backdrop. This block of material is thus a theological interpretation of Israel's history through the lens of ancient Israel's faithful prophetic tradition. Because of the prophetic concerns of this material, the Deuteronomistic history might also be appropriately called the **prophetic history.**

The writers of the Deuteronomistic history drew their information from various sources, such as "the book of the annals of the kings of Israel" and "the book of the annals of the kings of Judah" (for information see 1 Kings 14:19, 29; 15:7, 31). It is likely that various other lists, annals, and stories not specifically mentioned in the text were utilized by the writers as well. Nevertheless, when reading these and other history books (such as the chronicler's history, comprised of 1 and 2 Chronicles, Ezra, and Nehemiah), we should recognize that the primary concern of the writers is not to present a "colorless" list of disconnected events but rather a connected story that interprets the life of Israel from a theological perspective. For the Deuteronomistic history, that perspective is found in the sermons of Moses in Deuteronomy.

Date, Authorship, and Content of the Deuteronomistic History[1]

At what point in Israel's history would the Deuteronomistic history in its final form have been written, and who would have written this story? We will attempt to answer these questions before we study the Book of Joshua. The events reflected in the Deuteronomistic history go back to the time of the entrance of the Israelites into Canaan (ca. 1240 B.C.). It is likely that the written and oral sources utilized by the writers of the Deuteronomistic history would have had long histories themselves. Many scholars believe that the seeds of Deuteronomistic thought were planted late in the 10th century B.C. (ca. 922 B.C.), when the nation of Israel divided into two kingdoms. Jeroboam I, the first king of the Northern Kingdom, established worship sites at Dan and Bethel with a golden calf at each site, an act that would have outraged the prophetic traditionalists in that kingdom. It is reasonable to assume that these faithful members of Israel were the first to oppose and raise the outcry against Jeroboam I, who rebelled against God's chosen place of worship and the instructions (Torah) of Moses. Some scholars think that this prophetic circle preserved and transmitted Israel's ancient traditions and the history of the nation's apostasy.

It is likely that when the Assyrians destroyed the Northern Kingdom in 721 B.C., members of the northern prophetic circle migrated to the Southern Kingdom and continued their support of worship at a centralized location, the Temple at Jerusalem. In 621 B.C., during the reign of King Josiah, workers found a scroll of the Torah of Moses during a cleaning of the Temple in Jerusalem. Many scholars think that this scroll contained the core laws (chaps. 12—26) of the present-day Book of Deuteronomy. The reading of the Torah prompted Josiah to declare a time of repentance and reform, which included the destruction of all unauthorized worship sites in Judah.

It is likely that much of the Deuteronomistic history reached its present form during the time of this **Josianic** (or Deuteronomic) **reform.** The writing of such a history at this time would have served to demonstrate the way in which the people of God had strayed from Him throughout their history. The goal of this history would have been to call Israel to faithfulness and true worship of God. The history was also written to demonstrate God's continual faithfulness to the house of David in the Southern Kingdom to which King Josiah belonged. King Josiah's reform and reign embodied the Deuteronomic ideal of the Torah. The history (Joshua through 2 Kings 23:25) challenged the people to follow in the steps of Josiah by repenting wholeheartedly and putting their hope in God alone (see 2 Kings 23:24-25).

However, within a few years after the reform, the people once again strayed from God, returning to the worship of other gods. In just over a quarter of a century after the reform, the Southern Kingdom was also destroyed, with many of its citizens being taken into exile in Babylon. The

Chronology of Israel

Establishing the chronology of ancient Israel with precise dates has presented biblical scholars with difficulty. While biblical scholars hold varying views concerning specific dates, the two most widely accepted chronologies have been suggested by Thiele and Albright.[2] The two chronologies might be contrasted in relationship to major dates of the monarchic period.

Event	Thiele	Albright
Reign of Saul	1020-1000 B.C.	1020-1000 B.C.
Reign of David	1000—965 B.C.	1000—961 B.C.
Reign of Solomon	965-931 B.C.	961-922 B.C.
Division of the Kingdom	931 B.C.	922 B.C.
Fall of Northern Kingdom	723/22 B.C.	721 B.C.
Fall of Southern Kingdom	586 B.C.	587 B.C.

historians closed the story of Israel with the people and their king in exile (2 Kings 23:26—25:30). However, even this tragic conclusion held out hope that the God who had been faithful in the past would continue to hold the future open for His people. They in turn should repent and live faithfully.

The following general outline may be provided for the Deuteronomistic history:

Joshua 1—12	Entrance and settlement in the land of promise
Joshua 13—22	Distribution of the land
Joshua 23—24	Joshua's farewell
Judges 1—16	Stories of the judges

Deuteronomistic Theology

The Deuteronomistic history relates the following four dominant theological concerns:

First, the Deuteronomistic history relates religious and political alliances with neighboring nations as the primary sin of God's people. In Judges through 2 Kings, we find specific examples of the way in which Israel turned away from God and went after other gods (Baal worship). The various kings of Israel also made alliances with other nations or trusted in their own military might.

Second, the Deuteronomistic history perceives both the fall of the Northern Kingdom and the Babylonian exile of the people of Judah as the curses of Deuteronomy at work. The people turned to other gods, and kings made political alliances—both of which resulted in their destruction. Thus, this story of Israel answers the question, "Why are we in exile?"

Third, the Deuteronomistic history gives hope to the nation under God's judgment. Destruction is never the final word. The writers always hold out hope that God will ultimately deliver His people even from the destruction of their own making. The story ends with the report of the freedom of King Jehoiachin (2 Kings 25:27-30), which signaled the coming freedom of the nation as a whole.

Fourth, the writers call the nation to repentance. The Deuteronomistic history repeatedly leaves the invitation open to the people to turn from their dependency upon religious and political systems and to trust God. These same themes also serve as dominant theological concerns in the messages of the Latter Prophets.

The Book of Joshua

The Book of Joshua, the first book in the Deuteronomistic history, deals primarily with the manner in which the Israelites entered and possessed the land of promise. Following the death of Moses the covenant community found itself in the process of both formation and transformation. Up to this point, various events had taken place and instructions for future actions had been given. However, life together as a covenant community now had to be chiseled out on the anvil of real life in the land of promise.

Setting

The book in its present form presupposes a setting in the 13th century B.C. Joshua emerged as the leader of Israel following the death of Moses. The book deals with the entrance of Israel into Canaan from the plains of Moab, on the eastern side of the Jordan River. The stories of the book may be placed during the period between 1240 and 1225 B.C.

Content

The book depicts the stories of entering, possessing, and distributing the land as a solemn act of worship. Moses in Deuteronomy reminded the nation that the land would be a gift from God. The stories show that Joshua and Israel claimed the land as their worshipful response to God's faithfulness. The stories of Joshua can be arranged under four sections:

1. Entrance into the Land (1:1—5:15)
2. Possession of the Land (6:1—12:24)
3. Distribution of the Land (13:1—21:45)
4. Joshua's Farewell and the Covenant Renewal (22:1—24:33)

■ Entrance into the Land (1:1—5:15)

The opening chapter of Joshua demonstrates the direct correlation of Joshua's leadership to that of Moses. Although the entrance into the land began a new era for the people of God, the new era was directly related to what God has been doing in the previous generation. The book begins with God's encouragement of Joshua to complete the task of Moses by leading the Israelites into Canaan. God assured Joshua that He would be with him and commanded him to "be strong and courageous" as he carried out his task (1:6, 9; see v. 7).

Joshua began his task by instructing the Israelites to prepare for their entrance into Canaan (vv. 10-15). He sent two spies to Jericho to search out the land, where they were met and assisted by **Rahab**, a Canaanite woman (chap. 2). Rahab, though a non-Israelite,

A tower dated to 8000 B.C., located at the ruins of the ancient city of Jericho.

surely given the whole land into our hands" (Joshua 2:24).

Chapters 3—5 narrate the detailed story of the crossing of the Jordan River and the encampment of Israel at Gilgal. The priests, with the ark of the covenant at the head of the procession, led the way across the Jordan River. Once their feet touched the waters, the waters stopped flowing long enough for the people to cross on dry ground. In this story, this generation that entered the land is directly connected to the preceding generation that crossed the Sea of Reeds (Exodus 14). The two stories of divided waters demonstrate the full picture of God's saving activity for His people. God both delivered the people *from* the captivity of the Egyptians and delivered them *to* life in the Promised Land.

Once the procession across the Jordan was complete, the people responded in three significant acts. They set up 12 stones at the Jordan as a memorial of God's deliverance for future generations, just as Moses had commanded (Deuteronomy 27:2). Second, at the encampment at Gilgal, Joshua circumcised all male Israelites as a sign of their membership in the covenant community. Finally, the nation celebrated the Passover for the first time in the Promised Land.

The first section of Joshua ends with the story of Joshua's encounter with a "man." Joshua wanted to know on whose side this "man" stood. This mysterious being identified himself as a **"commander of the army of the Lord"** (5:13-15). This was an important reminder to Joshua that the battle belonged to the Lord.

recognized the power of God at work among the Israelites. The spies returned with a report quite different from the report of the 10 spies a generation earlier (see Numbers 13—14): "The Lord has

The Significance of "Connectedness"

The opening chapters of Joshua convey the Deuteronomic concern that every new generation must understand its connectedness to the previous generations. It would certainly have been easy for the generation entering the land to view itself as experiencing a totally new day under new leadership. However, Joshua is repeatedly connected to the former generation of Moses. While something new is taking place, it is a continuation of a greater picture that includes the previous generation.

Jericho was one of the oldest cities built in Canaan (8000 B.C.); this was the first city taken by Israel when they entered the land.

Holy War and the Kingdom of God

The various stories of battles in the Book of Joshua reflect the ancient practice of **holy war.** In this practice, people fought the war in the name of God. God gave them victory. Because the battle belonged to God, all that was conquered also belonged to Him. Therefore, everything conquered was dedicated or sacrificed to God through total destruction, or *cherem.*

These stories present modern Christians with a challenge. However, the stories of such wars must be understood first in light of their theological perspective. The Deuteronomistic emphasis upon holy war points to the necessity for the people of God to reject the ways of the world. God's people are truly resident aliens in the world (Hebrews 11:8-12). Though they are "in the world," they are not "of the world" (John 17:11, 14). Therefore, the stories of holy war should never be taken as a model for the establishment of the kingdom of God. The cross of Jesus demonstrates that the conquering power of the people of God is not found in killing the enemy but rather in giving up our own lives as a sacrifice for others.

The city of Gibeon, located five miles northwest of Jerusalem. The Gibeonites tricked Joshua and the Israelites into making a treaty with them.

■ Possession of the Land (6:1 – 12:24)

This section begins with the familiar story of the taking of Jericho. The narrative in chapter 6 shows great liturgical precision, with the repetition of the number seven throughout the story (e.g., seven priests with seven rams' horns; on the seventh day marching seven times around the city). The emphasis upon the total de-

Lachish, one of the oldest cities in Canaan (dated to 8000 B.C.), located 30 miles southwest of Jerusalem. Joshua and Israel conquered and took this city.

Israel's conquest of central, southern, and northern parts of Canaan.

struction of the city and all of its inhabitants points to the nature of the taking of Jericho as an act of worship. Everything was to be put under **cherem,** or the sacrificial ban.

The unsuccessful attack on Ai provides a direct contrast to the story of Jericho (chap. 7). God revealed to Joshua that Israel failed in this military campaign because they kept some of the "devoted things" for themselves. Through a process of casting lots, Joshua discovered the culprit in the person of **Achan.** Israel put to death Achan and his family and all his possessions. Once again, the Israelites moved against the city of Ai, and this time they were successful (chap. 8). Taken together, the stories of Jericho and Ai reflect the prophetic/Deuteronomistic conviction that the land of promise was never to be viewed as personal gain but always as the gift of God.

After building an altar on Mount Ebal and reading the Torah of Moses in the presence of the people (8:30-35), Joshua car-

The Conquest of Canaan

Various notations in the Book of Joshua and observations in the Book of Judges indicate that Joshua and the Israelites did not occupy the entire Promised Land. The first chapter of Judges describes specific inhabitants that remained in the land of Canaan.

Archaeological records do not indicate a massive destruction of Canaan or a complete cultural change in the 13th century B.C. However, there are good archaeological indications that various sites experienced violent destruction during this period. Various archaeological sites also show a change to a less-sophisticated cultural level. In many cases Israelites appear to have simply settled alongside native Canaanites, often living peaceably with and adopting the ways of their new neighbors.

Archaeological and historical indications as well as cultural and anthropological studies have led biblical scholars to postulate various theories about Israel's establishment in Canaan. Some biblical scholars suggest that Israel occupied the land not through a single unified invasion of the land but rather through the migration of various seminomadic tribes at different times. These seminomadic tribes of Israel entered the land in a more peaceful manner to seek a permanent agricultural setting for their life.[3] Others suggest that native Canaanites who were under the oppressive rule of Canaanite city-state kings would have welcomed the Israelites who entered the land in the name of the Lord. They also think that these Canaanites would have joined the Israelites and fought against their oppressors.[4]

Though these theories may have some validity, the biblical narrative does not support their conclusions. From the perspective of the Deuteronomistic history, the people of Israel possessed the land as an act of worship in response to the God who had brought them out of Egypt.

ried out two further military campaigns to occupy the remainder of the land. The first campaign was directed toward the five city-states in the south. Through a scheme, the **Gibeonites** deceived the Israelites into making a treaty that guaranteed their protection (chap. 9). Joshua later discovered the trickery of the Gibeonites and put them to labor as "woodcutters and water carriers" (v. 21). The five city-states of Jerusalem, Hebron, Jarmuth, Lachish, and Eglon attacked Gibeon in retaliation for its treaty with Israel. The Israelites came to the Gibeonites' aid and defeated these city-states. These city-states were incorporated into the southern Israelite tribe of Judah (chap. 10).

With the central and southern territories now under Israelite control, Joshua led a third campaign to the north (chap. 11). Under the king of the prominent city-state of Hazor, a coalition of city-states in the north fought against Israel. The victory decisively belonged to the Israelites, and Hazor was completely destroyed.

The narratives show that these central, southern, and northern campaigns enabled the Israelites to take possession of the Promised Land. The stories of conquest end with the statement: "So Joshua took the whole land, according to all that the LORD had spoken to Moses; and Joshua gave it for an inheritance to Israel according to their tribal allotments" (11:23, NRSV).

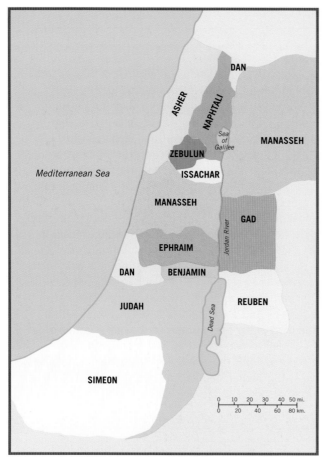

The settlement of the 12 tribes of Israel.

material can easily become monotonous, the claim being made by these details is of great value. From the Deuteronomistic perspective, the land did not belong to a particular nation, a political party, or a king. Ultimately, the land was God's property, and He had given to each tribe a plot of land as an inheritance to be kept within each family unit in perpetuity. For this reason, Israel's prophets such as Elijah, Amos, Micah, and Isaiah made harsh criticisms against the practice of stripping families of their inheritance of land (1 Kings 21; Amos 8:4-6; Micah 2:1-2, 9; Isaiah 5:8).

Once the land was distributed to the various tribes, Joshua established 6 cities of refuge (chap. 20) and 48 Levitical towns (chap. 21), according to the instruction of Moses (Deuteronomy 18:1-8; 19:1-10). The **cities of refuge** allowed for persons accused of capital crimes to have a fair hearing. The Levitical towns provided a place for the Levites to reside since no specific territory had been set aside for these traveling priests.

■ Distribution of the Land (13:1—21:45)

In chapters 12 through 21, we find specific details concerning the allotments of land to each of the tribes. While the reading of such

■ Joshua's Farewell and the Covenant Renewal (22:1—24:33)

The story of the conquest and settlement of Israel in Canaan

The First Mention of Israel

The *Hymn of Victory of Mer-ne-Ptah* contains the earliest mention of Israel that has been discovered. Near the end of the 13th century B.C., the Egyptian king Mer-ne-Ptah led a successful campaign against rebels in Canaan. In a hymn celebrating the victory, the statement is made that Israel has been laid waste and has no survivor. However, the term *Israel* in the hymn refers to a group of people rather than to a geographical location. At this point the people appear to have still been in the process of settling into the land.[5]

concludes with worship. After the settlement of the tribes, the people gathered for a farewell discourse from their leader (chap. 23) and a renewal of their covenant with God and each other (chap. 24). The leadership of Joshua ended in the same way as that of Moses had ended. The final act of both leaders was leading the nation in a covenant renewal service (see Deuteronomy 27—28).

Joshua's farewell sermon clearly echoes the admonitions of his predecessor. He instructed the people to observe carefully the Torah of Moses (23:6) and not to mix with the nations (v. 7) or to intermarry with foreigners (v. 12). Likewise, he reminded the people that it was God who fought for the people (v. 10).

In the closing chapter of the book, Joshua led the people in a renewal of their covenant at the central worship site at **Shechem**. The **covenant renewal** service began with an extensive review of the people's history with God (24:1-13). In this review, Joshua focused his attention on the activity of God himself. He concluded with the reminder that God had given His people a land on which they had not labored and towns that they had not built. The very identity of the Israelites was based upon the gracious activity of God toward them.

In response to the grace that God had demonstrated toward Israel, Joshua called the people to make a commitment to live a life of "complete" and "whole" devotion to Him (v. 14). He also challenged the people to cast aside any gods to whom they might turn. Yahweh (the LORD) alone was the God who saved them;

Suzerain-Vassal Treaty

The story of the covenant renewal depicted in Joshua 24 incorporates various elements of ancient treaties between suzerains and their vassals, often described as suzerain-vassal treaties. These elements include: a historical introduction providing the relationship between the suzerain and the vassal (vv. 2-13); requirements of the treaty (vv. 14-15); a written record of the treaty requirements (vv. 25-26); and the calling of witnesses to the treaty (vv. 22, 27).

therefore, the Lord alone would be the object of their reverence and service.

The people enthusiastically responded that they would never forsake God to serve other gods. Joshua concluded the service of renewal by making a covenant with the people, writing down various statutes, and finally by setting up a stone as a witness to the people's decision to serve God wholeheartedly (vv. 25-27).

The book concludes with the report about Joshua's death (vv. 29-30) and the burial of Joseph's bones at Shechem. Prior to his death, Joseph had anticipated that God would visit His people and bring them into the land that He had promised to give to their ancestors (Genesis 50:24-25). Here we find not only the fulfillment of that hope but also a proper closure to the story of Joseph. The exiled son of Jacob found a final resting place in the Promised Land.

Now that the promise of God to Israel had been fulfilled, the question remained: Would the people of Israel remain faithful to their covenant with God? Would they wholeheartedly serve Him?

Would they reject the gods of Canaan? Would they reject the culture of Canaan?

These questions receive attention in the next book, the Book of Judges.

Summary Statements

- The Deuteronomistic history interprets the life of Israel through the lens of Moses' sermon in Deuteronomy.
- The Book of Joshua seeks to directly connect the generation that entered the land to the generation of Moses.
- Israel entered Canaan and occupied that land as an act of worship, in gratitude to God, who had given the land to His people.
- The call to serve God in totality is based entirely upon the gracious act of God and the present identity of Israel as the people of God.

Questions for Reflection

1. In what ways can the people of God faithfully transmit the faith from one generation to the next?
2. How can the people of God remain distinct from the dominant society in which they live?
3. How can the people of God serve God "wholeheartedly" and "undividedly"?
4. In what ways does Joshua appear as a "second Moses"?
5. How does the Book of Joshua convey the possession of the land as an act of worship?

Resources for Further Study

Coote, Robert B. *The Book of Joshua: Introduction, Commentary, and Reflections.* Vol. 2 of *The New Interpreter's Bible* (Nashville: Abingdon Press, 1998), 553-719.
Hess, Richard S. *Joshua: An Introduction and Commentary.* Downers Grove, Ill.: InterVarsity Press, 1996.
Woudstra, Marten H. *The Book of Joshua. New International Commentary on the Old Testament.* Grand Rapids: Eerdmans, 1981.

13 Israel's Moral and Spiritual Crises: Judges and Ruth

 bjectives:

Your study of this chapter should help you to:
- Discuss the religious and cultural challenges the Israelites faced during the early years of their settlement in Canaan.
- Evaluate the threat of baalism to the worshipers of God.
- Describe the role of the judges.
- Explain the cycle of retribution in the context of the Deuteronomistic history.
- Make assessment of the portrayal of weakness in various judges.
- Describe the central messages of the Book of Ruth.

Questions to consider as you read:

1. What are some of the distinctive features of Christian culture that stand in opposition to the culture in which you live?

2. What happens to a people when they lose memory of their traditions or disconnect themselves from the previous generations?

 ey Words to Understand

Baal
Cycle of retribution
Fertility religion
Asherah
Judges
Ehud
Deborah
Song of Deborah
Barak
Gideon
Abimelech
Jotham's fable
Jephthah
Samson
Philistines
Nazirite
Ruth
Kethubim
Megilloth
Levirate marriage
Redeemer *(go`el)*

After the death of Joshua, the people of God began the long process of making the Promised Land their permanent home. The new beginning of Israel in the Promised Land was met with difficult challenges. The nation was somewhat settled in the land, though there were still many areas of the land still under the control of the Canaanites. It seems that the people of Israel became more and more concerned about adopting new strategies for survival in the land rather than continuing the conquest of the rest of the Promised Land. The Book of Judges shows that this stage in their history took the nation through great cultural, moral, and spiritual crises.

The Book of Judges

Title and Authorship

The title of the Book of Judges is appropriately named after the central characters in its stories. Though this book is part of the Deuteronomistic history composed at a later period, the stories in the book go far back to the time when the warrior-heroes and heroines of Israel lived. It is very likely that various tribes told and retold for generations the great feats, faith, and failures of certain warrior-judges. Each new generation would have learned

both the positive and the negative traits of these leaders, as persons to follow in some cases or as examples to avoid in other cases.

Setting

For about 200 years (approximately from 1220 B.C. to 1050 B.C.), Israel struggled to establish themselves in the land that was dominated by the religious, cultural, and political ideologies of the Canaanites. After Joshua's death, the tribes of Israel lacked unity and strong national leadership. Family, clan, and tribal leaders provided local leadership at various levels. This period presented the people of God with two significant challenges: first, the difficulty of making a transition from a seminomadic desert-dwelling way of life in the past to the settled life of agriculturalists; second, ordering life in the society as a covenant people without the assistance of a strong national leader. The story in the Book of Judges relates that in both of these areas, Israel succumbed to the pressures of the dominant culture that surrounded them.

Content

The characteristic feature of the Book of Judges is the repeated fourfold cycle lived out by the Israelites. In the first place, the Israelites repeatedly turned from their worship of God to worship **Baal,** or they did what was "evil in the eyes of the LORD" (2:11). In response to their apostasy, God handed them over into the hands of an invading nation (v. 14). As a result of the oppression by an enemy nation, the people cried out for help (vv. 15, 18). Finally God sent a deliverer or a "judge" to fight off

An ancient Canaanite altar at Megiddo.

the enemy (vv. 16, 18). For the remainder of the judge's life, the land remained at rest. However, when the judge died, the cycle was repeated once again. This **cycle of retribution** provides the general framework for the various stories of the judges.

This fourfold pattern of apostasy, deliverance into the hand of an enemy, outcry, and deliverance reflects very clearly the primary theological concerns of the Deuteronomistic history. With this paradigm as the backdrop, a large portion of the remainder of the book provides specific instances in which this cycle is played out.

The narratives in Judges can be outlined as follows:

1. Introduction (1:1—2:23)
2. The Judges of Israel (3:1—16:31)
3. Miscellaneous Narratives (17:1—21:25)

■ Strangers in a Foreign Land (1:1—2:23)

The opening two chapters set the stage for the story of the book. In spite of Joshua's final instructions, most of the tribes failed to continue the expulsion of the Canaanites from the land. God had already warned the Israelites that the Canaanites and

their gods would be a threat to their ongoing life in Canaan because the Israelites disobeyed His instructions. The narrator then summarizes the cycle of retribution that Israel experienced in the next 200 years.

■ Othniel, Ehud, and Shamgar (3:1-31)

Chapter 3 presents the stories of three "judges." The cycle of retribution began when Israel turned away from God to follow the worship of Baal. God handed them over to the king of Aram. When they cried out to God for help, the Spirit of the Lord empowered Othniel to overthrow the power of the king and to deliver the Israelites. For the remainder of his life, the Israelites were at peace.

The Law of Moses commanded the destruction of the Canaanite places of worship (Deuteronomy 12:3-4).

The Canaanite Religion

Baal worship was the characteristic of the Canaanite religion. As a **fertility religion,** baalism functioned to meet the needs of an agricultural people.[1] The worship of Baal was grounded in a cyclic myth in which Baal was taken captive into the underworld by the god of death (Mot). The Canaanites connected drought and famine, and the lack of productivity of the ground to the captivity of Baal. They also believed that in due time Baal's consort, **Asherah** (or in some accounts Ashtart or Anat), would descend into the underworld and release Baal. Baal and his consort subsequently engaged in sexual activity, which in turn made the ground to be fertile and productive. This cycle was repeated annually, which made it possible for the land to produce crops again and again.

The Alluring Attraction of Baalism

The problem of Israel's worship of Baal went deeper than the violation of the first commandment. God's people compartmentalized their existence and practiced both their traditional faith and the belief system of their Canaanite neighbors. Though they continued to view God as their Savior from enemies, Baal worship seemed to many Israelites to be the perfect way to make everyday life successful. In our consumer-oriented culture, baalism continues its seduction with attractive offers from economic, political, and religious systems. God's people must, however, live by the truth that "man does not live on bread alone but on every word that comes from the mouth of the LORD" (Deuteronomy 8:3; see also Matthew 4:4).

The Role of Judges

In the early days of Israel's life in Canaan, the 12 tribes were only loosely organized as a larger unit, perhaps more as a confederation of relatively independent tribes. It seems that family leaders or elders made important decisions that affected the clans and families within each tribe. However, intertribal disputes appear to have been left to the jurisdiction of **"judges"** (in Hebrew, *shophetim*) whom we find in the Book of Judges. Although some of the earliest leaders of the Israelites are not specifically identified as *judges*, the Hebrew verb used of their primary activity (*shaphat*, meaning "to judge") indicates this role. The one who does the activity of *shaphat* is one who renders justice or makes legal decisions.

The primary role of judges, however, was to lead the tribes in their fight against enemies who sought to take control of the land. Throughout the Book of Judges, the Spirit of God empowered various persons to lead in military campaigns. Once victorious, the military leader continued his role as "judge" over Israel for the remainder of his or her life.

Theology of Weakness

The various stories of the judges demonstrate two significant traits. The description of the enemies includes special mention of their strength, wealth, or power. The one whom God raises up as "judge" is often a person of weak or lowly status. In all of these cases, the Spirit of the Lord is the empowering agency. Judges gain victory not by their strength but by the strength of the Lord. The stories very clearly express the conviction that God demonstrates His strength through the weak and the powerless.

Centuries later the apostle Paul claimed that God's power is made perfect in human weakness. Reflecting on his own experience, he declared to the church at Corinth, "Whenever I am weak, then I am strong" (2 Corinthians 12:10, NRSV).

Following the death of Othniel, the Israelites once again turned away from God. King Eglon of Moab overran Israel and ruled for 18 years. In response to the outcry of the Israelites, God prepared Ehud, a left-handed man, to deliver the people. After **Ehud,**

Shamgar delivered Israel from the Philistines.

■ Deborah (4:1 – 5:31)

Chapter 4 contains the story of the prophetess/judge **Deborah.** This is followed by the **Song of Deborah** (chap. 5), which many scholars regard as one of the most ancient pieces of poetry in the Old Testament.

The story of Deborah begins with the usual description about Israel's apostasy and the subsequent oppression by Jabin, king of a Canaanite city-state at Hazor. The Israelites again cried out to God for help. Deborah, who already was settling legal controversies, appointed **Barak** to lead in battle against Jabin and his general Sisera. With God on their side, Barak's ill-equipped foot soldiers drove out the chariot forces of Sisera. Sisera fled to an ally, Heber the Kenite. Heber's wife, Jael, gave him a drink, and while he was sleeping, she hammered a tent peg into the temple of his head. As gruesome as the details are in this story, once again the emphasis is upon God's victory through the weak and powerless in the world.

■ Gideon and Abimelech (6:1 – 9:57)

God raised up **Gideon** to deliver the Israelites from the Midianite oppression. He gave victory to Gideon with the 300 most unlikely soldiers that He selected from the 32,000-member Israelite army. Gideon's success prompted the people to request him to be their king. However, he refused their request by citing his conviction about God's kingship over His people (8:23).

Chapter 9 narrates the attempt

of **Abimelech,** one of the many sons of Gideon, to become king. After slaying 70 of his brothers, Abimelech proclaimed himself king over Israel. Only Jotham, the youngest son of Gideon, escaped the massacre. Jotham stood at Mount Gerizim and presented a fable to the people of Shechem that acts as a great satire of those persons who exercise despotic power (see **Jotham's fable** in 9:8-15).

■ Tola, Jair, and Jephthah (10:1 – 11:40)

Following the very brief mention of Tola (10:1-2) and Jair (vv. 3-5), the story focuses on **Jephthah** in chapters 10 and 11. This time, the oppressors of Israel were the Ammonites. God sent Jephthah, the son of a prostitute and an outlaw, to be the next deliverer of the Israelites. Before going to battle, he vowed that he would sacrifice whatever came first out of his house to meet him upon a victorious return. When he returned home after his victory, the first person to greet him was his daughter, his only child. To fulfill his vow, Jephthah carried out human sacrifice, an act that was an abomination to the people of God.

Excavations at Hazor, located 10 miles north of the Sea of Galilee. During the period of the Judges, King Jabin of Hazor oppressed the Israelites.

■ Ibzan, Elon, Abdon, and Samson (12:1—16:31)

The narrator briefly mentions the judgeship of Ibzan, Elon, and Abdon (12:8-15), and then proceeds to give the detailed account of **Samson** (chaps. 13—16). In Samson, we see the ultimate degeneration of the office of the judge.

The story of Samson begins with a reference to the apostasy of Israel. This time, the oppressors were the **Philistines,** who occupied the southwestern part of the coastal plain of Canaan.

Samson's parents raised him as a **Nazirite** (see Numbers 6). Chapters 14—16 describe Samson's exploits of great strength and shrewd character. However, interwoven throughout these stories is the repeated thread of the hero's self-destructive actions. His activities showed that the Nazirite vow meant little if anything to him. However, in spite of the unfaithfulness of Samson, God remained faithful and filled him with His Spirit, thereby enabling him to do great wonders.

T Israel's Infidelity

The story of Samson vividly portrays Israel as a whole. The Israelites also had entered into a vow, a covenant with the Lord. At the heart of that vow was the commitment to serve God and to remain as a people separated from the world. However, over and over again, the people of God "flirted" with and often united with their neighbors and their gods. Nevertheless, God continued to be faithful by sending His Spirit upon the various judges who delivered the Israelites from their captors. In spite of the turmoil, the infidelity, and the insecurity during the early years in the land of promise, God never forsook His people.

■ The Final Days of the Judges (17:1—21:25)

In the closing five chapters of the Book of Judges, we sense just how loosely knit the tribes really were. Scattered throughout the book, we often catch a glimpse of the relative "independence" of each tribe. In this section, the narrator includes two specific examples of the growing tension that existed among the tribes. The tribe of Dan decided to migrate northward due to the increasing threat from the Philistines. However, on the way, the Danites not only stole objects of worship but also took a priest from the tribe of Ephraim. Once arriving in the north, this tribe established the city of Dan and set up the stolen object of worship as an idol. Eventually, the city of Dan became one of the two worship sites established by Jeroboam I as a rival to Jerusalem (see 1 Kings 12:26-30).

Chapters 19—21 relate the tragic events that led to Israel's war with the tribe of Benjamin. The rest of the tribes of Israel decided to punish the Benjamites, because some wicked members of that tribe had abused the concubine of a Levite who was passing through their territory. In the war, the Benjamites were nearly annihilated to the point that special provisions had to be made to repopulate the tribe.

The closing statement of the Book of Judges provides both a postlude to the premonarchic period and a prelude to the next chapter in the life of Israel: "In those days there was no king in Israel; all the people did what was right in their own eyes" (21:25, NRSV). Certainly, to do what was

A Nation Divided

The closing chapters of the Book of Judges show not only a lack of national leadership but also a lack of unity among the various tribes. Individuals and tribes began to make their own gods and their own shrines, and they hired their own priests. Individual and tribal survival became more important than national interests and preservation of a common faith. It is clear that, unlike in the earlier chapters of the book, the "undoing" of the community in the final chapters is not from *outside* but from *within*. The narrator's concluding remark that "all the people did what was right in their own eyes" reflects the result of the breakdown of communal identity within the people of God. When individualism takes priority over communal interests and identity, often the result is factions and struggle for survival.

"right in their own eyes" assumes that the people were not living according to the Torah as instructed by Moses and Joshua. In the absence of a king who promoted the Torah as the standard for the conduct of God's people (see Deuteronomy 17), Israel lived the first 200 years in Canaan by the law they had devised for themselves. The next chapter in Israel's history shows further steps that Israel took to declare their autonomy from God.

The Book of Ruth

Title and Authorship

The Book of **Ruth** is among one of the finest and best-loved short stories in the Old Testament. Characters such as Ruth, Naomi, and Boaz are some of the most colorful in the Bible. The book is appropriately named after the central character of the story. We do not know who wrote this book. Translators of the Septuagint placed the Book of Ruth between the Books of Judges and 1 Samuel. This was done most likely due to the reference in the opening verse that places the story of Ruth in the period of judges (see 1:1). However, the book was not originally a part of the Deuteronomistic history. Neither does Ruth reflect the familiar thought and language of the books of the Deuteronomistic history.

Within the Hebrew Bible, the Book of Ruth is found in the third major section known as the **Kethubim** or the Writings. This book and four other books (Song of Songs, Ecclesiastes, Lamentations, and Esther) are frequently referred to as the **Megilloth** (scrolls) or the Festal Scrolls. The Book of Ruth was traditionally read at the Feast of Weeks, later called Pentecost, which celebrated the giving of the Law at Mount Sinai.

Setting

Although the setting of the story is the premonarchic period, the writing of the story seems to have taken place at a later period. Some scholars think that the book was written during the early days of the monarchy, perhaps to trace the ancestry of King David (Ruth was David's great-grandmother). Others place the book during a period in the life of Israel when

Boaz instructed his servants to leave extra stalks behind for Ruth to glean.

narrowness and overt nationalism was prominent. Such an atmosphere of exclusivity emerged during the postexilic period (particularly the fifth century B.C.) when the people of God were attempting to redefine their identity often through narrow and rigid means. During this period, foreigners were kept at a distance, and Jewish men were even encouraged to divorce their foreign wives (see Ezra 10:1-5 and Nehemiah 13:23-27). In the midst of this situation, the Book of Ruth would have sought to combat a narrow nationalism by demon-

strating David's Moabite ancestry.

Content

The story of Ruth has the form of a play with four scenes. The story begins with famine, death, and tragedy; however, it ends on a happy note with marriage, home building, and children to keep posterity. The story has the following parts:

1. Naomi and Ruth (1:1-22)
2. Boaz and Ruth (2:1-23)
3. Naomi's Plan (3:1-18)
4. Boaz Marries Ruth (4:1-21)

■ Naomi and Ruth (1:1-22)

The opening chapter narrates the story of an Israelite family, Elimelech and Naomi and their two sons, Mahlon and Kilion. A famine at Bethlehem, their hometown, prompted the family to relocate to Moab where the sons married Ruth and Orpah, who were natives of Moab.

The death of her husband and her sons prompted Naomi to return home to Bethlehem. She encouraged Ruth and Orpah to stay with their families in Moab. Orpah decided to go back to her home, but Ruth responded in great fidelity: "Where you go I will go, and where you stay I will stay. Your people will be my people and your God my God" (1:16).

■ Boaz and Ruth (2:1-23)

Upon Ruth and Naomi's return to Bethlehem, Ruth encountered Boaz, a relative of Elimelech, when she went to collect leftover stalks in the field of Boaz. The law stipulated the practice of leaving the leftover stalks so that the poor may gather it for food (see Leviticus 19:9-10). Boaz was impressed

---

C

Levirate Marriage

In ancient Israel, the Law did not permit family properties to be sold because of the belief that God owned the land. If a family property had to be sold due to hardship, then the redeemer or *go`el*, the nearest relative, was responsible for buying it back or redeeming it (Leviticus 25:25-28). In the Deuteronomic law, the *go`el's* role includes marrying the widow of a childless brother. This custom is known as **levirate marriage** (Deuteronomy 25:5-10). The man who became the husband of his deceased brother's wife thus became her *go`el*.

Lessons from the Book of Ruth

Ruth's historical setting in the period of judges provides a significant theological corrective to the cultural, religious, and social attitude of that period. We point out here three important aspects of the Book of Ruth that offer insight into the fundamental convictions of Israel's covenant religion.

First, Ruth's story relates very clearly that God's providential care extends over all people regardless of their national origin. The stories of war and defeat of other nations in Judges might persuade one to conclude that Israel's God was simply a nationalistic God, siding with Israel against all others. However, the story of Ruth protests a narrow sense of nationalism that would limit the activity and the grace of God to any one particular national or ethnic group. The God who mysteriously intervenes in this story is the God of all peoples. The people of God today are challenged by this book to be a community without national, racial, or ethnic boundaries.

Second, Ruth depicts a sense of unity even in the midst of diversity. Both Moses and Joshua repeatedly reminded Israel of the need for unity. Family unity and the unity between an Israelite and a Moabite that we find in Ruth stand in great contrast to the warring factions and tribal competitions depicted in the Book of Judges. Ruth's famous words to Naomi, "Your people will be my people and your God my God," demolish the walls of division expressed in nationality, race, and socioeconomic status. We are reminded of Paul's words: "There is neither Jew nor Greek, slave nor free, male nor female, for you are all one in Christ Jesus" (Galatians 3:28).

Third, the story of Ruth is one of fidelity and communal concern at various levels. Such fidelity and communal concern were qualities lacking in Israel during the period of the judges. Ruth, a non-Israelite, modeled for the covenant community how to show loyalty and covenant fidelity at the social level. Throughout this story, we find the expressed desire not for individual concerns but for the well-being of the community, and particularly the well-being of weaker members within the community. Ruth in that sense is the ideal that God's people are to follow, whether they live with or without a human king.

by Ruth's devotion to her deceased husband's mother. He invited her to eat with him and instructed his servants to deal kindly with her when she gleaned in the field. When she came home, Naomi related to Ruth that Boaz was their **redeemer (go`el).**

■ Naomi's Plan (3:1-18)

Naomi instructed Ruth in ways to win the favor of Boaz so that he might marry Ruth. Taking Naomi's advice, Ruth endeared herself to Boaz. Boaz promised Ruth that he would seek means to act as her *go`el.*

■ Boaz Marries Ruth (4:1-21)

Boaz brought the matter to the city gate, where such official transactions were carried out. Since another man was nearer in kinship to Ruth's deceased husband, that relative first had to decline marriage to Ruth. Upon this man's decline, Boaz proceeded to act as Ruth's *go`el,* and he took her as his wife. The story concludes with the birth of a son to Boaz and Ruth, Obed. In the closing verse of the book, we discover that Obed is the father of Jesse, and Jesse is the father of David.

Summary Statements

- The Book of Judges portrays the repeated struggle and temptation of the Israelites to find religious systems they could manipulate.
- In the midst of the weaknesses of the judges, God's power is made visible.
- The cycle of retribution shows clearly the Deuteronomistic themes of religious rebellion, divine judgment, call to repentance, and hope for divine aid.
- In the story of Ruth, the kingdom of God is broadened beyond nationality or race.
- The Book of Ruth traces David's ancestry to Ruth, a Moabite woman.

Questions for Reflection

1. How does religious pragmatism affect believers today in the same way that it affected the Israelites?
2. Where do we see the cycle of retribution repeated in our own lives?
3. How do the stories of the judges reflect the Bible's perspective on human strength and weakness?
4. What lessons can we learn for our own lives from the story of Samson?
5. How does God use persons outside the community of faith as seen in the Book of Ruth?

Resources for Further Study

Boling, Robert G. *Judges*. Vol. 6A of the *Anchor Bible*. New York: Doubleday, 1975.

Grey, John. *Joshua, Judges, Ruth. New Century Bible Commentary*. Grand Rapids: Eerdmans, 1986.

Olson, Dennis T. *The Book of Judges: Introduction, Commentary, and Reflections*. Vol. 3 of *The New Interpreter's Bible*. Nashville: Abingdon Press, 1998. Pages 723-888.

Robertson Farmer, Kathleen A. *The Book of Ruth: Introduction, Commentary, and Reflections*. Vol. 3 of *The New Interpreter's Bible*. Nashville: Abingdon Press, 1998. Pages 891-946.

14 | Transition to Monarchy: 1 Samuel

O bjectives:

Your study of this chapter should help you to:

- Discuss the relationship of the stories of the early monarchy in 1 Samuel to the preceding stories of Israel in Joshua and Judges.
- Articulate the transitional role of Samuel in the story of Israel.
- Describe the two perspectives of kingship in 1 Samuel and how they relate to each other.
- Make assessment of Saul's kingship.
- Describe the manner in which David rose to power and the growing rivalry between David and Saul.

Q uestions to consider as you read:

1. Why do some people seek "to be like" others who are more affluent and accepted in society?
2. What does the idea of God's kingship convey?
3. What are some of the temptations of those who possess great power?

K ey Words to Understand

Elkanah
Hannah
Shiloh
Eli
Samuel
Song of Hannah
Hophni
Phineas
Philistines
Dagon
Ebenezer
Saul
Messiah
David
Jesse
Jonathan
Michal
Diviner at Endor
Mount Gilboa

The Book of Judges closed with the observation that Israel had no kings during the early days of the nation's existence in Canaan. This closing statement sets the stage for the next segment in the Deuteronomistic history. The Book of 1 Samuel relates the story of how Israel made the transition from the Spirit-equipped charismatic military leadership to the more permanent institution of kingship.

Title and Authorship

This book is named after Samuel, who was Israel's last judge and the first of the prophets. He occupied the place between the era of the judges (premonarchic period) and the era of statehood and kingship (monarchic period). He thus stood at the crossroads of divine rule and human rule. He, like Moses and Joshua, challenged Israel to trust in God alone.

Originally, the separate books of 1 and 2 Samuel were one book in the Hebrew Bible. In the Septuagint, the two books of Samuel and the two books of Kings are listed as I, II, III, and IV Kingdoms. The Septuagint translators evidently viewed the content of these books as one continuous story of the Israelite monarchies.

Although 1 Samuel is part of the completed work of the Deuteronomistic history, it is likely that various narratives within the book were part of Israel's oral tradition. It is equally possible that some of these narratives existed in written form long before the completion of the Deuteronomistic history itself.

Setting

The stories of 1 Samuel belong to a period approximately between 1050 and 1000 B.C. In the previous 200 years, Israel went through a series of national, cultural, and religious crises and a total breakdown of law and order in the society. The crises within the nation were compounded by the threat of external enemies, most notably the powerful Philistines who pushed their border in the southwest coastal region into the territories of Israel. The early chapters of the book also indicate that even the priestly family in charge of the Tabernacle at Shiloh was corrupt and abusive in their dealings with the worshipers. This is the context in which God called Samuel to give leadership to Israel.

Content

The story of 1 Samuel deals with the leadership of Samuel and Saul, Israel's two key national figures in its early history in the Promised Land. The content of this book can be divided into two major sections:

1. Samuel and the Transition to Monarchy (1:1—12:25)
2. The Kingship of Saul (13:1—31:13)

The early part of the book (chaps. 1—12) summarizes the story of the rise of Samuel as the nation's last charismatic leader. This part also shows how Israel made the transition from charismatic leadership to monarchy. The second part of the book (chaps. 13—31) focuses on the rise and fall of Saul, Israel's first king.

■ The Birth and Call of Samuel (1:1—4:1)

The account of the rise of the monarchy in Israel begins with the birth story of Samuel. The circumstances surrounding the birth

Shiloh

At this time during the history of Israel, Shiloh appears to have served as the central sanctuary for the 12 tribes. The ark of the covenant was housed in the Tabernacle. Heads of Israelite families made an annual pilgrimage to the central sanctuary to offer sacrifices to God. Reference to Eli and his sons indicates that a hereditary line of priests was responsible for officiating over the central sanctuary.

of Samuel somewhat reflect the birth accounts of other key figures in the Bible, such as Isaac, Jacob, Samson, and John the Baptist. The story begins with the background of Samuel's parents **Elkanah,** a Levite (see 1 Chronicles 6:27), and **Hannah,** his barren wife. Hannah was the subject of ridicule and harassment by Peninnah, Elkanah's second wife, who bore children to her husband. During an annual visit to **Shiloh,** Hannah made a vow to God that if He would grant her a son, she would consecrate him as a Nazirite. She returned home with an assurance from **Eli** the priest that God would answer her petition. Later she conceived and gave birth to a son whom she called **Samuel,** with the explanation that she asked God for a son. She returned to Shiloh later and offered her son back to God for His service. What she asked from God, she lent back to Him. This was truly an act of worship in which there was no selfishness or attempt to hoard God's gracious gift. The birth of Samuel concludes with Hannah's song of praise to God (2:1-10).

The second part of chapter 2 sets the stage for the rise of Samuel to leadership with a detailed description of the wickedness of Eli's sons, **Hophni** and **Phineas** (vv. 11-36). Samuel grew up as a

The Song of Hannah

The **Song of Hannah** contains her praise of God for elevating her from her lowly position. Also, it looks forward to God's exaltation of the humble and the humiliation of the proud in the world. This theme is reflected throughout the Deuteronomistic history. Appropriately, the Song of Hannah is later reflected in Mary's Magnificat (Luke 1:46-55). Paul echoes this theme in his analysis of the cross of Jesus Christ: "God chose what is weak in the world to shame the strong . . . so that no one might boast in the presence of God" (1 Corinthians 1:27, 29, NRSV).

young boy who found favor with both God and the people. As a result of the self-serving evil of Hophni and Phineas, an anonymous prophet declared to Eli that his sons would die and that his descendants would be removed from their priestly office.

With the doom of Eli's family now certain, the story moves to God's call of Samuel to the position of leadership in Israel (3:2—4:1). One night, while Samuel was lying down in the Temple (Tabernacle), God's call repeatedly came to him. Each time, Samuel responded to Eli thinking that his mentor was calling him. Finally, Eli understood that God was calling Samuel and gave him instructions as to what to say when God

T Samuel's Call

The story of Samuel's call reflects two Deuteronomistic concerns. First, *God would not abandon His people without proper leadership.* He provides for them His chosen leaders to guide them through the dark days of their existence. Second, *each generation is responsible for the faithful transmission of the faith to the next generation.* Although God was calling Samuel, Eli of the outgoing generation directed Samuel to be attentive to God. The faithfulness of Eli thus opened the way for Samuel to respond to the call of God.

Beth-shemesh, located 12 miles southwest of Jerusalem. The Philistines returned the ark of the covenant to Beth-shemesh, and from here the ark was sent to Kiriath-jearim.

called again. When Samuel finally did respond, God revealed to him the coming downfall of Eli's house. From this point on, Samuel assumed increasing responsibilities of leadership, and he became known to the people as a spokesperson for God.

■ Israel's Defeat and Victory (4:2—7:17)

Israel's defeat by the **Philistines** and the capture of the ark

serve as the immediate context of the rise of Samuel as a charismatic military leader. Israel's mistaken perception that the ark would guarantee their victory prompted them to take it to the battleground. Much to their surprise, the Philistines defeated them and took the ark as a trophy of their victory over the Israelites and their God. Israel learned the serious lesson that God would not allow himself to be a "good luck charm" or be manipulated by anyone.

With the ark taken away from the land of Israel, all hope appeared to be gone. However, the ark narrative (4:1—7:1) does not end with defeat! The Philistines brought the ark to Ashdod, and placed it inside the temple of **Dagon,** their chief deity and the god of grain. Soon the Philistines learned the valuable lesson that the idol of Dagon was not equal or superior to the God of Israel. The subsequent plague that came upon the Philistines prompted them to return the ark to Israel with gifts and offerings. In the midst of what appeared to be a great defeat for the people of God, God showed himself as sovereign and undefeatable.

Upon the return of the ark to the Israelites, Samuel gathered the people at Mizpah. Like his predecessors Moses and

Joshua, he called the people to return to God with all their heart, to put away the foreign gods that were among them, and to serve Him alone (7:3). The people responded by putting away their idols, and they gathered at Mizpah for a fast. As Samuel was making sacrifice on behalf of the people, the Philistines once again attacked. However, this time God intervened and empowered Israel to drive the Philistines back to their land. To commemorate this event of deliverance and to serve as a testimony to future generations, Samuel placed a memorial stone at the site of the victory. He called the stone **Ebenezer,** which means "stone of help." Samuel reminded Israel that God had been their help until that day.

■ Saul—Israel's First King (8:1—15:35)

In spite of the victory that God had brought to Israel, the people of God decided that they wanted to have a king over them. Their thinking was that kingship would bring them an identity similar to that of their neighboring nations (8:5, 19-20). Though at first Samuel was extremely reluctant, he fulfilled their request after God authorized him to do so. In His conversation with Samuel, God indicated that the people's desire to have a king was in reality the sign of their rejection of God himself.

Samuel solemnly warned Israel that they would face new challenges with a human being as their king. He listed various ways in which their king would enslave them and make their lives difficult. Israel's response was a firm determination to have a king regardless of Samuel's warning.

God himself selected Israel's first king. (chaps. 9—10). Through strange circumstances God brought **Saul** to Samuel's house (see the intriguing story in 9:3-14). Samuel announced to him

Two Perspectives on Kingship

Biblical scholars identify both a positive and a negative perspective on kingship in 1 Samuel. Some scholars suggest the writers have placed in this book two distinct sources regarding kingship. The source reflecting a negative estimation of kingship or the anti-monarchic perspective (1 Samuel 8; 10:17-27; 12) conveys Israel's desire for kingship to be a rejection of God's kingship. In this source, God yielded to the desire of the people and named Saul as king. The source reflecting a positive estimation of kingship or the pro-monarchic perspective (1 Samuel 9:1—10:16; 11) portrays Samuel as playing a very active role in naming Saul as king.

We think that both the positive and the negative perspectives together provided the subsequent generations with a realistic evaluation of the institution of kingship and more broadly of human power. The narrative in chapter 8 reflects the reality that God commissioned human beings to be rulers of His creation (see Genesis 1:28). However, as the history of the Israelite monarchy demonstrates, those persons entrusted with power abused their privilege and corrupted the office of kingship. Rather than being stewards and servants, and faithfully ruling God's people on behalf of God, they sought to be gods with absolute power (see the earliest pattern of this behavior in Genesis 3:5).

Anointing as a Ritual

Though other officials such as priests also were anointed with oil as part of their installation ritual, the anointing of persons as kings have a distinct meaning in the Old Testament. In this ritual, the officiating priest would pour olive oil upon the head of the person nominated to be the new king. This act symbolically conveyed the empowerment of this person by God's Spirit. Once the anointing with oil had occurred, the king would then be referred to as the *mashiach* **(messiah),** or literally the anointed one. The Greek equivalent of this term is *christos*, from which comes the title Christ.

that God had designated him as Israel's first king. Saul responded to Samuel with humility and acknowledged his unworthiness to be God's instrument (v. 21). The next morning, Samuel took a flask of oil and poured it upon Saul and thus anointed him as Israel's prince.

Another tradition depicts Saul's selection as a public event (see 10:17-27). Samuel brought all the tribes of Israel together and by casting lots, he chose the tribe of Benjamin. He then narrowed down the selection of the king by clan and family, and finally the lot fell upon Saul. But Saul was nowhere to be found. The people finally found him hiding out among the baggage. Samuel announced him as God's chosen one, and the people acknowledged him as their king. A third tradition about Saul's rise to kingship describes his leadership in the battle against the Ammonites, who had been threatening the people of Jabesh-gilead (see 11:1-15). Like the judges of the previous era, he brought freedom to the people of Jabesh-gilead. The people

brought him to Gilgal and made him king over Israel.

With Saul as king over Israel, Samuel retired from his office as Israel's judge. In a closing address to the people (chap. 12), Samuel proclaimed the core prophetic conviction that if the people and the king would live in obedience to God, all would be well. He challenged the people to fear God and serve Him faithfully with all their heart.

In spite of Saul's early military success over the Ammonites, the remainder of his reign was one of great tragedy. The downfall of Saul does not appear to be related to a despotic rule. In fact, unlike those kings who would come after him, Saul levied no taxes, conducted no military draft, and carried out little if any international trade. In many ways, Saul appeared much more like the judges before him than like the kings after him. However, the downfall of Saul was directly related to his outright disobedience to Samuel's explicit instructions. The narrator cites the following examples.

In preparation for battle against the Philistines, the Israelite warriors gathered at Gilgal and waited for Samuel to arrive and offer the priestly sacrifice (see 13:1-15). However, Samuel did not show up and the troops became restless. Saul increasingly felt the pressure to begin the battle. Therefore, he took matters into his own hands and carried out the sacrifice. Within moments, Samuel arrived. Hearing what Saul had done, Samuel rebuked him and announced that God had rejected him as king. God would raise up another person to take his place.

In a subsequent battle against

the Amalekites, Saul did not carry out the complete destruction *(cherem)* of the enemy camp (15:1-9). Rather, he permitted the Amalekites' king, Agag, to live, and he kept the healthiest of the livestock for himself. In response to Saul's action, God announced to Samuel His own regret about choosing Saul as king. The next morning, Samuel confronted Saul concerning the matter. When Saul claimed that he kept the healthy livestock in order to make a sacrifice to God, Samuel responded that God desired obedience more than his sacrifice (v. 22). Samuel announced God's final rejection of Saul as king over Israel.

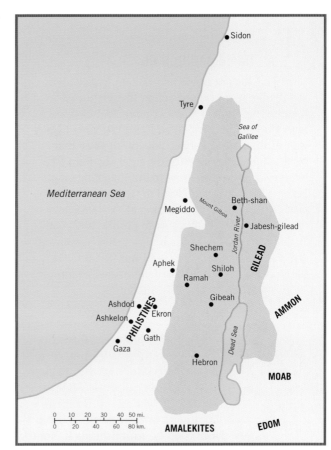

The boundary of Saul's kingdom.

■ Saul and David (16:1— 31:13)

Samuel had already indicated to Saul that God was seeking a person after "his own heart" to take over the leadership of Israel (13:14). Chapter 16 introduces **David** as that chosen person. God instructed Samuel to go to Bethlehem and anoint a son of **Jesse** as the next king of Israel. Though seven of Jesse's sons were brought before Samuel, God showed him David, the youngest son, as His choice. The story very clearly relates the truth that God looks at the heart of people and not their appearance when He calls them to do His special work. Also we find here the Deuteronomistic affirmation that God uses the weak to confound the strong. Samuel anointed David as the next king over Israel. At the moment of David's anointing, "the Spirit of the LORD came upon [him]," equipping and empowering him for leadership. At the same time, "the Spirit of the

LORD had departed from Saul" (16:13-14). The narrator relates the familiar story of David's victory over Goliath to authenticate the Spirit's empowerment of David as God's anointed one (chap. 17).

A shepherd's field. David was the Shepherd King of Israel.

David and Goliath

T he story of David and Goliath makes clear the Deuteronomistic conviction that victory is found not in human might or power but in the activity of God through human lives. The story begins with explicit details about Goliath, to show that from a human perspective the little boy from Bethlehem was no match at all to the Philistine giant. However, the words of David to Goliath affirm the Deuteronomistic understanding of "advantage" (see 17:45-47). David came to encounter Goliath "in the name of the LORD Almighty, the God of the armies of Israel" (v. 45). David was certain that the battle belonged to God. So he remained courageous and faced his enemy without fear.

Elah Valley, the site where David killed Goliath during Israel's battle with the Philistines.

From this point on, the story focuses on the rivalry between Saul and David, and the tragic events that led to Saul's death. Increasingly, Saul became estranged from everyone around him, and he found himself isolated in his own private, tormented

world. Meanwhile David shared an intimate friendship with Saul's son **Jonathan.** The people at large viewed David to be a greater warrior than Saul. Saul's jealousy toward David turned to fear, and he schemed different ways to bring David to his demise. He gave his daughter **Michal** to be David's wife and required as dowry the foreskins of 100 Philistines. His thought was that the Philistines would kill David when he attempted to get the dowry for his bride. David surprised Saul by bringing an extra hundred foreskins of the Philistines. This rivalry and hatred continued until the day of Saul's death.

Saul spent his final years attempting to restore his power and credibility as Israel's ruler. To establish his power, he needed to destroy David and defend the nation from the growing Philistine threat against his kingdom. On one occasion, he arranged to have David killed by Jonathan

and his servants, but both Jonathan and Michal helped him escape their father's plot. Although David easily could have taken Saul's life twice, he refrained out of respect for Saul's position as God's anointed (chaps. 24 and 26). The continued attempts of Saul to take his life prompted David to escape to the land of the Philistines, where he became their ally and a mercenary soldier for Achish, king of Gath (chaps. 25, 29, 30).

Samuel's Tomb.

Meanwhile the Philistines had made significant advance into the Israelite territory. Saul's army could not stop them from further invasion into the land. Having received no help from God, Saul turned to a **diviner at Endor** in a desperate attempt to make contact with the spirit of Samuel. He hoped that he would hear a word from God through the dead prophet's spirit. This act was a clear violation of the command set forth by Moses against divination (see Deuteronomy 18:10-11). When the spirit of Samuel showed up, the word to Saul was

Beth-shan. The Philistines fastened the body of Saul to the walls of Beth-shan. The old city of Beth-shan is the tell (mount) in the background; remains of the Roman city Scythopolis are in the foreground.

a confirmation of God's previous word to him about his removal from kingship.

The final chapter of Saul's life took place on **Mount Gilboa.** Three of Saul's sons, including Jonathan, were killed in the battle against the Philistines. Surrounded by the invading Philistine army, and facing certain defeat, Saul pleaded with his servant to kill him. As the servant refused to assassinate the king of Israel, Saul took his own sword and fell upon it. The following day, the Philistines cut off Saul's head and publicly displayed his corpse on a city wall in Beth-shan. The people of Jabesh-gilead, whom Saul saved from the Ammonites, showed their gratitude to him by giving their king a proper burial.

With Saul now dead, the stage was set for David to assume the role of king. However, as we shall see in the next chapter, the road to kingship was no easy path for David. The next book, 2 Samuel, begins with the trials of David before he finally established himself as Israel's second king. We shall now turn to this story.

Summary Statements

- Samuel gave leadership to Israel as judge, priest, and prophet in the period of transition between judgeship and monarchy.
- Israel's decision to have a human king was a sign of their rejection of God's kingship over them.
- The Song of Hannah and various stories of 1 Samuel reflect the conviction that God uses the weak in His service to overpower the strong and the proud.
- The role of Samuel in Saul's life reflects the nature of the prophetic ministry in that he was both a voice of promise and a voice of judgment.
- The story of Saul's downfall depicts the tragic results of the human attempt to take life into one's own hands.

Questions for Reflection

1. In what ways do the stories of 1 Samuel reflect the concern to love God wholeheartedly?
2. How does the call of God in Samuel's life relate to God's call in our lives today?
3. In what ways do we continue today to seek to have "kings" in place of God?
4. In what ways do we see the fall of Saul reflected in the world today? In the Church? In our own lives?

Resources for Further Study

Baldwin, Joyce G. *1 and 2 Samuel: An Introduction and Commentary. Tyndale Old Testament Commentary.* Downers Grove, Ill.: InterVarsity Press, 1988.

Birch, Bruce C. *The First and Second Books of Samuel: Introduction, Commentary, and Reflections.* Vol. 2 of *The New Interpreter's Bible.* Nashville: Abingdon Press, 1998. Pages 949-1198.

Brueggemann, Walter. *First and Second Samuel.* Louisville, Ky.: John Knox Press, 1990.

15 A Kingdom with a Royal House: 2 Samuel

Objectives:

Your study of this chapter should help you to:
- Describe the manner in which David consolidated his power.
- Describe the significance and meaning of the Davidic covenant.
- Articulate the manner in which David's household disintegrated.
- Understand the dual roles played by the prophets Nathan and Gad.

Questions to consider as you read:

1. What strategies do political leaders adopt to bring stability and unity to their government today?
2. Why is it important for a leader to have impeccable moral conduct?
3. What are some of the reasons for parent-child conflict within our society today?
4. What are some of the negative outcomes of mixing politics with religion?

Key Words to Understand

Ishbosheth
Abner
Hebron
Joab
Jebus
City of David
Jerusalem
Hiram
Zion theology
Bayit
Nathan
Davidic covenant
Royal theology
Mashiach
Mephibosheth
Succession narrative
Uriah
Bathsheba
Solomon
Amnon
Tamar
Absalom
Hushai
Ahithophel
Gad
Araunah

The Book of 2 Samuel traces David's consolidation of power over Israel and the subsequent disintegration of that power. In the story of David's rise and fall, we once again see the Deuteronomistic portrayal of God's promise of hope to His people as well as His judgment upon sin. As in 1 Samuel, here also we find the power of the blessings and curses in Deuteronomy at work in the history of Israel.

Title and Authorship

Although this book is named after Samuel, he was already dead, and the stories belong to the days of David as king over Israel. However, it is likely that the title conveys the Deuteronomistic conviction that the prophetic ministry of Samuel continued to give guidance to Israel during David's kingship.

The Book of 2 Samuel is a continuation of 1 Samuel, which concludes with the story of Saul's death. This book begins with another account of Saul's death and David's lament over Saul and Jonathan. Again, 2 Samuel belongs to the broader context of the Deuteronomistic history. However, it is very likely that some of the materials in this book may have existed as independent documents before they became part of the Deuteronomistic history.

Setting

The story of 2 Samuel covers the period approximately between 1000 and 960 B.C. The story shifts focus from Saul and the tribe of Benjamin to David, the tribe of Judah, and the whole nation of Israel. This book narrates the story of the establishment of David as king, first by the people of Judah and later by the rest of Israel. The threat of border invasions by the Philistines came to an end. During the reign of David, Israel became a kingdom-building nation by annexing neighboring countries and lands. Though David had to deal with some internal troubles, from a political perspective this period may be designated as the golden years in the history of Israel.

Content

The Book of 2 Samuel can be divided into four parts:
1. The Establishment of a Dynasty (1:1—8:18)
2. Covenant Faithfulness and Covenant Breaking (9:1—12:31)
3. David's Family Troubles (13:1—18:33)
4. Restoration of David's Reign (19:1—24:25)

■ The Establishment of a Dynasty (1:1—8:18)

Saul's death opened the way for David to set himself up as king over Israel. However, he proceeded with great caution, and his actions were methodical, well orchestrated, and showed appropriate respect to Saul's family. Second Samuel opens with another tradition about the death of Saul. David not only showed the traditional signs of mourning for the dead but also lamented over the death of Israel's mighty men in battle (see David's lamentation in 1:19-27). Though he was a victim of Saul's ruthless treatment, he demonstrated his love, mercy, and compassion for his enemy through this lamentation.

David was careful not to seize power immediately. He knew that Saul's surviving son **Ishbosheth** would be a legitimate contender for his father's throne. Also, he was well aware of the significant influence of **Abner,** Saul's military commander. We see in these narratives a reflection of both his respect for Saul's family and more importantly his political savvy, a trait that helped him later to secure his kingship.

David took the first step to establish his kingship by seeking the approval of his own tribe, Judah, who crowned him as king at **Hebron.** He made Hebron his capital and ruled there as king over Judah for the next seven years (1000 B.C. to 993 B.C.).

Meanwhile, Saul's son Ishbosheth began his rule as king over the remaining 11 tribes. He had on his side Abner, who was the real power behind the throne. With this faction among Israel's tribes, conflict, confrontation, and struggle for power were inevitable. Second Samuel 2—4 relates the tragic stories of treachery and bloodshed carried out by Abner and David's commander **Joab.** This civil war period saw the violent death of Abner and Ishbosheth, which finally cleared the path for David to consolidate his power as king over all Israel.

Early in his reign as king over Israel, David carried out numerous successful military campaigns. Although **Jebus** had been taken earlier by the Israelites, it remained a stronghold of the Canaanites. With his personal army, David was finally able to overcome the Jebusite stronghold and claim it as his own city. He renamed it the **city of David.** He also established this neutral city located between the tribes in the north and Judah in the south as the capital of his kingdom. At a later period, the city of David came to be called **Jerusalem** (meaning, "foundation of

The City of David (Jerusalem) during David's time.

peace"), a reflection of the role it played in bringing peace in the land.

David's early years as king over a united Israel proved positive both internationally and domestically. **Hiram,** the Phoenician king, sent carpenters, masons, and materials to build a palace for David. However, the narrator is careful to observe that his success was due to God's presence with him (5:10).

The Philistines, who had once been allies of David, initiated a confrontation to challenge David's strength. In the battles with the Philistines, David proved himself to be a capable military leader. He drove the enemy back to their territory and kept them confined to their land.

As a leader, David's next attempt was to establish a common identity for his people. He did this by bringing the ark of the covenant from Kiriath-jearim to Jerusalem. This initiative provided for Israel a central place to gather together to worship the God who brought them out of Egypt. Jerusalem thus became both the political and religious capital of his kingdom. Israel's later traditions recognized Jerusalem as the sym-

Jerusalem and Its Priests

Second Samuel 15:24-37 relates how Zadok the priest gained an equal place with Abiathar in Jerusalem's priesthood. Abiathar came from the line of Israel's Levitical priests, and he stood by the side of David during his struggle with Saul (see 1 Samuel 22:20-23). But we do not know the exact origin of Zadok or how he came to be priest in Jerusalem.[1] During David's reign, the families of both Zadok and Abiathar served as priests. When Solomon became king, he banished Abiathar from Jerusalem because he supported Solomon's rival Adonijah, who made the claim to kingship (1 Kings 2:26-27, 35). Zadok, who supported Solomon's kingship, became the chief priest, and his descendants later became the priestly family in Jerusalem.

Zion, the City of God

With the transfer of the ark, the "city of David" became "the city of God." In the next generation of the monarchy, the palace of the king and the Temple of the Lord sat side by side, often one providing legitimacy to the other. Religion and politics thus became inseparable twins, which later led to the rise of religious nationalism in Israel.

Jerusalem's establishment as the religious center led to the development of **"Zion theology"** in Israel's theological traditions. During the premonarchy days, Zion was a fortified hill within the Jebusite stronghold. Once the Temple was built on the hill at this location, the Temple Mount itself became known as Zion. This name later became the name for the entire city of Jerusalem. Zion in the Old Testament reflects the security found on the holy mountain of God. Reflecting the mighty kingship of God himself, the term evoked images of God's protection of His people and God's power in battle. It vividly embodied God's victory, sovereignty, and invincibility. Various psalms (see 46, 48, 76, 84, 87, 122, 125, 132) celebrate Zion's beauty and God's reign upon Mount Zion. Though this understanding evoked a deep sense of trust, it often led to a sense of false security and even invincibility of the people and the city itself. Later prophets, such as Micah and Jeremiah, preached against such false security.

bol of God's presence among His people because the ark resided in that city.

Once Jerusalem became the place for the ark of the covenant, David made plans to build a temple, which would be a "house" (in Hebrew, **bayit**) for the ark and thus a "house" for God (see 2 Samuel 7:1-3). Although at first supportive of David's plans, the prophet **Nathan** returned to him with the announcement that David's descendant who would sit on his throne would fulfill this desire. Through Nathan, God promised to make David's descendants a permanent, hereditary dynasty or royal "house" *(bayit)*. He also promised to enter into a father-son relationship with David's descendants. This oath of promise that God gave to David is known as the **Davidic covenant** (see 2 Samuel 7:12-17).

The narrator concludes this section of David's early years as Israel's second king with a detailed description of his conquest of the Philistines, the Moabites, the Syrians, and the Edomites (chap. 8). From these nations, David received war spoils of gold, silver, and bronze, as well as payments of tribute. The stories end with the

Royal Theology

God's covenant stands in direct continuity with the Sinai covenant and God's covenant with Abraham. However, the focus here is on a household rather than the entire Israelite community. The Davidic king was God's "son" who ruled Israel, God's "people," with whom He made the Sinai covenant. The development of this **royal theology** engendered the belief that the reign of the Davidic king represented God's reign over the people. Various psalms reflect this understanding of kingship (see 2, 18, 20, 21, 72, 89, 110, 132). Over time, the term *anointed one* (in Hebrew, **mashiach**) came to represent the ideal Davidic king who would properly embody the just reign of God over Israel.

Stele (inscribed stone slab) discovered at Dan in northern Israel showing reference to David's house.

The city of Jerusalem today.

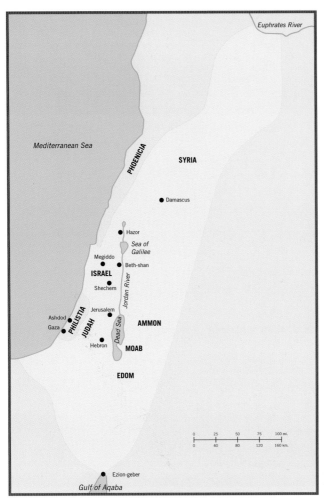

The area under the political and economic control of Israel during the reigns of David and Solomon.

■ Covenant Faithfulness and Covenant Breaking (9:1 — 12:31)

In this section, the stories of David include two examples of David's "just and right" actions, as well as an example of his tragic failure to keep justice and righteousness in his interpersonal relationships. In a display of lavish generosity, he invited Jonathan's crippled son, **Mephibosheth**, to remain under his custody for the remainder of his life and to receive income from his grandfather's property. Similarly, David sought to provide covenant faithfulness to the son of the Ammonite king following his father's death (see 10:1).

Chapter 11 shows how David, who exemplified covenant faithfulness to Saul's house, transgressed God's covenant and destroyed not only a marriage but also an innocent human life. In this familiar story of David's sin with **Uriah**'s wife, **Bathsheba**, we see the portrait of an oriental despot who manipulated people to accomplish his plans. Through careful scheming, he arranged for Uriah's death on the battlefield, so that the door would be open for him to marry Bathsheba, with whom he had committed adultery. When the news of Uriah's

note that "David reigned over all Israel, doing what was just and right for all his people" (8:15).

The Succession Narrative

Old Testament scholars describe 2 Samuel 9—20 and 1 Kings 1—2 as the **succession narrative** or court history. This lengthy narrative describes the struggle for power within David's family and the claims of various royal family members to David's throne. The stories graphically portray David's dysfunctional family and make no attempt to cover up for anyone. The presence of this material within Scripture demonstrates the manner in which the Bible is concerned with all of life. In these stories, there are no ideal heroes. However, we learn the lesson that the sinfulness of God's people brings only more brokenness to an already broken world.

death came, David did what seemed to be the most honorable thing for a "just and righteous" king to do. He married his dead soldier's widow, a shrewd public relations ploy and a cover-up for his sin. The narrator concludes this tragic story with the report that this matter "displeased the LORD" (11:27).

The prophet Nathan, who had previously spoken about God's covenant with David, confronted David and revealed to him God's judgment because of his sin. Through a parable of a rich man who took the beloved ewe lamb of a poor man, Nathan moved David unwittingly to condemn himself. The prophet announced that the evil that David had done to Uriah would come upon David and his household (12:11).

At this point in the story, David shows himself as a genuinely repentant sinner. He acknowledged his act as a sin against God. Though Nathan pronounced God's forgiveness, subsequent stories show the long-lasting results of David's sin, beginning with the death of Bathsheba's

T David: A Repentant Sinner

Psalm 51 has been associated with David's prayer for forgiveness when Nathan confronted him. In this prayer, the psalmist conveys his intimate acquaintance with human sin and its powerful influence upon his life from birth. The psalm also recognizes God's forgiving grace, cleansing from sin, and gift of a new heart as the solution to human depravity.

child. Later, she conceived once again and gave birth to a son. David named the child Jedidiah, who later received the throne name **Solomon.**

■ David's Family Troubles (13:1 – 18:33)

Although David repented of his sin, subsequent stories in 2 Samuel show that Nathan's word of judgment against his household came to fulfillment. Ironically, the first two acts of evil to take place within David's family were sexual misconduct (Amnon's rape of Tamar) and murder (Absalom's murder of Amnon). The royal

The Tomb of Absalom in the Kidron Valley.

palace became the setting for a great power play that involved adultery, murder, and rebellion.

Amnon, the eldest son of David and thus the successor to the throne, developed an unhealthy love for his half-sister, **Tamar.** He devised a scheme to molest her and afterward showed total contempt and hatred toward his victim. Two years later, Tamar's brother, **Absalom,** killed Amnon to retaliate the rape of his sister. Fearing that David might take action, Absalom became a fugitive and fled from Jerusalem (chap. 13). Later, through a well-planned scheme of Joab that involved a wise woman from Tekoa, David permitted Absalom to return to Jerusalem but refused to see him (chap. 14).

Two years later, David welcomed Absalom to his palace and the two were reconciled to each other. However, soon Absalom began to make aggressive moves to overthrow his father from the throne. Within four years, Absalom succeeded in gaining enough support to declare himself king at Hebron. David, fearing for his life, fled Jerusalem with his loyal supporters. Although both Abiathar and Zadok left Jerusalem with him, David persuaded them to return to Jerusalem with the ark of the covenant. David also sent back one of his advisers, **Hushai,** to join Absalom's forces on the pretext that he was a defector.

Absalom occupied Jerusalem with his supporters. Hushai returned to Jerusalem and convinced Absalom that he was a defector and pledged loyalty to him (chap. 16). Later, Hushai was able to dissuade Absalom from making an immediate attack against David, though **Ahithophel,** Absalom's trusted adviser, encouraged him to pursue David (chap. 17). Hushai also sent word to David to move quickly out of the area to escape Absalom's army. In the struggle that followed between the forces of David and Absalom, Joab killed Absalom, in spite of David's command to spare his son's life (18:5). Upon receiving word of Absalom's death, David raised a bitter lament for his son:

View of Jerusalem from the Mount of Olives.

"O my son Absalom! My son, my son Absalom! If only I had died instead of you—O Absalom, my son, my son!" (v. 33).

■ Restoration of David's Reign (19:1—24:25)

With the death of Absalom, the rebellion against David was put down. David returned to Jerusalem, and all those who stood against him came to him to make amends (chap. 19). One last opposition came from Sheba, a Benjamite, who openly rebelled against David's claim to kingship. Joab and his forces quickly moved in to put an end to Sheba's revolt (chap. 20).

In the closing chapters of 2 Samuel (21—24), we find various materials that reflect the final years of David's reign. These materials are not arranged in chronological order. The narrator recounts an event earlier in David's reign in which he avenged the bloodguilt of Saul by permitting the Gibeonites to hang seven sons of Saul (21:1-9). Another narrative recounts the story of David burying the bones of Saul and Jonathan and giving the seven sons of Saul a proper burial in their family tomb (21:10-14).

The final episode of 2 Samuel deals with David's census of Israel and the subsequent judgment that came upon him (chap. 24). When he realized that his action was not pleasing to God, he confessed his guilt. God sent the prophet **Gad** to David with the message that he could choose one of three calamities as judgment: three years of famine, three months of enemy assaults, or three days of pestilence. David requested God to spare him from his enemies. So God sent a pesti-

Nathan and Gad

The prophets Nathan and Gad play significant roles in 2 Samuel, one at the beginning and the other at the end of David's reign. Nathan gave a word of promise concerning the Davidic dynasty. Later, he brought God's judgment upon David because of his sin with Bathsheba and the murder of Uriah. Near the end of David's reign, Gad brought a word of judgment when David conducted a census. The story ends with Gad's word to David that directed him to build an altar on the threshing floor of Araunah. Later, this site became the place where Solomon built the Temple. Nathan and Gad thus spoke both words of promise and words of judgment. In the context of the Deuteronomistic history, it is clear that though God's judgment often comes upon His people, His dealing with them always begins and always ends with promise!

lence throughout David's kingdom that killed 70,000 persons in the land. David saw God's messenger, who was the agent of destruction, standing by the threshing floor of **Araunah**. He once again confessed his sin and pleaded that the pestilence be against him and not against those who were innocent (vv. 15-17).

As instructed by Gad, David went to Araunah and offered to buy his threshing floor. When Araunah offered to sell it at no cost to David, the king refused by saying that he would not make an offering to God that did not cost him anything. He purchased the floor and set up an altar there for future generations as the place of worship in Israel (vv. 18-25).

The Book of 2 Samuel ends with the optimistic note about God answering David's prayer for the land. In the end, a sinner confessed his sins, made amends, and pleaded for God's mercy. A gracious and compassionate God responded to his prayer with forgiveness and healing for His people. In the midst of sin and judgment, He made His presence known to a sinner under judgment. God's acceptance of David's offerings gave the king and his people the assurance that indeed God dwelt among them.

Would the next generation and the generations to come live by this truth about God? The Deuteronomistic history we find in 1 and 2 Kings answers this question. We shall now turn to this continuing story of Israel and her God in these two books.

Summary Statements

- Although Saul was his enemy, David grieved over the deaths of Saul and Jonathan.
- David became king after Saul's death, and he was careful to show due respect for Saul's family.
- David ruled as king over Judah for seven years before he consolidated his kingship over all Israel.
- David established Jerusalem as his capital and brought the ark to the city, thus making it also the nation's religious center.
- David sinned against God, but he also sought God's mercy and forgiveness.
- David suffered family troubles as the consequence of his sin.
- Nathan and Gad spoke to David both words of promise and words of judgment.

Questions for Reflection

1. What are some of the ways by which we can demonstrate faithfulness even to our enemies?
2. How does God demonstrate His continuing faithfulness in our lives even in the midst of our own disobedience?
3. In what ways does evil continue to play itself out beyond the initial act?
4. What are the steps that we need to take to bring stability and order within our family lives?

Resources for Further Study

Baldwin, Joyce G. *1 and 2 Samuel: An Introduction and Commentary.* Tyndale Old Testament Commentary. Downers Grove, Ill.: InterVarsity Press, 1988.
Birch, Bruce C. *The First and Second Books of Samuel: Introduction, Commentary, and Reflections.* Vol. 2 of *The New Interpreter's Bible.* Nashville: Abingdon Press, 1998. Pages 1199-1383.
Brueggemann, Walter. *First and Second Samuel.* Louisville, Ky.: John Knox Press, 1990.

16

The Kingdom Divided (Part 1): 1 Kings

bjectives:

Your study of this chapter should help you to:

- Describe the events leading to the coronation of Solomon as David's successor.
- Articulate the positive and negative features of Solomon's reign.
- Describe the nature and purpose of the temple in Jerusalem.
- Describe the factors leading to the division of the kingdom.
- Evaluate the political, economic, and religious impact of the Omride dynasty upon Israel.
- Discuss the role and message of the prophet Elijah.

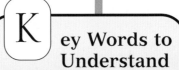ey Words to Understand

Adonijah
Abishag
Zadok
Benaiah
Hiram
Syncretism
`Ulam
Hekal
Debir
Jeroboam
Ahijah
Shishak
Rehoboam
Dan
Bethel
"Sin of Jeroboam"
Omri
Samaria
Ahab
Jezebel
Elijah
Mount Carmel
Micaiah

Questions to consider as you read:

1. How do you maintain loyalty to God?
2. What are some of the factors that contribute to political and religious instability?

Near the end of David's reign, rivalry and political intrigue developed within the house of David to settle the question of who would be the legitimate heir to the throne. The Book of 1 Kings narrates the developments that led to the rise of Solomon as David's successor. The rest of the narratives in this book show the continuing struggle for power in the land. This struggle led to the division of Israel into two kingdoms. As the political landscape changed, so did the religious culture of the covenant nation. In this first part of the story of the divided kingdom of Israel, we focus on the first hundred years of Israel's history since the days of David.

Title and Authorship

The Books of 1 and 2 Kings were originally one composition that continued the story of Israel's kingdom following the death of David. The title indicates that these books deal with the history of kingship in Israel. Again, these two books together make up the final part of the Deuteronomistic history. Deuteronomistic historians utilized various sources such as "the book of the annals of Solomon" (1 Kings 11:41), "the book of the annals of the kings of Israel" (14:19), and "the book of the annals of the kings of Judah" (v. 29) to compose their work. It is also likely that they drew from other written or oral sources that had circulated long before these books received their final form.

Setting

The Book of 1 Kings covers the story of Israel from about 960 B.C. to 850 B.C. The book begins with the declining years of David. The stage is thus set for the transition of power to the next generation. The closing story of 2 Samuel (David's purchase of the threshing floor of Araunah) anticipates the building of the Temple at the site where David offered burnt offerings to the Lord. Though the opening verses of the book attempt to paint a picture of relative calm and stability in the kingdom, the rest of chapter 1 suddenly shifts to shrewd political maneuverings and palace plots to establish a successor to the dying king.

Content

The first two chapters of 1 Kings serve as an appropriate introduction to the story of Solomon's reign. Scholars consider these chapters the conclusion to the succession narrative begun in 2 Samuel 9.

The Book of 1 Kings can be divided into the following two major sections:

1. The Reign of Solomon (1:1—11:43)
2. Divided Kingdoms and Their Kings (12:1—22:53)

The second part has extensive narratives about the ministry of Elijah the prophet, beginning with chapter 17.

■ The Selection of a Davidic Successor (1:1—2:46)

The question of the legitimate successor to David nearly divided the royal family and David's political and religious advisers into two camps. With the support of David's general, Joab, and David's high priest, Abiathar, his oldest living son, **Adonijah,** proclaimed himself king in Jerusalem. However, another rival priest Zadok, Nathan the prophet, and many of David's warriors did not support Adonijah. Plotting with Bathsheba, Nathan successfully convinced David to declare Solomon as the legitimate heir to the throne. At Gihon, Zadok anointed Solomon as the next king of Israel (960 B.C.)

Prior to his death, David challenged Solomon to walk in all the ways of God by keeping the Law of Moses (2:2-3). He further reminded Solomon that God's promise of an eternal Davidic dynasty was conditional. Fulfillment of this promise depended upon the future generations' obedience to God and their walk before God with all their heart and with all their soul.

Although Solomon was established as king, Adonijah, who had been forced to give up his kingship, made a final attempt to seek legitimacy to his claim to the throne. He requested that Solomon grant him permission to marry David's concubine **Abishag.** Solomon, who perceived this request as Adonijah's plan to make a claim to the throne, gave orders to murder his rival half-brother. Following Adonijah's murder, Solomon took further steps to strip power from all who had supported Adonijah's claim. He banished Abiathar from Jerusalem to the town of Anathoth and installed **Zadok** as the high priest of Jerusalem. Solomon further ordered the death of Joab as punishment for the murder of Saul's general Abner. In Joab's place, Solomon appointed **Benaiah** as commander of his army. Solomon thus secured his kingship by carrying out an extensive political housecleaning.

■ The Reign of Solomon (3:1—11:43)

The narrator begins and ends the story of Solomon by making reference to his mariage relation-

ships. The story begins with Solomon's marriage alliance with Egypt.[1] The concluding chapter of this narrative section observes Solomon's marraige alliances and love for foreign women whom he had taken from many of the neighboring countries (11:1-8). He thus violated the Law of Moses that sternly warned against Israel's intermarriage with pagan people (Deuteronomy 7:3-4). Solomon not only married pagan women but also worshiped their gods and became an influential patron of pagan religions in the land.

Early in his reign, Solomon traveled to Gibeon in order to make a sacrifice to the Lord. There he requested from God a "discerning heart" so that he would have the capacity to rule with wisdom and "distinguish between right and wrong" (3:9). Pleased with Solomon's request, the Lord not only gave wisdom to Solomon but also gave him wealth and honor.

Solomon's wisdom and fame spread throughout the ancient Near East. His wisdom surpassed the wisdom of all the eastern peo-

International Treaties and Marriage

The narrator of 1 Kings reports that Solomon had 700 wives and 300 concubines. In the ancient world, a king's possession of a large harem was not as much an expression of sensuality as it was international diplomacy. "Family ties" represented "political allies." Solomon's marriage relationship with other nations was thus a political strategy through which he secured stability to his kingship. The price Israel paid for this unholy alliance with pagan nations was the introduction of foreign gods into Jerusalem.

The Northern entrance to Megiddo built by King Solomon.

Syncretism in the Temple

The construction of the Temple shows evidence of **syncretism,** or the blending of religious ideas, during the reign of Solomon. Architectural features of the Temple reveal the strong influence of religious ideas from neighboring areas, especially Phoenicia. The two bronze pillars at the entrance door of the Temple perhaps stood as the symbol of the ancient Near Eastern view that the earth rested upon its foundation pillars. The molten sea supported by 12 oxen likely reflected the primeval waters conquered at creation. Engravings in the doors included cherubim, flowers, and palm trees, all Near Eastern symbols of fertility.

ples as well as that of the Egyptians. As a patron of wisdom, Solomon composed thousands of proverbs and songs and classified categories of both animals and plants. Later generations remembered this "enlightened king" as the very representation of splen-

Wisdom and Discernment

Throughout the Old Testament, we find both positive and negative treatment of human wisdom. On the one hand, human beings are encouraged to "get wisdom" or to "learn from wisdom." On the other hand, wisdom outside of its proper context has destructive consequences. The biblical invitation to wisdom is grounded in the conviction that the fear (honor/reverence) of the Lord is the necessary prerequisite to one's attainment of wisdom.

This two-sided understanding of wisdom is particularly evident in the story of Solomon. God granted Solomon wisdom when he sought wisdom by acknowledging His sovereignty. However, when he exercised wisdom outside of its appropriate context and entered into marriage relationships with pagan nations, it became a snare to him.

dor and wealth (e.g., see Jesus' words in Matthew 6:29).

Solomon's wisdom was evident in his skill as an effective administrator. He reorganized the northern tribes of Israel into 12 administrative districts for the purpose of taxation and conscription. This restructuring of the nation meant the subjugation of tribal and clan priorities to the larger interest of the nation and national identity. Solomon's administrative policy included the introduction of forced labor in his kingdom. Solomon's actions thus took the nation back to the days of slavery and political bondage.

Solomon's government rapidly grew, which required a lavish

supply of provisions for the royal entourage and increasing numbers of stalls for horses and chariots. Though a growing royal court and national army reflected Solomon's ability to organize, it also meant physical hardship and heavy taxation for the majority of the population. Though wise in many ways, Solomon thus resorted to unscrupulous political actions that planted in the nation the seed of discontentment and rebellion.

Solomon's greatest accomplishment was the construction of the Temple in Jerusalem on the plot of ground David had purchased from Araunah. This project took seven years to complete. Solomon depended heavily upon the architecture and artisanship of the Phoenicians for the building project. He not only traded food products for Phoenician building materials and craftsmen but also fulfilled his debt obligations to the king of Tyre, **Hiram,** by handing over a portion of land in the northern territory. His citizens also paid the heavy price of forced labor, taxation, and economic and physical hardship to complete the building of the Temple.

Solomon's Temple included not only the building itself but the outer precincts as well. A large bronze vat (the molten sea) supported by 12 bronze oxen southeast of the Temple entrance served as the site for ritual washings by priests. To the northeast of the Temple entrance was the altar of sacrifice. Ten steps led to the doors of the main entrance, which was flanked on both sides by two bronze pillars named Jabin and Boaz.

The Temple itself was approximately 100 feet in length and was

Model of the Temple.

constructed of stone overlaid with cedar paneling. it consisted of three rooms. The `ulam (the portico) served as a vestibule or an entrance into the nave, or the *hekal* (the main hall). As the central and largest room, the *hekal* was the site of most daily activities that occurred inside the Temple. In the *hekal* were 10 lampstands, a table that containing the daily bread of the Presence, and an altar for burning incense. At the end of the *hekal* were two stairs leading to the third and final room, the **debir** (the inner sanctuary). The *debir* was understood to be the throne

A horned altar found at Beersheba, the southern border of ancient Israel.

God and the Temple

The Temple and its precincts served as the symbolic representation of God's sovereignty over the universe and all creation. It was the palace of Israel's divine king, Yahweh of Hosts, who had overcome the chaotic waters both at the creation of the universe and at the creation of Israel in the Red Sea/Jordan River. Everything in the Temple, from its outer courtyard to the inner throne room, gave testimony to the fact that the Lord God reigned over the universe and the powers of chaos (see Psalm 93:1).

99:1). The ark of the covenant beneath the wings served as God's footrest.

Solomon's dedicatory prayer over the completed Temple (chap. 8) reflects Israel's conviction that God did not dwell in an earthly building. Throughout his prayer of dedication, Solomon declared that even the heavens could not contain the Lord, much less the Temple (v. 27).

Solomon committed 13 years to the construction of a royal complex, which included his own palace, a house for his Egyptian wife, and various other state buildings. In addition to numerous buildings in Jerusalem, he also constructed other royal buildings at Gezer, Hazor, and Megiddo.

In spite of the diverse accomplishments of Solomon, Deuteronomistic historians give a negative final evaluation of his kingship. He violated the prohibition against intermarriage with the nations and failed to walk in the ways of the Lord. Moreover, he became a worshiper and patron of foreign gods. His heart was di-

room of the Lord. The *debir* was a perfect cube in height, width, and length. It had no windows, and it was completely dark inside. This most holy place, frequently called the holy of holies, contained the ark of the covenant as well as two cherubim carved from olive wood and overlaid with gold. The wings of the cherubim stretched out to touch each other. Israel's faith maintained the view that God sat on the wings of the cherubim, which was His throne (see Psalm

Solomon fortified Megiddo and made it one of the most influential centers of his kingdom.

vided, and he did not follow God completely.

At the end of Solomon's reign, various rebellions against the Davidic house took place. Deuteronomistic historians relate these incidents as the beginning of God's judgment upon Solomon. Of particular significance was the rebellion of **Jeroboam,** Solomon's officer for slave labor. The prophet **Ahijah** announced to Jeroboam that God would give him 10 of the 12 tribes of Israel. Though Solomon sought to kill Jeroboam, he fled to Egypt and remained under the protection of Pharaoh **Shishak** until Solomon's death.

■ The Revolt of the North (12:1-33)

After Solomon's death (922 B.C.), the people gathered at Shechem to make Solomon's son, **Rehoboam,** his successor and king over Israel. At Rehoboam's coronation, representatives of the northern tribes along with Jeroboam, who recently returned from Egypt, requested the new king to give the people relief from their labor and heavy taxation. But Rehoboam listened to the counsel of his advisers who were his peers, and threatened to make the people's life even more difficult and burdensome than during the days of his father. In response to this threat, the northern tribes broke away to form their own kingdom under the leadership of Jeroboam. Rehoboam's kingship was confined to the tribes of Judah and Benjamin in the south. The 10 northern tribes (the Northern Kingdom) subsequently became known as Israel or Ephraim. The southern kingdom under the Davidic house came to be known as Judah.

Steps of Megiddo from the early Israelite kingdom period.

Early in his reign, Jeroboam reestablished Shechem as the political center of his kingdom. However, he was fearful that the people of the Northern Kingdom would continue to go southward to worship God at Jerusalem. To prevent his nation from becoming disloyal to his kingship, Jeroboam set up two worship sites—one at **Dan** in the northern border and another at **Bethel** in the southern border of his kingdom. At both locations, Jeroboam constructed a golden bull to serve as an alternative symbol to the ark of the covenant. The bull, which was the symbol of the Canaanite fertility god Baal, thus became for Israel the object of their worship. The

Deuteronomistic writers cast a negative judgment on Jeroboam's action by referring to it as the "sin of Jeroboam." In response to Jeroboam's act, a prophet came to Bethel from Judah and declared that a descendant of David by the name of Josiah would eventually destroy the sanctuary at Bethel. Three centuries later, under Josiah's reforms, the sanctuary at Bethel was destroyed (2 Kings 23:15-20).

■ The Divided Kingdoms (13:1—16:34)

Throughout the remainder of 1 and 2 Kings, the writers evaluate the various kings in light of their faithfulness or lack of faithfulness to God. For northern kings, the

Boundaries of the kingdoms of Israel and Judah.

writers describe subsequent rulers as continuing in the sin of Jeroboam. This meant that they did not abolish worship at the sanctuaries at Dan and Bethel. All of the northern kings receive a negative appraisal from the writers. On the other hand, some of the southern kings receive positive and some receive negative evaluations. Those who lived according to the instructions of the Torah were those who did what was "right in the eyes of the LORD." Those who continued in their idolatry were those who did what was "evil in the eyes of the LORD."

The Deuteronomistic writers also follow a typical pattern in describing the reigns of each of the northern and southern kings. For the Northern Kingdom, the writers date the king's first year on the throne according to the coinciding year of the king in Judah, followed by the length of the king's reign and the location of his capital. The narrative usually ends with a common negative evaluation of the king. In introducing the kings of Judah, the writers date the king's first year according to the coinciding year of the king in Israel, followed by comments on the king's age, the length of his reign, and the name of the queen mother. The final evaluation sometimes includes a comparison to David or to the immediate predecessor.

The lack of a permanent dynasty resulted in volatile and violent political conditions in the Northern Kingdom. Assassinations and relatively brief reigns of kings were characteristic of the first half century. In contrast, the Southern Kingdom of Judah reflects relative stability, since successors to the throne were already determined by means of the Davidic dynasty.

In rapid succession, the writers comment upon the reigns of the southern kings Abijah and Asa and the reigns of the northern kings Nadab, Baasha, Elah, and Zimri. After Zimri had ruled only seven days, the commander of the Israelite army, **Omri,** assassinated him. Up until the time of Omri, the Northern Kingdom had been unable to establish a permanent succession of kings. However, with Omri, relative political stability and economic prosperity was achieved for over three decades. Although the Deuteronomistic writers give little information concerning Omri's reign (16:24-28) and describe Omri as having sinned "more than all those before him." Omri had great successes both domestically and internationally.

Omri not only established a dynasty that would last through four kings but also built **Samaria** as his new political capital. In proximity to the major north-south travel route, the city was located at the top of a steep hill, which protected it from enemy invasions. Archaeological excavations reveal a city that was well

Mesha Inscription[2]

The significance of Omri in the larger ancient Near Eastern context is evident from a ninth century B.C. inscription by King Mesha of Moab. This inscription contains the record of the Moabite victory over the Northern Kingdom. Included in this inscription is a reference to the manner in which Omri had subjugated the Moabite people for a long period of time. However, under Mesha the bonds of the Israelites had been broken. Of particular importance is the fact that this stone was erected long after Omri's death; yet the land of Israel continued to be called "the land of Omri."

fortified, with buildings constructed by well-trained masons and with furnishings having inlaid ivory.

Although the Deuteronomistic writers give Omri's reign only minimal attention, they describe Ahab's reign in great detail. In order to seal the political relation with Phoenicia, Omri married his son, **Ahab,** to the Phoenician king's daughter, **Jezebel.** As an ardent supporter of the Phoenician god, Baal, Jezebel imported hundreds of prophets of Baal into Israel and subsequently constructed numerous sanctuaries for these prophets. Soon, the

Northern and Southern Kings in 1 Kings[3]

Northern Kings			Southern Kings	
Jeroboam I	922-901	**900**	Rehoboam I	922-915
			Abijah	915-913
			Asa	913—873
Nadab	901-900			
Baasha	900—877			
Elah	877-876			
Zimri	876			
Omri	876-869			
Ahab	869-850	**850**	Jehoshaphat	873-849

masses of Israelites were worshiping Baal alongside Yahweh.

■ Prophet Voices (17:1—22:53)

When baalism was running rampant in Israel, God sent the prophet **Elijah** to the Northern Kingdom to champion the cause of Yahwistic faith in that nation. His name, which means "My God is Yahweh," demonstrated his mission. At a time when the people of Israel served whatever gods were promoted by the royal household, Elijah made no compromise. His mission was to challenge the dominant system of baalism and to declare Yahweh alone to be the God of Israel. Subsequently he was to instigate the ultimate overthrow of the Omri dynasty.

Elijah's mission began appropriately as he called for a drought in the name of Israel's God. During the drought, God provided bread, meat, and water to the prophet just as he had provided for Israel's ancestors in the wilderness. When the water finally dried up, Elijah made his way to Zarephath, a city in Sidon. Ironically, while at the very center of Jezebel's homeland, Elijah ex-

T Divided Loyalties

The first commandment, "You shall have no other gods before me" (Exodus 20:3), had become irrelevant to Israel in the 9th century B.C. They lived with the idea that "other gods," such as Baal and Asherah and gods of other neighboring cultures, were necessary for their life, productivity, prosperity, and security. In our 21st-century culture, the temptation to go after other gods is as powerful as in the ancient world of Israel. We, too, are prone to live a compartmentalized existence with sacred and secular boundaries, with divided loyalties and alternative choices. Elijah's story shows to us the implications and challenges of a life that is totally committed to God.

tended life-giving miracles to a widow and her son by providing an endless supply of food and by bringing the widow's son back to life. Once again, Elijah demonstrated that only Israel's God has the power to provide for and sustain life.

After three years of drought, Elijah declared a showdown between Baal and Yahweh at **Mount Carmel.** Challenging 450 prophets of Baal and 400 prophets of Asherah, Elijah called upon the people to make a decisive choice as to whom they would serve. For Elijah, the problem was not necessarily the people's refusal to serve God. Rather, their hearts were divided between the Lord

Wadi Qelt in the Judean desert; tradition holds that Elijah stopped here on his way to Horeb.

and Baal. Elijah challenged the people, "If the LORD is God, follow him; but if Baal is God, follow him" (18:21).

At Mount Carmel, the prophets of Baal attempted to show Baal as the supreme god over nature. They sought to manipulate Baal through various rituals, dancing, and laceration of their bodies. However, Baal made no response. Elijah followed by pouring water around his sacrifice to God. This wastefulness of water took place during a severe drought! This act of worship shows Elijah's utter confidence in the power of God as the Creator and the Sustainer of the universe. In response to Elijah's prayer, God consumed the sacrifice. Subsequently, Elijah destroyed the prophets of Baal, along with their places of worship.

Seeing Elijah as a threat to her religious, political, and economic agenda, Jezebel vowed to take his life for what he had done to her prophets. The prophet escaped to the wilderness in the southern part of the land and arrived at Mount Horeb. God, who appeared to Moses and Israel at this same location in thunder, earthquake, and smoke (Exodus 19:16-18), spoke to Elijah in a "gentle whisper" and gave him the com-

An Israelite storehouse at Hazor, probably dated to the period of King Ahab.

mission to return and continue his prophetic task.

Near the end of his reign, Ahab made an alliance with Judah's King Jehoshaphat to regain the city of Ramoth-gilead, which was lost previously to Syria. He consulted 400 false prophets concerning the prospects of a joint military campaign against Syria and received from them a unanimous favorable report. However, when he consulted a true prophet by the name of **Micaiah** ben Imlah, the prophet declared that the venture would be unsuccessful and that Ahab would die in the battle. Despite Micaiah's counsel, Ahab and Jehoshaphat proceeded to wage battle against Syria. In the battle, not only were they defeated, but Ahab was fatally wounded as well.

T True and False Prophets

In the story of Micaiah and the false prophets, we observe how easily prophets themselves could fall prey to nationalism and to the mundane service of the king. They spoke in the name of God a message of optimism and "God is on our side" theology. They spoke what the politicians wanted to hear in their day. Micaiah reminds us today that God is not on the side of politicians and leaders who seek Him only when they need religious legitimacy and sanction to their schemes. True prophets seldom made compromises with political establishments.

The Book of 1 Kings begins and ends with narratives that deal with Israel's splendor and downfall. Both the Solomonic and the Omride kingdoms represent opulence, wealth, security, and national splendor. Ironically, both periods also show tremendous injustice, corruption, and utter disloyalty to God. In 2 Kings, the final book of Deuteronomistic history, we shall see the tragic outcome of Israel's breaking of the Mount Sinai covenant, and their determination not to walk in the ways of Yahweh, their God.

Summary Statements

- Although the political and economic developments of Solomon's reign were far-reaching, they also provided the seed for destruction.
- Rehoboam's stubborn refusal to ease the burden of forced labor led to the division of the kingdom.
- Jeroboam's establishment of sanctuaries at Dan and Bethel became the "measuring rod" for the Deuteronomistic writers' evaluation of the northern kings.
- The Southern Kingdom experienced relative stability due to the permanence of the Davidic dynasty.
- The Northern Kingdom experienced a rapid succession of military overthrows until Omri established a dynasty in the ninth century B.C.
- The Solomonic and Omride periods were characterized by international alliances, domestic prosperity, syncretism, and royal marriages to foreigners.
- The message and ministry of the ninth century B.C. prophet Elijah reflect the central Deuteronomistic conviction that the people of the Lord must serve their God with an undivided loyalty.

Questions for Reflection

1. How do our subtle alliances with the world in which we live lead to divided hearts?
2. How might symbols of God's presence, such as the Temple in Jerusalem or Jeroboam's golden bulls, become worshiped as idols in our lives? What might some of these symbols be?
3. How might we, like Solomon, import foreign elements into our worship settings? In what situations is this appropriate, or is it ever appropriate?
4. Where might we "limp between two opinions" in relationship to our serving the Lord?
5. When is an appropriate time to take a stand for God, as the prophet Elijah did?

Resources for Further Study

Bright, John. *A History of Israel,* 4th ed. Louisville, Ky.: John Knox Press, 2000.
DeVries, Simon J. *1 Kings.* Vol. 12 of *Word Biblical Commentary.* Waco: Word, 1985.
Wiseman, Donald J. *1 and 2 Kings: An Introduction and Commentary.* Tyndale Old Testament Commentary. Downers Grove, Ill.: InterVarsity Press, 1993.

17 The Kingdom Divided (Part 2): 2 Kings

Objectives:

Your study of this chapter should help you to:

- Discuss the role of Elisha as the prophetic successor of Elijah.
- Evaluate the impact of Jehu's revolution upon Israel's politics, economy, and religious practices.
- Describe the political, economic, and religious developments during the reigns of Jeroboam II and Uzziah.
- Describe the reforms of Joash, Hezekiah, and Josiah.
- Discuss the ways in which the stories of the people of God in 2 Kings reflect core Deuteronomistic convictions.

Questions to consider as you read:

1. What are the reasons for military and political revolutions in many parts of the world today?

2. What role does religion play in bringing about radical changes within a culture?

3. What are some of the modern-day examples of national tragedies because of corrupt and oppressive leadership?

Key Words to Understand

Ahaziah
Elisha
Jehu
Jezreel
Athaliah
Jehoash
Jeroboam II
Uzziah (Azariah)
Jotham
Tiglath-pileser III
Ahaz
Syro-Ephraimite war
Shalmaneser V
Hezekiah
Siloam tunnel
Sennacherib
Manasseh
Josiah
Huldah
Jehoiakim
Jehoiachin
Zedekiah

As we have observed in 1 Kings, the people of God and their kings repeatedly made alliances with other nations and turned to other gods. The Book of 2 Kings resumes the story of covenant breaking that has become a characteristic way of life for the citizens of both the Southern and Northern Kingdoms. We shall see later in this chapter how both of these kingdoms lost their national and political existence due to God's judgment that came upon them as punishment for their sin.

Title and Authorship

Second Kings is the second part of the story of Israel's kingdoms and kingship. This book continues the story of 1 Kings and narrates the events that led to the destruction of both nations. Although the two Books of Kings were originally one scroll, the present break between the two books is appropriate, since 2 Kings begins with a major turn of affairs that resulted in the overthrow of the Omri dynasty in the Northern Kingdom. Again, this is the final part of the Deuteronomistic history that covers Israel's history from the theological perspectives of the Book of Deuteronomy. The historians who compiled this book very vividly portray God's judgment that came upon Israel and Judah as the unleashing of the covenant curses stated in Deuteronomy.

Setting

Second Kings continues the story of Israel's divided kingdoms. The narratives reflect the ongoing conditions of religious apostasy and political instability in both Israel and Judah. The continued ministry of Elijah in the opening chapter of the book indicates that a small minority of people remained as faithful champions of the traditions and the covenant with God. The narratives cover the period from around 850 B.C. to 587 B.C.

Content

The content of the Book of 2 Kings can be divided into the following two major sections:

1. The Downfall of Israel (1:1—17:41)
2. The Downfall of Judah (18:1—25:30)

■ The Overthrow of a Dynasty (1:1—12:21)[1]

Following Ahab's death in the battle against Syria (1 Kings 22), **Ahaziah** succeeded his father to the throne. Ahaziah clearly continued in the way of his father, who had turned his back on God to serve Baal. Israel's prospects of returning to God under Ahaziah appeared to be no better than they had been under his father Ahab.

One of the final tasks of Elijah was to transfer the prophetic ministry to his disciple **Elisha** and to appoint him as his successor. When the time came for Elijah to end his ministry, he took Elisha with him and went to Jericho, and from there to the eastern side of the river Jordan by parting the river with his mantle. As the two walked along, Elijah disappeared into the heavens in a fiery chariot. Elisha picked up the mantle of his "prophetic father," which symbolized the transfer of prophetic activity and the power to perform miraculous things. On his way back, he also parted the Jordan River with Elijah's mantle. When he reached Jericho, the fellow prophets who were disciples of Elijah recognized that the spirit of Elijah was upon Elisha.

In contrast to Elijah, who made his mark by religious and political confrontations, the stories of Elisha focus upon various miracles performed by the prophet. His miracles for the most part were directed to helping the people who needed water and food, healing the sick, and raising the dead. More specifically, his primary ministry was to instigate a revolution to overthrow the Omri dynasty. He played a vital part in the rise of **Jehu** as Israel's king. Jehu, who was anointed king by one of Elisha's followers, made his way to **Jezreel** to lead a thorough and violent coup d'etat of the house of Omri. Not only did Jehu assassinate Ahab's son, Joram, but also he went as far as to kill Judah's king, Ahaziah, who was in Israel visiting his ally Joram. Jezebel was cast out of an upper-story window. Horses below trampled upon her body, and she suffered the fate pronounced upon her by Elijah. Jehu completed the bloody purge of the royal family by assas-

Elijah parted the Jordan River with his mantle (cloak).

The Valley of Jezreel has been the site of many battles in the Old Testament period.

The Prophet Elijah and Messianic Expectations

The role of Moses and Elijah as the ones who prepared the way for God had a long-lasting impression upon the people of God. The stories of both Moses and Elijah end mysteriously on the eastern side of the Jordan. In light of the unusual way in which his life came to an end, later generations thought that Elijah would return to prepare the way for the establishment of God's kingdom. As early as the fifth century B.C., the prophet Malachi declared that God would send "the prophet Elijah before that great and dreadful day of the LORD comes" (4:4-5; see also 3:1). As this understanding of Elijah continued to develop in early Judaism, it naturally found its way into the thought of early Christians. Some thought that John the Baptist fulfilled the mission of Elijah (Matthew 11:7-15; 17:10-13; Mark 6:14-16; Luke 1:17). At Jesus' transfiguration, he appeared along with Moses (Mark 9:2-8). When Jesus asked His disciples how people viewed Him, they responded that some thought He was John the Baptist or Elijah (Mark 8:28).

The entrance to Dan, in the Northern Kingdom of Israel.

sinating the 70 sons of Ahab along with persons even remotely related to Ahab. Subsequently, he destroyed the worship sites of Baal and restored the proper worship of Yahweh in Israel.

The religious renewal in the Northern Kingdom was matched by a renewal in Judah a few years later. By a strange twist of events, **Athaliah** (queen mother of Judah's king Ahaziah and daughter of Jezebel) had usurped the Davidic throne in Judah after Ahaziah's assassination. Though she attempted to exterminate all rivals to the throne by wiping out the male members of the Davidic family, a royal family member saved the life of **Jehoash** (Joash), the one-year-old son of Ahaziah. Under the care and tutelage of the priest Jehoiada, Jehoash was kept hidden for the following six years. This priest was eventually successful in overthrowing the wicked queen mother and installing Jehoash as Judah's king. With the support of conservative landowners outside of Jerusalem and under the guidance of the Jerusalem priests led by Jehoida, the young king led the nation through a revival of Yahwism. He removed the places of Baal wor-

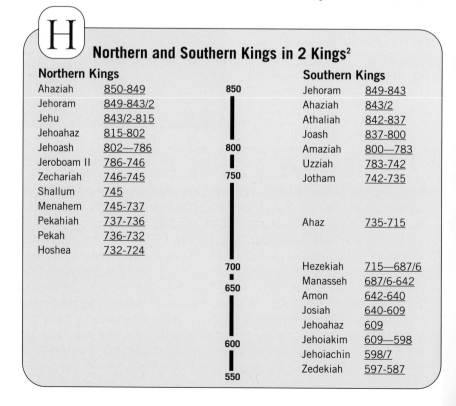

H Northern and Southern Kings in 2 Kings[2]

Northern Kings			Southern Kings	
Ahaziah	850-849	850	Jehoram	849-843
Jehoram	849-843/2		Ahaziah	843/2
Jehu	843/2-815		Athaliah	842-837
Jehoahaz	815-802		Joash	837-800
Jehoash	802—786	800	Amaziah	800—783
Jeroboam II	786-746		Uzziah	783-742
Zechariah	746-745	750	Jotham	742-735
Shallum	745			
Menahem	745-737			
Pekahiah	737-736		Ahaz	735-715
Pekah	736-732			
Hoshea	732-724			
		700	Hezekiah	715—687/6
		650	Manasseh	687/6-642
			Amon	642-640
			Josiah	640-609
			Jehoahaz	609
			Jehoiakim	609—598
		600	Jehoiachin	598/7
			Zedekiah	597-587
		550		

ship and repaired the Jerusalem Temple. Jehoash is one of the few kings in the Deuteronomistic history to receive a highly positive evaluation by the writers of the text. Nevertheless, even this reformer did not remove the high places of worship (12:3). Tragically, his servants murdered him, and his son Amaziah succeeded him to the throne.

■ The Downfall of the Northern Kingdom (13:1—17:41)

The dynasty that Jehu established ruled Israel for the next four generations. Although the Deuteronomistic writers praised Jehu's attempt to wipe out Baal worship, in the final evaluation of his reign they observed that he "did not turn from the sins of Jeroboam" (10:29, 31).

Jehu's revolution resulted in significant diplomatic and political changes in Israel's relation to their neighboring nations. Relationships with Phoenicia developed by Omri and Ahab were severely broken with the murder of Jezebel. Likewise, Jehu's murder of Judah's king severed Israel's relation with Judah. Without the support of Phoenicia and Judah, Israel became considerably more vulnerable to the attacks of Syria.

After the account of Jehu's reign, the writers rapidly continue the story of the people of God through the reigns of the northern kings, Jehoahaz and Jehoash (son and grandson of Jehu) and the southern king, Amaziah (son of Jehoash). During the days of Jehoahaz, Israel suffered enormously from successful Syrian invasions. However, during the reign of Jehoahaz's son, Jehoash, the situation changed once again.

During his reign, Israel was able to recapture the lands taken over by Syria.

During the reign of the southern king Amaziah, bitter rivalry once again broke out between Israel and Judah. The Northern Kingdom defeated Judah during military invasion, broke down the walls of Jerusalem, took hostages, and plundered the Temple treasury. However, Amaziah was able to remain on the throne of Judah. Although he received a positive evaluation from the Deuteronomistic writers, they also indicted him for not removing the high places of worship.

For the next 50 years, the stage was set for a period of growth and prosperity in the Northern Kingdom. Israel reached its political and economic pinnacle under the reign of **Jeroboam II**. Although the writers provide the characteristically negative judgment on Jeroboam II, Israel expe-

High Places

High places, often mentioned in 1 and 2 Kings, were sanctuaries located on high hills surrounded by green trees. Israel established such places of worship patterned after the Canaanite high places where the Canaanites worshiped Baal and Asherah. The Law of Moses prohibited such places of worship in Israel. However, as a practice, these places provided the people with local shrines, in addition to the established and legitimate place of worship in Jerusalem. These places were furnished with altars for sacrifice, pillars, and poles and other objects of idol worship. According to 1 Kings, Solomon was the first king of Israel to build such places of worship in Israel. This practice was continued by his son Rehoboam and many of the northern kings (see 1 Kings 11:7-8; 14:23; 2 Kings 17:9).

rienced tremendous economic prosperity and development during his reign. Under Jeroboam II, Israel recovered significant tracts of land that had been lost in the previous decades, and they ultimately controlled the trade route in the Transjordan. Under his leadership, Israel resumed vigorous international trade. The capital city of Samaria became the center of luxury and lavish lifestyle. However, these were the days of extreme economic inequity, social injustice, moral corruption, and religious hypocrisy in the Northern Kingdom. It was in this context that God sent a Judean prophet named Amos to preach the message of justice and righteousness to the northern nation. God also raised up Hosea, a citizen of the Northern Kingdom, to pronounce judgment against the nation's covenant unfaithfulness and religious harlotry.

Jeroboam's reign of economic prosperity and political advancement coincided with similar wealth and development in Judah. Under King **Uzziah** (also called **Azariah** in the biblical text), the Southern Kingdom expanded its borders eastward across the Jordan and westward into the Philistine territory, putting Judah in control of major commercial thoroughfares. With Edom under Judah's control, a seaport was built at Ezion Geber so that Judah could actively engage in sea trade. During the lengthy reign of Uzziah, Judah also reached the pinnacle of its military, economic, and political power. Although Uzziah was later stricken with leprosy (see the cause of this judgment in 2 Chronicles 26:16-21), this much-loved king remained on the throne until his death, alongside

his son **Jotham** as coregent. Though Uzziah received high praise from the historians, he, too, was indicted for not removing the high places of worship in Judah.

Following nearly a half century of peace and prosperity under the reigns of Jeroboam II in the north and Uzziah in the south, the situation changed dramatically. Soon after the death of Jeroboam II, the Northern Kingdom returned to its earlier practice of royal assassinations and coups. After only six months on the throne, Jeroboam's son Zechariah was assassinated and replaced by Shallum, who reigned for only one month until Menahem murdered him. For a decade, Menahem succeeded in maintaining power. During his reign, the Assyrian king **Tiglath-pileser III** forced Israel to pay a large tribute in order to preserve its relative independence. Although Menahem's son Pekahiah followed his father to the throne, his two-year reign came to an end when Pekah assassinated him.

During Pekah's reign large portions of territory were lost to Tiglath-pileser III. In order to defend the kingdom against the Assyrian invasion, Pekah entered into an alliance with the Syrian king Rezin. Together, Pekah and Rezin attempted to force King **Ahaz** of Judah to join them against the Assyrians. The joint **Syro-Ephraimite** (Syria and Israel in alliance) **war** against Jerusalem prompted the Judean King Ahaz to seek help from Assyria. He did this against the wise counsel of the prophet Isaiah, who called Ahaz to put his trust in the Lord. Though the Assyrians delivered Judah, they entered Damascus and brought an end to Syrian power. Judah thus became a vassal of Assyria and was forced to pay tribute as well as to adopt Assyrian practices of worship (16:5-16).

In contrast to many of the kings of Judah, the Deuteronomistic writers particularly single out Ahaz for condemnation. Not only did Ahaz not do what was right in the sight of God, but also he worshiped at the worship sites of Baal (high hills and green trees) and went as far as to offer his own child as human sacrifice (v. 3).

During the reign of Ahaz over Judah, the Northern Kingdom experienced its final violent coup d'etat, which resulted in the murder of Pekah by Hoshea. Though Hoshea remained a vassal of Assyria during the early part of his nine-year reign over Israel, he later joined Egypt in a plot against Assyria and subsequently withheld tribute from Assyria. In retaliation against this breach of loyalty, the Assyrian king **Shalmaneser V** besieged Israel for three years. Following Shalmaneser's death, his successor, Sargon II, completed the task of

A water tunnel at Megiddo built during the days of King Ahab; this tunnel carried water into the city from a spring outside the city.

Remains of King Ahab's palace at Samaria, capital of the Northern Kingdom.

Samaritan-Jewish Conflict

The sharp division between Samaritans and Jews present in the New Testament texts goes as far back as the last part of the eighth century B.C. With Assyria's repopulation of the Northern Kingdom territory with various ethnic groups, and the origin of a racially mixed population, the Southern Kingdom's citizens came to view the northern population as religiously and racially unclean. Though both the southern and the northern people shared a common ancestry, the southern people regarded themselves as the only racially pure and Yahweh worshiping people in the land. This religious and racial superiority maintained by the south gradually led to bitter religious and ethnic rivalry and ongoing conflict between the two segments of the Israelite nation. This rivalry reached its climax during the postexilic period when the northerners (the Samaritans) attempted to disrupt the Temple rebuilding program undertaken by the Jews in the south.

bringing an end to the nation of Israel in 721 B.C.

When the Assyrians conquered Samaria, they not only deported many Israelites from their homeland and dispersed them throughout the empire but also settled other ethnic and national groups in their place in Israel. This Assyrian practice of resettlement prevented future uprisings by the people. At first those persons who were resettled in Israel continued to worship their own gods. When concern was expressed to the Assyrian king that the people living in the land did not know the requirements of the god of the land, the king sent a priest back from exile to Bethel to train the people in the ways of the Lord (see 17:25-28). Nevertheless, religious syncretism continued in the land along with Israel's social relations with the newcomers from various

parts of the Assyrian Empire. As a result of the marriage relationship between Israel and other ethnic groups, a racially mixed population known as the Samaritans came into existence in the north.

■ Final Southern Reformers and the Destruction of Jerusalem (18:1—25:30)

While his father Ahaz had yielded to Assyria by not only paying regular tribute but even building an Assyrian altar in the Jerusalem Temple, **Hezekiah** led the people of Judah into an era of religious renewal and political strength. He removed the places of Baal worship, including the Asherah poles and Baal altars. Furthermore, Hezekiah moved to centralize all worship at the Temple in Jerusalem. These religious reforms clearly signaled Hezekiah's intent to liberate Judah from its political bondage to Assyria.

The construction of the **Siloam tunnel** was a major engineering achievement during Hezekiah's reign. Over 1,700 feet in length, this tunnel conducted water from outside the city wall of Jerusalem at Gihon into the Pool of Siloam within the city walls. He undertook this project so that the city could survive a lengthy siege during military invasion by foreign armies. Hezekiah also strengthened the fortifications of the city of Jerusalem and repaired the city wall.

In 712 B.C., Egypt and Philistia attempted to revolt against Assyria. Fortunately Hezekiah, with the counsel of the prophet Isaiah (Isaiah 20), did not become engaged in the revolt and was spared the vengeance of Assyria. However, a decade later, in 701 B.C., Hezekiah did join a revolution against Assyria, supported by both Babylon and Egypt. Just as Isaiah had counseled Hezekiah's father Ahaz against revolt, so, too, he counseled Hezekiah to remain neutral. The prophet encouraged Hezekiah not to place his trust in human beings but in God (30:15; 31:1-3). In spite of Isaiah's counsel, Hezekiah joined the revolt. The Assyrian king **Sennacherib** responded quickly (1 Kings 18—20; also Isaiah 36—39) and surrounded Jerusalem with his army. Though Sennacherib's army laid siege against the city, through God's intervention, his army withdrew and the city was miraculously spared destruction.

The Deuteronomistic writers have given Hezekiah an unqualified positive evaluation. They observed that no one before or after Hezekiah was like him in his faithfulness to God. However, this was not the case with **Manasseh,** Hezekiah's son, who succeeded his father to the throne. Manasseh ruled for nearly 45 years, one of the longest reigns of any of the kings of Israel or Judah. Throughout the reign of Manasseh, Assyria dominated the entire ancient Near East, including Egypt. Manasseh sought to appease the Assyrians by being a subservient vassal. He rebuilt the high places that Hezekiah had destroyed, and thus reversed the reform policies of his father. Manasseh practiced and promoted astral worship, human sacrifice, and sorcery. It is

Hezekiah constructed this tunnel to bring water into Jerusalem from a spring outside the city.

likely that Manasseh's loyalty toward Assyria accounts for the apparent lack of Assyrian military attacks against Judah during this period.

After Manasseh's death, his son Amon succeeded him on the throne of Judah and continued his father's pro-Assyrian policies. Two years later, members of the royal court murdered him and placed on the throne his son **Josi-**

The Annals of Sennacherib

In a clay prism, Sennacherib described his victory over the rebellious nations. Celebrating his siege of Jerusalem, Sennacherib observed that he had shut up Hezekiah within the city of Jerusalem "like a caged bird."[3]

ah, who was only eight years old. Eighteen years later, Josiah gave instructions to refurbish the Temple, which by this time had become Judah's symbol of religious and national identity. This was the beginning of a massive religious reform intended to restore true worship in Judah and to shake the nation free from its bondage to Assyria. During the repair work, workers found the "book of the law" in the Temple, which was then promptly brought before the king. As the king listened to the words of the Torah, he asked Hilkiah the priest and other royal officials to seek God on behalf of the nation. They consulted the prophetess **Huldah**, who announced that disaster would certainly come upon the people of God because of their repeated abandonment of the Lord. This word of judgment further compelled Josiah to undertake a covenant renewal and further reform activities. Most scholars think that the "book of the law" that instigated the Josianic reform contained the core of the present Book of Deuteronomy (chaps. 12—26).

Following the covenant renewal ceremony, Josiah purged the Temple of all objects dedicated to other deities and religions. Furthermore, he ousted all religious

The Assyrian Empire in the mid-seventh century B.C.

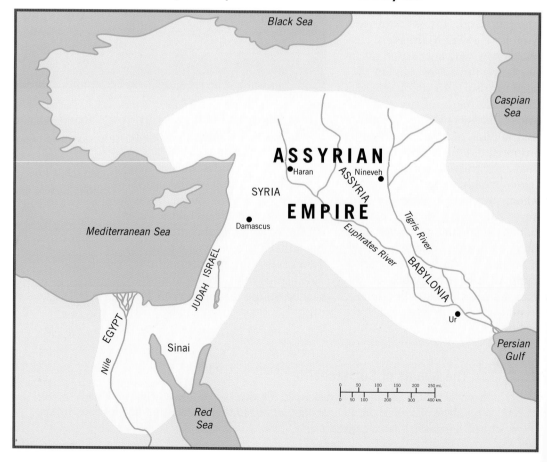

leaders who had worked at the numerous high places throughout the land, and he removed all cultic objects and buildings that were objectionable to the pure worship of God (2 Kings 23:4-14). This included the destruction of the shrine and the altar established by Jeroboam I at Bethel. The reform of Josiah finally was culminated in the national observance of the Passover, the first of its kind since the time of the judges. The historians observe that there was none like Josiah, either before him or after him, who served God wholeheartedly and with undivided loyalty.

Meanwhile, changes in international politics prompted Josiah to become involved in the affairs of the ancient Near East. Toward the last quarter of the seventh century B.C., a major assault was launched against Assyria by the Medes, which was soon joined by the Babylonians. The allied forces were able to bring the downfall of the Assyrian Empire and the eventual destruction of Nineveh, its capital city, in 612 B.C. The allies moved westward and captured Haran, Assyria's last major stronghold. Egypt, under the leadership of Pharaoh Neco II, set out to offer assistance to Assyria to recapture Haran from the Babylonian-Mede allied forces. King Josiah, who saw the destruction of Assyria as the long-awaited opportunity for Judah's freedom, attempted to stop the Egyptian army that was on its way to Haran. Josiah was mortally wounded in the battle at Megiddo in 609 B.C. by the Egyptian army. The Egyptians removed Jehoahaz, Josiah's son, who was on the throne for only three months, and replaced him with his brother

Jehoiakim. He remained a loyal vassal of Egypt during the first six years of his reign. Though Egypt could not help Assyria, it gained control of the Syria-Palestine region.

The Egyptians tried to prevent the Babylonians from marching southward to the Syria-Palestine region. But in 605 B.C. at the battle of Carchemish, the Babylonian army defeated the Egyptians and made its way down to the Philistine plain. Babylon's victory over the cities of Philistia and the helpless condition of Egypt prompted Jehoiakim to transfer his allegiance to Babylon's king Nebuchadnezzar in 603 B.C. Two years later, when the Babylonian army suffered a temporary setback in the war with Egypt, Jehoiakim decided to rebel against Babylon. Nebuchadnezzar sent his army against Judah to punish the rebellious vassal. However, Jehoiakim's death in 598 B.C. spared him from seeing the outcome of the Babylonian invasion of Judah. **Jehoi-**

Wholehearted Devotion to God

T Wholehearted devotion to God is a major theological theme in 1 and 2 Kings. This emphasis in the Deuteronomistic history is the central concern of the Book of Deuteronomy. The good kings of Judah who attempted to reform the nation received positive evaluation from the historians for their faithfulness and commitment to the law of the Lord. Kings of both kingdoms who were evil received negative evaluations. The writers repeatedly refer to Deuteronomic phrases such as doing "what was evil in the sight of the LORD" or doing "what was right in the eyes of the LORD." The writers were also careful to note that obedience to the Law brought blessings and prosperity, and disobedience brought the curses of the covenant.

achin, his son who assumed the throne, could keep his kingship for only three months. The Babylonians carried Jehoiachin and many of Jerusalem's prestigious political and religious leaders into captivity in Babylon in 597 B.C.

The Babylonians installed **Zedekiah** as king over Judah with the understanding that he would encourage faithfulness to Babylon. However, when Zedekiah rebelled, Nebuchadnezzar returned to Jerusalem in 587 B.C. and carried out its final destruction. The Babylonians looted the Temple treasury and set fire to the Temple, the royal palace, and other adjacent buildings. Zedekiah was forced to witness the murder of his sons, and he was blinded and taken captive to Babylon. The majority of the population was carried into exile, and the Babylonians left in the land only the poorest and weakest members of the nation. Even among this group there was treachery and violence. A rebel group murdered Gedaliah, who was appointed by Babylon as Judah's governor. This rebel group finally escaped to Egypt fearing reprisal from Babylon.

The story of Kings in a real sense is the story of failed leadership. For the most part, Israel's

T Kings and Prophets

The Deuteronomistic historians give significant place to the ministry of the prophets in their narratives. In their final evaluation of the destruction of both Israel and Judah, the historians include the report that both nations came to an end according to the words spoken by the prophets (see 2 Kings 17:13, 23; 24:2). As God's servants and spokespersons, the prophets confronted evil kings, gave warnings, made threats about judgment, and even challenged the kings to make political decisions trusting in the power of God. The historians make it very clear that the national tragedies that happened in 721 B.C. and 587 B.C. were the direct outcome of rejecting the message of the prophets.

A Story That Continues: Grace in the Midst of Judgment

The tragic destruction of Jerusalem is not the final story of 2 Kings. Though the covenant nation Israel lost its political existence and religious freedom, the future was not filled with gloom and despair. The final narrative in this book casts a glimmer of hope for the nation in exile. The Deuteronomistic historians who compiled this book and other parts of Israel's past history knew very well that the exile was not God's last word to His people. Time and time again, they recalled for the nation God's gracious dealings with His people and His mighty deeds of salvation performed for them since He brought them into the land of promise. They were convinced that God would again return to His people with His grace and mercy during the darkest days of Judah's exile in Babylon. They saw the release of Jehoiachin from prison by the Babylonian king Evil-Merodach as the harbinger of the good days to come for the exiled community. The writers note that the Babylonian king "spoke kindly" to the exiled king of Judah and gave him "a seat of honor higher than those of the other kings who were with him in Babylon" (25:28). This note of optimism is, in the final analysis, the message of 1 and 2 Kings. Judah's future is with her God, who is her covenant God. And that future depends solely on the gracious compassion of God, who had long ago promised to restore His scattered people from the lands of their exile (Deuteronomy 30:1-5).

leaders failed to model before their nation godliness and true piety. More than that, they introduced paganism and idolatry in the land and made political alliances for the sake of survival. They often disregarded the Sinai covenant and rejected the law of the Lord. As a result, God's judgment came upon both kingdoms. At a much later time, Ezekiel reminded the exiled nation that their judgment was brought upon them by the "shepherds of Israel" who showed no concern for their flock (Ezekiel 34:1-6).

Summary Statements

- Elisha carried out the successful overthrow of the Omri dynasty and the establishment of the Jehu dynasty.
- The rise of the Jehu dynasty represented a dramatic shift in political, economic, and religious policies in the kingdom of Israel.
- In spite of the thoroughgoing reforms of Jehu, Jehoash, Hezekiah, and Josiah, the people of God were not capable of ultimately changing their ways.
- The ultimate consequence of Israel's covenant breaking with God was the loss of their political and religious freedom.
- The destruction of Samaria and the destruction of Jerusalem were evidence of the covenant curses at work.
- The Deuteronomistic history concludes on a note of optimism that God holds the future open.

Questions for Reflection

1. What is the responsibility of an "Elijah" generation to the "Elisha" generation among the people of God? What is the responsibility of an "Elisha" generation to the "Elijah" generation?

2. What can be accomplished through religious revivals or reforms? What are their limitations?

3. What brings exile to the lives of the people of God? Why should the people of God face "exile-type" experiences?

Resources for Further Study

Bright, John. *A History of Israel,* 4th ed. Louisville, Ky.: John Knox Press, 2000.

Hobbs, T. R. *2 Kings.* Vol. 13 of *Word Biblical Commentary.* Waco, Tex.: Word, 1985.

Wiseman, Donald J. *1 and 2 Kings: An Introduction and Commentary. Tyndale Old Testament Commentary.* Downers Grove, Ill.: InterVarsity Press, 1993.

18 The Exile and Restoration

bjectives:

Your study of this chapter should help you to:
- Describe the main events and key people involved in the exile and restoration of Israel.
- Envision the setting in which the exilic and postexilic books of the Bible were written.
- Recognize the theological issues facing the descendants of Abraham during the exile and restoration.

ey Words to Understand

Babylonian exile
Restoration period
Nebuchadnezzar
Babylonians
Nabonidus
Belshazzar
Persians
Cyrus the Great
Sheshbazzar
Zerubbabel
Cambyses II
Darius the Great
Haggai
Zechariah
Xerxes I
Esther
Artaxerxes I
Ezra
Nehemiah
Malachi
Samaritan Pentateuch
Elephantine

Questions to consider as you read:

1. How would you respond if your nation was destroyed and you had to live in a refugee camp in another country?
2. How do you feel when things do not get better as quickly as you hoped they would?

The **Babylonian exile** was a watershed event in the history of Israel both politically and spiritually. Things were never the same after that. Following exile, a slow period of recovery known as the **restoration period** emerged. These were times of testing and rethinking the ancient faith of Israel. Fortunately prophets and other spiritual leaders rose up once again to provide encouragement and guidance for a new community. Many of the books of the Old Testament took their final shape in these years. The development of some of the significant theological perspectives of Judaism and the Jewish institutions we encounter in the New Testament may also be traced to the period of restoration.

The Ishtar Gate, the main gate of Babylon built during the reign of Nebuchadnezzar II (605-562 B.C.).

The Exile of Judah[1]

In the spring of 587 B.C. the Babylonian army ended their siege of Jerusalem and breached the walls of the city.[2] The hours that followed this breach were filled with violent death and destruction. **Nebuchadnezzar,** king of Babylon, determined that Jerusalem would no longer be a seedbed for rebellion in his empire. So he crushed it thoroughly.

Babylon the Great

The ancient city of Babylon was located along the Euphrates River about 50 miles south of modern Baghdad. It was an impressive city with massive double walls and decorated gates. Among its many places of worship, the most important was Etemenanki, the ancient tower of Babel. It was a ziggurat-styled artificial hill topped by a temple.

The palace complex included lavishly decorated rooms and courts with a throne room over 100 feet in length and 50 feet wide. Most breathtaking, however, were the hanging gardens, one of the seven wonders of world. Nebuchadnezzar constructed them for his Median princess, whose mountainous homeland was lush with vegetation. Hundreds of varieties of plants and trees were brought in to please the princess. Slave labor pumped water from the Euphrates in shifts each day in order to keep them watered.

Babylonian soldiers systematically burned and looted the city of Jerusalem and the Temple. The leaders of the rebellion against Babylon were executed, and most of the nation was deported to Babylon. A few, like Jeremiah, were treated favorably because of their apparent support of Babylon.

The exiles joined the Israelites from previous deportations in 604 and 597 B.C. They settled in villages like Tel-abib, Tel-melah, and Casiphia located east of Babylon along the Kebar River toward Nippur. The **Babylonians** allowed the exiles to build houses, engage in agriculture and commerce, and form their own communities (see Jeremiah 29:5-7). It is likely that some of the exiles gained employment in the government, military garrisons, and building projects in Babylon.

Survivors in Judah

Not all Israelites were taken into exile in Babylon. Some of the poorest and least skilled remained in the land, while others fled to neighboring countries to live as refugees.

The plight of those left in the land of Judah was meager. Most cities and villages had been ravaged by the Babylonian conquest. Those who remained in the land attempted to resurrect a destroyed economy. Worship at the Temple ruins in Jerusalem continued, but it contained mixed elements (see Jeremiah 41:5). The Babylonians established an administrative center about seven miles north of Jerusalem at Mizpah. Gedaliah, a man whose family had served in the royal court of Judah, was appointed regional governor. Gedaliah's leadership lasted only briefly. A rebel leader by the name of Ishmael assassinated Gedaliah, took captive those who were at Mizpah, and attempted to escape to the Ammonite region. However, Johanan, another local leader, pursued him with his supporters and rescued the captives. Ishmael escaped and went to the Ammonites (see Jeremiah 41).

Refugees in Egypt

Some Israelites escaped the Babylonian sword by fleeing to surrounding countries. These refugees went east across the Jordan River to the Ammonite land, and south to Egypt. A group under the leadership of Johanan wanted Jeremiah to go with them to Egypt. Jeremiah pleaded with them to remain in Judah. He told them that God would prosper them if they remained in their land. However, they forced the prophet to go with them to Egypt (see Jeremiah 42). They settled in the Delta region at Tahpanhes. Other groups settled in Migdol and Memphis (Noph) in the north while still others moved to villages in southern Egypt.

Theological Crisis and Its Outcome

The events of the Exile precipitated a major theological crisis for those who survived. The descendants of Abraham remained without the symbols of God's special blessings—their Temple, the kingship, and their nationhood. This crisis led them to reflect and raise questions about the nature of God and His relationship to the descendants of Abraham.

Central to their concerns were questions about God's fairness and trustworthiness. Survivors of Jerusalem's destruction wanted to know why this evil had happened. All appearances suggested that God had failed or abandoned them. Perhaps the Babylonian gods were more powerful than Israel's God.

Also important were questions about identity. How could the exiles or refugees be Israelites if there was no nation called Israel? Without the Temple and kingship, could the Israelites still be God's people? Such questions led to concerns about the future. These people needed to know what they might be able to expect from God. Was there any basis of hope for something different in their future?

These questions led the exilic community to reflect on their past, present, and future. Their reflection of the past led them to the great historical and theological traditions of their ancestors. In these ancient traditions they found evidence of God's power and faithfulness. The Books of

Moses most likely received their final canonical shape during the Exile. The Books of Joshua, Judges, 1 and 2 Samuel, and 1 and 2 Kings were also compiled at this time to provide an extended narrative explanation for the Exile (Deuteronomistic history). As the people contemplated their present conditions, they composed highly emotional poems such as Lamentations and Psalm 137 to express deep feelings of living the nightmare of exile. Also, they gathered the writings of the prophets and recognized their credibility and authenticity as God's true prophets to Israel. They found in the words of these prophets God's plans and purposes for their future. The words of these previous prophets were reiterated and recast into new words of hope and comfort by their own prophets who were in exile (see Isaiah 40—55). A number of other books, such as Psalms and Job, also received their final form during the Exile.

The Exile was thus a turning point in Israel's history. It gave the people a new vision for their future. We know from their later history that they took the identity of Yehudites (Jews) during this period. Also, they learned Aramaic, the language of their Babylonian captors, and made it their spoken and commercial language. We also think that the Exile introduced them to commercial and business enterprises, which became the primary vocation of their later descendants.

The absence of the Temple and rituals prompted the exilic community to meet together in private homes for prayer and praise and reading of Scripture. This gathering eventually led to the es-

H Excerpt from Psalm 137

By the rivers of Babylon we sat and wept
  when we remembered Zion.
There on the poplars
  we hung our harps,
for there our captors asked us for songs,
  our tormentors demanded songs of joy;
    they said, "Sing us one of the songs of Zion!"
How can we sing the songs of the LORD
  while in a foreign land?
If I forget you, O Jerusalem,
  may my right hand forget its skill.
May my tongue cling to the roof of my mouth
  if I do not remember you,
if I do not consider Jerusalem
  my highest joy.

(vv. 1-6)

tablishment of the synagogue, the educational and teaching center of later Judaism.

Decline of Babylon

The Babylonian Empire tee-tered on the brink of disaster af-ter the death of Nebuchadnezzar in 562 B.C. A series of his succes-sors were assassinated until **Nabonidus** came to power in 556 B.C. He was neither a member of the royal family nor a worshiper of Marduk, the patron god of Babylon. He preferred the wor-ship of the moon god Sin, which angered the establishment of Babylon. He eventually left Baby-lon and lived in the Arabian Desert in Teman while his son **Belshazzar** ran the affairs of the empire.

The Persian Conquest of Babylon

As Babylon was weakening, a gifted prince among the **Persians**, who became known as **Cyrus the Great**, was beginning to gain prominence in the lands to the east. He rebelled against the lord-ship of the Medes and took con-trol of their vast empire in 550 B.C. This included most of modern Iran. Then he conquered areas in modern Turkey in the west and

Afghanistan in the east before turning his attention to Babylon. In October of 539 B.C. the armies of Persia conquered the city of Babylon. The gates of the city were opened wide to the Persians, according to ancient historians, and Cyrus was viewed by the peo-ple of Babylon as a liberator from the oppressive and ineffective rule of Nabonidus.

The Jewish exiles saw the rise of Cyrus as God's plan for their liberation from Babylon (see Isa-iah 44:28—45:6). The Persians took a different policy toward their captives than the Babylo-nians. Instead of relocating con-quered people to other areas of the empire as the Babylonians had done, Cyrus returned them to their homelands. He determined that people living and worshiping in their own lands would be bet-ter subjects. The Persians ac-knowledged the significance of all gods and thus encouraged each group of people within their king-dom to honor their own god by

Cyrus Cylinder—contains King Cyrus's proclamation of freedom to the exiled Jews.

The Cyrus Cylinder
The Cyrus Cylinder records the capture of Babylon in 539 B.C. and refers to new poli-cies instituted by Persia's king Cyrus the Great. Part of the text of the cylinder reads: "As far as Ashur and Susa, Agade, Eshnunna, the towns of Zamban Me-Turnu, Der, as well as the region of the Gutians, I returned to these sacred cities on the other side of the Tigris, the sanctuaries of which have been ruins for a long time, the images which used to live therein and established for them permanent sanctuaries. I [also] gathered all their (former) inhabitants and returned [to them] their habitations."[3]

Modern Jewish settlement in Israel.

The Glorious Days of the Persian Empire

When Cyrus died in 530 B.C., his son **Cambyses II** took over rule of the empire and continued to expand its boundaries. By 525 B.C. Cambyses sacked Thebes and gained control of Egypt. Cambyses died while dealing with a false claimant to the throne, and his cousin Darius I took over leadership of the empire in 522 B.C.

Darius I brought the Persian Empire to its greatest strength and most glorious days, and so became known as **Darius the Great.** He pushed the boundaries westward into modern Turkey and eastward to the Indus River. Darius also reorganized the system of satrapies (provinces) that Cyrus had introduced. Judah was located in the satrapy called "Beyond the Euphrates," which included the areas of Syria and Palestine.

building temples for them (see Cyrus's proclamation in 2 Chronicles 36:23; Ezra 1:2-4).

Freedom to the Jewish Exiles

Under this new Persian policy, some of the Jewish exiles began their return journey to Jerusalem and the surrounding regions in 538 B.C. Though many in the exiled community remained behind in the secure and familiar environment of Babylon, a significant number made the perilous journey to reclaim their homeland. According to Ezra 1:8, **Sheshbazzar** led one of the earliest groups around 538 B.C. They brought items that the Babylonians had taken from the Temple. The Persians returned these in order to reestablish worship in Jerusalem. Other groups later followed. Ezra mentions in particular the group led by **Zerubbabel,** a Davidic descendant who became governor of the province (2:2).

The first returnees rebuilt the altar at Jerusalem and lay the foundation for the Temple. Soon, however, the Temple rebuilding work was halted because of opposition from neighboring peoples and raw economic realities.

The Temple Rebuilding

During the reign of Darius two Jewish prophets, **Haggai** and **Zechariah,** began to challenge the people of Judah to rebuild their Temple. In the fall of 520 B.C., Haggai began preaching and a few months later Zechariah joined him. The question of official Persian approval of the project was resolved by a search of the royal archives. Darius affirmed Cyrus's decree that not only approved the project but also called for assistance from Persian sources. Despite continued opposition, in 515 B.C., the new Temple was dedicated. Though it was not of the scale and grandeur of Solomon's Temple, it served as the center for worship of Israel's God for nearly 600 years.

Jews Escape Annihilation

At the death of Darius I in 486 B.C., **Xerxes I** became ruler. The Book of Esther calls him Ahasuerus. About 479 B.C., Xerxes chose a beautiful Jewish girl named **Esther** to be his queen. According to the Book of Esther, the entire Jewish population of the empire was nearly annihilated because of a plot by a high royal administrator named Haman. Through Esther's intervention the plot was averted and the Jews were able to defend themselves against their enemies.

Ezra's Reform

Xerxes eventually fell victim to another plot and was assassinated by the captain of the guard in 464 B.C. Following further intrigue in the royal palace, **Artaxerxes I** emerged as Persia's new ruler. About 458 B.C., Artaxerxes sent his special adviser for Jewish affairs, a scribe named **Ezra,** to Jerusalem. His mission was to teach the Law of Moses to his people. As a result of his teaching, major reforms in marriage practices and in daily living took place.

Walls Rebuilt

About 12 years after Ezra arrived in Judah, Artaxerxes sent his Jewish cupbearer, **Nehemiah,** to serve as governor of the land and accomplish the rebuilding of Jerusalem's walls. Though opposed by many neighboring communities, who feared Judah would become too strong, Nehemiah accomplished the repair and rebuilding of the walls within two months.

Nehemiah also encouraged reli-

Cardo—rebuilt Roman street with underground shops in the Old City of Jerusalem.

gious reform. According to the Book of Nehemiah, he and Ezra led the Jewish community in a dramatic covenant renewal ceremony. Nehemiah governed Judah for about 12 years and then returned to Susa. After a brief absence, he came back to govern Judah for several additional years.

Joining Ezra and Nehemiah in their reform efforts was the prophet **Malachi.** Somewhere between 450 and 430 B.C. Malachi ministered to people who were lax in their worship of God. He challenged them to take their faith seriously and honor God appropriately.

The End of the Persian Rule

At the death of Artaxerxes I in 424 B.C., Darius II (423-404 B.C.) gained control of the empire by murdering Xerxes II, the legitimate successor to the throne. The years of Persia's next emperor, Artaxerxes II (404-358 B.C.), were filled with questions about the endurance of the empire. The internal struggle for power continued to weaken the once mighty Persian Empire. In 331 B.C., Alexander the Great defeated Darius III of Persia (336-331 B.C.) and annexed the provinces of Persia, including Judah, as part of the Greek Empire.

Challenges to Restoration

Life in Judah throughout the Persian period did not turn out as bright and hopeful as Jeremiah, Ezekiel, and the exilic writer of Isaiah 40—55 envisioned it. The stability and benevolence of the Persian government did allow for some restoration of Judah. People returned, the Temple was rebuilt, and Jerusalem's walls were repaired. However, there were community tensions, economic hardships, and spiritual lapses that thwarted full recovery.

Relations with Samaritans to the north, Ammonites to the east, and Arabs to the south were mostly hostile throughout this period. Eventually the Samaritans erected a rival temple in Shechem and created their own scriptures, known as the **Samaritan Pentateuch.** This edition of the Pentateuch is essentially an altered version of the Pentateuch of the Jews, aimed to give legitimacy to the peculiar theological beliefs of the Samaritan Jews. Additionally, the Jewish community itself experienced internal factions. Besides the ordinary divisions along economic lines, tensions existed between those who had remained in the land and those who had returned from exile or from refugee situations.

Most serious of Judah's problems during the Persian period were its spiritual lapses. Unrealized dreams of the glorious renewal projected by earlier prophets apparently led people to distrust the God of their fathers. They resisted building the Temple and the walls of Jerusalem, married nonbelievers, and withheld tithes and offerings. Some scholars also think that this period witnessed the rise of party movements within Judaism and conflicts within the community on matters of worship, rituals, and other religious issues (see Isaiah 56—66, Haggai, Zechariah, Ezra, Nehemiah, and Malachi).

Despite such problems, the community of Israel discovered new depths to their faith through this time of testing. There were periods of renewal with the rebuilding of the Temple, the deliverance under Esther, the revival with Ezra and Nehemiah, and the rebuilding

A　Jews in Egypt

Excavations on the island of **Elephantine,** near the first cataract of the Nile, brought to light a Jewish military colony from the fifth century B.C. called Yeb. This community consisted of mercenary soldiers serving in the Egyptian army and stationed on the southern front of Egypt. Some think that the origin of this colony goes back to Assyrian period in the mid-seventh century B.C.

Papyri documents found during the excavations reveal the existence of a temple where the Jews worshiped not only Yahweh but also other deities. These included a female consort for Yahweh named Anatyahu. Obviously this Jewish community had not remained true to the monotheistic emphasis of the biblical faith. Among the documents, scholars also found a letter asking for help from the Jerusalem community in rebuilding a temple at Elephantine, which was destroyed by local Egyptian priests around 407 B.C.

of Jerusalem's walls. In addition, the institution of the synagogue, which became a vital element for nurturing the community for centuries, began to develop during this time. In this context, the importance of sacred Scripture as a guide to daily life gained new emphasis and became a distinguishing feature of Judaism.

Summary Statements

- The Babylonian invasion stripped Judah of all symbols of God's special blessing—its Temple, its holy city, its king, and its nationhood.
- The Babylonian exile pushed Israel into a theological crisis of major proportions.
- Persian policy allowed exiled Israelites to return and restore their nation.
- The community of Israel struggled to gain economic strength and to maintain spiritual stability during the Persian period.

Questions for Reflection

1. How was Judah's questioning during exile similar to the response of people today who face a major crisis in life?
2. Why did the community of Judah experience spiritual disillusionment during the restoration?
3. In what ways was Israel restored during the Persian period?
4. How does knowledge of the Persian period help a person understand the New Testament?

Resources for Further Study

Bright, John. *A History of Israel,* 3rd ed. Philadelphia: Westminster, 1981. Pages 391-401.
Kaiser, Walter C., Jr. *A History of Israel.* Nashville: Broadman and Holman, 1998. Pages 438-39.
Yaumauchi, Edwin M. *Persia and the Bible.* Grand Rapids: Baker, 1990.

19 History Revisited: 1 and 2 Chronicles

bjectives:

Your study of this chapter should help you to:
- Describe the content of Chronicles.
- Articulate the message of these books to their first audience.
- Understand the way biblical history can be read for theological meaning.

uestions to consider as you read:

1. What lessons can you learn about your relationship to God by looking at your nation's history?
2. How significant are symbols for your faith?
3. Why is worship such an important part of a relationship to God?

Key Words to Understand

Deuteronomistic history
Postexilic history
David
Priestly history
Priests
Levites
Prayer of Jabez
Solomon
Asa
Jehoshaphat
Hezekiah
Josiah
Manasseh

Chronicles begins the second section of the historical books of the Old Testament. We have already reviewed the first section, which contains the **Deuteronomistic history** (Joshua through Kings) in chapters 12 through 17. The second section is made up of Chronicles, Ezra, Nehemiah, and Esther. These books are often called the **postexilic history** because they were all written after the Exile and contain records of the events of that period. However, the narrative section in Chronicles begins with **David**'s rise to kingship around 1000 B.C. and ends with the time of Nehemiah around 430 B.C.

The two Books of Chronicles offer one more overview of Israel's history before the Exile. While they repeat information from previous books of the Old Testament, they do not simply rehash the same thing. There is new material and a fresh look at Israel's experience with God. More than simply recording events, these books contain new theological perspectives aimed to give the present and future generations direction for life as God's people.

Why Is Chronicles at the End of the Hebrew Bible?

The Books of Chronicles are located at the end of the Hebrew Bible. This may be because these were some of the last books to be written. They also function as a fitting summary and conclusion to the Hebrew canon. The following points illustrate this role of Chronicles: (1) Chronicles summarizes the Old Testament history from Adam to Israel's restoration by making reference to the patriarchs, the Exodus, the conquest, the monarchy, the Exile, and the restoration. (2) Chronicles draws materials from the Pentateuch, the Deuteronomistic history, the Prophets, and the Psalms. (3) Finally, many of the key ideas of the Old Testament are reaffirmed in Chronicles. Some of these are: Israel's God is the Lord; judgment of the wicked; blessing to those who seek God; and hope for all who worship God with humility.

Chronicles as Priestly History

Chronicles, along with Ezra-Nehemiah, could be called the **priestly history** because it presents Israel's history from the perspective of the **priests.** By contrast, the Deuteronomistic history analyzes Israel's past from a prophetic viewpoint.

It is this difference in perspective that accounts for the kind of material that is either included or omitted in Chronicles. A large amount of material in Chronicles focuses upon the Temple, its ritual, and its personnel. The Deuteronomistic history shares some of this material, but Chronicles adds much more. The lists of **Levites** in 1 Chronicles 24—26 and the worship service of Jehoshaphat in 2 Chronicles 20 are good examples.

The narrative section in Chronicles begins with David, the one who prepared for building the Temple. The history from Joshua to Saul is omitted since it was prior to the Temple era. Chronicles further focuses upon the nation of Judah, where the Temple was located. This is one of the major differences between Chronicles and Kings. Chronicles gives little attention to the Northern Kingdom and omits most stories about its kings and people. The stories of the prophets Elijah and Elisha are missing from Chronicles as well. Chronicles also tends to omit negative stories about David, such as his sin with Bathsheba and the rebellion of Absalom.

Authorship and Date

The author of Chronicles is unknown and is often simply called the chronicler. Some scholars have suggested that the chronicler may have been either Ezra or Nehemiah. Though this could be possible, we simply do not have enough evidence. These books do not appear to have much in common with the Books of Ezra and Nehemiah, so it is unlikely that Chronicles is the work of either Ezra or Nehemiah. Some scholars suggest that the chronicler may have been a Levite since he gives so much attention to the ministry of the Levites.[1]

The Books of Chronicles were some of the last books of the Old Testament to be written. Evidence in the text suggests they were composed sometime around 400 B.C.

Setting

The Books of Chronicles were composed during the time of unrest in the western part of the Persian Empire (around 400 B.C.). A number of provinces were in revolt against the empire, and the people of Judah were caught in the middle. The future of the Persian Empire, and the Jews as well, was uncertain. Further, the Jews still remained disillusioned with their lot in life. Restoration of their community had not come about as hoped. The economy still struggled, and foreign powers still dominated. The first audience to hear Chronicles was wrestling with questions of God's interest in His people and their future.

Contents

The two Books of Chronicles are a unified composition. They were originally written as one unit and only later were divided for convenience.

The chronicler relied upon many sources to compose his history. Most obvious is the material from 2 Samuel, 1 Kings, and 2 Kings. About half of Chronicles is drawn directly from these books. The chronicler, however, was selective in using the material. He employed only those parts that fit his purposes and rearranged them as needed.

Other materials were available to the chronicler as well. The text mentions sources that are no longer extant, such as the "Records of Nathan," the "Prophecy of Ahijah," the "Visions of Iddo," and the "Annals of the Kings of Judah and Israel." Additional material seems to have come from military lists and other state records. It appears that the author may have also used the genealogies in the Book of Genesis. The purpose of the writer was to show certain clear patterns and themes in Israel's history. This is evident in the careful selection and arrangement of the above sources.

Chronicles focuses upon the lives of David and Solomon. They are the primary examples of faithful worshipers of God. Introductory and concluding sections frame the stories of the reigns of these two kings. The books divide into the following four sections:

1. Genealogies (1 Chronicles 1:1—9:44)
2. David Narratives (1 Chronicles 10:1—29:30))
3. Solomon Narratives (2 Chronicles 1:1—9:31)
4. Kings of Judah Narratives (2 Chronicles 10:1—36:23)

■ Genealogies (1:1—9:44)

The first nine chapters of 1 Chronicles give a list of Israel's ancestors from Adam to Saul. This seems unusual to the modern reader. To the ancient Jew, however, genealogies were significant. They clarified relationships and emphasized connections to the past. Genealogies also affirmed that God's blessing rested upon His people. A list of generations meant that God had made them fruitful and increased their number (see Genesis 1:28).

Genealogies are a kind of history writing.[2] They can cover a vast amount of time quickly. Chapter 1 moves from Adam to Israel, and so connects the Israelites to the entire human race. God's salvation is not reserved for a few; it is universal. All members of humanity, as well as "all Israel," may participate in God's redemption.

Chapters 2—8 delineate the descendants of the various tribes of Israel. Two groups, the Levites and the Judahites, are highlighted by the amount of space given to them and by the arrangement of the text. Both groups are significant in the book—the Levites because of their relationship to the Temple, and the Judahites because they were the tribe of David.

Chapter 9 brings the history down to the time of the first readers. It mentions those who returned to Judah after the Exile and lists descendants into the fifth century B.C. This section closes with the genealogy of Saul, which prepares the reader for the narrative in chapter 10.

The genealogies of this section are punctuated with historical, geographical, and spiritual comments. One of the most important of the latter type is the **prayer of Jabez** in 4:10. His prayer for blessing, empowerment, and protection provides a model for the faithful. Another significant comment is that Israel suffered exile "because of their unfaithfulness" (9:1). Blessings and curses, the major emphasis of Deuteronomistic history, thus receive attention in these early chapters of Chronicles.

■ Reign of David (10:1—29:30)

The second section of Chronicles focuses upon the life of David. It deals first with the establishment of David's kingdom and then turns to how David prepared to build the Temple. David served as the chronicler's best example of a godly king.

Chapters 10—12 relate how the kingdom was transferred from Saul to David and became established. Saul's tragedy contrasted with David's prosperity. Saul failed because of his unfaithfulness and failure to keep God's word (10:13-14). As a result God

Priests and Levites

The tribe of Levi was responsible for care of the holy sanctuaries and leading worship in ancient Israel. Both Levites and priests came from this tribe. Priests were descendants of Moses' brother, Aaron. Levites were all other descendants of Levi that were not priests.

Priests focused primarily upon sacrifice and general oversight of the ritual. Levites performed a number of other functions that were part of the daily operations of the Temple. They were gatekeepers, musicians, cooks, craftsmen, accountants, teachers, and caretakers. Thus, Levites and priests worked together to assist Israel in the worship of their God.

View of the Temple Mount from the Mount of Olives. The Second Temple was located where the Dome of the Rock is today.

gave the kingdom to David. The chronicler makes it clear that David did not gain leadership by shrewd maneuvering or human scheming. It was a gift from God. A significant sign of God's blessing was the many people who came to surround David. God provided him with support from many caring and capable people from all over Israel.

The reason God prospered David, according to the chronicler, was because of his godly character. Chapters 13—16 describe the salient points that make David the ideal leader of God's people. He inquired regularly of the Lord and placed a priority on worship. His efforts to bring the ark of the covenant to Jerusalem symbolized his deep desire to place God at the center of his kingdom. David's hymn in chapter 16 stands as a model for true worship. It lifts up God and confesses total reliance upon Him.

Chapter 17 forms a climax for this section of Chronicles. David desired to build a house for God (the Temple). But God determined to build a house for David (a dynasty of kings). David's faithfulness brought divine blessing, a promise of an everlasting kingdom. For the first readers of Chronicles, this was an important word of hope. David's earthly dynasty did not last past 587 B.C., but one of his descendants, the Messiah, was destined to rule again. This promise found its fulfillment in Jesus Christ. He was the descendant of David who would reign forever.

The final chapters of this section focus upon David's preparation for building the Temple. The first step in the process was to provide resources and acquire land. Chapters 18—21 describe

H   The Jerusalem Temple

The Temple symbolized significant ideas about God and Israel's relationship to Him. The palacelike structure of the Temple declared that the Lord was king over His people. Only the specially consecrated personnel were allowed to be in its sacred areas. Everything in the Temple and about the Temple affirmed the separateness or holiness of God.

The Temple was a reminder of God's covenant relationship with Israel. It embodied the essence of the ancient covenant expression, "You will be my people, and I will be your God" (Jeremiah 30:22). Through the rituals of worship, people acknowledged God's forgiving and healing presence among them.

Finally, the Temple also stood as a constant testimony of God's covenant faithfulness in the past. The annual feasts recounted major moments in Israel's history with God: the Exodus from Egypt, the Law at Sinai, and guidance in the wilderness. As long as the Temple stood, the people could not forget their spiritual heritage.

The Western Wall, known as the Wailing Wall, is the only part of the Second Temple complex that exists today.

how David did this by subduing enemies and purchasing the threshing floor of Araunah.

Most of the material in chapters 22—29 is unique to Chronicles. It records how David organized the Levites for worship

service and charged Solomon to carry out the plans for the Temple. Worship of God was no afterthought. Extensive plans were made because worship at the Temple was a primary means of demonstrating faithfulness to

God. As Moses made certain that the holy traditions continued from himself to Joshua (see Deuteronomy 31), so also David passed his treasure into the hands of **Solomon.** Solomon was more than a political successor to David. He was his spiritual successor as well.

■ Reign of Solomon (2 Chronicles 1:1—9:31)

The chronicler presents in these chapters an ideal picture of Solomon by careful selection of material. As with David, his intention was not to gloss over imperfections or realities. Rather, he simply sought to highlight the ways in which Solomon did things right. He saw patterns in David's and Solomon's lives that served as models for believers.

Solomon was a true seeker of God (chap. 1). He, like his father David, went before God to receive direction for life. As a result he was blessed with tremendous wealth in chariots, precious metals, and international trade.

Chapters 2—4 describe Solomon's efforts in building the Temple. He was not fully adequate to construct God's house. He had to call upon the Phoenicians, the world's finest architects and builders, to accomplish this task. This emphasized the majesty of Israel's God, who deserved only the best that humans can offer.

Solomon led the worship at the dedication of the Temple (chaps. 5—7). He brought the ark of the covenant to the Temple, affirmed God's faithfulness to Israel, offered sacrifices, gave thanks, and prayed. His prayer was an urgent plea for regular communication with God. The Temple was to be a place of healing, forgiveness, and genuine encounter between God and His people. God's response to the prayer laid out the conditions to continue that relationship.

The key verse for this section, and the entire book, is the well-known verse in 7:14. It reads, "If my people, who are called by my name, will humble themselves and pray and seek my face and turn from their wicked ways, then will I hear from heaven and will forgive their sin and will heal their land." It concisely expresses the central theme of the book. A forgiving, healing relationship with God depends on a humbling, seeking, repentant posture before God. This text invites us to examine our hearts when we come before God through prayer and worship.

God responded to Solomon with blessing and favor. Chapters 8 and 9 detail the many evidences of God's favor in Solomon's life, including his building projects, his international standing, his strong nation, his legendary wisdom, and his exceptional wealth.

■ Reigns of the Other Kings of Judah (10:1—36:23)

The final section of Chronicles illustrates the main points of the book by means of a survey of the rest of Judah's kings. The fortunes of each king are told in reference to how well they followed David's model. Those who imitated David were blessed, but those who pursued other patterns were cursed.

Positive examples are given the most space. These include **Asa** (chaps. 14—16), **Jehoshaphat** (chaps. 17—20), **Hezekiah** (chaps. 29—32), and **Josiah** (chaps. 34—35). They are characterized by doing what was right in eyes of

Theological Themes of Chronicles

Like most historians, the chronicler selected material in order to highlight important theological ideas and themes. Some of these are: (1) God rewards faithfulness, the kind modeled in certain kings such as David and Solomon. (2) Faithfulness meant complete devotion to God and His laws. (3) The best expression of such devotion is demonstrated in the posture of genuine worship. In proper worship, God's people should humble themselves, seek God, pray, and turn from wickedness (2 Chronicles 7:14). (4) Though the prophets of Israel called people to this kind of relationship, their voices went unheeded. (5) The chronicler's hope was that "all Israel" (repeated 43 times), not only Judah, would listen and humble themselves before God.

God, like David. The chronicler noticed when these kings sought the Lord, prayed, or humbled themselves before God. Their attention to the Temple and worship was especially highlighted. The results for each were blessings from God. Typical of these kings is what is said of Hezekiah in 31:21, "In everything that he undertook in the service of God's temple and in obedience to the law and the commands, he sought his God and worked wholeheartedly. And so he prospered."

Negative examples of kingship are found in Jehoram (chap. 21), Ahaziah (chaps. 22—23), Ahaz (chap. 28), Amon (chap. 33), Jehoiakim (chap. 36), Jehoiachin (chap. 36), and Zedekiah (chap. 36). Their pattern was to do evil in God's eyes and walk in the ways of the kings of the Northern Kingdom. They characteristically would not humble themselves or seek God. They set up foreign idols and worshiped other gods. The outcome in each case was disastrous, for the king and for the nation.

Other kings of Judah provided mixed examples. They either started good and turned bad, or vice versa. In either case, God rewarded each king according to his faithfulness to the pattern of David and Solomon. One of the most interesting kings in this category is **Manasseh**. According to 2 Kings 21, he was one of Judah's

The Problem of Numbers in Chronicles

The numbers in the genealogies, military lists, and other parts of Chronicles present a problem that is not easy to assess. Sometimes Chronicles varies considerably from the parallels in Samuel or Kings. Its numbers are often much bigger. We cannot adequately explain this problem. We offer the following general observations:

1. Numbers in the Bible often have symbolic meaning. *Forty* conveys a generation. *Seven* stands for perfection. *Four* indicates completeness.

2. The words for "thousand" (`eleph) and "hundred" (*me´ah*) can also refer to a family or military unit.

3. Scribes made errors in copying numbers sometimes. Such is clearly the case of Jehoiachin's age at the time of his succession (8 in 2 Chronicles 36:9 and 18 in 2 Kings 24:8). The number 10 was either accidentally added or dropped at some point.

In no case does the interpretation of numbers dramatically change the message of the text. We do not suspect that the chronicler was trying to be misleading. We only acknowledge that our understanding of the numbers is limited.

worst kings, leading the nation into its darkest period of apostasy. The chronicler, however, records his humbling before God when the Assyrians took him as a prisoner, and God's answer to his prayer. Manasseh was restored to his kingship and he became a true servant of God (2 Chronicles 33:1-20). This confirms that God holds out hope even for the most treacherous sinner.

The final verses of the book (36:15-23) confirm the message of judgment and hope found throughout Chronicles. God brought the Babylonians to destroy Jerusalem because the people refused to listen to the warnings of the prophets. Yet, God also raised up the Persians to offer new hope. A proclamation from Cyrus provided for the rebuilding of the Temple. The people of Israel could once again seek God if they desired. The chronicler invited "anyone of his people among you . . . let him go up" to build the Temple and worship God (36:23).

Summary Statements

- Genealogies are a kind of history writing that emphasizes connections to the past.
- David was an ideal king because he sought God's guidance and put a high priority on worship of God.
- The blessings of Solomon were a result of following the pattern of his father.
- The Temple was so important to Israel because it was the place where people could humble themselves and seek God's forgiveness and healing.
- Kings who did not follow the model of David brought disaster upon themselves and their nation.

Questions for Reflection

1. What are the ways to connect with our past Christian traditions and heritage, since we cannot trace our ancestry to particular individuals who lived 2,000 years ago?
2. Why does the chronicler not include some stories from David and Solomon's life that are found in Samuel and Kings?
3. What are some of the important symbols of faith and God's presence in our lives?
4. What is the basis of hope for a nation that suffers from adversity?

Resources for Further Study

Selman, Martin J. *1 Chronicles: An Introduction and Commentary. Tyndale Old Testament Commentary.* Downers Grove, Ill.: InterVarsity Press, 1994.

————. *2 Chronicles: An Introduction and Commentary. Tyndale Old Testament Commentary.* Downers Grove, Ill.: InterVarsity Press, 1994.

Williamson, H. G. M. *1 and 2 Chronicles. New Century Bible Commentary.* Grand Rapids: Eerdmans, 1982.

20 The Building of Community Life: Ezra, Nehemiah, and Esther

Objectives:

Your study of this chapter should help you to:

- Describe the historical setting of the Books of Ezra, Nehemiah, and Esther.
- Discuss the content of the Books of Ezra, Nehemiah, and Esther.
- Evaluate the significance of the messages of Ezra, Nehemiah, and Esther to their first audiences.
- Assess the biblical prescription for reforming and maintaining a vital community of faith.

Key Words to Understand

Ezra
Nehemiah
Syncretism
Esther
Xerxes I
Mordecai
Haman
Additions to Esther
Purim

Questions to consider as you read:

1. What are some ways past events have influenced the world we live in today?
2. What risks are involved in following God completely?
3. How do God's people fit into the scheme of nations and world politics?

The Books of Ezra, Nehemiah, and Esther speak of events during the fourth and fifth centuries B.C., when Persia dominated the affairs of Israel. This was a time in which the survivors of Israel's exile were trying to reestablish themselves as a community of faith in and around Jerusalem.

These three books provide selected glimpses of the Jewish community's struggle to survive under adverse circumstances. In the process, they extend hope to all of God's people in any era where earthly powers threaten existence. Various obstacles confronted the Jews of the Persian period. Yet, as these three books indicate, God had a plan, not only to preserve a remnant of His people but also to shape them into a vital community of faith.

Ezra—Nehemiah

The main characters in these books are a scribe named **Ezra** and a layperson named **Nehemiah**. Ezra came from a family of high priests and apparently held a position in the Persian court as an adviser on Jewish affairs. Jewish tradition holds Ezra almost on par with Moses. Nehemiah was cupbearer to the king in the Persian court in Susa.

Authorship and Date

Ezra and Nehemiah are treated as a unified work in the Hebrew tradition. The division of the two books obscures the interrelation of ideas in these books. They are also similar in structure, themes, and literary techniques. Here we will deal with these books as one unified work.

We do not know for sure who composed Ezra—Nehemiah. Tradition places Ezra as the author. It is also likely that Nehemiah or an unknown person may have compiled these books. The last dated event in these books is the beginning of Nehemiah's second term as governor of Judah (Nehemiah 13:6-7). This would have been around 430 B.C. It is likely that the materials were compiled into Ezra—Nehemiah around 420 to 400 B.C.

Setting

The biblical text presents the ministry of Ezra and Nehemiah during the reign of the Persian king Artaxerxes I (464-424 B.C.). Some scholars think that Ezra served under Artaxerxes II (404—359 B.C.). It is likely that Ezra came to Jerusalem in 458 B.C. and Nehemiah in 444 B.C. We do not know much more about Ezra's dates except that he was present at the wall dedication in 444 B.C.[1] Nehemiah was governor for 12 years, and then he went back to Susa in 432 B.C. His next term as governor probably began a few years later and did not last as long as the first.

The ministry of Ezra and Nehemiah took place at a crucial period in the postexilic history. The Jewish national and religious life was in crisis. Though the Temple was rebuilt and worship restored, the Jewish community fell victim to spiritual apathy and community tensions. The restored community needed religious instruction in the Law of Moses. Intermarriage with non-Jewish people and lack of covenant commitment seriously affected the spiritual condition of the nation. These spiritual lapses also affected the social life of the Jewish community.

Content

Ezra-Nehemiah is composed of various materials. Diary-like writ-

T Decrees of Pagan Kings

The message of Ezra 1—6 is that God's people can trust the sovereignty of God. Throughout these chapters God's purposes are accomplished through the decrees of kings. "The LORD moved the heart of Cyrus" (1:1) and directed Darius (6:1-12) to make decrees that benefited God's people. God used foreign rulers to rebuild the community of faith.

These chapters also affirm the importance of one's spiritual heritage. The returnees brought with them artifacts from Solomon's Temple to maintain their connections to the old ways. After the exiles arrived in the land, they celebrated the religious festivals of their ancestors. The focus upon genealogies in these chapters also underscores this message. No one stands alone in the stream of history. God's promises and patterns of the past were still relevant to the community under reconstruction. The past is part of the present.

ings by Ezra and Nehemiah are among the sources of these books. The Ezra memoirs may be found in Ezra 7—10 and possibly Nehemiah 8—9. The Nehemiah memoirs consist of Nehemiah 1—7 and 11—13.

The Ezra—Nehemiah material may be divided into the following four major sections:

1. Restoring the Temple (Ezra 1—6)
2. Restoring Purity (Ezra 7:1—10:44)
3. Restoring the Walls (Nehemiah 1:1—7:73)
4. Restoring Law (Nehemiah 8:1—13:31)

Each of these sections contains a pattern of four regularly occurring elements. There is a focus upon (1) kingly decrees, (2) a return of the people, (3) opposition to rebuilding, and then (4) success over the opposition. The sections also parallel one another. Nehemiah 1—7 recalls Ezra 1—6 by its focus upon a physical building project. Both sections also include celebrations of feasts and dedication ceremonies. Nehemiah 8—13 echoes Ezra 7—10 by emphasizing the role of law in rebuilding God's community.

■ Restoring the Temple (Ezra 1:1—6:22)

The first section of Ezra—Nehemiah tells of the trials and triumphs of those who first returned to build the Temple in Jerusalem. An edict from the Persian king Cyrus allowed the return.

Sheshbazzar, a member of the royal family, led the first group of returnees in 538 B.C. Like the Exodus from Egypt hundreds of years earlier, Israel once again made their way to the Promised Land, but this time from the homeland of their ancestor Abraham. When Zerubbabel came with another group, he took over leadership of the community along with Jeshua the high priest.

Model of the city of Jerusalem during the first century A.D.

Model of the
Jerusalem Temple

His people. The rebuilding ended with celebration of the Temple dedication and the Passover.

■ Restoring Purity
(Ezra 7:1—10:44)

There is a gap of 50 years between Ezra 6 and 7. The focus shifts to the return of Ezra the scribe in 458 B.C. and the reforms he undertook upon his arrival.

The Persian king Artaxerxes I commissioned Ezra to return, along with others who wished to go, and teach the law of their God. Such a commission fits with what historians know of Persian policies and practices. The effect of Ezra's teaching of the Law was a new awareness of the problem of mixed marriages. Ezra was heartbroken by this sin and repented. Others followed his lead, and the community confessed its sin. Then specific steps were taken to deal fairly with each improper marriage.

■ Restoring the Walls
(Nehemiah 1:1—7:73)

The story of the rebuilding of the walls of Jerusalem is the subject of Nehemiah 1—7. About 10 years after the events in Ezra 10, Nehemiah received news of the conditions of Jerusalem's walls and set out to rebuild them.

Through divine providence, the

They built an altar and began laying the foundation of the Temple. Opposition from neighboring peoples brought an abrupt halt to the project, and work on the Temple ceased.

About 18 years after the first returnees arrived in the land, the prophets Haggai and Zechariah began to inspire the Jews to take up the task of rebuilding the Temple once again. This evoked questions from Tattenai, the governor of the Trans-Euphrates satrapy. Darius the Great reissued the decree allowing the Jews to rebuild the Temple. The Jews completed the Temple around 515 B.C. This was an important event in the history of God's people. It affirmed once again God's presence with

T   Mixed Marriages

Ezra's call to dissolve mixed marriages does not reflect racism or separatism. The threat posed by mixed marriages during Ezra's time was **syncretism**—the incorporation of pagan beliefs and customs into Israel's monotheistic faith. Mixed marriages meant mixing with the pagan religions. Ezra's attempt was to remedy the sin committed by Israel. We are challenged here to be cautious in choosing marriage partners. Our decision to enter into a marriage covenant with a nonbelieving person may ultimately lead to the loss of a vital relationship with God. Our conduct in marriage relationship reflects the nature of our covenant with God. God calls us to live distinctive lives of holiness because He is a holy God.

The Broken Walls of Jerusalem

In the ancient world, city walls were a symbol of strength and stability. Jerusalem was scarcely populated because of its broken-down walls. A city without secure walls was vulnerable to attack. But the ruined walls meant more than lack of security to Israel. Nehemiah called the broken-down walls of Jerusalem a disgrace (Nehemiah 1:3 and 2:17). The ruined wall and the unprotected city portrayed Israel's God as powerless among the nations. They also signified that restoration had not fully taken place. The rebuilding, on the other hand, symbolized God's continued blessings upon Israel and His protection of His chosen city.

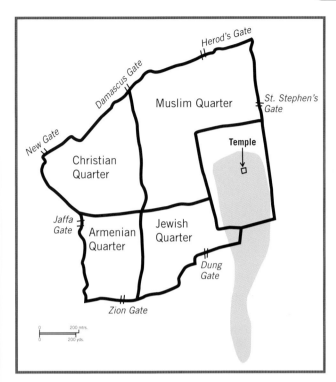

Map of Jerusalem in the 4th century B.C. (shaded areas). The outline shows the modern boundary of the Old City of Jerusalem.

Nehemiah was concerned with the rebuilding of Jerusalem's walls. The walls around Jerusalem today were built by Suliman the Magnificent in the 16th century A.D.

Persian king granted permission to Nehemiah to accomplish his goal. When he arrived in Jerusalem, he laid out a plan for the project but immediately encountered opposition. Neighboring peoples evidently feared that the Jews might gain too much strength and influence in the region.

Showing exceptional tenacity and leadership skills, Nehemiah eventually overcame the opposition and completed the restoration of the walls in 444 B.C. As with the Temple, this success came about not because of Nehemiah's skills, but because of God (6:16). The message of Nehemiah 1—7 echoes Ezra 1—7. We can trust in God's control over His world.

■ Restoring the Law (Nehemiah 8:1—13:31)

The final section of Nehemiah focuses on the reading of the Law of Moses (Torah) and the renewal of the covenant with God. This is what the rebuilding of the community was all about. The ultimate aim was recommitment to the God who continued to work in the history of His people.

Ezra read the Law to the community, evoking responses of mourning, celebration, confession, and finally commitment. This section emphasizes the importance of the Mosaic Law for rebuilding the community. It is the foundation for community order and relationships. Ezra's primary mission had been to teach the Torah to the people (Ezra 7:13-26). The results of his teaching were a revival of social (9—10) and spiritual relationships (Nehemiah 8—10). When the community took the Law seriously, changes took place in their lives, and they es-

tablished social and spiritual priorities.

Nehemiah 9 rehearses the story of Israel's faith emphasizing the uniqueness, power, and compassion of God. This prayer reflects on God's graciousness toward His people from the time of creation to the Exile. The lesson of this history is that apart from God's grace, there is no hope for the community. The future of the restored community rests upon the character of God, not only upon faithfulness to His instructions. Such a God, then, is the hope of the community.

In a dramatic moment, the community recommitted themselves to follow the Law. They determined to avoid mixed marriages, to take care of the Temple, and to repopulate the city of Jerusalem. Once the commitments have been made, the community celebrated the dedication of the wall.

The final chapter of Nehemiah summarizes the main themes of the previous sections of Ezra—Nehemiah. This gives the effect of closure to these books. The various themes in this chapter include the significance of rebuilding the Temple, the restored wall, and mixed marriages.

The main goal of Israel's restoration was not an ideal societal structure, but a committed, trusting relationship with the living God. The material of Ezra—Nehemiah points us in that direction.

Israel understood the character of God as "a forgiving God, gracious and compassionate, slow to anger and abounding in love" as the basis for covenant renewal (Nehemiah 9:17). References to God's compassion and goodness are abundant in the Old Testament. The possibilities of restored covenant hinged on God's faithfulness and compassion toward His people. Because God is who He is, we have hope in becoming who we should be—a forgiven and redemptive community in the world in which we live today.

Esther

The Book of Esther is a well-told story of the dramatic deliverance of the Jews that took place during the Persian period. This drama unfolds with considerable intensity, and affirms throughout that God is in control of this world and that He cares for His people.

By contrast with Ezra and Nehemiah, the events in this book takes place solely in Susa, one of the three main administrative centers of the Persian Empire. Originally the ancient capital of the Elamites, Susa became the winter capital when Darius I built a large palace complex there. **Esther** and Nehemiah lived in Susa, along with numerous other Jews who had high positions in the royal court.

Authorship and Date

The events of the book took place during the reign of **Xerxes I** (in Hebrew, Ahaseurus) who ruled over the Persian Empire from 486 to 464 B.C. One may assume that the author of this book wrote soon after the events and that this person would be one of its main characters, either Esther or **Mordecai.**

This assumption may be right,

The Persian Empire.

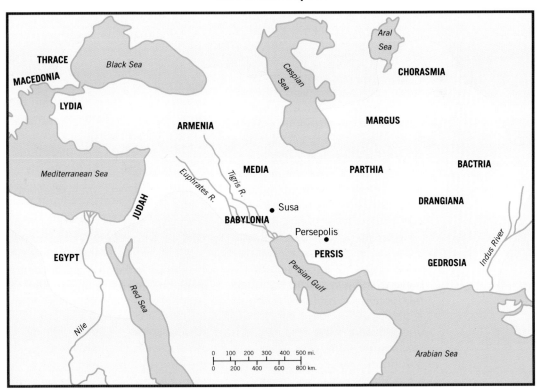

but there is little evidence to confirm or deny it. Consequently scholars have suggested various other possibilities for the author and time of writing. Most of the suggested dates fall within a time frame beginning just after the events in the book to the end of the Persian period in 330 B.C.[2]

Setting

Esther's story belongs to the early part of the fifth century B.C. The story takes place in Susa. During the time of the story of Esther, we assume that Jews were settled in various parts of the Persian Empire. Babylon, which became a part of the Persian Empire, was most likely a center of the Jewish life. The story of Nehemiah indicates that Jews might have gained high positions in the Persian government. We do not know anything about the religious condition of the Jews of this period. Ironically, the book does not mention God or any of the traditions of Israel.

Content

Esther contains many of the elements that traditionally make for a good story. There is characterization, life-and-death suspense, comic relief, skillful use of irony, and a happy ending.

In addition to good story technique, the author of Esther employed other devices to make the book more memorable. One dominant feature is the recurrence of banquets. There are 10 banquets mentioned throughout the book, which tends to heighten the sense of celebration. They are also occasions for significant turns in the plot of the story. Further, there are a number of couplets and

double references in the story. Examples of couplets are: Esther gives two banquets for the king; the king issues two decrees; Mordecai sends two letters about commemoration of these events. Double references are made of such things as Esther concealing her Jewish heritage, the people fasting for Esther, and the listing of the sons of **Haman**. This pairing feature provides a sense of balance as well as emphasis to certain aspects of the story.

The story of Esther may be outlined as follows:

1. The Setting (1:1—2:23)
2. The Conflict (3:1—5:14)
3. The Climax (6:1—7:10)
4. Final Resolution (8:1—10:3)

■ The Setting (1:1—2:23)

The first two chapters of the book establish the background for the events in the story. The Persian king Xerxes I gave a royal banquet and displayed his vast wealth and power. His queen, Vashti, refused to attend his banquet, and so the king banished her from her position. This led to a search for a new queen and the opportunity for Esther to enter the king's court.

These chapters introduce three key characters of the story. The Persian king Xerxes I is portrayed as a pompous and impetuous person. Esther the queen came from a poor Jewish background. Though she rose to high position, she remained as a woman of principle with a teachable spirit and loyalty to her heritage. Mordecai raised his orphaned cousin Esther and continued to give her guidance. He uncovered a plot to assassinate the king and thus rescued him from death.

■ The Conflict (3:1—5:14)

Dramatic tension in the story develops with the introduction of Haman, the arrogant villain. He held a powerful position in Persian politics, second only to the king. His hatred for Mordecai the Jew evolved into a sinister plot to exterminate not only Mordecai but his people as well. Xerxes was deceptively drawn into the evil plan, a date for the extermination was selected, and a decree sent throughout the kingdom.

In response, Mordecai challenged Esther to take advantage of her position in order to rescue the Jews. Esther rose to the occasion and designed a counterplan. She called her people to fast and took the risk of presenting her request the king.

At this point in the story the battle lines are drawn. Evil and good come face-to-face. Though God's name is not mentioned, there is no question that He is the key player. His people, the Jews, are endangered by the powers of this world. Esther's call for a fast (4:16) is an obvious acknowledgement that this is God's battle. Mordecai affirmed the same when he said, "For if you remain silent at this time, relief and deliverance for the Jews will arise from another place" (v. 14). In the context of the biblical story, from the Garden of Eden to the restoration, God is the only source of deliverance for those who trust Him.

Though God is sovereign and will achieve His purposes, these chapters emphasize the importance of human responsibility. Esther's role was vital. She could participate in God's deliverance or miss an opportunity. Her decision did matter.

Haman the Agagite

The identity of Haman as an Agagite connects the story of Esther to the long-standing feud between the Israelites and the Amalekites. The Amalekites were the first people to battle with the Israelites during Israel's journey to the Promised Land (see Exodus 17:8-16). See further conflicts between these two people in 1 Samuel 15 during the days of Saul. Haman may have been a descendant of Agag, who was the king of the Amalekites during the reign of Saul. Mordecai was a descendant of Kish, as was Saul. Thus the conflict between Haman and the Jews had its origins in biblical history. The victory of the Jews over Haman and his family indicates the ultimate triumph of Israel over their ancient enemies.

God in the Book of Esther

The lack of reference to God in Esther prompted an unknown author in the second century B.C. to add six major **additions to Esther** with explicit reference to God. The Septuagint translators added this version of the story to their work. These additions are part of the apocryphal books.

The secular character of Esther reminds us of how important it is to read all Scripture within the larger context of the canon. The book makes sense only within this setting. Though God is never mentioned by name, and such terms as *covenant*, *election*, and *promise* cannot be found, these ideas are assumed in the narrative. The speeches and actions of the book's key characters would not have significance without the setting of the biblical worldview.

Purim

The Book of Esther explains the origins of the Feast of Purim and its regular observance. This holy day became known as **Purim** because lots (*purim*) were cast to determine what day the Jews would be destroyed. Purim is celebrated on the 14th and 15th of Adar (February or March). The Feast of Purim celebrates God's sovereign hand in the history of His people. It affirms His special selection of Israel as His people, and His constant protection of Israel throughout the generations. The Book of Esther is read during the feast.

Nationalism in the Book of Esther

Some may ask the question: How can the nationalism of this book be reconciled with Paul's assertion that Abraham's true descendants are not blood-related but faith-related (Romans 9:6-30)?

Paul's definition of true Israel (the spiritual descendants of Abraham) does not altogether eliminate the significance of the ethnic nation Israel. The Bible as a whole attests to the possibility that the Jews would continue to play a vital role in human history. Having said this, we must also affirm that political or ethnic entities are not God's final concern. Those who possess a faith like Abraham's are the primary focus of God's plans. They are the true Israelites (or Jews).

■ The Climax (6:1—7:10)

The tables turned quickly in the narrative with an ironic, comical twist. Haman, whose hatred drove him to build a gallows on which to hang Mordecai, ended up showing honor to Mordecai. Haman's evil plot to exterminate the Jews was revealed at Esther's banquet. Haman suffered the fate he intended for Mordecai. He was entrapped by his own plans. The story confirms the proverbial saying that "the wicked are brought down by their own wickedness" (Proverbs 11:5).

■ Final Resolution (8:1—10:3)

Though the villain was removed, the consequences of his actions continued. The plan to exterminate the Jews remained in effect since Persian law was inviolable. Esther and Mordecai received permission from the king to issue another decree allowing the Jews to defend themselves. The result was the elimination of thousands of enemies of the Jews throughout the kingdom.

Jews celebrate Purim to commemorate their deliverance from the plot of Haman.

The final verses of the book encourage those who experienced God's deliverance, as well as future generations, to commemorate this event regularly. The things God has done must not be forgotten.

The Book of Esther provides a fitting conclusion to the historical narrative of the Christian Bible (Genesis through Esther). It emphasizes once more that God will not abandon His people. The book affirms God's promise to Abraham, "I will bless those who bless you, and whoever curses you I will curse; and all peoples on earth will be blessed through you" (Genesis 12:3). The faithfulness of God to His people is one of the primary themes of biblical history.

Summary Statements

- The Books of Ezra and Nehemiah should be read together as one unit.
- The first readers of Ezra—Nehemiah were the Jews who struggled to survive the hardships of the restoration period.
- Ezra—Nehemiah communicates five important messages to its original audience: (1) trust God's sovereignty; (2) connect to your spiritual heritage; (3) let God's Law shape your life; (4) be holy; and (5) rely on God's grace.
- The Book of Esther is a well-told story that affirms God's sovereignty in this world and His faithful protection of His people.

Questions for Reflection

1. Compare and contrast the issues that confronted the Jews of the fifth century B.C. with the issues that God's people face today.
2. What are some principles in these books that can guide societies today into renewal?
3. In what practical ways does Scripture give guidance for organizing and maintaining societies?
4. Why is obedience to God's word alone not enough to establish a just and functioning society?
5. Why can Christians feel a sense of peace even when world powers are hostile toward them?

Resources for Further Study

Baldwin, Joyce G. *Esther: An Introduction and Commentary. Tyndale Old Testament Commentary.* Downers Grove, Ill.: InterVarsity Press, 1984.

Clines, David J. A. *Ezra, Nehemiah, Esther. New Century Bible Commentary.* Grand Rapids: Eerdmans, 1984.

Kidner, Derek. *Ezra and Nehemiah: An Introduction and Commentary. Tyndale Old Testament Commentary.* Downers Grove, Ill.: InterVarsity Press, 1979.

UNIT IV

DISCOVERING THE POETIC AND WISDOM BOOKS

This unit introduces the reader to:
- The characteristic features of Hebrew poetry
- Israel's wise men and their contribution
- The various issues in the Book of Job
- Psalms as Israel's hymnbook
- The teachings of Proverbs, Ecclesiastes, and Song of Songs

■ Israel's Poetry and Wisdom

■ Suffering of the Righteous: Job

■ Israel's Songs of Praise: Psalms

■ Instructions on Life: Proverbs, Ecclesiastes, and Song of Songs

21 | Israel's Poetry and Wisdom

O bjectives:

Your study of this chapter should help you to:
- Identify the main characteristics of Hebrew poetry.
- Describe the interests of wisdom literature.
- Explain the theological basis of wisdom thinking.
- Trace the sources of wisdom literature.
- Explain how Israelite wisdom literature relates to the wisdom literature produced in other areas of the ancient Near East.

K ey Words to Understand

Parallelism
Synonymous parallelism
Antithetical parallelism
Formal parallelism
Alliteration
Assonance
Acrostic
Meter
Paranomasia

Q uestions to consider as you read:

1. Why is it important to pay attention to the language of poetry?
2. Who is considered wise in our culture?
3. What is wisdom in our cultural thinking?

Hebrew Poetry

There are only a few passages written in poetry in the Books of the Law and in the Deuteronomistic history of Joshua, Judges, Samuel, and Kings. Yet most of the works of the Prophets, the books of wisdom, and all of the Psalms are composed of poetry. To understand these books, a basic knowledge of how the Israelites composed their songs and sayings is needed.

Our understanding of the elements of Hebrew poetry has come about rather recently. Bishop Robert Lowth (1753) was the first to make a significant contribution to our understanding of Hebrew poetry.[1] Translations prior to that date, such as the King James Version, treated the text, even the Psalms, as prose. Modern translations, however, set the lines in poetic verse.

The basic building block of Hebrew poetry is parallelism of thought. **Parallelism** refers to the relationship between two or more lines of verse. The three basic forms of parallelism are: synonymous, antithetical, and formal. Several other types of parallelism occur, but these three forms dominate and are easily recognizable in English translations.

Synonymous Parallelism

In **synonymous parallelism,** the first line makes a statement and the second line repeats the thought. The parallelism exists in the concepts, not necessarily in the words. Because of this shift of words, sometimes this form is called complimentary parallelism. Compare the following examples:

Show me your ways, O LORD,
teach me your paths (Psalm 25:4).

Come near, you nations, and listen;
pay attention, you peoples!
Let the earth hear, and all that is in it,

the world, and all that comes out of it (Isaiah 34:1).

Yet how often is the lamp of the wicked snuffed out?
How often does calamity come upon them? (Job 21:17).

Antithetical Parallelism

In **antithetical parallelism** the first line makes a statement and the second stands in contrast to it. Many of the Proverbs use this form and often, but not always, translators will start the second line with the adversative conjunction *but.* Compare the following examples:

The sluggard craves and gets nothing,
but the desires of the diligent are fully satisfied (Proverbs 13:4).

For the LORD watches over the way of the righteous,
but the way of the wicked will perish (Psalm 1:6).

Better to live on a corner of the roof
than to share a house with a quarrelsome wife (Proverbs 21:9).

Formal Parallelism

In **formal parallelism,** sometimes called synthetic parallelism, the first line makes a statement and the second carries the thought on or expands it without repetition or contrast. Compare the following examples:

Do not be quickly provoked in your spirit,
for anger resides in the lap of fools (Ecclesiastes 7:9).

A besieging army is coming from a distant land,
raising a war cry against the

cities of Judah (Jeremiah 4:16).

Look on my suffering and deliver me,
  for I have not forgotten your law (Psalm 119:153).

In addition to parallelism, there are a number of literary devices in Hebrew poetry that cannot be reproduced in a translation. The use of these devices not only enriched the poetry but often enabled the speaker to deliver a message in a more memorable and thought-provoking manner. **Alliteration,** the repetition of the same consonantal sounds, and **assonance,** the repetition of the same vowel sounds, are two such devices. Some poems were written as an **acrostic.** The first word of a verse or stanza began with the first letter of the Hebrew alphabet, the first word of the second verse with the second letter, and so on, through the 22 letters of the alphabet. Psalm 119 is made up of 22 sections of eight verses each. Each verse of a section begins with the same letter. The first section of eight verses begins with the first letter *(aleph),* and the pattern continues to the last section where each verse begins with the last letter *(tav).* The first four chapters of the Book of Lamentations are each an acrostic poem. Notes in study Bibles will often identify these poems for the reader.

Hebrew poetry has a type of **meter,** although there is still discussion on this issue. In one method each word or group of words is given an accent or a beat. The number of accents in a line is compared with that of other lines. Some scholars suggest that the individual syllables of a

line should be counted and then a comparison made. Whichever method is followed, the meter of Hebrew poetry is not like that of modern, western poetry.

Another important Hebrew poetic device is **paranomasia,** or a play on words. Hebrew poets often used similar-sounding words to create an impact on the audience through a memorable message. In Jeremiah 1:11-12 the Hebrew words for almond tree *(shaqed)* and watching *(shoqed)* sound much alike. The poem in Micah 1:10-16 is made up of a number of plays on words on the names of the towns. Sometimes translations will identify when a pun occurs in the text. Modern translations and study Bibles often include notes that indicate the use of parallelism and other literary techniques to help the reader understand more fully the message of the poet.

What Is Wisdom?

The Books of Job, Proverbs, and Ecclesiastes are the product of Israel's wisdom teachers. Who were the wise and from where did they receive their wisdom? Moses brought down from Mount Sinai the Ten Commandments, written by God himself. The prophets stood in the presence of God to receive their messages. However, in wisdom literature there is little appeal to divine revelation as its source. Rather, wisdom looks to the created order. The arguments of the wise (see Job and Ecclesiastes) come from observing how God has structured the world. One studies the world to gain understanding and insight into how to live well.

The Book of Proverbs opens with a statement of purpose of the wise:

For attaining wisdom and discipline;

for understanding words of in-
  sight;
for acquiring a disciplined and
  prudent life,
  doing what is right and just and
  fair;
for giving prudence to the simple,
  knowledge and discretion to the
  young—
let the wise listen and add to their
  learning,
  and let the discerning get guid-
  ance—
for understanding proverbs and
  parables,
  the sayings and riddles of the
  wise (1:2-6).

Wisdom includes discipline, knowledge, discretion, learning, discernment, and understanding. The simple and young may learn it. The wise may increase and add to their understanding. Its pur-

Solomon asked for wisdom, and God granted his request.

pose is to provide the discipline and prudence to live a life that is right, just, and fair. Also, there is a mystery about life that one may explore in the sayings and riddles of the wise. This is a wide-ranging statement of purpose.

Categories of Wisdom

While the word *wisdom* (*hok-mah*) appears often in the Scripture, its meanings can generally be grouped into four broad categories.

Skill of an Artisan

One who is skilled as an artisan or craftsman is said to possess wisdom in making things. Huram (or Hiram) constructed the bronze furnishings of the Temple for Solomon because "he was full of wisdom, understanding, and skill, for making any work in bronze" (1 Kings 7:14, RSV). This use of the word *wisdom* would apply even today to carpenters, computer technicians, mechanics, artists, and so forth.

Encyclopedic Knowledge

The Old Testament mentions those who possessed encyclopedic knowledge among the wise in ancient Israel. Solomon became the patron of wisdom, seeking out knowledge and creating proverbs. He had a vast knowledge of animal and plant life and was the author of a large number of proverbs and songs (1 Kings 4:32-33). Today we have people who have given themselves to long years of study to master the information of their specialized field of study.

Insight Concerning People and Relationships

A third use of wisdom concerns those who understand people in their social interactions within the community. They are adept in social skills. The Book of Proverbs contains many insights into what to do or not to do.

A fool gives full vent to his anger,
but a wise man keeps himself
under control (29:11).

Seldom set foot in your neighbor's
house—
too much of you, and he will
hate you (25:17).

The wise in ancient Israel included those who spoke well and were able to negotiate agreements (see the example of the woman of Tekoa in 2 Samuel 14:1-20, and the woman of Abel Beth Maacah in 2 Samuel 20:16-22). Wise counselors advised rulers on matters of state (compare the advice of Ahithophel and Hushai to Absalom in 2 Samuel 17:1-14). In our modern societies, this type of information or wisdom is gathered, structured, and taught in a number of areas of study including psychology, sociology, management, marketing, and so forth.

Reverence for God

Biblical wisdom, for the most part, focuses on understanding of one's obligations to God and service to God with awe and respect. The religious principle of wisdom is found in Proverbs: "The fear of the LORD is the beginning of wisdom" (1:7). As wisdom developed in Israel, it came to be identified with God's revelation of the Torah or Law. To know the Law was to know God's revealed wisdom. This wisdom included not only knowing what was written in the Law but also applying it to everyday life (Psalm 119). A person with such wisdom would find the favor of God and enjoy an abundant life (Psalm 1).

The Sharing of Wisdom

In Israel, the family was the first social order to preserve the sayings of the wise. Parents created sayings and used them to teach their children about the world and their place in it. They taught their children how to behave in society and imparted to them the collected knowledge and wisdom of the family and community. Wisdom was shared with others as members of various families, villages, clans, or tribes mingled, carrying on trade

Wisdom was taught at the city gate in ancient Israel.

Instruction is an integral part of Jewish religious life.

or attending other social or religious occasions.

With the rise of monarchy in Israel, wisdom became a profession similar to that of the priest and the prophet (Jeremiah 18:18). Royal counselors gave political wisdom to kings (compare Rehoboam's older and younger counselors, 1 Kings 12:6-11). Also, there were the scribes who kept court records. This group of skilled government and religious workers trained their apprentices in the art of writing and copying records as a profession. They also taught the young of the nobility how to conduct themselves in the king's court and how to advise him in affairs of state. The Book of Proverbs may have its origin in this class of servants, who compiled proverbs to teach the young of the rich and powerful in the society (25:1).

Wisdom as an International Art Form

Wisdom as an art form did not arise with the people of Israel. Other cultures and peoples of the

Egyptian and Israelite Wisdom Sayings

Instructions of Amen-em-Opet
Give thy ears, hear what is said,
Give thy heart to understand them.
To put them in thy heart is worth while,
See [you] these thirty chapters: They entertain;
   they instruct.
Do not associate to thyself the heated man.
Do not carry off the landmark at the boundaries of
   the arable land.

Sayings of the Wise
Pay attention and listen to the sayings of the wise;
apply your heart to what I teach
for it is pleasing when you keep them in your heart.
Have I not written thirty sayings for you,
   sayings of counsel and knowledge.
Do not make friends with a hot-tempered man.
Do not move an ancient boundary stone

(These parallel passages show some of the similarities between the *Instructions of Amen-em-opet* and the *Sayings of the Wise* in Proverbs).[2]

Theology of Wisdom

In the above discussion of wisdom, it appears that God has little to do with its origin or even with much of its content. Biblical wisdom, though it appears to be secular, has a theological foundation. Israel connected wisdom with God's creation of the universe. Jeremiah 10:12 and 51:15 state: "God made the earth by his power; he founded the world by his wisdom and stretched out the heavens by his understanding."

This theme is further developed in Proverbs 8 where wisdom is personified. She was God's first creation and was the craftsman by which all of the created order came into being (vv. 22-31). Whatever was created in the heavens, in the seas, and on the earth came through her. Her present task is to invite humanity to come learn of her in order to know how to live well (vv. 32-36). The theological points can be stated simply. When God created all things, His first creation was wisdom. God did not create the world by some outside standard called Wisdom. To hold such a position would mean that there is some principle higher than God to which He must conform. Rather, He determines what wisdom is, just like He determines what is good, beauty, and truth.

By wisdom God created all things. At the time of creation, He placed the principles of wisdom—a divinely established moral order—within the universe so that it functions or works according to those principles. The "fear of the LORD" includes one's recognition of this truth. What are those principles that tend to make life longer, safer, healthier, more successful, and prosperous? One discovers them by studying the created order and seeing what works. The wise who structure their lives according to these principles enjoy a long and good life. Fools never learn the principles. Even when they are taught wisdom, they reject it to live a pleasure-seeking, self-willed life. The end of such a life is poverty, illness, disgrace, and death. Thus ultimately wisdom comes from God. To study His created order is to learn about God himself and His will for humanity and the created order.

ancient Near East also had their own proverbs, sayings, riddles, stories, and poems from their study of the universe. As these peoples were in constant contact through trade, diplomatic missions, and even wars, they shared with each other their insights. Since Israel was situated on the main trade routes between Egypt and Mesopotamia, the two main ancient cultural centers, she also shared in this cultural interchange. One example of this migration of knowledge may be found in the *Sayings of the Wise* in Proverbs 22:17—24:34 to the Egyptian work titled *Instructions of Amen-em-Opet*. The two literary works have so many parallel

sayings that it appears that some type of borrowing took place between them. Works similar in theme to Job and Ecclesiastes, but shorter in content, are found in the Mesopotamian cultures.[3] The wise of many nations observed and recorded their insights and then were willing to share with others their wisdom.

Scope of Wisdom Literature

There are several types of wisdom literature in the Old Testament. The Book of Proverbs communicates wisdom through short, easy-to-remember statements that deal with the practical issues of life. We may label this book as an example of practical or proverbial wisdom. There is also a speculative side to wisdom. The Book of Job explores whether or not one may live a blameless life before God, and if so, why does one who is innocent suffer evil? Ecclesiastes examines the question of the purpose of life and finds that it is vanity, that is, empty of meaning. These books are examples of speculative or philosophical wisdom in the Old Testament.

Wisdom, however, is not confined to a select group of books. It is found throughout the Bible. For example, the story of Joseph (Genesis 37, 39—45) reflects the wisdom emphasis on good prevailing evil. A number of psalms are classified as wisdom psalms because of the contrast between the godly and the wicked (Psalms 36, 37, 49, 73, 78, 112, 127, 128, 133). The Wisdom of Solomon and the Wisdom of Jesus Ben Sirach are two wisdom books included in the Apocrypha. This tradition continues into the New Testament. The teachings of Jesus are often cast in the form of wisdom sayings (see the Beatitudes in Matthew 5:3-12). Finally, the Book of James is also part of the wisdom tradition. It even encourages one to seek wisdom: "If any of you lacks wisdom, he should ask God, who gives generously to all without finding fault, and it will be given to him" (1:5).

Interpreting the Wisdom Books—Some Guidelines

- Wisdom books are different from the Law and the Prophets. The goal of these books is to impart wisdom with which one may live a produc-

tive and meaningful life in society.
- The operating principle of wisdom is the "fear of the LORD," and the source of wisdom is God's created order.
- Job and Ecclesiastes focus on difficult existential issues without providing answers to the questions raised in these books. Proverbs deals with practical issues of life.
- When dealing with the Book of Job, follow the structure of the book and the pattern of the organization of its materials. The book is for the most part a dialogue. Conclusions we make about a particular speech should take into account other theological issues that are central to the book.
- When dealing with a particular speech in the Book of Job, attempt to understand what the speaker really intended to say. In a number of cases, the apparent meaning may not be what the speaker intended to convey. We may need to read into the text to discover the meaning and implications of a particular speech.
- Consult commentaries and study Bibles to get a somewhat accurate reading of the Book of Job. This book is well known for its textual difficulties.
- Ecclesiastes contains a pessimistic attitude, doubt, and despair because of the human inability to alter God's created order. The underlying message is that only God can bring about any change in our human situation.
- Proverbs are instructions and not promises from God. Look for the moral and ethi-

cal principles in the proverbs. Avoid strictly literal interpretations.

- Some proverbs may need to be translated into our thought forms and ideas for the purpose of applying the message to our context.

Summary Statements

- A substantial portion of the Old Testament is poetry.
- Parallelism is a common feature of Hebrew poetry.
- Various literary devices enrich and give beauty to Hebrew poetry.
- The wise derived wisdom by observing how God has structured the world and established an order for its existence.
- Wisdom in the Old Testament includes four broad categories, one of which is the "fear of the LORD."
- Wisdom was taught in Israel by the various social groups and by the trained professionals.
- Wisdom was a shared phenomenon in the ancient Near East.
- Job, Proverbs, and Ecclesiastes are the primary examples of wisdom literature in the Old Testament.

Questions for Reflection

1. Read Psalm 37 and attempt to identify the various types of parallelism (synonymous, antithetical, and formal) in this psalm.
2. Compare and contrast the four types of wisdom and show which type needs to be sought out first.
3. Why does wisdom seem to be more secular than religious? How can one learn about God by studying wisdom?
4. What do we learn today by observing the created order of things?
5. What wisdom have you learned from others around you (parents, teachers, or others with life experience)?

Resources for Further Study

Crenshaw, James L. *Old Testament Wisdom: An Introduction*. Atlanta: John Knox Press, 1981.
Gottwald, N. K. *"Poetry, Wisdom."* Vol. 3 of *Interpreter's Dictionary of the Bible*. Nashville: Abingdon Press, 1962. Pages 829-38.
Von Rad, Gerhard. *Wisdom in Israel*. Trans. James D. Martin. Nashville: Abingdon Press, 1972.

22 Suffering of the Righteous: Job

Objectives:

Your study of this chapter should help you to:
- Identify the major persons in the book.
- Outline the content of the book.
- Compare the arguments of the main characters.
- Trace the way an argument based on wisdom is developed.
- Explore ways to comfort those who are suffering.

Key Words to Understand

Job
Genre
The Satan
Eliphaz
Bildad
Zophar
Elihu

Questions to consider as you read:

1. What thoughts go through your mind when you hear about tragedy and loss of life?
2. Why do bad things happen to good people?

Many have heard that **Job** patiently endured great suffering (James 5:11). How many, however, know him as a man of protest? Did you know that his patience was not cheerful and his suffering was not done in silence? Rather, he became quite angry over his situation and directed his anger toward God. Most people hold an image of Job based on the first two chapters of the book. When we turn to chapter 3, we encounter a different Job. The rest of the book is made up of long, wordy poems. What happened? Welcome to the world of wisdom poetry.

What we studied in the last chapter about poetry and wisdom now meets the actual text. The characters in the book draw their arguments from nature, comparing and contrasting how God deals with the world, particularly the righteous and the wicked.

The following passage shows how the wise often formulated arguments from their observation of the world:

*Can papyrus grow tall where
   there is no marsh?
  Can reeds thrive without water?
While still growing and uncut,
  they wither more quickly than
  grass.
Such is the destiny of all who forget God;
  so perishes the hope of the god-
  less* (Job 8:11-14).

Authorship, Date, and Composition

Scholars have proposed various views on the date and authorship of the Book of Job, ranging

C | The Ancient Near Eastern Background and Literary Parallels

The Book of Job was not the first work in the ancient Middle East to ask questions about the suffering of the righteous. Egypt produced a number of works that dealt with this problem during the 12th dynasty (1990—1785 B.C.). A good example is *The Admonitions of Ipuwer.* This work contains the lament of Ipuwer over the strife and social turmoil in the land. He complained that even the gods did not take notice of the situation. "There is no pilot in their hour. Where is he [God] today? Is he then sleeping? Behold, the glory thereof cannot be seen."[1]

Mesopotamia also produced several similar works. The poem *A Man and His God,* a Sumerian work of the second millennium, describes the complaint of a sufferer to the gods about his tormented situation. The Babylonian poem *I Will Praise the Lord of Wisdom* deals with a sufferer's struggle with the inscrutable will of deity. He had performed the rituals required by the gods but was uncertain that they would have any effect.[2] *The Babylonian Theodicy* (1100 B.C.) is similar to Job in that it is a dialogue between a sufferer and his friend. The friend maintained an orthodox position while the sufferer listed his grievances against the gods. In the end he offered up a prayer that the gods might take note and help him.[3]

The Book of Job shows no direct dependence on any of these works. Job, however, is similar to these works in that it represents Israel's attempt to grapple with the problem of the suffering of the righteous. What sets Job apart from other ancient wisdom works is its comprehensive treatment of the topic. Job also shows a variety of literary forms or **genres,** such as laments, disputations, lawsuits, hymns, wisdom instructions, petitions, avowals of innocence, and affirmations of trust in God. In summary, we believe that Job's intellectual roots lie in the wisdom tradition that spanned many cultures. Its theological concepts, however, belong to Israel's religious traditions contained in the Old Testament.[4]

from Moses in the 13th century to someone in the 2nd century B.C. The patriarchal setting in the first two chapters has led some to conclude that the book is quite old, possibly the first book of the Old Testament to have been written. The sophisticated theological arguments in the rest of the book compel us to place the book at a much later period in Israel's history. Many scholars tend to date the book in the 7th or the 6th century B.C.[5]

The composition of the book also raises questions. The first two chapters and the last 11 verses are prose, while the rest of the book is poetry. Was there an earlier prose story to which the poetry was introduced? If so, then we might think that the author wove the two together so tightly to make it a seamless work. However, chapters 22 to 27 seem to lack continuity. The poem on wisdom (chap. 28) shows no continuity with the preceding or following chapters. The speech of Elihu in chapters 32 to 37 seems to be an intrusion into the book. It seems that the book has gone through a process of writing, compiling, editing, and expansion. It is likely that the book reached its final form during the Babylonian exile.

Content

The following is a general outline of the Book of Job:
1. Prologue (1:1—2:13)
2. Job's monologue (3:1-26)
3. The first cycle of speeches (4:1—14:22)
4. The second cycle of speeches (15:1—21:34)
5. The third cycle of speeches (22:1—27:23)
6. Poem on wisdom (28:1-28)

7. Job's final response (29:1—31:40)
8. Elihu's speech (32:1—37:24)
9. God's response (38:1—42:6)
10. Epilogue (42:7-17)

■ The Prose Introduction (1:1—2:13)

The first two chapters contain five scenes alternating between earth and heaven. The opening scene describes Job's wealth and his piety, portraying him as a blameless and upright man who feared God and shunned evil. The scene quickly shifts (v. 6) to a day when the angels (literally, "the sons of God") gathered to present themselves to Yahweh. **The Satan** was among the angels.

In Job, the Satan appears as a member of the heavenly court. When God called the Satan's attention to Job's piety, he contend-

Names of God in Job

In the first two chapters the deity is named Yahweh, the LORD. This is the covenantal name of God given to Moses at Mount Sinai (Exodus 3:14). In the dialogue section, the Hebrew terms for God are *El* or *Eloah*. The only exception to this is found in 12:9. Chapter 42 reverts back to the name Yahweh, or the LORD.

Satan

The term *satan* means adversary, opponent, one who brings accusations. The New Testament identification of Satan with the devil is lacking in the Old Testament. In the Book of Job, the term is always used with the article (*the* Satan), in order to designate an office. From the conversation between God and the Satan it appears that his job was to investigate persons and bring offenders to God's notice. He functioned as the heavenly prosecuting attorney, hence the title "the Satan," meaning the adversary.

On Serving God

The theological issue being tested in the prologue chapters is whether or not a person can serve God out of disinterested holiness. Can one love and serve God even if one receives no personal benefit from such service? Only the grace of God can transform a self-seeking sinner into one who willingly serves God out of love. Some suggest that this issue just "sets the stage" for the real discussion of the problem of suffering. Such an approach undermines the theological basis of the test. Without this theological dimension, the story merely becomes a test of Job's personal strength and courage in the face of great loss. It becomes a story about humanity, and not God.

God's Omniscience

The "cosmic wagers" in Job 1—2 seemed to be based on the premise that neither the Satan nor God knew how Job would respond to his crisis. While God was confident of the outcome of the trial, He did not know what Job's initial reaction would be. This raises the question about God's omniscience, His knowledge of all things. Has God limited His knowledge of human decisions and allowed humanity true freedom to choose?

ed that God protected Job and blessed him with wealth and prosperity. The Satan also challenged God to take away Job's wealth to see if he would still keep his piety before God. God accepted the challenge and allowed the Satan to take away all that Job had.

The next scene (vv. 13-22) returns to earth. Through a succession of calamities Job's children were killed and his wealth swept away. In response Job made one of the greatest confessions of faith in the Bible:

Naked I came from my mother's
    womb,
    and naked I will depart.

The LORD gave and the LORD has
    taken away;
may the name of the LORD be
    praised (1:21).

Scene four is another meeting of the angels in heaven. Again God questioned the Satan about Job. The Satan claimed that Job would curse God if he was inflicted with pain and suffering. In response, God allowed the Satan to make Job suffer.

The final scene on earth portrays Job's intense suffering. Even though his wife encouraged him to curse God, he did not sin. His three friends—**Eliphaz** the Temanite, **Bildad** the Shuhite, and **Zophar** the Naamathite—came to comfort him. They sat in silence with Job seven days, the normal time of mourning in the ancient world.

■ The First Cycle of Speeches (3:1—14:22)

At the end of seven days, Job broke the silence with a lament. He cursed the day he was born, and wished he had been stillborn so that he would not have to suffer. He preferred death and rest to the turmoil of life.

Eliphaz the mystic addressed Job first (chaps. 4—5). Though he did not have an answer to Job's suffering, he asked if humanity can be righteous before God. This thought came to him through terrifying visions in the night. Humans are mortals and their destiny is trouble and hardship. They cannot understand the ways of God, so they must submit to His judgment. God will restore those who humble themselves and seek Him.

Job responded to Eliphaz (chaps. 6—7) with an accusation that God was responsible for his suffering. He pleaded with his friends to be true to him and not turn against him. He then addressed his complaint to God. His nights were filled with misery and his days had no hope. The comfort of sleep was robbed from him by disturbing dreams sent by God. Death was preferable. Job closed his complaint by asking God to pardon him if he had sinned, and leave him alone.

Bildad's speech (chap. 8) focused on God's justice. He implied that Job's children died as punishment for their sins. He affirmed the traditional view, the wisdom of former generations, that God punishes the wicked. They die like an uprooted plant. Bildad's clear implication was that Job was suffering due to his sin and he needed to repent.

Job response (chaps. 9—10) affirmed Eliphaz's view that humans cannot be just before God (9:1). The issue for Job was that God would not allow anyone, righteous or wicked, to stand before Him. Yet as a blameless man, he could not understand why God was punishing him. Since a human is not capable of arguing his case against God, Job asked for an arbitrator to stand in the court and assist him in his defense before God (vv. 32-35). He

Artist's depiction of Job and his friends.

The problem of the suffering of the innocent has no easy answer.

continued his defense by asking God for the charges against him. Job reminded God that he was the work of God's hand, molded like clay and clothed with skin and flesh. Yet God concealed from him the plan to bring calamity upon his life. It would have been better if he had died at birth than to continue to live without a moment of joy.

What Bildad implied, Zophar made explicit (chap. 11). He challenged Job's claim of innocence and self-righteousness. Zophar thought that Job's punishment was much less than what his guilt deserved. But if Job would put away his sin, God would restore him and then "life will be brighter than noonday" (v. 17).

Job's reply (chaps. 12—14) shows his lack of patience with his friends. He mocked their claim of wisdom. Job insisted that God was not just. God is powerful and can do what He wants. No one can resist Him. Job thought his friends were "worthless physicians" (13:4). Their wisdom was empty. Job wanted to plead his case directly with God. Though he was faced

Resurrection of the Dead

In the early traditions of Israel, there was no thought about the resurrection of the dead. When people died, they simply joined their ancestors who were "asleep." Job's wish that God would hide him in his grave and bring him out after His anger subsided reflects the early stage in the development of resurrection belief in ancient Israel. Job was also confident that even after death, he would see God (see 19:26-27). During the Exile, Ezekiel spoke about God reviving the dead bones —the raising up of the exilic community from their death to life. Though Judaism continued to debate the resurrection of the dead (see Acts 23:8), during Jesus' time it was a popular religious conviction among most Jews.

Sheol

Sheol in the Old Testament is the grave or the dwelling place of the dead. The Old Testament also uses terms such as "the pit," "abaddon," and "the earth" to describe Sheol. Both the good and the bad went to Sheol. It is a place of gloom and darkness (Job 10:21-22). In Sheol, everyone is free from trouble and hardship (3:17-19). There is no return from Sheol (7:9; 16:22). The Septuagint translates Sheol as *Hades.* In the Old Testament, Sheol does not convey the idea of punishment or suffering. The concept of suffering in Sheol and its association with hell are postexilic in origin.

with the threat of death, he wanted to defend his integrity and innocence. Job lamented the frailty of human life, as well as hopelessness after death (chap. 14). He wished that God would hide him in Sheol until His wrath was over and remember him afterward at the appointed time.

■ The Second Cycle of Speeches (15:1—21:34)

Eliphaz's second speech (15:1-35) reiterated the theme that humans cannot be pure before God. He cited the wisdom of the past. God is just and the wicked will eventually suffer a horrible judgment at His hands. Job's response (16:1—17:16) characterized the words of his friends as long-winded speeches of his "miserable comforters." He quickly turned his address to God himself, blaming Him for his situation. Job claimed that he did have a "witness," an "intercessor" who would plead his case with God. Job, however, lamented that his death was near. He would go to the grave without hope.

Bildad was offended by Job's rejection of the friends' counsel. He argued (18:1-21) that the wicked suffer horrible terrors from God, many of which he described. The implication was that since Job was suffering these terrors, he was also wicked and needed to repent. Job would not accept Bildad's arguments (19:1-29). God had wronged him and there was no justice for him. Not only had God rejected him, but so also had his family, friends, servants, and wife. Job cried out to his friends for comfort and called for his words of protest to be engraved forever in stone (vv. 23-24). Earlier Job had called for an arbitrator (9:33) and intercessor (16:20). Now in a strong statement of faith he called God his Redeemer (*go'el,* a kinsman who defends and delivers) and confessed with assurance that even after death he would see God (19:25-27). Although the Hebrew in these verses is difficult, it is still clear that Job in his suffering had risen to a new level of faith and spiritual insight.

Zophar was unimpressed with Job's words. He continued (20:1-29) with the standard wisdom that God would punish the wicked. The bulk of the poem describes the many punishments God would bring upon them. Job directly contradicted Zophar's arguments (21:1-34). He took a hard look at what actually happens in life and described how the wicked did not suffer but prospered in life and died in peace. They meet the same final destiny as the righteous people, who suffer in their life. He concluded that God was partial to the wicked. Even in death, the wicked enjoyed safety and fame.

■ The Third Cycle of Speeches (22:1—27:23)

Eliphaz opened the third cycle of speeches (22:1-30) with a direct attack on Job's moral character. Humans are of no benefit to God. Even if humans were righteous before God, it would not give Him pleasure. Eliphaz produced a catalog of sins Job must have committed. However, if Job would repent, God would restore him. In Job's reply (23:1—24:25), he requested that God meet him at the bar of justice. There he would plead his case and be delivered. Yet however diligently he sought God, he could not find Him. He complained that God did not keep the appointed time to bring judgment on the wicked. He also presented a catalog of the crimes of the wicked. The verses at the end of the passage (24:22-25) are difficult to understand, but it appears that Job called upon God to judge the wicked and bring their evil to an end.

Bildad's last speech (25:1-6) proclaimed again that humans cannot be righteous before God. Job beautifully described the awesome power of God, before which he himself was powerless (26:1-14). Yet Job maintained his righteousness and complained that God had denied him justice

(27:1-10). The last part of the chapter (vv. 11-23) presents a problem. Either Job mockingly took up the arguments of his friends, or perhaps these verses contain the final speech of Zophar. The verses describe the fate of the wicked as God brings judgment on them.

■ The Poem on Wisdom (28:1-28)

Chapter 28, a fine poem on the nature of wisdom, presents a pause in the discussion. It begins with a description of how precious metals and stones are brought out of deep mines. Wisdom, more precious than either, however, is not found there. Wisdom can be found only in the God who has created all things. Humans are to fear God, stand in awe and obedience. This is the true source of wisdom.

■ Job's Final Response (29:1—31:40)

The debate hangs in the air unresolved. The arguments seem to present inadequate answers to the problem of God's moral governance of creation. Job opened his last defense by remembering how good the former days were when he had the favor of God (chap. 29). His had been a respected voice in the gate of the city where justice was conducted. He had taken up the cause of the poor and defended the widow. He had great honor in the society. But things had changed (chap. 30), and instead of being honored, Job was mocked by even the base and nameless of society. He suffered physical pain and mental terrors. He cried to God and received no answer. Even when he turned to the assembly where formerly he had sat as an honored member, no one would help him. Yet still Job maintained his innocence (chap. 31). In a confession of innocence he listed the evils he had not committed. To the end he held that he had not sinned and that his punishment was unjust.

■ Elihu's Speech (32:1—37:24)

The author introduces **Elihu,** a new speaker, who felt compelled to speak because Job's friends failed to give an adequate answer to his complaints (chap. 32). He rejected Job's claim of innocence and stated that God punishes humanity to turn them back from sin (chap. 33). But, if they pray to God, He would restore them. Elihu defended zealously God's honor (chap. 34). He argued that it is impossible for God to make a mistake in judgment since He knows all things. He noted that whatever humanity does, either good or evil, it does not affect God (chap. 35). Elihu reiterated the theme that God sends punishment to instruct and discipline the wicked (chap. 36). Punishment is remedial, to call the sinner back to God who is exalted in power as demonstrated in His ordering of nature. This description of God's majesty revealed in nature continues into chapter 37. The argument in some sense anticipates God's speeches.

■ God's Response (38:1—41:34)

The final segment of Elihu's speech sets the stage for God's speech out of the storm. God's response to Job is couched in traditional wisdom form. The argument looks at nature and asks for an explanation as to how everything is ordered. If Job could not explain how the physical universe was run, how could he hope to advance to the more difficult moral questions?

God began His speech not by answering Job but by demanding that Job answer Him (38:2-3). He asked where was Job when the world was created, when the boundaries of the seas were established? Could he bring the dawn or visit the gates of death or order the storms with their hail, snow, water, and lightning? Did he know the laws of heaven that govern both stars and clouds? Chapter 39 contains illustrations of God's providential care even for the animal world. Job began his answer to God (40:3-5) but was cut short as God continued to question him. If Job could explain how to order the moral world justly, then God would recognize that Job was able to save himself (v. 14). The next two poems (40:15-24 and 41:1-34) describe in hyperbolic poetry two of God's mighty creations, the behemoth and the leviathan. These animals that are so terrifying to humans are God's creations. The contrast between

God and humanity is again being concretely illustrated. God creates and controls that which terrifies humanity. A great gulf separates the two.

■ The Conclusion (42:1-17)

Job responded to God in humility and repented (vv. 1-6). He repented not because of evil or sins committed, but because he spoke of things he did not understand (v. 3). He recognized the truth that he was human and that he could not understand how God ordered the universe. All that God does and the ways by which He relates to the universe remain a mystery. From now on, Job would aban-

God asked Job: "Do you know when the mountain goats give birth?" (Job 39:1).

Divine Justice

The book closes without answering the question of divine justice. The question, "Why do the righteous suffer?" remains an enigma. Yet it does illustrate a proper response to evil. Job passionately questioned God's justice, yet God did not count it as sin. He learned from God's speeches the greatest truth about God. God is intimately involved with His creation. The relationship of God to the world included Job and his suffering. Job's world of suffering was within God's providential care. Job's response was repentance, a turning away from anger and back to trusting God. It is difficult to trust God when we are angry and hurt. Jesus later experienced the bitterness of human injustice and the agony of divine silence in the moment of suffering. There is a quiet comfort to be gained through trusting the One who knows the depth of human affliction.

don presumptive thinking about God. He would take the path of trust rather than protest. Faith would replace anger.

The story ends with God restoring to Job double for all the possessions and wealth he had lost. He received all his children back. Is there a subtle hint here that even in death, Job and his wife had not ultimately lost their children?

Summary Statements

- The Book of Job is a wisdom book.
- The Book of Job is mostly poetry, and it is for the most part in the form of a dialogue.
- It is difficult to determine the date and authorship of the Book of Job.
- Job's friends defended the traditional doctrine that suffering is the evidence of sin in one's life.
- Job maintained his innocence and hoped to be vindicated by God.
- Elihu's speeches relate suffering to the idea of divine discipline and instruction.
- God's speeches emphasize His relationship to the world and His governance of everything He has created.
- Job repented of his presumptive words about God, and God restored him to full life and prosperity.

Questions for Reflection

1. List some of the reasons that might help explain why good people suffer.
2. Is it possible to be angry with God when tragedy strikes and not sin? What does your answer say about your concept of God?
3. Is human suffering the consequence of sin? Explain your answer based on the lessons of the Book of Job.
4. What lesson do we learn from the example of Job's friends about how not to comfort one who is suffering? What might be more helpful approaches?
5. In your informed opinion, what was the ultimate objective of the writer of the Book of Job?

Resources for Further Study

Hartley, John. *The Book of Job*. New International Commentary on the Old Testament. Grand Rapids: Eerdmans, 1988.

Janzen, Gerald J. *Interpretation: A Bible Commentary for Teaching and Preaching: Job*. Atlanta: John Knox Press, 1985.

Newsome, Carol A. *Job: Introduction, Commentary, and Reflections*. Vol. 4 of *The New Interpreter's Bible*. Nashville: Abingdon Press, 1996. Pages 319-637.

23 Israel's Songs of Praise: Psalms

Objectives:

Your study of this chapter should help you to:
- Understand the history of the formation of the book.
- Identify the various types of psalms.
- Analyze the message of individual psalms.

Questions to consider as you read:

1. What are the various themes of songs and hymns we sing during our corporate worship on Sundays?
2. Should complaints to God be a regular part of our corporate worship? Explain why or why not.
3. What are the various reasons why you praise God?

Key Words to Understand

Tehillim
Psalmoi
Liber Psalmorum
Ledavid
Orphan psalms
Selah
Hermann Gunkel
Form criticism
Hymn
Lament
Song of thanksgiving
Royal psalms
Mashiach
Zion psalms
Enthronement psalms
Wisdom psalms
Psalms of trust

The Book of Psalms is one of the most widely read and appreciated books in the Bible. Both the synagogue and the Church continue to read, sing, and pray the Psalms. Whereas other books of the Old Testament represent God's word to humanity, the Psalms bring humanity's voice to God. They articulate our cry to God for help or express our gratitude for His care and deliverance. The Psalms explore our depth of need and the height of our praise. Worshipers are able to locate their various phases of life in the words of the psalmists, and find comfort in praying them anew. These ancient words also provide us with the language to express our hope and confidence that God's grace will sustain us in the midst of difficult experiences of life.

This chapter will examine Psalms as a whole, with attention given to individual psalms only for the purpose of illustration. The discussion will begin with an examination of the authorship of the psalms and the development of the book. The psalms will then be divided into literary categories according to form and/or content. Individual psalms will be examined as examples of form or theological content. The size of the book, 150 psalms, prohibits a detailed analysis of each individual psalm.

Authorship and Date

The Hebrew title for the Psalms is *tehillim,* meaning "songs of praise." *Psalmoi,* which also means "songs of praise," is the title of the book in the Septuagint. The Latin version called it *Liber Psalmorum.* The Greek and Latin versions are thus the source of the title "Book of Psalms." The ancient titles convey that the book contains Israel's songs of praise to God.

The development of the book covered a long span of time, perhaps over a thousand years. The earliest psalms reach back to the beginning of the nation. Psalm 90 is attributed to Moses, and Psalm 29 may have been adapted from an earlier Canaanite psalm. Coming much later, Psalm 137 is set during the time of the Exile.

While most of the psalms come from the time of the monarchy, it was not until after the Exile that the book as a whole took final shape. There are presently five sections or books of Psalms, each ending with a doxology. These sections are Psalms 1—41, 42—72, 73—89, 90—106, and 107—150.

In the first and the second books (Psalms 1—72), 45 psalms are attributed to David, 7 to Korah, and 1 to Asaph. The sons of Korah and Asaph formed guilds of musicians who passed down their songs to succeeding generation. The first psalm, a Torah psalm, and the second, a messianic psalm, may have been added later as introductions to the whole book. It appears that the first two books circulated together, possibly as early as the time of the monarchy, as a group of mainly Davidic psalms.

Book three is composed of 11 psalms of Asaph, 4 from Korah, and 1 each attributed to David and a certain Ethan. These, too, were probably written and compiled during the monarchy and then attached to the first two books. While a number of the psalms in books four and five were written during the time of the monarchy, they probably were not compiled and attached to the others until sometime after the completion of the second Temple (515 B.C.). The last book contains the Songs of Ascents or Pilgrim psalms (120—134), and the *haleluyah* psalms (146—150). Psalms in the second group each begin and end with the Hebrew word *halelu-*

yah, which is translated "praise the LORD." The Book of Psalms probably took its final shape during the fourth century, but no later than the third century B.C.

Most of the psalms have titles or captions. These titles often identify the person or group with whom the psalm is associated. They also contain some instructions for musical accompaniment. The meaning of the instructions has mostly been lost to us. For example, the caption of Psalm 88 includes the phrase "According to *mahalath leannoth.*" The last two words may indicate a now unknown tune to which the psalm was to be sung.

The reference to authorship in the titles presents another problem. Of the 73 Davidic psalms, 18 have notes associating them with events of David's life as recorded in 1 and 2 Samuel. This would indicate that the titles were not added until after those books were written and thus sometime after the psalms themselves were first created. Also, we do not know what was meant by the term **ledavid.** It can be translated "by David" (meaning a psalm written by him), "for David," "of David," or "belonging to David." The latter translations indicate that a psalm might have been composed for one of the Davidic rulers. Several psalms attributed to David mention the sanctuary or Temple (e.g., 18:6; 20:2; 63:2; 68:29), but Solomon built the Temple of Zion after David's death. Thus, these psalms were written about David or for the Davidic ruler, but not by David. In addition to the Davidic psalms, 1 is attributed to Moses (90), 1 to Ethan (89), 2 to Solomon (72 and 127), 11 to the sons or guild of Korah, and 12 to the guild of As-

aph. Fifty psalms have no authorship and are sometimes called **orphan psalms.**

In addition to the caption statements, often we find the term *selah* in a number of psalms. We do not know the exact meaning of this term. One suggestion is that *selah* may indicate a pause for a musical interlude.

It is likely that psalm writing and singing of songs were activities associated with worship in Israel that go back to the premonarchy period. Later, many psalms were most likely written specifically for the shrine erected by David and the Temple built by Solomon. An organized choir, musicians, and psalm singing were part of the Temple worship in the postexilic period. Most scholars refer to the Book of Psalms as the hymnbook of the Second Temple, thus giving it a prominent place in Israel's worship in the postexilic period.

Types of Psalms

The modern study of Psalms took a major step forward with the work of a German scholar named **Hermann Gunkel.** He noted that many of the psalms were structured according to identifiable patterns or forms. This analysis of literary works according to structure is known as **form criticism.** By identifying the form of a psalm, a reader is able to understand how its thought and message are developed. The form also indicates how the psalm was used in worship. Gunkel realized that, while not all psalms could be classified by their forms, a sizable number of them could be placed into the categories of hymns, laments, and songs of thanksgiv-

Steps that lead to a ceremonial bath *(mikveh)*. Ceremonial bathing was a required ritual to maintain holiness in ancient times in Israel.

given. Psalm 117, the shortest psalm in the collection, is a hymn.

Praise the LORD, all you nations;
extol him, all you peoples.
For great is his love toward us,
and the faithfulness of the LORD
endures forever.
Praise the LORD.

The first two lines, using synonymous parallelism, form a call to praise. The word *for* introduces the two motive lines, which are also in formal parallelism. The psalm closes with the single Hebrew word *halelu-yah,* meaning "Praise Yahweh." The word *for* is usually missing from the creation hymns, such as 8; 19:1-6; and 104. However, the creation hymn Psalm 148 repeats the regular form twice.

Other hymns celebrate Yahweh's rule over creation and history (33; 145; 146; 147). Hymns that proclaim the kingship of Yahweh (93 and 95—99) may have been part of a ritual where the recognition of the kingship of Yahweh over the created order was reenacted.

ing. Scholars have accepted his classification with minor adjustments. Gunkel's work helps us understand that Israel's psalms were not just expressions of individual piety but were situated in the worship of the community. They belonged to the congregation of the faithful who used them to express both their praise and their needs to God.

Hymns

The simplest category is that of a **hymn,** which first called the community to praise God. The initial call to praise God is often followed by the Hebrew word *ki,* usually translated *for.* Reasons or motives for praising God are then

Laments

Over a third of the psalms may be classified as **laments,** or cries to God for help. This category is comprised of both community and personal laments. When the community faced military defeat, famine, pestilence, drought, or some other difficulty, it expressed its need of God in the form of a prayer for deliverance. The crises forced the community to raise agonizing questions. Was God with them? Was He angry over sin? Was He just in His treatment of His people? Psalm 44 expresses this agony. It begins by recalling the mighty deeds God performed for His people (vv. 1-8).

*We have heard with our ears, O
      God;
   our fathers have told us
what you did in their days,
   in days long ago* (v. 1).

With dramatic suddenness the poem shifts to recount the plight of the people (vv. 9-16).

*But now you have rejected and
      humbled us;
   you no longer go out with our
      armies* (v. 9).

God had sold them to their adversaries, and they were forced to bear their taunts. Yet all of this was not deserved (vv. 17-22). Protesting their innocence, they reminded Yahweh of their faithfulness and denied that they had turned after other gods.

*All this happened to us
   though we had not forgotten
      you
   or been false to your covenant*
      (v. 17).

The poem closes with a call to God to awaken and take note of their situation (vv. 23-26). They called upon His "unfailing love," trusting that He would redeem them. Other community laments include Psalms 58, 60, 80, 90, 94, and 137.

The authorship of most of the laments may be attributed to individuals who called upon God in times of personal misfortunes and trials. These laments reflect the contexts of sin, illness, economic distress, betrayal by a friend, false accusations, infertility, death, abandonment by God himself, and oppression by enemies. Often the precise situation cannot be identified. A number of psalms refer to the enemies of the worshiper. The use of stylized language and metaphors cloak the identity of the enemy, as in Psalm 22:12-14:

*Many bulls surround me;
   strong bulls of Bashan encircle
      me.
Roaring lions tearing their prey
   open their mouths wide against
      me.
I am poured out like water,
   and all my bones are out of
      joint.
My heart has turned to wax;
   it has melted away within me.*

Or Psalm 35:26:

*May all who gloat over my dis-
      tress
   be put to shame and confusion;
may all who exalt themselves over
      me
   be clothed with shame and dis-
      grace.*

This use of stylized and metaphorical language allows other worshipers who feel threatened by problems of life to pray the lament, reading their situations into the language. Thus the psalms have continued to be used by new generations of distressed worshipers to articulate their cries of anguish.

The form of the lament contains

Jews praying at the Western (Wailing) Wall; psalms are prayers of the faithful who trust in the mercy of God.

a great deal of variation. It usually begins with (1) a cry to God:
How long, O LORD? Will you forget me forever?
  How long will you hide your face from me? (13:1).

Save me, O God, by your name;
  vindicate me by your might (54:1).
Hear, O Lord, and answer me,
  for I am poor and needy (86:1).
The cry for help may be followed by (2) a description of the situation, sometimes called the complaint:
Strangers are attacking me;
  ruthless men seek my life—
  men without regard for God (54:3).

The arrogant are attacking me, O God;
  a band of ruthless men seeks my life—
  men with out regard for you (86:14).
Following the complaint there may be (3) a protestation of innocence:
I do not sit with deceitful men,
  nor do I consort with hypocrites;
I abhor the assembly of evildoers
  and refuse to sit with the wicked (26:4-5).
Or a confession of sin:
Then I acknowledged my sin to you
  and did not cover up my iniquity.
I said, "I will confess my transgressions to the LORD"—
  and you forgave the guilt of my sin (32:5).
A dramatic turn often occurs in a lament when (4) the worshipers confess their trust in God. In spite of the situation they cling in faith to the steadfast love of God, believing that He will maintain the cove-

nant and come to their rescue.
Surely God is my help;
  the Lord is the one who sustains me (54:4).

But I trust in you, O LORD;
  I say, "You are my God" (31:14).
The lament may close (5) with another prayer for help:
Listen to my cry,
  for I am in desperate need;
rescue me from those who pursue me,
  for they are too strong for me.
Set me free from my prison,
  that I may praise your name (142:6-7).
Or with a vow to praise God:
I will praise you, O Lord, among the nations;
  I will sing of you among the peoples.
For great is your love, reaching to the heavens;
  your faithfulness reaches to the skies (57:9-10).
The lament has many variations, which are not difficult to recognize. The cry to God for help and the description of some type of difficult situation are distinctive markers. The variations displayed in the individual psalms arise out of the creativity of the composers as well as the change of circumstances. Underlying the variations, however, is a consistent belief that the God of Israel would hear the petitions of His worshipers and act in their behalf. They trusted in His faithfulness and loyalty to the covenant. When they had sinned, they had an assurance that He would forgive and restore them. However difficult their situation might be, they still approached God with the sureness of being heard. Out of that confidence praise and thanksgiving arose. The laments

Hate Language in the Psalms

A number of psalms contain strong language of hatred toward enemies. Such psalms call for God's merciless judgment upon those who persecute and oppress the faithful. Psalm 137 is an example of psalms that contain the language of vengeance and hatred. We may not feel comfortable today when we read,

O Daughter of Babylon, doomed to destruction,
happy is he who repays you
for what you have done to us—
he who seizes your infants
and dashes them against the rocks (137:8-9).

When we encounter such hateful language, we must keep in mind that calling God to carry out judgment was an important part of Israel's religious beliefs. The helpless people of God saw God as the only source of justice and help. They did not take matters into their hands, rather trusted God with His righteous judgment. As Christians reading the psalms, we should apply the love commandment as the basis of our relation with those who hate and persecute us (Matthew 5:43-45).

---

thus did not end in despair, but in hope and worship.

Songs of Thanksgiving

While the lament looks forward to the help of God, the **song of thanksgiving** arises as a response of gratitude for God having responded to prayer. Some psalms reflect the context of sin and forgiveness.

I said, "I will confess my transgressions to the LORD"—
and you forgave the guilt of my sin (32:5).

Others make reference to healing that had taken place.

O LORD my God, I called to you for help
and you healed me.
O LORD, you brought me up from the grave;
you spared me from going down into the pit (30:2-3).

Some others indicate that deliverance had come.

This poor man called, and the LORD heard him;
he saved him out of all his troubles (34:6).

Not only the individual but also the community as a whole expressed its joy for God's blessing, particularly for bountiful harvests (65 and 67), victory over enemies (75 and 124), and for bringing pilgrims safely to Jerusalem for one of its times of annual festivals (107).

These psalms were sung in the presence of the congregation as the opening indicates. They begin with a statement of intent to praise God. The individual may begin with a personal statement:

I love the LORD, for he heard my voice;
he heard my cry for mercy (116:1).

Or the community as a whole may be called to give thanks.

Give thanks to the LORD, for he is good;
his love endures forever.
Let the redeemed of the LORD say this—
those he redeemed from the hand of the foe (107:1-2).

The main body of the song of

Waves in the Mediterranean Sea. The psalmist trusted in the presence of God even in the midst of all natural calamities (Ps. 46:1-3).

thanksgiving is made up of three movements: (1) a description of the distress that the worshiper experienced:

The cords of death entangled me;
the torrents of destruction over-
whelmed me.
The cords of the grave coiled
around me;
the snares of death confronted
me (18:4-5).

(2) The supplication to God:

In my distress I called to the LORD;
I cried to my God for help (v. 6).

(3) God's answer to the prayer:

He reached down from on high
and took hold of me;
he drew me out of deep waters.
He rescued me from my powerful
enemy,
from my foes, who were too
strong for me (vv. 16-17).

There is no standard form for the conclusion; rather there are several possibilities. Examples may include a celebration of praise to God:

The LORD lives! Praise be to my
Rock!
Exalted be God my Savior!
(vv. 46-50).

Or a prayer for continued help:

Give us aid against the enemy,
for the help of man is worthless.
With God we will gain the victory,

and he will trample down our
enemies (108:12-13).

Or a pledge to fulfill vows:

I will sacrifice a thank offering to
you
and call on the name of the
LORD.
I will fulfill my vows to the LORD
in the presence of all his people
(116:17-18).

Or a wisdom saying:

Whoever is wise, let him heed
these things
and consider the great love of
the LORD (107:43).

The song of thanksgiving may be confused with the hymn, as both open with a statement of intent to give praise to God. It is the next movement, however, that differentiates the two. In the hymn the call to praise is followed by a series of reasons for praise whereas thanksgiving songs rehearse the problems that need divine intervention and then relate how God responded. Both hymns and songs of thanksgiving make positive statements about the graciousness of God, who does marvelous things for His people.

Other Types of Psalms

Many of the psalms cannot be classified by their form but by their rhetoric or content. Some have a common theme that binds them together. The **royal psalms** represent one such group. These psalms were written by or for the king and often have the superscription "By David." Psalms 2, 72, and 110 were sung at the coronation of the king, Psalm 45 at a royal wedding. In Psalm 118 the king led the congregation in worship. In Psalm 20 the king prepared to go to war; in Psalm 21 he returned in victory. Psalm 18 is a royal psalm of thanksgiving. The Tem-

Jewish and Early Christian Interpretation of Psalms

What happened when the monarchy was swept away with the fall of Jerusalem in 587 B.C.? How could these psalms be reinterpreted so as to be meaningful to the new society that had no native king? After the Exile, the people returned to Judea, which became a part of the greater Persian Empire. Then came the Greek Empire of Alexander the Great, followed by the Seleucid rulers, and finally the Romans. There was no Jewish monarchy for God to bless, no king to lead the people in battle. The psalms were reinterpreted as having a future meaning. They became the voice of expectation. The people longed for God to bring forth a royal leader who would once again, like David, restore the kingdom to Israel. The king was the "anointed one," in Hebrew the ***mashiach*** or messiah. In the postexilic community, these psalms were read as prophetic descriptions of the messiah whom God would send to redeem His people. Instead of looking backward to a historic kingdom, they were viewed as looking forward to God's new act of redemption, which He would inaugurate with a messianic king. The early Christians applied many of the royal psalms to the life and ministry of Jesus the Messiah.

ple of Jerusalem was a royal chapel, financed, built, and maintained by the king. That many of the psalms concern the king should be no surprise. The king was God's chosen representative. In particular David had been elevated to the throne over Saul and had been promised an eternal throne with an unbroken succession of descendants (see 2 Samuel 7; Psalms 89, 132).

While the royal psalms deal with matters concerning the earthly monarchy, the **enthronement psalms** (47, 93, 95—99) celebrate the kingship of Yahweh. Beyond all earthly rulers sits enthroned in heaven the King of Kings. To Him all nature and humanity bows. He is the absolute sovereign. This is a cause of rejoicing, for He brings victory to His people. These psalms by content form a distinctive group, but each is also by form a hymn. Here content and form overlap.

The **Zion psalms** celebrate the choice of Jerusalem as the location of Yahweh's Temple (Psalms 46, 48, 76, 84, 87, 122). In these rather short psalms, Jerusalem is described as the place God has chosen for His dwelling. No city can compare to her in beauty. It is the ideal place to live, and those born in her are blessed. In time of danger God himself will defend her.

There are a number of psalms that celebrate the Davidic kingship (Chalcolithic crown).

"On his law he meditates day and night" (Psalm 1:2).

teous as opposed to the foolish and wicked (Psalms 37, 112), looking to human experience as the source of knowledge. Psalm 1, which serves as an introduction to the entire book, focuses on the two ways of life—the way of godliness and the way of wickedness. In Psalms 49 and 73 the psalmists struggled with the complexities of the world. The common thought of the day was that God would insure justice—the righteous would be rewarded and the wicked punished. Yet the wicked prospered and suffered no punishment. This inequity pushed the psalmists to look beyond the present and into a confession of hope for life beyond the grave (Psalms 49:15; 73:26). While this thought seems obvious from the standpoint of the New Testament, in the Old Testament it was innovative.

The **wisdom psalms** were written later, toward the end of the monarchy or during the exilic and postexilic periods. They reflect the concerns of wisdom: seeking success in life (Psalm 128), dividing people into the wise or righteous.

The **psalms of trust** are some of the best-loved psalms of the Bible. Psalm 23 is probably the best known of all the psalms. Oth-

Theology of Psalms

The Psalms may be humanity's prayer to God, but at their center is God, not humanity. There is one God, Yahweh, who delivered Israel from Egypt, established His covenant with His special people, gave them the land, chose David as king and Jerusalem as His place of habitation. Yahweh jealously guards His people from their enemies but will not allow their sin to go unpunished. A primary task of Yahweh is the moral governance of this world. The righteous can rest secure in His justice that the wicked will be punished and the righteous rewarded. Israel's covenant relationship will be sustained by Yahweh's steadfast love (in Hebrew, *hesed,* which also means "covenant loyalty, unfailing love, faithfulness").

The Psalms view humanity as dependent creatures in need of God's help. The world has become a hostile place with powerful forces opposed to Israel. Even in the covenant community, the wicked seek to destroy the righteous. Only Yahweh can provide an adequate shelter. He sustains the warrior, brings justice to the oppressed, and defends the holy city. There is little hope beyond this life, so worshipers cry for immediate relief from oppression, the powers of death, and the infertility of the earth. Psalms shows only faint hopes that the justice of God might reach beyond the grave. Sin will bring the wrath of God, yet restoration is possible through repentance. While the laments seem to color the emotional tone of Psalms in dark hues, the joy of the presence of God stands in contrast. Even the laments ring with a confidence that God will hear and answer prayer. Life will be good again.

er songs of trust include Psalms 11, 16, 62, 63, 91, 121, 125, and 131. The lament will often contain a section that proclaims the worshiper's confidence that Yahweh has heard and will answer prayer. The song of trust is a more explicit proclamation that celebrates God's goodness and dependability in the midst of the troubles of life. At points the exuberance overflows into excessive claims of divine protection, particularly for the king, from all of life's calamities (Psalm 91).

Summary Statements

- Praise of God is the overall objective of Psalms.
- Psalms originated in the context of Israel's worship.
- Psalms provide us with the language to pray and praise God.
- The Book of Psalms in its present form represents over a thousand years of writing, compiling, and composition.
- Psalms once existed as five separate books or sections.
- The Book of Psalms reached its final form during the postexilic period.
- David's name is associated with about half of the psalms.
- Gunkel pioneered the study in classifying the psalms according to their form.
- Hymns, laments, psalms of thanksgiving, royal psalms, enthronement psalms, wisdom psalms, and psalms of trust are some of the major types of psalms.

Questions for Reflection

1. Read through the Psalms and describe the psalmists' portrait of humanity.
2. Read through the Book of Psalms and describe the psalmists' portrait of God. Look at the various descriptions of God and make assessment of the psalmists' faith in God.
3. What is significant about the way most laments end? What lesson does it teach us about prayer?
4. Why is it helpful to be able to analyze a psalm by its form?
5. Write a personal prayer of trust and confidence using the language of the psalmists.

Resources for Further Study

Brueggemann, Walter. *The Message of the Psalms: A Theological Commentary.* Minneapolis: Augsburg Publishing House, 1984.

McCann, Clinton J., Jr. *The Book of Psalms: Introduction, Commentary, and Reflections.* Vol. 4 of *The New Interpreter's Bible.* Nashville: Abingdon Press, 1966. Pages 641-1280.

Mays, James L. *Interpretation: A Bible Commentary for Teaching and Preaching: Psalms.* Louisville, Ky.: John Knox Press, 1994.

24 Instructions on Life: Proverbs, Ecclesiastes, and Song of Songs

Objectives:

Your study of this chapter should help you to:

- Understand the issues concerning the authorship and dating of Proverbs, Ecclesiastes, and Song of Songs.
- Apply proverbial wisdom to life situations.
- Analyze different approaches for gaining meaning for life.
- Develop a biblical view of human sexuality and its proper function.

Key Words to Understand

Righteous
Wicked
Numerical sayings
Proverb
Qoheleth
Canticles

Questions to consider as you read:

1. What are some of the meaningful proverbial sayings in our contemporary world?
2. What is the common attitude toward life in secular society today?
3. How do people view sex and sexuality in our contemporary society?

Israel's wise men and poets address different aspects and concerns of human existence with eloquence and style in Proverbs, Ecclesiastes, and Song of Songs. Proverbs asks the question, What should one do to succeed in life? Ecclesiastes challenges the conventional or traditional ideas about life. It asks the question, What is the purpose of life? The Song of Songs celebrates the passion of life. We live in a world that continues to grapple with the existential issues addressed in these books. A reflective reading of these books will help us gain biblical insight and guidance on living a meaningful and relevant life in our postmodern world.

Proverbs[1]

How does one discover the way to the good life? Israel maintained the view that God had placed within creation itself the principles of wisdom (Proverbs 8). By studying the outcomes of the choices people had previously made, one could discern what tended to make life long or short, prosperous or poor, and peaceful or troublesome. The wise could see the lessons before them and structure their lives for good. The foolish would reject wisdom and live an undisciplined life that leads to destruction. In Israel's

"Righteous" and "Wicked"

The terms *righteous* and *wicked* are often used in the Old Testament to designate relationships rather than moral conditions. The individual lived as a member of the family, clan, tribe, community, and so forth, and each area imposed certain expectations. When one discharged the obligations demanded in each situation, then the person was righteous. A person is righteous only when obligations are met in all levels of relationships. In Proverbs the term *wicked* is used for those who are immoral (12:12) as well as those who violate social obligations (v. 26).[2]

wisdom tradition, those who fulfilled God's pattern were the righteous and wise; those who did not were the wicked and foolish.

Authorship and Date

While many Old Testament books are anonymous, Proverbs begins by stating: "The proverbs of Solomon son of David, king of Israel." In addition 10:1 has the title, "The proverbs of Solomon." These statements might lead one to think that Solomon wrote the book as we have it. However, 25:1 notes: "These are more proverbs of Solomon, copied by the men of Hezekiah king of Judah." This note tells us that the book was not completed until at least the time of Hezekiah (715 to 687 B.C.). The book also contains other collections of sayings such as "Sayings of the Wise" (22:17—24:22), "Further Sayings of the Wise" (24:23-34), "Sayings of Agur" (chap. 30), "Sayings of King Lemuel" (31:1-9), and a poem on "The Wife of Noble Character" (31:10-31). There is no reason to doubt that some of the material goes back to Solomon, and probably some even earlier. However, the book as we have it today went through a process of editing and compiling, perhaps taking final form sometime during or just after the Babylonian exile.

Content

The following is a broad outline of the materials in the Book of Proverbs:
1. Poems on the Way of Wisdom (1:1—9:18)
2. Proverbs of Solomon and Other Sayings of the Wise (10:1—29:27)
3. Closing Material (30:1—31:31)

◼ Poems on the Way of Wisdom (1:1—9:18)

The prologue (1:1-7) states the purpose of the book: to give wisdom and discipline for both the simple and the young and to enable the wise to learn more. The foundation of wisdom is in one's respect and reverence for the Lord.

The first main section (1:8—9:18) is composed of longer poems, a style similar to some of the Egyptian wisdom materials. This section is made up of 10 instructions, usually beginning with the formula "Listen, my son."

The first instruction (1:8-19) warns the youth to avoid the enticement of sin and sinners. The rest of this chapter presents wisdom as a woman who walks the streets calling on all to listen and learn from her.

The second instruction describes the need to seek wisdom, which is more precious than wealth (2:1-22). It protects the young from the snares of life. The third instruction (3:1-12) encourages the youth to trust God and walk humbly in His teachings. The fourth instruction emphasizes sound judgment and discernment that will lead to safety and security (vv. 21-35).

In the fifth instruction (4:1-9) the youth is directed to gain understanding. The sixth instruction (vv. 10-19) describes the twofold path and encourages the youth to choose the way of wisdom and avoid the path of the wicked. The seventh instruction (vv. 20-27) calls upon the youth to choose the morally right path of life and avoid evil.

The eighth instruction is a warning to the youth to avoid sexual immorality (5:1-23). One is to "drink

water from your own cistern" (v. 15), that is, be faithful to one's spouse. Chapter 6 includes admonitions on sound business practice, diligence in work, and a numerical list of things that the Lord hates (vv. 1-19).

A Jewish family begins a shabbat, or sabbath, meal with the breaking of bread.

C "Listen, My Son"

Why is only the son and never the daughter addressed in the Proverbs? This address shows the patriarchal orientation of the Israelite society. Though at home both young men and women received instruction, instruction in the public arena was reserved for the men. We do not think that patriarchal society was the norm that God intended for all human cultures. His revelation consists of a message that transcends cultural barriers. It would be more appropriate in a western, egalitarian society to translate "my son" as "my child."

I Numerical Sayings

Numerical sayings are found in several places in Proverbs and in other Old Testament books (see Amos 1:3—2:6). In this literary device, we find different matters listed in numerical order, usually giving the last mentioned item more significance or seriousness than the rest.

The 9th instruction (6:20-35) is again on sexual fidelity. What seems like an opportunity for secret enjoyment of sensual pleasure will turn out to be public disgrace and destruction. The 10th instruction (7:1-27) develops this same theme in the form of drama.

In chapter 8, wisdom is again personified as a woman (Lady Wisdom). She calls the people to enter her house and receive life, honor, and wealth. She was with God in creation, and through wisdom God brought everything into existence. The personification of wisdom is continued in chapter 9. Those who enter her house will feast on the finest of foods (vv. 1-6). With her, life will be good. In contrast Dame Folly invites the simple to her house where stolen food is delicious (vv. 13-18). Hers, however, is the house of the dead.

■ Proverbs of Solomon and Other Sayings of the Wise (10:1 — 29:27)

This part of the book is composed of short, two- to four-line sayings. These are the types of sayings usually associated with the term *proverbs*. A **proverb** (Hebrew, *mashal*) is a short, pithy saying that contains an idea or truth. There seems to be no connecting or unifying theme to this section.

This section covers a wide range of topics. We find in this section warnings against illegal business practices, laziness, idle chatter, dishonest scales, pride, sexual indiscretion, gossiping, slandering, foolish talk, false witnesses in courts, fraud, gluttony, envy, lying, and rulers who oppress the poor. Also there are proverbs here that call for trust in God, disciplining oneself, one's children, and one's servants, generosity, care for the poor, maintaining right relations within the family, diligence in working, thrift, patience, and above all attaining wisdom. Basic to wisdom is the fear (respect and obedience) of God.

■ Closing Material (30:1 — 31:31)

The final material of the book comes from several sources. The sayings of Agur make up chapter

---

T Contemporary Relevance of Israel's Proverbs

How trustworthy are these ancient proverbs for guiding a person's actions today? Are they absolute truth? How are they to be understood when some proverbs seem to contradict each other, such as those contained in 26:4-5.

Do not answer a fool according to his folly,
*   or you will be like him yourself.*
Answer a fool according to his folly,
*   or he will be wise in his own eyes.*

Should one answer or not answer a fool? Wisdom knows the answer. These proverbs illustrate that while all proverbs are true in that they capture an aspect of life, not all are universal and applicable in all circumstances. The wise know not only what to say or do but also the appropriate time. The fool does not. Wisdom is not purely an intellectual endeavor, gained by memorizing lists of proverbs, but a pragmatic application of insight into how to live well.

30. Agur's sayings include a poem on God's greatness (vv. 2-6), and two numerical sayings (vv. 7-9 and 15-31). The sayings of King Lemuel begin the final chapter (31:1-9). The sayings are a recital of the teachings of his mother. Instructions focus on the responsibilities of a king. The final collection in this book is an acrostic poem on the qualities of a worthy wife (vv. 10-31). The woman's qualities are described in typical wisdom pattern. While her piety is noted, it is her industry that receives emphasis and praise in this poem. Choose a wife (and the advice relates to choosing a husband as well) not according to physical beauty, but according to the person's ability to work diligently, to conduct business shrewdly, and to run the household efficiently. Such a choice is wise.

Ecclesiastes

Israel's wisdom sages were proponents of the tradition that promoted the reward of good life for the righteous and destruction for the wicked. However, they also knew that human existence was far more complex than this neatly packaged religious doctrine. They questioned, argued, and proposed new perspectives that would shed light onto the complexities of human existence. The disparities and disillusionment of life made some pessimistic even about their view of the world and human existence. Can any human really know the purpose of life? Does life have any meaning? These questions seem to occupy the thoughts of the writer of Ecclesiastes.

Authorship and Date

The writer called himself **Qoheleth**, sometimes translated "Teacher." The term has something to do with one who collects or gathers. Does Qoheleth gather a group to hear his words, students to teach, or sayings to publish? It is not certain, but it may have been that he did all three. The superscription (1:1) states that he was a son of David and, according to 1:12, a king over Israel in Jerusalem. Because of these statements, tradition has assigned this book to Solomon, suggesting that Qoheleth was a type of pen name. In other places, however, the author speaks like a subject, not a ruler (4:1-2; 5:8-9; 8:2-4). Also, the Hebrew reflects the style of postexilic developments, including some words that may be Persian in origin.[3] For these reasons, most scholars today place the book in the postexilic period and suggest that the author assumed the role of a king to test intellectually the various opportunities that life presents.[4]

Content

There has been much discussion over the plot of Ecclesiastes, but scholars have come to no consensus. The book moves from one topic to another with little internal structural development. The book also contains diverse literary forms such as poetry, prose, rhetorical questions, proverbs, curses and blessings, and autobiographical narrative. This variety adds to the richness of the thought but detracts from the book's purposeful development. The reader is thus confronted with an anthology of assorted materials compiled for the purpose of demonstrating the emptiness of life.

Ecclesiastes can be generally divided into three parts:

1. Prologue (1:1-11)
2. The Futility of Life (1:12—11:6)
3. Epilogue (11:7—12:14)

The second section and bulk of the book (1:12—11:6) contains loosely connected literary units that cannot be outlined without making numerous exceptions. The final part begins with an epilogue on youth and aging (11:7—12:7). The book concludes with an appendix that reflects traditional wisdom and an orthodox perspective (12:9-14).

■ Superscription and Prologue (1:1-11)

"Meaningless! Meaningless!"
    says the Teacher.
"Utterly meaningless!
    Everything is meaningless"
    (1:2).

So the author begins. Life is meaningless, vain, and empty of purpose. The prologue (vv. 3-11) develops this thought by describing the endless cycle of life. People are born, die, and are forgotten. Nature continues on its ceaseless cycle of seasons and nothing new arises. What is accomplished?

■ The Futility of Life (1:12—11:6)

The Teacher explored the various facets of life in order to dis-cover its purpose. His great wisdom brought only sorrow and grief (1:12-18). He then indulged himself with things that brought pleasure. Everything seemed meaningless. He realized that both the wise and the fool die in the end (2:1-16).

The Teacher also found work to be meaningless (vv. 17-26). He concluded that nothing is better than enjoying life by eating, drinking, and finding satisfaction with work. Enjoyment of life is God's gift to humanity.

The discussion about work is interrupted by what may be the most famous poem of the book (3:1-8):

There is a time for everything,
    and a season for every activity
        under heaven (v. 1).

Matched antithetical pairs fill out the poem: a time to be born and to die, to plant and to harvest, to kill and to heal. There is a time for each. The problem is, of course, knowing when is the proper time to engage in each activity. Is now the time for war or for peace? How do we know? Perhaps the intent of the author is to show that humans cannot alter the divinely established order of time for everything that happens. If this is the case, what, then, is the purpose of human existence? The writer thus paints before us an image of despair and pessimism.

The author reiterates the theme of work and enjoyment of life in 3:9-15. Humanity labors and thinks about eternity but cannot figure out what God is doing. So, enjoy life, which is a gift from God.

What about justice in the world (vv. 16-22)? Surely God guarantees that justice will be done. But the wicked prosper and in the end all die, just like the animals.

No Life After Death?

One of the theological limitations of this book is its lack of belief in life after death. The grave is the end. Whatever rewards or punishments one is to receive must come in this life. Therefore, the best that the Teacher finds in life is that one should enjoy one's work and take delight in one's spouse.

Who knows what happens next? The best a person has to hope for is to enjoy one's work.

The Teacher saw that oppression, envy, and discontentment were all around him (chap. 4), and everything was meaningless, a grasping after the wind. The Teacher thought that one should not be too zealous even in serving God (5:1-7). If one is so rash as to make a vow to God, then that person should certainly pay it.

The Teacher next explored the folly of wealth, because it does not endure (5:8—6:12). The wealthy are not content but are driven by an insatiable appetite. The Teacher concluded that humanity can't discover what is good in life.

Yet chapter 7 begins with a series of seven things that are called good or better (vv. 1-14). A good name, death, sorrow, mourning, rebuke of the wise, wisdom, and inheritance are among the good things in life. The last saying (vv. 13-14) calls for contentment in all circumstances, for both good and evil times come from God. Traditional wisdom, which the Teacher agreed with at this point, taught that there is only one God and that He is good. Yet paradoxically all things, whether good or evil, come from Him. How can this be? This is the problem Job struggled with, and it still puzzles modern thinkers.

The next section (7:15—8:1) is composed of a number of proverbs that do not appear to have any common theme. The Teacher recommended moderation in all things, even in righteousness and wickedness. He included sayings not very flattering to either women or men.

The next chapter includes instructions to the young on court etiquette (8:2-8) and a dialogue concerning justice (vv. 9-17). The Teacher had observed in life that an immediate punishment did not come to the wicked, but he concluded that a God-fearing life was better than a life filled with wicked schemes. Again, life seemed meaningless.

The end of life is the grave, for both the wicked and the righteous (9:1-10). So, what is the advantage of one over the other? With the living there may be hope, but it is tarnished with the thought that all will die and their memory be forgotten. The best one has is this life, so one should enjoy it as fully as possible.

The material in 9:13—11:6 presents a collection of proverbial sayings, the first few verses in prose and the rest in poetry. The first part (9:13—10:7) contrasts wisdom and folly. The balance of the mate-

A Mesopotamian Parallel to Ecclesiastes

The words of the Teacher are similar to the advice given to Gilgamesh, a Mesopotamian hero whose epic was recorded as early as the beginning of the second millennium B.C.

Thou, Gilgamesh, let full be thy belly,
Make thou merry by day and by night.
Of each day make thou a feast of rejoicing,
Day and night dance thou and play!
Let thy garments be sparkling fresh,
Thy head be washed; bathe thou in water.
Pay heed to the little one that holds on to thy hand,
Let thy spouse delight in thy bosom!
For this is the task of [mankind]![5]

It is not likely that the Teacher borrowed directly from the Gilgamesh epic, but it does demonstrate that wisdom writers of all ancient cultures wrestled with the same existential questions.

Orthodox children attend Yeshiva to receive religious instruction.

rial provides more traditional advice to the young on how to succeed in life. Yet even if the advice is heeded and one works diligently and wisely, in the end all things are in God's hands and no one can understand what He will do.

■ Epilogue (11:7—12:14)

The final word of the Teacher comes in the form of instruction to the young, perhaps his students (11:7—12:8). They are to enjoy life, a continuing refrain of the book. Yet all restraint is not to be cast off. One must still be aware that God brings one into judgment. Also, old age comes and one must live with the end as well as the beginning in mind. A beautiful poem describes pictorially the aging process (12:2-7). Finally, the opening words of the book are echoed again:

"Meaningless! Meaningless!" says the Teacher.
"Everything is meaningless" (v. 8).

The book ends with two additional sections, perhaps added later by an editor. The first (12:9-12) speaks about the Teacher, his diligence, and careful work. The last two verses bring the book to

Proverbs vs. Ecclesiastes

The Both Proverbs and Ecclesiastes deal with God, humanity, and critical concerns of human life. Proverbs is more positive about these matters. God's will is knowable. One may succeed in life by working diligently according to the divine will. While life may have some difficulties, in the end God will bring justice by rewarding the righteous and punishing the wicked. The Teacher is not as confident as the author of Proverbs. God seems more remote, unknowable, and wrapped in mystery. Whatever proposals are made, one is never sure how God will respond. One should be cautious in life and live in moderation, even in serving God. God does not appear to be interested in justice. In the end, both the righteous and the wicked suffer the same fate; they die and are forgotten. However, even in the midst of his pessimistic thinking, the Teacher recognizes the need for worship, ethical values, and enjoying the simple pleasures of eating, drinking, and work.

Proverbs approaches life with optimism. However, the Teacher is pessimistic. Death hangs over every aspect of life. The Teacher comes close to espousing the idea of **carpe diem,** "seize the day." What separates him from this philosophy of living only for the moment is his recognition that there is a God and that it would be foolish to live so as to anger Him.

Both books are Scripture and require the believer to come to grips with their teachings. Neither presents God's final revelation, so they must be held as incomplete and partial. They also indicate that our understanding of life and of God's dealing with His creation is only partial. There is a mystery that goes beyond human knowledge. These books recognize our human finitude and invite us to worship our God who has revealed himself only partially, trusting that He is good.

a close. The purpose of humanity is known: keep God's commandments. Why? God will bring everything into judgment. These words reflect a more traditional approach to the religion of Israel, more in keeping with the pragmatic wisdom of Proverbs and the theology of Deuteronomy.

Song of Songs

The Song of Songs celebrates human sexuality as a normal part of the love and affection shared by a married couple. The book captures in beautiful poetry the sexual passion and intimate conversations between lovers. Its view of love is consistent with other parts of the Bible in that love and sexuality are seen as normal expressions of human life, and thus gifts of God. It is only one of two books that never mention God, the other one being Esther. Because of its passionate subject matter, its place in the canon has been the subject of debate. Its presence in the Bible, however, enables us to maintain an appropriate view of sexuality as a blessing of God whenever other voices seem to cheapen, denigrate, or pervert its purpose.

Authorship and Date

The phrase "song of songs" is a Hebrew expression meaning "the greatest song." From the Vulgate or Latin translation the book took the name **Canticles.** The first verse of the book associates the work with Solomon, the patron of wisdom literature, and is thus often called the Song of Solomon.

Who authored the book is an open question. The traditional view ascribes the authorship to Solomon (1:1). Sometimes scholars can date a book by its style of poetry or by historical references contained in the book. Neither of these methods offers a secure means for dating this book. Suggestions as to date of writing vary from the 10th century, written by Solomon himself, to the 4th century B.C. The dominant voice in the book is that of a woman, not a man.

Interpretation of this book has a long history.[6] Early Jewish scholars followed the allegorical method and interpreted it as an expression of God's love for Israel. Early Christian scholars followed the same pattern, only recasting it as Christ's love for the Church. Modern approaches have varied, some seeing it as a type of Greek drama complete with a chorus, or as originally coming from a pagan cultic ritual that celebrated the union of a god and goddess. Marvin Pope relates the song to the funeral festivals in which life and love were celebrated as the most powerful force that can cope with the fear of death.[7] A better way to view the book is to see it as a collection of love songs. While some poems may have been composed as songs for wedding festivals, others may simply be love poems composed by various individuals. When and by whom the diverse materials were brought together as a collection of love poems is unknown.

Content

The book consists of a number of seemingly disconnected poems, and therefore, it is difficult to give a thematic outline to the book. The first verse was added to give it the authority of Solomon, the patron of wisdom literature. The book itself is firmly located within

Song of Songs is a celebration of love.

the wisdom tradition as it derives its content from the world of humanity. Its images are drawn primarily from nature: gardens, animals, perfumes, spices, and trees. With expansive and redundant expressions, the poetry builds vivid word pictures of passionate love.

The speakers in the first two chapters alternate between the woman and the man. First the

woman sings (1:2-7) of her love for her husband whom she honors as a king and seeks as a shepherd. The man answers by praising her beauty (vv. 8-11). She in turn rejoices in his presence (vv. 12-14), and he again responds by praising her (vv. 15, 17; 2:2). Fantasizing about the expressions of his love toward her, the woman sees him approaching like a wild gazelle. He then entices her to depart with him (2:3-17).

The scene shifts in chapter 3; the woman seeks her lover through the streets of Jerusalem. Finding him, she entices him into the wedding chamber (3:1-5). The last half of the chapter describes a wedding procession with the groom portrayed as Solomon (vv. 6-11).

Chapter 4 begins with the groom describing the physical attractions of his bride. Most of the comparisons are drawn from nature: doves, ewes, pomegranates, and fawns. In the last half of the chapter and into the next (4:9—5:1) the groom extols the love of his bride, again comparing it to the fruits and spices of nature.

In 5:2 the scene shifts again back to Jerusalem where she opens her door to her lover only to find him gone. She calls on the "daughters of Jerusalem" to assist her (v. 8). The chorus then asks why she loves him so (v. 9). The woman then describes his physical charms (vv. 10-16). When the chorus asks where they might seek him, she responds that he has gone to his garden; that is, he has been with her (6:1-3). Again the groom's voice is heard extolling the physical beauty of his bride, who is more beautiful than all the women in the harem of a king (vv. 4-10).

Chapter 7 begins with a poem

Theology of the Song of Songs

The book is unusual in that it lacks any divine voice, prophetic voice, or reference to Israel's laws, covenant, or sacred history. We hear only human voices that extol the pleasure and passion of sexuality. What theological message does it contain? Israel viewed Yahweh as the Creator of the physical universe. Whatever He created was a gift and a blessing to His creation. This includes our physical bodies and the physical enjoyment we receive in sexual love. Sexuality used as an expression of love and affection within the bounds of marriage becomes both a creative act, issuing in the birth of children, and an expression of companionship between a man and woman. Exploitation of sexuality outside of marriage or in unnatural or perverse ways is a perversion of God's gift. The song celebrates the goodness of God's gift of love.

celebrating the beauty of the maiden (vv. 1-5). The groom speaks of the pleasure of her physical love (vv. 6-9). The woman responds by inviting him into the vineyards where she will give him her love (vv. 10-13). Her song continues into 8:1-4, where she expresses the desire to be with her lover openly as with a brother. The rest of chapter 8 consists of a number of short songs by the groom, the woman, and brothers or friends of the woman.

Summary Statements

- According to Israel's wisdom tradition, God placed the principles of wisdom in the created world.
- Proverbs, Ecclesiastes, and Song of Songs deal with issues of humanity and human existential concerns.
- Proverbs contains a collection of Israel's proverbial sayings.
- Proverbs focuses on the theme of living a good life and living up to one's potential as a responsible member of society.
- Proverbs proposes the view that wisdom is a gift from God.
- Ecclesiastes takes a pessimistic view of life.
- Ecclesiastes calls for moderation in everything one does and for the fear of God.
- Song of Songs celebrates human sexuality and the love shared by a man and a woman.

Questions for Reflection

1. God's revelation came through the patriarchal Israelite society. What does this mean for structuring gender relationships in modern society?
2. In a secular society that rejects political arguments supported by quotations from Scripture, how can one build an argument using the methods of wisdom? Why have organizations such as MADD been successful in getting their message heard?
3. How is sexuality viewed differently in the Bible than in secular culture?
4. Is life as meaningless as the Teacher thought? How does one discover life's purpose?
5. What risks does one take by being sexually promiscuous? How wise is a person who runs such risks?

Resources for Further Study

Garrett, Duane A. *Proverbs, Ecclesiastes, Song of Songs. New American Bible Commentary.* Nashville: Broadman, 1993.

Kidner, Derek. *The Proverbs: An Introduction and Commentary. Tyndale Old Testament Commentary.* Downers Grove, Ill.: InterVarsity Press, 1964.

Kinlaw, Dennis F. *Song of Songs.* Vol. 5 of *The Expositor's Bible Commentary.* Grand Rapids: Zondervan, 1991.

Scott, R. B. Y. *Ecclesiastes. Anchor Bible.* New York: Doubleday, 1965.

Whybray, Roger N. *The Book of Proverbs. Cambridge Bible Commentary.* Cambridge, Mass.: University Press, 1972.

UNIT V

DISCOVERING THE PROPHETIC BOOKS

This unit introduces the reader to:

- An understanding of prophets and prophecy in Israel
- The ministry and message of Israel's canonical prophets
- The significance of the prophetic message to the Christian Church today

■ Israel's Prophetic Voices

■ Isaiah

■ Jeremiah and Lamentations

■ Ezekiel

■ Daniel

■ Hosea, Joel, Amos, and Obadiah

■ Jonah, Micah, Nahum, and Habakkuk

■ Zephaniah, Haggai, Zechariah, and Malachi

25 Israel's Prophetic Voices

Objectives:

Your study of this chapter should help you to:
- Compare and contrast prophecy in Israel with prophecy in other ancient Near Eastern religions.
- Summarize the history of the development of prophecy in ancient Israel.
- Describe the identity, mission, and function of Israel's prophets.
- Identify the key literary types *(genres)* found in the books of the prophets.
- Describe the formation of the books of the prophets.
- Describe the guidelines for interpreting the prophetic books.

Questions to consider as you read:

1. What is your view of the current interest in the end times (through books, movies, etc.)?
2. When you hear the words "prophet" and "prophecy," what thoughts come to your mind?

Key Words to Understand

Gad
Nathan
Micaiah
Elijah
Elisha
Noncanonical prophets
Classical period of prophecy
Canonical prophets
Court prophets
Temple prophets
Ro`eh
Oracle
Forthtelling
Foretelling
Eschatology
Prophetic eschatology
Apocalyptic eschatology
Genres
Messenger-style speech
Vision accounts
Symbolic actions
Woe oracles
Legal disputes
Funeral songs
Parables
Riddles
Redactors

Prophets occupy a unique place in Israel's faith traditions. They have contributed to one-third of the content of the Old Testament. The phenomenon of biblical prophecy, which began with Israel's prophets, continues to be a subject of great interest today.

Were there prophets in other religions of the ancient Near East? What prompted the appearance of prophets as religious leaders in Israel? What characteristics set them apart from other religious leaders? What was the nature and purpose of their ministry? We will begin with some of these questions.

Israel's prophets were God's spokespersons to their nation during national crises. When Israel was in bondage in Egypt, God called Moses as His spokesperson. Scholars think that the ministry of Moses laid the foundation for the prophetic office in Israel (see Deuteronomy 18:15-22; Hosea 12:13).

Who Were the Prophets Since the Days of Moses?

We do not have any record of prophetic activity in the early days of Israel's settlement in Canaan (see 1 Samuel 3:1). Samuel seems to be the first person to hold the prophetic office since Moses (3:20-21). He was known throughout Israel as a prophet. The last mentioned prophet in the Old Testament is Malachi, who is dated to the mid-fifth century B.C.

The Old Testament mentions individuals such as **Gad, Nathan,** Ahijah, Jehu the son of Hanani, **Micaiah, Elijah,** and **Elisha** among Israel's prophets during the 200 years after Samuel. Most of these individuals (except perhaps Gad and Nathan) were visionaries and miracle workers. Sometimes prophets of this period traveled as a group as the "sons" of a leading prophet (see 1

Prophecy in the Ancient Near East[1]

Other ancient cultures also had their share of prophets and prophetic activity. The following is a brief overview of prophecy in the ancient Near East.

The Prophecy of Neferti and *The Admonitions of Ipuwer* are two of the well-known prophetic materials from Egypt. The first text contains predictions concerning a future king, and the second gives negative evaluations of the rulers of Egypt. Revelation from God, a unique feature of Israel's prophecy, is lacking in both of these materials.

The Old Testament makes reference to the prophets of the Canaanite religion (1 Kings 18), but we know very little about their activities. Israel's traditions describe these prophets as worshipers and promoters of the Canaanite god Baal.

Literature from Mesopotamia includes "prophecies" and extensive collections of omen texts. Prophecies from Mesopotamia mostly contain predictions that scholars regard as "after the fact" statements. Some of these are oracles given to kings as divine responses to specific inquiries. The Mesopotamians used omens to predict the future by observing unusual occurrences. They understood signs and objects as a means of communication from gods who controlled various aspects of the natural world.

In contrast to that of other ancient Near Eastern religions, prophecy in Israel was a well-developed phenomenon. Its most distinguishing feature is the message that moral and ethical integrity is demanded by the covenant God of Israel. This emphasis is completely lacking in prophecy outside of Israel.

Samuel 10:1-13; 2 Kings 2:3, 5, 15). The Old Testament does not contain any writings that come from the prophets of this period. Amos's book, dated to the mid-eighth century B.C., is considered to be the first literary product of Israel's prophetic tradition. Therefore, scholars assign the label **noncanonical prophets** (non-writing/literary prophets) to those who ministered before Amos.

When Did Prophecy Emerge in Israel as an Ongoing Activity?

During the eighth century B.C., prophecy became an ongoing religious phenomenon in Israel. Literary activity, prophetic leadership, and prophecy as an ongoing phenomenon continued through the mid-fifth century B.C. Scholars label this period as the **classical period of prophecy** in Israel (800—450 B.C.). Israel's **canonical** (writing) **prophets** belong to this period.

Court Prophets and Temple Prophets

In Israel, in addition to the authentic, God-called persons who functioned as God's spokespersons, there were also **court prophets** and **temple prophets.** As institutional prophets, they served the interests of the palace or the Temple. Scholars think that the Temple prophets gave oracles during worship in Israel. Court prophets gave political counsel to the kings. Gad and Nathan were David's seers and counselors. Nathan was influential in both religious and political affairs, and he indicted the king for his moral

Elijah challenged the Baal prophets on Mount Carmel.

lapse (2 Samuel 12:1-15). Gad also was not hesitant to communicate the divine judgment to David (24:10-14).

In later history, the court prophets became strong advocates of national and royal policies. These prophets often harassed and attempted to invalidate the message of the true prophets. Moreover, they claimed that they also spoke on behalf of God. Jeremiah referred to them as false prophets because they spoke visions and dreams of their heart.

Hebrew Terms and Meanings

The Hebrew vocabulary contains several terms that describe the role of the prophet. The terms *ro`eh* and *hozeh* (meaning "seer" or "visionary") were popular designations for nonwriting prophets. Often the prophet declared messages that came through visions and dreams. The classical prophets of Israel were known by the title *nabi* (a spokesperson for God). The Greek equivalent of *nabi* is *prophētēs* (which means "one who speaks for another"), the source of the English term *prophet*. Prophets were individuals called and commissioned by God, and their primary vocation was to faithfully proclaim God's word to a contemporary audience.

Prophets Were God-Called Individuals

Israel's prophets were recipients of a special call from God to undertake a special mission for

Him. Amos, Isaiah, Jeremiah, and Ezekiel give us the record of their call and commission (Amos 7:10-15; Isaiah 6:1-13; Jeremiah 1:4-10; Ezekiel 1:1—3:15). The call compelled them to deliver messages that were often contrary to what their audience wanted to hear. As God-called individuals they were not attached to any religious or political institution. God's call did not mean an immediate recognition of these individuals as prophets by their nation. It is likely that most of the prophets of Israel became recognized as true prophets only after their prophecies came true at a later time.

Prophets Were Mission-Driven Individuals

The prophets were passionately concerned about Israel's election, destiny, and mission to the world. The goal of their preaching was to remind the nation of its identity and relation to God. This goal is evident in the following three important aspects of the prophetic message.

First, the message of the prophets was grounded in the historical and theological traditions of Israel. Prophetic books make references to the mighty acts of God such as God's call and covenant with Abraham, the Exodus, the Sinai covenant, the wilderness journey, the conquest of Canaan, and God's covenant with David. The prophets sought to help the people of Israel to reclaim their great theological heritage.

Second, Israel's relationship to God was of utmost concern to the prophets. They called the nation to show forth devotion to God through obedience, repentance, and life-transforming worship.

Israel's prophets strongly condemned the worship of idols, such as this Canaanite calf.

Third, the prophets challenged the people to respond to their moral, ethical, and social obligations to others. They appealed to their nation to live a life of covenant loyalty by demonstrating care and concern for the widow, the orphan, and the alien in the land.

Prophets Were Preachers and Foretellers of the Word

Prophets often introduced their message as a "word" *(dabar)* from God. We may call this "word" an **oracle** from God. Often the "word" dealt with contemporary moral, social, or religious conditions, and conveyed the message that God was concerned about the way His people lived their everyday lives. This focus on the present realities of life through preaching or **forthtelling** was an important part of the prophetic ministry. Prophets preached about Israel's sins and called the nation to repent and restore her relationship with God.

Though the preaching of an immediate message was a main feature, prediction **(foretelling)** was also an important component of the prophetic message. Prediction in the Old Testament is an announcement about the future. In the prophetic thinking, Israel's present way of life shaped the nation's future. The prophets reiterated the Deuteronomic theology that God would send His blessings as the reward for faithfulness and curses for breaking the covenant (see Deuteronomy 28). Salvation and judgment are thus integral parts of prophetic predictions.

The Prophets and the End-Time Statements

The end-time (in Greek, *eschaton*) oracles in the prophets deal with God's actions in the future of Israel and the nations in the world. (**Eschatology** is the study of the end-time events). They described the future as "days that are coming" or "that day."

For the most part, Israel's prophets thought of the end time in terms of God's establishment of His righteous kingdom on earth. They preached that God would bring judgment upon Israel's sins. The result would be the loss of political and religious freedom, destruction, and Israel's exile to foreign lands. However, the Exile would not be forever. God would bring His people back to their land. He would place an

Old Testament prophets more often spoke about present conditions than about future events.

Micah proclaims God's judgment on a corrupt society and oppressive leaders.

tology originated among the faithful people who saw God's own sudden coming to destroy evil as the hope of their salvation from political and religious oppressors. The Book of Daniel is the most fully developed apocalyptic work in the Old Testament.

Prophets Used a Variety of Literary Forms to Communicate God's Word

ideal ruler from the Davidic family *(mashiach)* on the throne of David. There would be justice, righteousness, and peace throughout the land. The land would become fruitful and prosperous. God would also reestablish His covenant with Israel. This perspective focuses on the total earthly transformation as the goal of God's judgment. We may call this end-time teaching **prophetic eschatology.** This perspective is the dominant view of the end time in the books of the prophets.

However, in some prophetic books we also find traces of **apocalyptic eschatology,**[2] a different perspective about the end time. The end-time events in this mode of thinking include universal judgment, annihilation of the wicked, and the ultimate destruction of evil. The outcome will be the establishment of a heavenly kingdom (a new heaven and a new earth) for God's faithful people. Isaiah 24—27, Ezekiel 38—39, and Zechariah 9—14 contain some elements of this mode of thinking about the end time. It is very likely that apocalyptic escha-

Israel's prophets often used various literary forms **(genres)** to convey the content of revelation they received from God.[3] The most common genre of prophetic speech is the **messenger-style speech.** In the messenger-style speech, the prophet speaks God's word with the introductory formula "Thus says the Lord." Messenger-style speeches contain messages of judgment and warning or messages of salvation. A primary purpose of judgment speeches was to draw the audience to repentance and reconciliation with God. Messages of salvation brought hope and comfort to those under judgment.

In addition to the messenger-style speeches, prophets utilized a variety of other literary forms. Narratives or accounts of events contain historical or biographical or autobiographical details (Isaiah 36—39; Jeremiah 32—44; Hosea 1:2-9; 3:1-5). Some texts show dialogue between God and the prophet as a literary form (Jeremiah 15:15-21). **Vision accounts** deal with the message received through visions (Jeremiah 1:11-19; Amos 7:1-9; 8:1-3; 9:1). **Symbolic actions** are actions carried out in a symbolic way by a prophet to demonstrate the seriousness of the message being conveyed (Isaiah 20:1-5; Jeremiah 13:1-7; 19:1-13). **Woe oracles** contain words of utter destruction and ruin (Isaiah 5:8-23). Through **legal disputes,** the prophets aimed to show that God's people were on trial for breaking their covenant with God (Micah 6:1-16). Wisdom sayings contain proverbial statements and instructions for proper conduct in society (Amos 3:3-8; Jeremiah 17:5-8). **Funeral songs** are eulogies given in advance and in anticipation of impending destruction and death of a society (Amos 5:2). **Parables** serve to communicate the message in a story form in which the listeners also play a part as characters in the story (Isaiah 5:1-7; Ezekiel 15—16). **Riddles** keep the message hidden but challenge the audience to reflect on the meaning of the riddle (Ezekiel 17:1-10).

The Making of a Prophetic Book

How did the oracles of a prophet become a book? Who gave the prophetic books their present shape? We now turn to these and other related issues on the making of the prophetic books.

We begin with the generally accepted understanding that the prophetic books are collections of oracles that the prophets gave at various times during their ministry. That means, at a later time, either the prophet or someone else collected these oracles and committed them to writing. We find very few illustrations of writing activity in the prophetic books. A notable exception is the account of Baruch the scribe writing on a scroll the oracles Jeremiah dictat-

ed to him (Jeremiah 36:1-32). It is also likely that those who followed the ministry and teaching of the prophets (we call them "disciples"; see Isaiah 8:16) would have initiated the writing of the words of the prophets for future generations.

Modern scholars think that most prophetic books contain extensive revisions and additions by later **redactors** (editors). They conclude that each successive generation modified and even expanded the earlier message of the prophets to meet the theological issues and challenges of later times. They view the prophetic books as theological documents that were shaped and reshaped over a long period of time in Israel's history. Redaction criticism

I Prophecy—Principles of Interpretation

- Prophetic words originated in particular historical settings. We should pay careful attention to the political, social, cultural, and religious setting of the prophetic word.
- The message of the prophets has often been the focus of various New Testament writers. Therefore, we should seek to understand how New Testament writers appropriated, understood, and interpreted the prophetic words to the Early Church community.
- Relating the prophetic texts that deal with the Davidic messiah to Jesus should be done with proper understanding of what those texts meant to the original audience.
- We should assess of the fulfilled and unfulfilled predictions in light of the New Testament story and faith.
- We need to recognize the element of difficulty in deciphering figurative language and mysterious names and numbers related to the end-time events. When dealing with these elements, we should attempt to evaluate the overall message of the text.

seeks to isolate later additions and expansions by the redactors of a particular book. Though we recognize the possibility of later editorial expansions, we also think it is important to consider the present canonical shape of the books of the prophets. Our attempt in the following chapters is to focus on the final canonical form of the prophetic books.

Summary Statements

- Prophecy in Israel was distinctly different from prophecy among Israel's pagan neighbors.
- The classical prophets belonged to a period between 800 B.C. and 450 B.C.
- The prophets were committed to the shaping of their nation to be God's people with a mission to the world.
- The prophets were both forthtellers and foretellers.
- The prophets spoke about the earthly transformation of God's people under the rule of a Davidic king as well as the sudden destruction of the earth and all evil.
- Prophets utilized various literary forms to communicate God's word.
- Prophetic books are composed of individual oracles that often do not follow any logical or chronological arrangement.

Questions for Reflection

1. Read the story of Elijah in 1 Kings 17:1—18:46 and the message of Amos in 5:1-27. Compare and contrast the ministry of these two prophets of Israel.
2. Why is it important to have a correct understanding of the eschatology that we find in the books of the prophets?
3. What lessons do we learn about "prophetic" ministry today based on the discussion of the mission of the prophets of Israel?
4. Make assessment of the literary skill of the prophets as both speakers and writers of God's word.
5. What presuppositions do we need to have to understand the end-time statements of the prophets?

Resources for Further Study

Beegle, Dewey M. *Prophecy and Prediction*. Ann Arbor, Mich.: Pryor Pettengill, 1978.
Lindblom, J. *Prophecy in Ancient Israel*. Philadelphia: Fortress Press, 1973.
Scott, R. B. Y. *The Relevance of the Prophets*. New York: McMillan Publishing Company, 1973.

26 Isaiah

Objectives:

Your study of this chapter should help you to:

- Describe the various parts and content of the Book of Isaiah.
- Describe the setting of the various parts of the Book of Isaiah.
- Discuss the major themes of the Book of Isaiah.
- Identify specific themes in Isaiah that have particular importance to the teachings of the New Testament.

Questions to consider as you read:

1. What is your perception of God?
2. What is worship all about? What is the most important ingredient of worship?
3. What is the relation of spirituality to social concerns?

Key Words to Understand

Isaiah
Uzziah
Tiglath-pileser III
Pekah
Jotham
Ahaz
Hezekiah
Second Isaiah
Third Isaiah
The daughter of Zion
Zion
The day of the LORD
The remnant
Zion theology
Shear-Jashub
Holiness of God
Immanuel
Immanuel oracle
The Spirit of the Lord
Davidic king
Isaiah's apocalypse
Servant of the LORD
Bel-Marduk
Nebo
Identity of the Servant
New heaven and new earth

Isaiah's Personal Background

The Book of Isaiah is undoubtedly the greatest prophetic book in the Old Testament. Both Judaism and Christianity regard this book as a highly significant theological work. The New Testament quotes this book more than any other Old Testament book.

The opening statement of the book labels the content of the book as the visions of **Isaiah** ben Amoz, of whom the book gives few details. The name *Isaiah* means "the LORD is salvation." Some scholars think that his family belonged to Jerusalem's aristocracy. The book tells us that he was married and had two sons (7:3; 8:3). He gave his sons symbolic names that conveyed God's message to Judah.

According to chapter 6, Isaiah received the call to be a prophet in the year of king **Uzziah's** death (742 B.C.). The opening statement of the book (1:1) indicates that he was a prophet during the reigns of Uzziah, Jotham, Ahaz, and Hezekiah, who were all kings of Judah. Scholars think that his ministry lasted until 690 B.C.

Setting

God called Isaiah to be a prophet during a critical time in the history of the Southern Kingdom (Judah). Both Israel and Judah existed under the threat of the Assyrian empire-building program initiated by **Tiglath-pileser III** (745-727 B.C.). Israel's king **Pekah** joined Syria and formed a coalition army to fight against Assyria. Judah maintained a neutral policy, and that prompted the Syrian-Israelite army to attack Jerusalem. Meanwhile Judah's king **Jotham** died, and his son **Ahaz** (735-715 B.C.) was left with the responsibility of dealing with the crisis. Ahaz also had military pressure from the Edomites who recaptured the town of Elath (see 2 Kings 16:5-9). Chapters 7—8 describe Isaiah's involvement during this national crisis.

Isaiah challenged Ahaz to trust God and not be afraid of his enemies (7:3-17). Ahaz's lack of faith, however, prompted him to seek help from Assyria. The Assyrian army invaded Syria and Israel, which eventually led to the destruction of Israel in 721 B.C. (2 Kings 16:5—17:6).

Isaiah also gave sound political counsel to Judah's next king, **Hezekiah** (715—687 B.C.). Isaiah was opposed to Hezekiah's attempt to make political alliances with neighboring nations (chaps. 20, 30). The Assyrian invasion of Judah in 701 B.C. is the setting of chapters 36—37. The prophet chastised Hezekiah for welcoming Merodach-Baladan's envoys from Babylon (perhaps around 703 B.C.). Isaiah said that Babylon would eventually carry off Judah's wealth and her people in to exile (chap. 39). In 587 B.C., Babylon destroyed Jerusalem and took Judah into captivity.

Oracles in chapters 40—66 focus on God's redemption and the return of the exiled Judah from Babylon. Judgment, which is a dominant theme in chapters 1—39, is completely lacking in chapters 40—66. This section depicts the land of Judah and Jerusalem as destroyed and uninhabited. Oracles in chapters 40—66 also anticipate the rebuilding and repopulation of Jerusalem/Zion. These oracles, therefore, reflect a later historical situation.

Scholarly opinion on the setting of chapters 40—66 is not unanimous. Scholars who prefer to see chapters 40—66 as the work of a prophet during the Babylonian exile label this section as **Second Isaiah**. There are still others who limit the Second Isaiah section to chapters 40—55 and view chapters 56—66 as the work of a postexilic prophet **(Third Isaiah).** They place chapters 56—66 in the religious and social context of the last quarter of the sixth century B.C. There is no unanimous opinion on this issue among conservative evangelical scholars. Some prefer the multiple authorship view. Others view the entire book as the work of Isaiah of the eighth century B.C.

Content

Although the materials in the Book of Isaiah may belong to two or perhaps three different historical settings, the book in its present canonical shape is the focus of our study, and for that reason we shall treat the book in its entirety in this chapter. As we have mentioned earlier, the judgment theme dominates chapters 1—39.[1] The assurance of salvation and the restoration of Zion unify the various oracles in chapters 40—66.[2]

We group the various oracles of Isaiah under the following themes:

1. Rebellion and Judgment (1:1—39:8)
2. Redemption from Babylon (40:1—55:13)
3. Universal Salvation (56:1—66:24)

■ Rebellion and Judgment (1:1—39:8)

Judah's Rebellion (1:1—5:30)

Isaiah's book begins with a description of rebellion against God by His covenant people (1:2-9). God's judgment resulted in the destruction of virtually all the cities of Judah, except Jerusalem **(the daughter of Zion).** The prophet

announced God's willingness to be reconciled with His people and remove the deep stains of their sins if they would repent and live a transformed life (vv. 10-20). Those who continued to live as God's enemies were destined for total destruction (vv. 21-31).

Isaiah proclaimed that God will redeem **Zion** and out of Zion will go forth God's Law (Torah) to all the nations (1:27; 2:1-5). This eschatological hymn is followed by several oracles on **the day of the LORD**—a day of terror, destruction, and end to all who are proud and arrogant (2:6—4:1). Through a parable, the prophet portrayed Judah and Israel as unworthy to be kept as God's vineyard. God's

Isaiah said, "The ox knows his master, the donkey his owner's manger, but Israel does not know, my people do not understand" (1:3).

T

God's Grace in the Midst of Judgment

God's grace in the midst of judgment is the hope of our salvation. God's desire is that we should live our lives free from the power of sin. Performance of religious rituals can neither save nor cleanse us from our sinfulness. When we repent, we receive not only reconciliation but also cleansing from the guilt of our sins.

Isaiah described Israel as God's vineyard.

people who were to promote justice and righteousness were guilty of bloodshed, violence, greed, self-indulgence, materialism, perverted moral thinking, pride, and bribery (5:1-31). We find in the middle of these judgment speeches another oracle about Zion (4:2-6) as the refuge for those who have survived the purifying judgment of God **(the remnant).**

Isaiah's Call (6:1-13)

Isaiah saw God as the King above the kings and kingdoms of this world, in the year of Uzziah's death (742 B.C.). God was seated in His heavenly throne room surrounded by the seraphs, His heavenly guardians and messengers. The seraphs' song of God's holiness conveyed the truth about God's absolute purity and glory. This vision prompted Isaiah to confess his sinfulness and his unworthiness to stand before the holy and awesome God. Through a symbolic act, God granted pardon

H Zion Theology in Isaiah

Zion (Jerusalem) was the concrete reality of God's presence among His people. Isaiah calls Zion "the mountain of the LORD" (2:3) and "the City of the LORD" (60:14). Scholars think that Isaiah developed a **Zion theology** that focuses on the restoration of Jerusalem. New Testament writers described Zion/Jerusalem as "the heavenly Jerusalem" and "the new Jerusalem," the city of God's dwelling with His people forever (Hebrews 12:22; Revelation 21:2).

T Holiness of God

The **holiness of God** is a dominant theme in Isaiah. God is "the Holy One of Israel," a description found in the book about 26 times. Holiness is the very essence of God. Holiness means separation from sin and includes the idea of God's judgment of sin. The holiness of God is also the hope of humanity. Isaiah's experience of forgiveness and cleansing from his sinfulness can be our experience also. The holy God calls us to "wash and make [ourselves] clean" from sin (1:16).

T Remnant

Isaiah often spoke about God preserving a remnant. In some texts, the remnant refers to those who are left in Jerusalem, whose names are recorded for life (4:2-6). Other passages describe the remnant as a penitent group that God would bring back to Jerusalem from their exile. The prophet gave his son the name **Shear-Jashub** ("a remnant shall return") to convey this message (7:3; 10:20-23; 11:11 ff.; 27:12-13).

and cleansing to Isaiah. He heard God's call for someone to be His messenger and responded without hesitation. God warned Isaiah that though Judah would not respond to the message, he must continue to preach until the judgment comes. After the judgment, God would raise up a holy seed—a faithful community of people.

Judah, Israel, and Assyria (7:1–12:6)

Chapters 7—12 probably belong to the early part of King Ahaz's reign. Ahaz was panic-stricken because of the Syrian-Israelite army in Jerusalem (7:1-2). Isaiah, accompanied by his son Shear-Jashub, met with Ahaz and assured him that the plan of the enemy would fail. Establishment of his kingship depended on his faith in God's word (vv. 3-9).

Though God was willing to give a sign to Ahaz to confirm His word, the king piously refused. Isaiah offered the sign that a "young woman" will give birth to a son to be called **Immanuel** (meaning "God with us"). To Ahaz and to Judah, the child was to be a symbol of God's presence with His people even in the midst of their lack of trust in Him. Before the child reached the age of conscious decision making, Assyria would devastate the lands of Syria and Israel. Judah would go through painful and tragic days (7:10—8:8).

The prophet maintained firm trust and hope in the God whom the people rejected. Though the nation dwelt in spiritual darkness and political bondage, he anticipated the arrival of light, joy, and the end of warfare through "a child" who would be God's gift to His people (8:9—9:7). The child

The Immanuel Oracle

The **Immanuel oracle** has significance to both the Old and the New Testaments. The identity of the "young woman" (in Hebrew, *almah*; in the Septuagint, *parthenos*, meaning "virgin") in Isaiah 7:14 is not known. Some scholars think that she was Ahaz's wife. Others think that Isaiah was speaking about his own wife. The Gospel writer Matthew related this oracle to the manner in which Jesus was born of a virgin (Matthew 1:23).

Messianic Rule

The coming messiah and his messianic rule is the theme of 9:2-7 and 11:1-9. The prophet anticipated that the ideal Davidic ruler would truly represent God for His people. As Israel's history shows, human rulers from David's family failed to realize this hope. From our Christian perspective, the full scope of this text is to be found in the kingship of Jesus the Son of David and the Son of God.

would be called "Wonderful Counselor," "Mighty God," "Everlasting Father," and "Prince of Peace." God would establish His peaceful kingdom, an eternal kingdom marked by the qualities of justice and righteousness.

Israel's destruction by the hand of the Assyrians is the theme of 9:8—10:4. There are four oracles in this section, each of which ends with the same words about God's anger (see the final part of verses 9:12, 17, 21; 10:4). The prophet described Assyria as the instrument of God's judgment against both Israel and Judah (10:5-11). God would also bring judgment upon Assyria and remove the Assyrian burden from His people (vv. 12-27). Chapter 10 ends with the description of the enemy's march against Israel and Judah.

There are two major sections to

The Spirit of the Lord

Isaiah understood the **Spirit of the Lord** as the active agency in the messianic kingdom. The primary ministry of the Spirit is to bring wholeness and well-being (in Hebrew, *shalom*) to our broken lives. The symbolic description of the wolf living with the lamb (11:6-9) conveys the idea of a peaceful order of life in the messianic kingdom. Graceful and grace-filled life will be the characteristic of this kingdom. Only the Spirit of the Lord can bring about this radical transformation to our sinful and self-centered lives.

chapter 11. The first part (vv. 1-9) describes the **Davidic king** ("a shoot from the stump of Jesse" [v. 1]) as a Spirit-filled ruler who shall rule with righteousness. The messianic kingdom will be a peaceful and transformed kingdom. The second part (vv. 10-16) reiterates the theme of the return of the remnant to live under the messianic rule. This is followed by a song of thanksgiving in anticipation of the coming salvation (12:1-6). The source of joy for us is God who is our salvation, and for that we must be grateful.

Universal Judgment and Universal Salvation (13:1—27:13)

Isaiah's oracles against the nations focus on judgment upon Babylon, Assyria, Philistia, Moab, Syria, Egypt, and Edom (13:1—23:18). This theme of God's judgment of the world is continued in what is known as **Isaiah's apocalypse** (24:1—27:13). The prophet anticipated a worldwide catastrophe that will affect all humanity. God will bring an end to all evil and defeat His enemy. God's people will be free from death and suffering. God will plant the remnant

gathered from the four corners of the world as His new vineyard.

Six Woe Oracles (28:1—33:24)

The prophet delivers in these chapters six woe oracles—pronouncements of doom and destruction—addressed to Ephraim/Israel (28:1), Ariel/Jerusalem (29:1), those who hide God's counsel (v. 15), those who make political alliances (30:1; 31:1), and treacherous destroyers (33:1). Mixed with these woe oracles are also words about God's intent to lay in Zion a cornerstone aligned with justice and righteousness (28:16-17) and a king who will rule with righteousness and justice (32:1). God will also pour out His Spirit upon His people, and the land will experience justice, righteousness, peace, quietness, and trust in God forever (32:15-20). God's people will see their "king in his beauty" and Zion will be a peaceful and quiet place of dwelling for God's people (33:17-22).

Zion's Deliverance (34:1—39:8)

Judgment on the nations and the return of Judah to Zion dominate the content of chapters 34 and 35. The language of chapter 35 has many parallels to several passages in chapters 40—55. Both sections (35 and 40—55) point to the return of the captives from Babylon to Zion. The materials found between these two sections (chaps. 36—39) narrate the sequence of events that culminated in the prophetic word about the exile of Judah to Babylon.

Assyria laid a siege around Jerusalem during the reign of Hezekiah (around 701 B.C.), and Sennacherib, the Assyrian emperor, demanded that Hezekiah surrender to his army (36:1-22). In response to Hezekiah's prayer, God sent Isaiah with the word of Jerusalem's deliverance and the destruction of the Assyrian army (37:1-38). God's intervention in the life of Hezekiah during his near-death illness is the story of chapter 38. Chapter 39 deals with the royal reception Hezekiah gave to the envoys from Babylon, and Isaiah's repudiation of the king's unwise alliance with Babylon. The prophet warned that Babylon would carry away Judah and her wealth to Babylon.

Now we turn to the second part of the book, which deals with the impending deliverance of Judah from Babylon and her return to Zion (chaps. 40—66).

■ Redemption from Babylon (40:1−55:13)

God the Comforter Is Coming (40:1-31)

With a profound sense of urgency and deep conviction in the redemptive power of God, the prophet told the exiled Jews that God would lead them on a highway back to their homeland. The God who is coming like a gentle shepherd to gather His flock is none other than the Creator who is incomparable in power and majesty. He is the source of strength to the weary and the weak. Though weakened by the hardship of the Exile, the people of God who wait for Him will receive strength for their journey home.

God Shapes and Controls History (41:1-29)

Using a legal dispute genre, the prophet announced that idols of the nations have no power to shape and control history. Historical events of the day (the rise of the Persian Empire and the im-

The Dead Sea Scrolls of the Book of Isaiah.

pending doom of Babylon in the second half of the sixth century B.C.) were the work of the Lord, who is "the first" and "the last" (41:4). The purpose of the Lord is the redemption of His people.

The Servant Individual and the Servant Nation (42:1-25)

Isaiah's book portrays two ser-

God the Creator and the Redeemer

The announcement of the coming of God the Redeemer is good news for humanity. The goal of redemption is to bring comfort to those who are bound to the slavery of sin. Comfort comes through freedom from judgment. Salvation of sinners is the gracious will of God. He has the power to save because He is the Creator of the universe. The prophet connects redemption with creation in chapters 40—45. No other gods have the power to create or redeem us. The creative power of God is at work when we receive His salvation. "So if anyone is in Christ, there is a new creation" (2 Corinthians 5:17, NRSV). This is the heart of the message of the Bible.

vant figures in chapter 42. The first one is that of an individual God has called and endowed with His Spirit to bring forth justice to all the earth (vv. 1-4). This is the first of four poems in Isaiah that deal with the mission and ministry of the **Servant of the LORD.** The mission of the Servant is to be "a light to the nations" (v. 6, NRSV), to give sight to the blind and freedom to those in bondage (v. 7). In the second part of this chapter, the servant is Israel, a blind and deaf nation that refuses to understand God's word and His work among them (vv. 18-25). The Gospel writer Matthew related the first servant figure to the person of Jesus (see 12:18-21). The second figure applies to Israel in exile because of her rejection of God.

The Lord, the Gracious Redeemer (43:1—45:25)

God promised the salvation of His servant nation Israel, whom He has created to be His witnesses in the world. His presence would make it possible for them to go through even the worst trials of life. Isaiah announced God's forgiveness to His people who sinned against Him. His desire for Israel was that she would acknowledge God as the only Savior. One of the spiritual blessings of God's redemption is the gift of His Spirit (43:3), which would bring life and vitality to the redeemed people of God.

The prophet announced that the Persian king Cyrus would be God's "shepherd" and "anointed" and would free Judah from Babylon (44:28; 45:1, 13). Nations that serve idols would come to acknowledge God as the Creator and the only God who can save humanity. Isaiah also spoke about God as a God of life and not of chaos. His will for His people was their freedom from chaos, brought upon them by the idols they served.

Babylon's Fall (46:1—47:15)

Babylon's judgment is the theme of these two chapters. Judgment would begin with the humiliation of the principal deities of Babylon, **Bel-Marduk** and **Nebo.** The nation that depended on idols, magic, sorcery, and stargazing would be faced with sudden destruction.

Flee from Babylon (48:1-22)

Isaiah described Israel's salvation from Babylon as one of the "new things" (v. 6) that God would create for His people. The judgment of the Exile was God's refining fire to purify His people. Obedience to God's instructions would result in peace that flows like a river. The prophet challenged Israel to flee from Babylon—the world of sin and idolatry—and proclaim their redemption to the whole world.

The Servant: A Light to the Nations (49:1-26)

The second Servant poem (vv. 1-6) describes the call of the Servant even before His birth. The mission of the Servant was twofold: to bring Israel back to God and to be a light to the nations. God will lead and guide those who dwell in darkness and will bring comfort to the afflicted. God promised that He would never forsake or forget Zion.

The Servant: God's Obedient Disciple (50:1-11)

God's judgment came upon Israel because of her sins and lack of trust (vv. 1-3). Obedience to God is necessary to maintain a proper relationship with God. In the third Servant poem (vv. 4-9), the Servant is the model of trust and obedience to those who remain in darkness (see v. 10). His ministry is to speak words that will comfort the weary and afflicted. He is obedient to God's teaching though he is the object of opposition and attack by his enemies.

The Coming Deliverance (51:1—52:12)

God promised that He would be faithful to His calling of Abraham, Israel's ancestor. The true author of comfort and deliverance is God, who promises salvation to all who listen to His instructions. The result of this salvation from God is "everlasting joy" (51:11).

The Suffering Servant (52:13—53:12)

In the fourth Servant poem, the focus is on the redemption that would come through the suffering of the Servant. The prophet portrayed the Servant as despised and rejected and wounded for the sins of humanity. Though He was innocent, He voluntarily submitted to suffering. However, His suffering fulfilled God's plan to bring healing and wholeness to sinners. The Servant, through His obedience to God, opened the way for sinners to be counted as righteous by God. The Servant's ministry included intercession for the transgressions of humanity.

God Extends His Grace to the Exiled Nation (54:1—55:13)

The prophet compared Israel in exile to a barren woman, a woman forsaken by her husband. Though God was angry with His people, He promised to love them with His everlasting love and maintain His "covenant of peace" with them

The Identity of the Servant

There are various views about the **identity of the Servant** in Isaiah's Servant poems. The eunuch's question to Philip the evangelist reflects the Jewish uncertainty over this matter in the first century A.D. (see Acts 8:26-40). Some scholars see the nation Israel as the servant. In their thinking, Isaiah was speaking of the sufferings of the Jews in their long history as part of God's redemptive plan for the whole of humanity. Some even think of the holocaust in terms of its redemptive purpose. Others think that the prophet was speaking about himself. A third view popular among evangelical Christians is that the prophet was speaking about the suffering of the future Messiah—events that were fulfilled in the life of Jesus of Nazareth. Philip found in the story of the Servant "the good news about Jesus" (Acts 8:35). The Church proclaims Jesus the crucified as God's Suffering Servant through whom He demonstrates His suffering love for humanity.

(54:10). Moreover, His salvation is free to all who seek it (55:1). The good news in Isaiah 55:1 is that God does not attach a price tag to our salvation. Those who seek the Lord with repentance will find Him. God will fulfill His word and lead His exiled people in joy and peace to their homeland.

■ Universal Salvation (56:1—66:24)

There is no unifying theme to the oracles in Isaiah 56—66. These chapters focus on worship and rituals, issues of justice and righteousness, restoration and rebuilding of Zion, God's kingdom, and the universality of salvation. Some scholars see here the work of several prophetic voices.[3] However, salvation to all who are righteous—both Jews and Gentiles—seems to be a connecting link in these chapters.

A Jewish worshiper prays at the Western or Wailing Wall in Jerusalem.

to please God (58:1-5). The prophet announced that rituals do not please God. He blesses those who promote justice and righteousness and who are contrite and humble in their hearts (56:1-3; 57:15; 58:6-7). God's house is a "house of prayer for all nations," even those who were once barred by the law (56:4-8). The mark of true religion is not false piety or one's racial purity but a commitment to bring wholeness to the society. However, along with social concerns, the community of faith must honor God by their careful observance of the Sabbath (58:13-14).

Is God Indifferent to His People's Cry? (59:1-21)

The prophet responded to those who thought that God did not care about the plight of His people. What separated God from His people and their cry for help was their sin (vv. 1-8). The prophet, rather than preaching, confessed the sinfulness of the nation (vv. 10-15). He assured those who were willing to turn away from their sins that God would come as their Redeemer and that His Spirit and His word would be with them forever (vv. 16-21).

God the Everlasting Light (60:1-22)

The prophet announces the lifting of darkness and the arrival of God as the "everlasting light" (v. 20). Israel shall become the light to the nations. Zion, "the City of the LORD" (v. 14), will be ruled by peace and righteousness. The walls of the city will be called "Salvation" and her gates "Praise" (v. 18). God will accomplish His plan in the time appointed for it to become a reality.

Proper Worship (56:1—58:14)

The postexilic community most likely included people who were sinful, oppressive, and sectarian in their thinking (56:9-12; 57:1-21). They were, however, very religious and performed rituals to try

True Religion

There is an essential relationship between one's life of faith and social consciousness. God's gift to us is His shalom—wholeness and well-being that comes through His redemption. The recipients of the gift of shalom must show gracious and compassionate concern for the oppressed, the hungry, and the homeless in the society. James calls this "religion that is pure and undefiled before God" (1:27, NRSV). Paul admonishes his readers, "Let each of you look not to your own interests, but to the interests of others" (Philippians 2:4, NRSV).

Good News to the Poor and the Afflicted (61:1-11)

This poem announces the mission of the Servant, commissioned by the Spirit of the Lord. The Servant declared total freedom for all who were bound, broken, and oppressed. His ministry was to restore justice and thereby usher in God's sovereign rule on earth. The ruined land would be rebuilt. Those who spent their days in mourning and weeping would rejoice with "everlasting joy." God would clothe them with garments of salvation and righteousness. All nations in the world would see the work of the Lord through His Servant.

Zion Redeemed (62:1-12)

It is possible that the exiles who returned to their homeland were disillusioned because of their continued struggle for existence and the ongoing strife within their community. The prophet spoke about an end to all the past and present conditions. God's relationship with Israel will be like a marriage relationship in which God will rejoice over His bride. His bride will take up a new identity—a new name that characterizes God's passion and love for His people.

A Community Lament (63:1—64:12)

The postexilic community became cynical and skeptical about God's power to restore Zion and their community life. The prophet announced the coming of God the Divine Warrior with victory and salvation to His people. Isaiah 63:7—64:12 is a community lament. The prophet mediated for the people and appealed to God's mercy by recalling His past deeds of compassion. He confessed the

> ## T The Gospel in Isaiah
>
> The ministry of Jesus focused on giving freedom to the oppressed and harassed, sight to the blind, hearing to the deaf, healing to the sick and the demon possessed—bringing wholeness (shalom) to humanity. He saw himself as the fulfillment of Isaiah 61:1-3 (see Luke 4:16-21). Through Christ, God pronounces total forgiveness and freedom—the jubilee year—to our broken world that is in turmoil, bondage, and despair. That's good news to us today.

sins of his people, who were unrighteous through and through. The lament ends with a passionate plea to God the Father and the Potter to restore His city and His people to wholeness.

A New Heaven and a New Earth (65:1-25)

God's plan is to restore for His creation wholeness and well-being characterized by joy, long life, prosperity, and peaceful coexistence. The prophet gave assurance to the true servants of God that they would inherit the land. God will create a **new heaven and new earth**. This world will be not only a restored world but also a transformed world. Prophetic hope expressed here is not just idealism but rather vision of a reality that only God can bring about.

No Substitute for Moral and Spiritual Integrity (66:1-24)

Isaiah said to the postexilic community, which was divided over the Temple rebuilding program, that God required from His people humility and contriteness and not their meaningless sacrifices. God would bless those who trembled at His word, and He would punish His enemies. He would restore joy, comfort, and prosperity to Zion and would bring the scattered Jews to their homeland. God's restoration includes the nations (the Gentiles). Both Jews and Gentiles will worship God in Jerusalem. Isaiah's oracles end with the eternal destiny of the wicked in unquenchable fire.

Jesus' words about the eternal destiny of sinners echo Isaiah's final words (see Mark 9:42-50). When we rebel against God, we are shaping our eternal destiny. Isaiah's book ends with an implicit challenge and invitation to choose life and not death and hell, where "worms" do not die and "fire" burns forever.

Summary Statements

- Various parts of the Book of Isaiah address communities of faith that belonged to different historical settings.
- Judgment is the dominant theme in chapters 1—39.
- Chapters 40—66 focus on the theme of salvation.
- God is a holy God, and He is the Creator and the Redeemer of His people.
- The remnant, Zion, the Davidic Messiah, and the Servant of the Lord are important themes in Isaiah.
- Jesus through His life and ministry fulfilled the mission of the Servant in Isaiah.
- Isaiah challenged the people to practice true spirituality integrated with social concerns.
- God will ultimately vindicate the righteous and bless them with wholeness and well-being.
- The destiny of the wicked is eternal judgment.

Questions for Reflection

1. Discuss practical ways to express trust in God when we are overwhelmed by difficult and complex issues of life.
2. What lessons do we learn from Isaiah's encounter with God's holiness (chap. 6)?
3. Describe Isaiah's portrait of God. Give illustrations.
4. Discuss practical ways to promote wholeness and well-being (shalom) in our society.
5. Describe the Servant in Isaiah and develop a philosophy of the Christian life based on the Servant's model.
6. Discuss the significance of Isaiah's vision of universal salvation to the Church and its mission to the world.

Resources for Further Study

Hanson, Paul D. *Isaiah 40—66: Interpretation.* Louisville, Ky.: John Knox Press, 1995.

Motyer, J. Alec. *The Prophecy of Isaiah: An Introduction and Commentary.* Downers Grove, Ill.: InterVarsity Press, 1993.

Oswalt, John N. *The Book of Isaiah: Chapters 1—39. New International Commentary on the Old Testament.* Grand Rapids: Eerdmans, 1986.

Seitz, Christopher R. *Isaiah 1—39: Interpretation.* Louisville, Ky.: John Knox Press, 1993.

27 Jeremiah and Lamentations

O bjectives:

Your study of this chapter should help you to:

- Summarize the historical setting of Jeremiah's ministry.
- List the key events in the life of Jeremiah.
- Discuss the major theological teachings of the Books of Jeremiah and Lamentations.
- Evaluate the ministry of Jeremiah as a prophet of great courage and hope.
- Identify the new covenant passage and discuss its significance to the message of the New Testament.

Q uestions to consider as you read:

1. Often Jeremiah is referred to as a "weeping prophet." What does this label mean?

2. What do people think of those who proclaim the coming of God's judgment?

3. Why should a faithful preacher today agonize over the message of judgment?

K ey Words to Understand

Anathoth
Abiathar
Josiah
Jehoahaz
Jehoiakim
Jehoiachin
Zedekiah
Deuteronomic editors
Temple Sermon
Valley of Ben Hinnom
"Confessions"
Shalom
Hananiah
"Seventy years"
Book of Consolation
New covenant
Babylonians
Branch
Recabites
Baruch
Ebed-Melech
Nebuchadnezzar
Gedaliah
Ishmael
Tahpanhes
Megilloth
Ninth of Ab
Acrostic

Jeremiah

Jeremiah's Personal Background

Jeremiah (Hebrew meaning, "exalted by the LORD") was the son of Hilkiah, a member of the priesthood that lived in **Anathoth,** a village near Jerusalem. His family may have descended from **Abiathar,** David's high priest who was later dismissed by King Solomon (see 1 Kings 2:26). Jeremiah began his ministry in the 13th year of King **Josiah** (627 B.C.), and he prophesied during the days of Josiah, **Jehoahaz, Jehoiakim, Jehoiachin,** and **Zedekiah.** According to 16:2, God commanded him not to marry and have sons and daughters. He was an eyewitness of the destruction of Jerusalem by the Babylonians in 587 B.C. Soon after that, he was forcefully taken by a group of rebel Jews to Egypt where he spent the remainder of his life.

Setting

Jeremiah's call came at a crucial time in Judah's history and world politics. The weakening of the Assyrian Empire and the emergence of the Neo-Babylonian Empire under Nabopolassar (ruled from 625 to 605 B.C.) meant changes in political conditions in the Fertile Crescent. Judah was under the rule of Josiah, a young king who was making plans to free the nation from Assyrian bondage. Five years after Jeremiah's call, Josiah (640-609 B.C.) began the religious reformation prompted by the discovery of the Book of the Law (2 Kings 22—23; 2 Chronicles 34—35). However, this reform did not produce any lasting change, except a resurgence of nationalism and spiritual pride. The political instability that followed Josiah's death (609 B.C.) serves as the backdrop for much of Jeremiah's ministry. As we saw in chapter 17, Judah's religious and political conditions deteriorated during the days of Jehoiakim, and eventually the nation was destroyed by Babylon. The prophet witnessed the tragedy of Jerusalem's destruction in 587 B.C. by the Babylonian army.

Content

The Book of Jeremiah is not arranged in chronological order. Jeremiah utilized both poetry and prose, frequently switching back and forth from one to the other. There are a number of historical and biographical accounts and prose sermons in the book. Historical accounts parallel the accounts in 2 Kings. Jeremiah's prose sermons reflect the teachings of the Book of Deuteronomy. Some scholars attribute these sermons to the **Deuteronomic editors** of the book.

We give the following outline to the Book of Jeremiah:

1. Oracles of Judgment (1:1—29:32)
2. Oracles of Hope (30:1—33:26)
3. Historical and Biographical Accounts (34:1—45:5)
4. Oracles Against the Nations (46:1—51:64)
5. Historical Appendix (52:1-34)

■ Oracles of Judgment (1:1—29:32)

Jeremiah's Call (1:4-19)

The biographical and historical introduction to the book (vv. 1-3) is followed by the account of Jeremiah's call, which we find in the form of three dialogues between God and Jeremiah. In the first dialogue with Jeremiah, God appointed him to be a prophet to the nations (vv. 4-10). God told

Jeremiah that He had consecrated him to be a prophet before his birth. Jeremiah resisted the call by claiming that he was only a youth. God, however, touched the mouth of Jeremiah and equipped him with His word. He commissioned Jeremiah "to pluck up and to pull down, to destroy and to overthrow" the existing corrupt conditions and "to build and to plant" (v. 10, NRSV) a new moral order in the world (see also 12:14-16; 18:7-9; 24:6; 31:28, 40; 42:10; and 45:4).

In the second (vv. 11-12) and third (vv. 13-19) dialogues, God confirmed Jeremiah's call and authenticated His word. These dialogues took place in the context of two separate visions. The vision of the almond branch conveyed the assurance that God is "watching to see that [His] word is fulfilled" (v. 12). The vision of the boiling pot conveyed God's plan to bring political disaster upon Judah because of the nation's wickedness (v. 16).

Sermons on Sin, Judgment, Love, and Forgiveness (2:1—6:30)

This section contains a collection of Jeremiah's oracles, all connected with the theme of Israel's apostasy and God's response. Most commentators place these oracles in the early part of the prophet's ministry.

Jeremiah announced God's indictment against Israel for forsaking her devotion to God (2:1-37). The nation as a whole followed Baal and abandoned God, who is the source of life. He compared this to someone leaving "the spring of living water" to collect

God showed Jeremiah a branch of almond blossoms to confirm the fulfillment of His word (Jeremiah 1:11).

Jeremiah's Call

Jeremiah's call illustrates the freedom of God's grace to call whomever He wishes to be His spokesperson (1:5). God in His sovereign freedom calls us to be His servants. He seldom counts our personal worth or our religious qualifications. God's word, "Do not say, 'I am only a child'" (v. 7), challenges us to examine our established way of perceiving the call to ministry. Does a person's age or gender prevent God from calling that individual to His ministry?

God, the Fountain of Living Water

Jeremiah brings the charge that God's people have abandoned Him, the Fountain of Living Water, and have followed idols that have no worth (2:13). God alone is the Source of our life and salvation (see Jeremiah 17:13; Psalm 36:9; Isaiah 55:1; John 4:13-14; 7:37). We must always remember this truth about God. Nothing in the world can compete with and be compared with God who has the richest resources to satisfy our deepest spiritual needs. Self-sufficiency and dependency on other gods will lead only to stagnation and frustration.

water in "broken cisterns that cannot hold water" (v. 13).

Jeremiah 3:1—4:4 deals with Judah's adultery, but the central idea is God's willingness to take His adulterous wife back to himself. Jeremiah called Israel to accept God's mercy and love and return to her true husband and thereby to become a source of blessing to the nations.

Judgment is the theme of 4:5—6:30. Jeremiah warned his nation that God was about to carry out His judgment through an enemy, a political nation coming from the "north." The prophet agonized in his heart and soul because he knew that judgment would bring terrible destruction. The whole universe would return to chaos, darkness, death, and ruin because of the sins of God's people. Chapter 6 ends with God's appointment of Jeremiah as a "tester" of Judah. Jeremiah found the nation far beyond the point of redemption. God's people did not respond to His refining methods and they remained corrupt and impure.

Sermons on the Outcome of Judah's Depravity (7:1—10:25)

Jeremiah's **Temple sermon** (most likely preached in 609 B.C.; see 26:1) is an indictment against Judah's worship (7:1—8:3). Judah was confident in God's eternal presence, and the nation thought of the Temple as the sure guarantee of this hope. However, they lived their life by violating the prohibitions of the Ten Commandments. Jeremiah said that God would dwell with His people only if they stopped oppressing the aliens, widows, and orphans. God's worshipers have made the Temple a "den of robbers" (7:11). Therefore it will be destroyed just

True Worship

As other prophets, Jeremiah also emphasized the importance of integrating spirituality with social concerns. True worship is not an occasional event but rather a way of life. A person who is transformed by God's grace should be attentive to the needs of the oppressed and the needy in our world (7:6). "Hunger and thirst for righteousness" is the characteristic of those who integrate spirituality with social concerns (Matthew 5:6; cf. James 1:27).

as God destroyed the Tabernacle at Shiloh.

Judgment was upon Judah because of her stubborn refusal to respond to God's word spoken through Moses and the prophets. Instead, the nation followed other gods through idolatry. When the judgment came, the **Valley of Ben Hinnom** (Topheth), where Judah practiced child sacrifice to please the Assyrian gods, would become the nation's burial ground.

Jeremiah described his audience as an unrepentant and backsliding people who thought they were wise in their own ways (8:4-17). The prophet wept bitterly because of Judah's sin and appealed to the dying nation to seek God, their "physician" and "balm in Gilead" (v. 22; see 8:18—9:3). He compared everyone in the land to "Jacob," the ancestor known for his deceit and falsehood. God's refining judgment is coming upon His deceitful people, the outcome of which will be total devastation of the land. Moreover, this is the des-

tiny of all who are "uncircumcised in heart" (9:26; see 8:4—9:26).

The God of Israel is the true, living, and eternal King and Creator God (10:1-16). Judah's leaders, who failed to seek God's guidance, were responsible for

T ## Repentance

The only prerequisite to salvation is repentance. Repentance is action taken to restore relationship with genuine contriteness and acknowledgement of guilt (3:12, 14, 19, 22; 4:1). Repentance unleashes God's healing power and brings wholeness to sinners who are incurably sick. Repentance cancels the death sentence upon us and prepares us to fully embrace God's grace that comes through Jesus Christ.

the coming Exile and the scattering of the nation (vv. 17-22). The prophet agonized over the impending destruction of Judah and called upon God to be merciful in His judgment (vv. 23-25).

The Covenant with Yahweh Is Broken (11:1—15:21)

Israel has broken the covenant with God; therefore, punishment is certain. This section begins with an announcement of the curses of the covenant upon rebellious Judah (11:1-17).

We find the first in the series of several complaints **("confessions")** of Jeremiah in 11:18—12:6. The people of his hometown planned to kill the prophet, but he committed his life to God. God assured Jeremiah that He would punish his enemies. The prophet complained about the prosperity of the wicked. God challenged Jeremiah to build up strength during his personal struggle, so he could withstand more severe crises later in life.

Jeremiah proclaimed that Judah's rulers were responsible for the desolation of God's vineyard (12:7-17). Judah's humiliation is the theme of chapter 13. Through a symbolic act, Jeremiah announced that Judah was no longer the object of God's pride and delight. The judgment of the Exile would bring humiliation and pain upon Judah's royal family and the city of Jerusalem. Judah's sin has become an inherited condition like the blackness of an Ethiopian's skin or the spots on a leopard. The real remedy for this depravity is healing and cleansing that God offers to the nation (vv. 23-27).

Chapter 14 begins with an announcement about a severe drought. Jeremiah confessed the nation's sins and sought mercy and forgiveness from God. God announced to Jeremiah that neither intercession nor rituals would change His mind. The prophet represented the nation once again and confessed their sins and placed his hope in God who alone can send rain and save the nation from the drought. Chapter 15 continues the theme of intercession (vv. 1-4). God had already appointed His people to destruction. No one, not even Moses and Samuel, would be able to persuade God to change His mind.

Jeremiah 15:10-21 is another "confession" of the prophet. He perceived himself as a failure, becoming despondent and self-righteous. He wondered if he could really trust God, who seemed to be deceptive in His dealings with him. God's response to Jeremiah was a stern challenge to stay on course and remain true to his calling.

Sin, Judgment, and Grace (16:1—17:27)

God commanded Jeremiah not to marry and have the joy of normal family life. This personal experience symbolized the end of all joyous occasions in the land, because God withdrew His **shalom** from His people (16:1-9). However, there would be grace at the end of judgment. God would bring His people to their homeland from the lands of their exile (vv. 10-15).

Jeremiah characterized idolatry as the sign of the powerful influence of sin on the lives of God's people (17:1-4). The prophet pronounced God's curse on those who have forsaken God. He portrayed the righteous as prosperous, like a tree planted by water (vv. 5-8; see Psalm 1). Jeremiah warned the wicked that God, who sees their corrupt and wicked heart, would bring them to judgment (Jeremiah 17:9-13). In verses 14-18 is another "confession" of the prophet with an appeal for protection from those who persecute him. Jeremiah challenged Judah to show faithfulness to God through their commitment to the law of the Sabbath (vv. 19-27).

God's Sovereignty (18:1—20:18)

God sent Jeremiah to the potter's house, where he received a word about the absolute sovereignty of God and His gracious freedom to shape and determine the destiny of the nations (18:1-12). Using the illustration of the potter who reworked the spoiled clay into another vessel, Jeremiah said that God was free to change His plans concerning Judah and the nations. God's chosen people stood under the threat of destruction. The reason for this was their corruption and the rejection of God's plans for them.

Jeremiah described the coming Exile as the consequence of Judah's idolatry and her forgetting of God (vv. 13-17). Chapter 18 ends with another "confession," in which the prophet sought divine judgment against those who schemed to silence him (vv. 19-23; see v. 18).

Jeremiah performed a symbolic act of breaking a flask into pieces to show God's determination to destroy Jerusalem (19:1-13). The place of worship that they have abandoned (Jerusalem) will be destroyed; the place of worship that they have chosen for themselves (the Valley of Ben Hinnom) will become their burial ground.

God the Divine Potter

Jeremiah portrayed God as the divine potter who comes to us with His sovereign freedom of grace. The message at the potter's house shows that our ultimate destiny depends on the way we respond to God. Saying yes to God will lead to the fulfillment of His plans for our lives. Saying no, as Judah did (see v. 12), will only lead to death and destruction. Though God is our Potter, we also play a part in sealing our destiny by our positive or negative response to His will at work in our lives. The good news here is that sinners under God's judgment can hope in His grace and mercy and receive a new lease on life through their repentance.

The religious leaders who thought the Temple was an indestructible place arrested Jeremiah and put him in the stocks (v. 14—20:6).

Jeremiah complained that God had deceived him with His word and that he had become the object of ridicule and laughter (see the "confession" in 20:7-12). He also knew that the fire of God's word would consume him, if he refused to be God's prophet. The next "confession" (vv. 14-18) is very much like Job's cry of despair (Job 3). Life had become unbearable, so Jeremiah cursed the day of his birth.

Ungodly Kings and Other Leaders (21:1—23:40)

This section contains two parts: oracles in the first part are directed against the kings who have ruled Judah in the final days of her history (21:1—23:8). The second part of this section consists

Jeremiah described God as the potter and Israel as the clay (18:1-10).

of Jeremiah's indictment against those who have illegitimately assumed the prophetic role for their own profit (23:9-40).

When King Zedekiah sought God's word during the Babylonian siege of Jerusalem, Jeremiah challenged him and the nation to surrender to Babylon. God's judgment was upon the royal family because it failed to provide justice to aliens, orphans, and widows in the land. Jeremiah also said that God would establish over the nation a "righteous branch" from the house of David, who would initiate a new relationship between God and His people (vv. 1-8). Jeremiah pronounced judgment upon those who have made false prophecies and the priests who have abused their office (vv. 9-40). He charged the false prophets with lack of loyalty to God and with speaking visions and dreams of their own heart.

To Build and to Plant (24:1-10)

The vision of two baskets of figs outlines God's plan for those who were left in the land and those who were exiled from the land. Those who were left in the land had no future. The Exile of 597 B.C. was God's way of preparing a future for Judah. God would restore, build, and plant the exiled community in their homeland. They would also receive from God the gift of an obedient heart and would enter into a new covenant relationship with Him.

God's Wrath on the Wicked (25:1-38)

For 23 years Jeremiah relentlessly preached to Judah, calling the nation to repentance. The nation refused to accept the mes-

senger or his message from God. God's patience was exhausted. He would send Babylon, a pagan nation, to carry out His wrath against Judah. God's wrath was also upon all the ungodly nations and the wicked in the world.

Jeremiah Under Trial (26:1-24)

Chapter 26 describes the consequence of Jeremiah's Temple sermon (see 7:1-15). The people were outraged that the prophet spoke about the destruction of the Temple. They demanded his death. During the trial that followed, some of the royal officials and certain elders spoke in favor of Jeremiah, citing Micah's speech about Zion's destruction nearly a century before. In the end, Jeremiah's life was spared.

Controversy over the Babylonian Yoke (27:1—28:17)

This narrative has two sections: Jeremiah's symbolic act of wearing a wooden yoke to symbolize the coming Babylonian captivity and the subsequent message to King Zedekiah (27:1-22), and his confrontation with **Hananiah,** the false prophet who attempted to discredit Jeremiah's message (28:1-17). Jeremiah put yoke bars on his neck to convey the message to Judah that submission to Babylon meant submission to God's will. Hananiah, a false prophet, took the yoke bars, broke them, and declared that God had broken the yoke of Babylon. Later, God revealed to Jeremiah that Hananiah spoke falsehood and therefore would suffer judgment.

The Letter to the Exiles (29:1-32)

Jeremiah sent a letter to the Judeans who were exiled to Babylon in 597 B.C. In his letter

Jeremiah challenged the exiled community not to give up hope. He described the time of judgment as a time to build and to plant themselves among the heathens. They must pray for the welfare of their captors. God has set a time (**"seventy years"**) for the punishment of the exiles. When that set time is completed, He would return to them. God offered to give them a future, if they would call upon His name and seek Him with all their heart.

■ Oracles of Hope (30:1 — 33:26)

Scholars label chapters 30—33 as the **Book of Consolation** or Book of Hope. Various oracles in this section are connected by the theme of Israel's restoration.

God's offer of comfort will be realized in the future. Jeremiah thus spoke of Israel's restoration as an eschatological (end-time) event. God will restore Israel and the Davidic kingship. The covenant with God will be reestablished. God's love for Israel is everlasting, and He will build up the nation.

The most significant part of the Book of Consolation is Jeremiah's announcement of God's **new covenant** with Israel (31:31-34). The old covenant was broken. However, God's purpose remained the same. He would once again establish himself as Israel's God and Israel as His people. The covenant is new in that the heart will become the depository of God's instruction (Torah). Jeremiah anticipated that the instructions God would place within the heart would direct God's people to know Him in an intimate way. An added dimension of this new covenant is the promise that God

> ### T The New Covenant
>
> God fulfilled His promise of the new covenant through Jesus, His Son. The Lord's Supper reminds the Church of the "blood of the covenant, which is poured out for many" (Mark 14:24; see 1 Corinthians 11:25). The new covenant is a covenant of God's love, grace, and forgiveness. This covenant gives hope to our sinful world.

would forgive and forget the sins of His people.

Jeremiah bought a property from his cousin Hanamel shortly before the fall of Jerusalem to fulfill his obligation to redeem the land (chap. 32). Through this legal transaction, the prophet conveyed the message that normal life would return again to the land. Though God was about to deliver the city to the **Babylonians,** He would bring His people back from their Exile. The theme of restoration is continued in chapter 33. God would restore the Davidic kingship with a just and righteous ruler ("a righteous **Branch**" [v. 15]) and Israel's worship under the Levitical priesthood.

■ Historical and Biographical Accounts (34:1 — 45:5)

A Lesson on Covenant Faithfulness (34:1 — 35:19)

Jeremiah described King Zedekiah and Judah as examples of covenant unfaithfulness (chap. 34). During the time of the Babylonian siege of Jerusalem, the people renewed the covenant with God and let their fellow Jewish slaves go free in obedience to the Law of Moses. However, they turned around and made them slaves again when the danger was over. Jeremiah declared that the nation was under the covenant curses because of such acts of insincerity and unfaithfulness. The next chapter contrasts the hypocrisy of Judah with the loyalty of the **Recabites** (chap. 35). Jeremiah offered wine to the Recabites, but they refused to drink it because their ancestor Jonadab ben Recab had commanded his children not to drink wine. Jeremiah urged Judah to learn from the Recabites a lesson on faithfulness. God's judgment was coming because of the nation's persistent disregard for the Sinai covenant.

Baruch wrote the words of Jeremiah the prophet.

Jehoiakim Burns the Scroll (36:1-32)

Around 605 B.C., Jeremiah's scribe **Baruch** wrote down on a scroll the words Jeremiah dictated to him—the content of his first 22 years of preaching about Judah's sin and the coming judgment. Baruch read the scroll to the people who came to worship in the Temple. He read it again before the royal officials and princes, who urged Baruch and the prophet to go into hiding for their safety. A royal official read the scroll to King Jehoiakim, who cut the scroll, threw it into the fireplace, and ordered the arrest of Baruch and Jeremiah. God protected the prophet and his scribe. Jeremiah dictated his words again to Baruch, who prepared another scroll, to which many other oracles were added later.

Jeremiah in Prison (37:1—38:28)

The Babylonians placed Zedekiah as a puppet king over Judah in 597 B.C. Zedekiah showed no regard for God's word. When Jeremiah was in prison on charges of desertion to the enemy, Zedekiah secretly questioned Jeremiah about God's plan. Jeremiah replied that the king himself would be a prisoner of Babylon. Jeremiah was later thrown into a cistern; but **Ebed-Melech**, an Ethiopian servant of the king, saved the prophet from death. He remained in the royal guardhouse until the Babylonian invasion.

The Fall of Jerusalem and Other Related Events (39:1—44:30)

The account of the fall of Jerusalem to the army of **Nebuchadnezzar** (chap. 39) includes the tragic fate of Zedekiah. The Babylonians put his sons to death and took him to Babylon along with the rest of the nation. The Babylonians offered Jeremiah freedom and safe passage to Babylon; however, he opted to stay in Judah with the poor who were left in the land.

The Babylonians appointed **Gedaliah** as governor over Judah. A few months later, **Ishmael** and his supporters murdered Gedaliah and took several people as hostages. Gedaliah's loyal supporters planned to escape to Egypt, fearing reprisal from Babylon. The prophet strongly advised them to remain in the land. He promised that God would build this remnant community and plant them in the land. However, they forced Jeremiah to go with them to Egypt. This community settled down at **Tahpanhes.** While in Egypt, Jeremiah prophesied the death and destruction of the Jews who escaped to Egypt (43:8—44:30).

A Message to Baruch (45:1-5)

Baruch perhaps expected great things from God for being Jeremiah's faithful scribe and loyal friend. God told Baruch not to expect great things because he was sending evil upon the whole land. God, however, promised to preserve his life during war.

■ Oracles Against the Nations (46:1—51:64)

These chapters contain the prophetic words of judgment against Egypt (46:1-26), Philistia (47:1-7), Moab (48:1-47), Ammon (49:1-6), Edom (vv. 7-22), Damascus (vv. 23-27), Kedar and Hazor (vv. 28-33), Elam (vv. 34-39), and Babylon (50:1—51:64). There is a brief oracle of salvation addressed to Israel in 46:27-28.

Jeremiah focused on God's sovereignty over the nations in his oracles against the nations. God is incomparable, and no nation can challenge His authority. The primary sin of these nations was their idolatry and refusal to acknowledge the God of Israel (50:17-18). Though God used these nations as His instruments of judgment against Israel, they, too, would be judged. However, God's plan of restoration included not only Israel but also the nations that He judged.

■ Historical Appendix (52:1-34)

This chapter summarizes the story of the destruction of Jerusalem and the Exile of Judah (see the parallel account in 2 Kings 24:18—25:30). This concluding chapter presents the tragedy of the destruction of Jerusalem as the outcome of God's anger (Jeremiah 52:3). The chapter ends with a note about Jehoiachin's release from prison by the Babylonian king Evil-Merodach.

Jeremiah's book began with a word of judgment (1:14-16), but at the conclusion we find the anticipation that the exiled nation would be released. The ultimate goal of prophetic preaching is to announce God's grace and the hope of salvation to sinners. In that regard, this last chapter is a fitting conclusion to Jeremiah's book.

Lamentations

We live in a culture that has lost the capacity to cry out and express deep emotional distress over sudden death and destruction. So it is difficult for us to understand the depth of agony, suffering, and the fragmented world portrayed in the Book of Lamentations. Such lament poems were a part of the religious and literary tradition of the ancient world.[1] The Book of Lamentations introduces us to a world that knew how to express grief and how to cope with the reality of pain and suffering when horrifying tragedy occurred.

Authorship and Setting

Lamentations is part of the Writings (Kethubim), the third division of the Hebrew canon. This book, together with Song of Songs, Ruth, Ecclesiastes, and Esther make up the five festival scrolls (Megilloth). Readings from Lamentations are part of the liturgy of the Ninth of Ab, the Jewish remembrance of the Roman destruction of the Jerusalem Temple in A.D. 70.

Ancient versions such as the Septuagint and the Vulgate attributed the authorship of Lamentations to Jeremiah and placed this book after the Book of Jeremiah. The introductory statements of both the Septuagint and the Vulgate cite the fall of Jerusalem and the captivity of Judah as the occasion for the writing of Lamentations. This tradition is followed in the English Bible. Most scholars today regard this book as the work of an anonymous writer who was an eyewitness of the tragedy of 587 B.C.

Content

The book is made up of five carefully crafted and structured poems that utilize a rich and elegant variety of metaphors. Each poem, except the last one, is constructed as an acrostic, using the 22 letters of the Hebrew alphabet. As typical of dirge poems, the thoughts of the author are often mixed, moving from one theme to another and showing discontinuity and fragmentation. However, the acrostic structure of these poems also shows the author's intention to deal with the details of the tragedy carefully and systematically without glossing over pain and suffering.

▆ No Comfort to Jerusalem (1:1-22)

The author lamented the desolation of Jerusalem and recognized the truth that the pagan desecration of the Holy City and the Temple was the direct consequence of the sins and uncleanness of God's people. God had withdrawn His presence, which left Israel with no rest or comfort. The poet invited the nation to admit that God is righteous in all that He does, and to confess their rebellion against Him.

▆ God's Anger (2:1-22)

The author saw the destruction of the Temple and other symbols of God's holiness as the sign of God's anger against His people who were no longer holy to the Lord. Moreover, God withdrew His communication through the Law and the prophetic visions. However, God would have pity for them if they would come into His presence with a broken heart and tears of sorrow.

▆ A Personal Lament (3:1-66)

Like Job, the author complained to God about his suffering. But unlike Job, the writer was convinced that he and his nation were suffering because of their sins. Nonetheless, he maintained hope in God's great love, compassion, and faithfulness. In the midst of suffering, he proclaimed that God is good, and he called his people to wait quietly for their salvation. The true character of God's people is best revealed through their patient waiting upon the Lord (see Romans 5:3-5). The poet challenged the people to confess their sin and to acknowledge their guilt before God so that they would once again experience His unfailing love.

■ The Wages of Sin (4:1-22)

The poet reminded the people that they were paying a terrible price for their sins. During the famine caused by the Babylonian siege, even the mothers lost compassion for their children. The responsibility for this tragedy was on the prophets and priests, who failed to give the nation proper direction and leadership.

■ A Prayer for Mercy (5:1-22)

The poet once again acknowledged sin as the cause of the present misfortune of God's people. The community was under judgment because of the sins of both the present generation and the previous generations. The lament ends with an earnest appeal for the restoration of God's people. The poet was certain that the Eternal King and the Sovereign Lord would not reject or be angry forever with a repentant sinner.

T Theology of Grief

This little book reminds the Christian community of the tragic consequences of breaking covenant with God. Though the suffering of God's people is a major issue in this book, we must place it in its proper context. God's wrath is poured out upon those who have been unfaithful to Him. Though the book offers no clear solution to the problem of suffering in the world, we find here some practical guidelines to encounter both personal and communal suffering.

Grief is not a private matter. The author challenges us to speak openly about our agony and pain and the chaos that surrounds our human existence. This is the courageous way to encounter suffering. We must also take time to examine, reflect, and come to grips with our pain. We must take time to pray, confess, and seek God's forgiveness. In the end, what sustains us in our suffering is the faithfulness and the love of God that surrounds us in the midst of the trials and tribulations in life (3:23, 32; Romans 8:28, 38-39).

Summary Statements

- God called Jeremiah to be a prophet during the final years of Judah's political existence.
- Jeremiah preached the message of judgment with passion and tears.
- Jeremiah appealed to God's people to repent of their sins.
- Jeremiah spoke about the necessity of integrating spirituality with social concerns.
- Jeremiah described the human heart as corrupt and evil.
- Jeremiah described God as a merciful God who would restore His people from their exile.
- Jeremiah anticipated God's new covenant with Israel.
- The author of Lamentations acknowledged sin as the cause of the destruction of Jerusalem and pleaded for God's mercy.

Questions for Reflection

1. In what ways do we tend to forsake God today? What are the areas in our life where this is a crucial issue?
2. Discuss the notion that God is on our side. What are the conditions for this claim to be true?
3. Discuss ways in which one can integrate spirituality with social concerns today.
4. What lessons do we learn from Jeremiah as a preacher filled with passion for God?
5. How do we maintain hope and courage in the midst of despair and hopelessness?

Resources for Further Study

Feinberg, Charles L. *Jeremiah: A Commentary.* Grand Rapids: Zondervan, 1982.
Harrison, R. K. *Jeremiah and Lamentations. Tyndale Old Testament Commentaries.* Downers Grove, Ill.: InterVarsity Press, 1973.
Thompson, J. A. *The Book of Jeremiah. The New International Commentary on the Old Testament.* Grand Rapids: Eerdmans, 1980.

28 Ezekiel

bjectives:

Your study of this chapter should help you to:

- Summarize the historical setting of the ministry of Ezekiel.
- Describe the content of the Book of Ezekiel.
- Describe the key theological teachings of Ezekiel.
- Relate the significance of Ezekiel's message to the New Testament.

 ey Words to Understand

Ezekiel
Buzi
Kebar
Son of man
"Idol of jealousy"
Tammuz
Mount Seir
Gog
Magog

Questions to consider as you read:

1. Describe the feeling of displacement from home, church, and religious traditions that are important to you.

2. What would you say to a person who lives without any hope for the future?

3. What are some of your convictions about the end time?

Ezekiel's Personal Background

Ezekiel's book begins with a brief reference to the prophet's background. The name **Ezekiel** means "God strengthens." His father was **Buzi,** perhaps an influential member of Jerusalem's priesthood. Ezekiel was among the 10,000 Judeans who were taken to exile in Babylon in 597 B.C. by Nebuchadnezzar's army (2 Kings 24:14). He made his home in Babylon near the river **Kebar** at a place called Tel Abib (3:15). He was married and his wife died in 587 B.C. as a sign to the people concerning the fall of Jerusalem (24:15-17).

God's call came to Ezekiel in the fifth year of his captivity (593 B.C.). It is very likely that "the thirtieth year" (1:1) refers to his age, when he would have entered the priesthood. God's call took him from being a priest to being God's spokesperson. From 593 to 587 B.C., he prophesied the impending judgment of God. After the destruction of Jerusalem in 587 B.C., he spoke about God's plan to restore His city and the people. His last dated prophecy comes from around 571 B.C. (29:17).

Ezekiel described very vividly the activities in Jerusalem, while he was in exile in Babylon (8:1-18; 11:1-13). The book relates that he saw these things when the Spirit transported him to Jerusalem from Babylon. Some scholars speculate that Ezekiel had never been to Babylon and that his ministry took place in Judah. There is no compelling reason to adopt this view.

Setting

Ezekiel's ministry took place during the darkest days of Judah's history. Judah continued in her stubborn resistance to God's word even after the exile of the leading citizens in 597 B.C. Those who took over the leadership also were corrupt and wicked. King Zedekiah succumbed to the political pressure to join an alliance with Egypt against Babylon. The leaders gave false hopes to the people of Jerusalem about re-building the city (11:1-15). Idolatrous worship and pagan rituals continued even in the Temple precinct (8:1-18). Ezekiel's initial task was to address the stubborn and rebellious nation and warn them about the impending destruction of the city and the deportation of the people to Babylon (chaps. 1—24).

The fall of Jerusalem in 587 B.C. is the setting of Ezekiel's oracles of restoration in chapters 33—48. The Babylonians devastated the land and deported the nation to Babylon. During the latter part of his ministry, Ezekiel spiritually prepared the nation for God's redemption.

Content

A few scholars have questioned the unity of the Book of Ezekiel. They think there were many additions to the book by later editors. The book in its present form, however, has a balanced structure, uniformity of style and language, and a clear chronological sequence.[1] Except for the opening verses, the book is written in autobiographical style. We regard the entire book as the product of Ezekiel the prophet.

The following is a general outline of the major parts of Ezekiel's book:

1. Ezekiel's Call and Commission (1:1—3:27)
2. Oracles of Judgment Against Judah (4:1—24:27)
3. Oracles Against the Nations (25:1—32:32)
4. Promise of Restoration (33:1—39:29)
5. New Jerusalem (40:1—48:35)

Ezekiel's Call and Commission (1:1 — 3:27)

God's call came to Ezekiel through a supernatural vision. In the vision, Ezekiel saw God seated on His throne on a platform supported by four half human and half animal creatures. Ezekiel also saw four bright and sparkling wheels, one beside each creature. The movement of the creatures and the wheels in any direction was completely under the control of the Spirit. Ezekiel saw God's chariot moving in all directions without being confined to an earthbound route.

Ezekiel could not adequately describe in detail the majestic glory of God, who was seated on His throne. He caught only a glimpse of the radiance and splendor of God. In shock, and in fear and awe, he fell on his face before God's holy presence.

God addressed Ezekiel as "son of man" (2:1) and commissioned him to speak to Judah, a rebellious and stubborn nation. He warned Ezekiel not only about the difficulty of his mission but also of the need to be obedient to the call. God commanded Ezekiel to eat a scroll to symbolically express his obedience to Him. This meant defiling himself with an

Son of Man

God addressed Ezekiel over 90 times as **"son of man."** This term simply refers to Ezekiel as a mortal being, a part of humanity. In Daniel 7:13 and 8:17, this term designates a heavenly figure. In the intertestamental period, this designation became a messianic title. Jesus frequently used this title, perhaps to suggest both His human nature and His messianic role.

unclean object. But God's word was written on the scroll. Ezekiel must consume it, digest it, and assimilate it. Obedience to the strange demand of God was necessary for him to be God's faithful spokesperson. When he obeyed, the Word tasted like honey. Though obeying God's will is not always easy, the outcome of obedience is total satisfaction and fulfillment of life.

God appointed Ezekiel to be a watchman over Israel. His task was to give warning to the wicked and call them to change their lives. He was also to warn the righteous not to sin. Whether or not the people responded to God's word, Ezekiel was to faithfully deliver the message. He would otherwise be held account-

God's Chariot Throne

Ezekiel's vision of God's chariot throne relates the theological perspective that God's presence is not confined to a particular location. The Israelites of Ezekiel's day thought that God remained within the boundaries of His Holy City. So it must have been an unbelievable thing for Ezekiel to experience God in a foreign land, in an unclean place, in the midst of sin and judgment. God is dynamic, and His presence may be experienced regardless of who we are or where we live in the world today. Even though sin separates humanity from God's holy presence, the holy and gracious God visits sinners with the offer of salvation. This is the mystery of God's grace.

God asked Ezekiel to eat a scroll that contained words of judgment (3:1-2).

who lived in Jerusalem. These were: (1) portrayal of the siege of the city with a diagram on a brick; (2) lying like a paralyzed person for a total of 430 days; (3) eating unclean food; and (4) shaving his head and beard.[2] The details of each action showed the severity of God's judgment upon sinners. Jerusalem, the center of the world, had become more corrupt than the pagan nations around her. Punishment of sinners would fulfill God's demand for justice. Both Israel and the nations would recognize that God had carried out His judgment.

able for the death of sinners. God also said to Ezekiel that the people would restrain him with ropes to show their opposition to his preaching. Moreover, God would restrain him from speaking by making him speechless. His period of silence would last for seven and a half years, until the fall of Jerusalem (see 33:21-22). During this period of silence, he would speak only when God opened his mouth to speak His word.

■ Oracles of Judgment Against Judah (4:1 — 24:27)

Symbolic Actions (4:1—5:17)

Ezekiel performed four symbolic actions to convey the fate of those

> ## T Symbolic Actions
>
> Ezekiel, like other prophets, sometimes communicated God's word through strange and unusual actions. By observing Ezekiel's symbolic actions, his audience would have learned that the days ahead would be days of enemy invasion, exile, lack of freedom, destruction, and death. Why did Ezekiel do such unusual and strange things? We think that he submitted even his body to be used by God, and he subjected himself to the reality of judgment in the hopes of saving sinners from their impending destruction.

End to All Abominations (6:1 — 7:27)

God announced His judgment upon the mountains because they represented Judah's idolatry and unholy alliance with the Canaanite religion. Ezekiel said that the

"They Will Know That I Am the LORD"

Ezekiel frequently used the phrase "they will know that I am the LORD" to describe the goal of God's judgment and the coming salvation. To know God means to experience the reality of God in a personal way. The invitation of God's word to us is to know Him as our Savior, and that experience is possible through Christ, who suffered and died for us (see the intense desire of the apostle Paul in Philippians 3:10-11).

few who would escape the judgment would recognize that indeed God had fulfilled His word. Idolatry had infiltrated all levels of society, including the Temple. Judgment would bring an end to all evil and abominable practices of worship in Israel.

The Departure of God's Glory from Jerusalem (8:1—11:25)[3]

The visions in these chapters occurred in 591 B.C. The main message of the visions is the departure of God's glory from Jerusalem because of the abominations and idolatry in the city. The Spirit took Ezekiel to Jerusalem in a supernatural vision, and there he found idolatry in the Temple. He saw an **"idol of jealousy"** in the outer court. Some scholars think it was the idol of Asherah, one of the major female deities of the Canaanite religion. The elders of the people were engaged in animal worship, and the women were involved in the worship of **Tammuz,** the Mesopotamian god of vegetation. In the inner court, 25 men were worshiping the sun.

In the visions Ezekiel heard God commanding executioners to slay those who were idolaters. The slaughter of the guilty began in the sanctuary. Afterward, the city was purified by fire. Once again he saw God's chariot-

throne, the living creatures, and the wheels, as in his initial vision (chap. 1), now ready for its departure from the city. The final part of the vision includes Ezekiel's confrontation of the complacent leaders who had misguided the people. He rebuked them and pronounced God's judgment upon them. While he prophesied in his visions, a leader by the name of Petaliah died in Jerusalem. This would have confirmed the authenticity of Ezekiel's visions.

Ezekiel was alarmed at the finality of God's word of judgment. He appealed to God not to completely destroy His people. God responded with His plan for the future of those who were under judgment. He promised to restore

A New Heart and a New Spirit

The promise of a new heart and a new spirit (see also Ezekiel 18:31; 36:26) is God's remedy for the sickness of sin that plagues humanity today. Our rebellion against God has its root in the sinful condition of our heart. A new heart means the end to our rebellious condition and the beginning of a life in conformity to God's word. A new spirit means an attitude of loving obedience to God (Matthew 22:37; cf. Deuteronomy 6:5). God fulfills this promise now through His Holy Spirit, who makes all things new in Christ (2 Corinthians 5:17).

the exiled people to their land and give them the gift of a new heart and a new spirit. God would remove their heart of rebellion and give them a heart of flesh. He would also reestablish His covenant with Israel.

The visions ended with the departure of the glory of God from the city. The glory of God stood on the mountain east of the city (the Mount of Olives). God's departure made the city vulnerable and defenseless before the invading army of Babylon.

More Symbolic Actions (12:1-28)

As instructed by God, Ezekiel prepared baggage for his exile and dug a hole through the wall of his house and escaped at night. This action conveyed the message that in the same way, Judah would go into exile. Ezekiel announced that King Zedekiah himself would try to escape through the wall of Jerusalem, but he would be brought to Babylon and face death there (see also Jeremiah 39:4-7). In the second symbolic act, Ezekiel ate bread and drank water with fearfulness and shaking to convey the message that the land would suffer terrible violence and destruction.

The people of Judah had been hearing about judgment over a long period of time. Through two popular proverbs, the nation expressed skepticism about God's intent to carry out His threats. Ezekiel responded to this with his own proverbs and warned the people that God would fulfill His word in their own lifetime.

False Prophecy and Idolatry (13:1—14:23)

Both Jeremiah and Ezekiel had to deal with false prophets who preached smooth words of peace and prosperity. The people believed such words and rejected God's true prophets. Ezekiel announced God's judgment upon all the false prophets, magicians, and diviners for their part in encouraging the wicked and disheartening the righteous in the land.

Ezekiel appealed to the idolatrous nation to quit their wickedness and turn to God. He reminded the nation that they cannot presume to be saved because of the righteous in the land. Even if Noah, Daniel, and Job—the three great examples of righteous living in Israel—were in the land, only those three would be saved through their righteousness. The destiny of the wicked is destruction.

Three Parables (15:1—17:24)

Ezekiel illustrated God's judgment and the future of Judah through three parables. He compared Jerusalem to the vine in the forest (chap. 15). The quality of the vine depends on the quality of the fruit it produces. Israel, God's choice vine, became worthless; so God would destroy His people like the worthless wood of the forest (see Matthew 3:8-10).

The second parable (chap. 16) summarizes the spiritual history of Jerusalem. Though Jerusalem was once a Canaanite city with no future, God showed His favor toward this city and chose her as His bride. However, God's chosen city became unfaithful through idolatry. Ezekiel announced God's judgment upon His unfaithful wife. The parable ends with the promise that God would again restore the city and enter into an everlasting covenant with her.

The third parable (chap. 17)

deals with King Zedekiah's rebellion against Babylon and its consequence. Zedekiah was the epitome of indecisiveness and infidelity. Ezekiel warned that Zedekiah, who sought support from Egypt, would die in Babylon. The narrative ends with the promise that God would place on the throne of David an ideal messianic ruler.

The Soul That Sins Shall Die (18:1-32)

A popular proverb ("The fathers eat sour grapes, and the children's teeth are set on edge" [v. 2]) implied that God was punishing the children for the sins of their ancestors. Ezekiel affirmed the truth that everyone is accountable to God. He punishes individuals for their own sins and not for the sins of their ancestors. The righteous would live, and the wicked would die. The prophet reminded the exiles that they must follow their covenant obligations in Babylon. He challenged them to repent, quit being a sinful people, and receive the offer of "a new heart and a new spirit." God has no delight in the death of a sinner. This is the greatest truth in Ezekiel 18. An intentional commitment to break away from the world of sin is the key to the gift of life that God offers us. God's will for His creation is life, not death (18:32; see John 3:16).

A Lament over Judah's Kings (19:1-14)

Ezekiel mourned over the disastrous fate of the Judean kings Jehoahaz, Jehoiachin, and Zedekiah. Both Jehoahaz and Jehoaichin met their fates because of their wickedness. Zedekiah would soon be taken out of power and be exiled. None of these kings provided good leadership to Judah.

God's Response to Israel's Sins (20:1–24:27)

God's response to the sin of His people was to hide His counsel from them. Ezekiel described the impending Babylonian invasion as the wielding of God's sharpened sword against His people, who have defiled themselves with idolatry throughout their history. Using the names Oholah for Samaria, and Oholibah for Jerusalem, Ezekiel described Israel in the north and Judah in the south as two sisters who pursued the life of idolatry. God punished Samaria for her sins. He warned the younger sister Judah, who did worse than the older sister, that she would suffer judgment by the hand of the Babylonians.

When the Babylonians laid siege around Jerusalem on January 15, 588 B.C., Ezekiel gave an allegory of a boiling pot and two woe oracles to convey the message that God's wrath was coming upon the city. The cooking pot imagery showed the intensity of the judgment that was about to take place. Jerusalem had rejected God's offer of cleansing. God was left with no other option but to burn the city in His anger and destroy the rusty scum and filth that filled the city.

God warned Ezekiel about the death of his wife and commanded that he should not mourn for her. She died as a reminder that God was about to hand His own pride and glory—the Temple—over to be destroyed by the Babylonians. God also said to Ezekiel that a fugitive would bring him the news of Jerusalem's destruction and that he would no longer be unable to speak.

■ Oracles Against the Nations (25:1—32:32)

Ezekiel's judgment oracles against Israel's neighboring nations continue the pattern we have already noticed in Isaiah and Jeremiah. The nations addressed by Ezekiel were Ammon, Moab, Edom, Philistia, Tyre, Sidon, and Egypt. Tyre (26:1—28:19) and Egypt (29:1—32:32) received the most attention in Ezekiel's judgment speeches. Both nations were symbols of wealth and glory in the ancient world. They boasted in their wealth and power. Ezekiel predicted that God would send Nebuchadnezzar, king of Babylon, to destroy Tyre and Egypt because of their pride and arrogance.

God described Israel as a sheep without shepherd (Ezekiel 34:1-6).

■ Promise of Restoration (33:1—39:29)

God's Watchman (33:1-33)

God once again appointed Ezekiel to be His watchman to give warning to Israel concerning their life-and-death choices (see also 3:17-21). This time the commission was to give a final warning before the fall of Jerusalem. Even at the last hour, God gave the people an opportunity to repent and be saved. Ezekiel said that repentance would lead the wicked to their salvation regardless of the depth of their sin. He also reminded the righteous that they have a responsibility to remain righteous. God would hold them accountable if they turned away from their righteous living.

Ezekiel received the word that Jerusalem had fallen (587 B.C.). This news marked the end of his dumbness. The people who were left in the land of Judah after the Babylonian invasion claimed that the land was given to them to possess. Yet they showed no repentance but continued in the sins of those who were deported. Ezekiel warned them of their destruction by the sword. God's plan was to make the land totally desolate.

The Good Shepherd (34:1-31)

Ezekiel charged the shepherds of Israel (political and religious leaders) with failure to give faithful leadership to God's people. The prophet announced that God himself would come to gather His sheep that were scattered by the unfaithful shepherds. He would rescue them and bring them to His good pasture. God would be their shepherd. Moreover, the people themselves would be

Faithful Leadership

Faithful leadership is the responsibility of everyone called into leadership positions. When leaders become preoccupied and even obsessed with self-serving agendas, the people under their leadership pay the price. In the biblical model of leadership, a leader is first and foremost a servant. The "shepherd" imagery in the Bible conveys the idea of self-giving and self-sacrificing qualities necessary for those who aspire to be leaders of God's flock. Jesus' words, "Whoever wants to become great among you must be your servant" (Mark 10:43), are a timely reminder to Christian leaders today (see Mark 10:35-45).

God the Good Shepherd

The coming of God as the good shepherd is one of the greatest promises in the Old Testament. This promise is rooted in the Sinai covenant tradition. Through the covenant, God became the Shepherd of Israel and Israel became the sheep of His pasture (see Psalms 23:1; 100:3). Ezekiel announced that this experience would be a reality to God's people. Jesus said, "I am the good shepherd" (John 10:14). Through Christ we now have the privilege of living under the watchful care and providence of God our shepherd.

judged for their antisocial conduct and uncaring attitude toward each other. God would also establish His messianic ruler over His flock. The people of God would dwell in peace and security in God's ideal kingdom filled with blessings and prosperity.

An Oracle Against Edom (35:1-15)

Ezekiel singled out Edom again to pronounce God's judgment. He referred to this country by the name **Mount Seir,** the mountainous and rocky region south of the Dead Sea. Edom maintained a long history of hatred toward Israel. During the Babylonian invasion of Jerusalem, they showed no pity. Ezekiel said God would make Edom a desolate place.

The Reversal of Israel's Disgrace (36:1-38)

In His anger, God punished Israel. The people suffered judgment because of their idolatry, with which they profaned God's holy name. But God would gather

The Theology of Cleansing

The idea of divine cleansing is an important part of Ezekiel's understanding of restoration. According to Mosaic Law, ritual cleansing from defilement was necessary to restore an individual's membership in the holy community of Israel (see Leviticus 14:52; Numbers 19:11-22). Ezekiel anticipated that God himself would cleanse His people by sprinkling clean water upon them. The holiness of God's people would no longer be determined by a cultic and ceremonial act done by the priests but by God's own activity of cleansing. Moreover, he connected this cleansing with the gift of a new heart and a new spirit. The object of divine cleansing is the human heart defiled with sinfulness and impurity. A clean heart has pure motives, right attitude, and love for God and neighbor. Peter described the Pentecost experience as having "purified their hearts by faith" (Acts 15:6-9; see 2:1-4). God's gracious work in our lives includes not only our redemption from sin but also the cleansing of our hearts through the blood of Jesus Christ (Hebrews 9:13-14; 1 John 1:7-9). The Bible invites us to live a holy life by appropriating this gift through our faith in Jesus Christ.

"The bones came together . . . tendons and flesh appeared . . . and skin covered them" (Ezekiel 37:7-8).

Life to the Dead (37:1-28)

Ezekiel's audience and perhaps even Ezekiel himself thought that the restoration of Israel would be difficult or impossible. God assured Ezekiel of His power to fulfill this promise through a vision of a valley filled with dry bones. The bones that were dry and scattered meant no possibility of life again. However, God showed Ezekiel His power to bring life in the midst of death and destruction. This vision gave Israel the hope and confidence in their restoration from the Exile and the reemergence of their nationhood. Ezekiel anticipated that both Judah and Israel would be reunited under the Davidic kingship.

Gog and Magog (38:1—39:29)

These two chapters are difficult to interpret primarily due to our lack of understanding of the identities of **Gog** and **Magog** and the many nations listed here as enemies of Israel. We do not know if these were nations that existed in the seventh and sixth centuries B.C. Revelation 20:8 also mentions these names, so perhaps they symbolize all the evil powers in the world that are hostile to God's plans and purposes.

The setting of these chapters is the end time, and thus the oracles

them from the lands of their exile. He would act to restore the sanctity and credibility of His holy name. Ezekiel announced that God would make Israel clean from their uncleanness and give them a new heart and a new spirit. The covenant would be reestablished, and the people would live under blessed and prosperous conditions.

T The Valley of Dry Bones

The vision of the valley of dry bones helps us understand two key aspects of biblical faith. First, God has the power to give life to those who are dead in their sins. Sin alienates us from God and leads to our spiritual death. The vision promises the reality of the power of God to make us "alive with Christ" (Ephesians 2:4; see vv. 1-5). Second, the vision provides the Old Testament foundation for our faith in the resurrection of the dead. Up until the Exile, Israel for the most part thought of death as the end of one's existence. This vision together with its historic fulfillment gave the postexilic community the basis for developing the concept of resurrection. Paul speaks of the resurrected Jesus as "the firstfruits of those who have fallen asleep" (1 Corinthians 15:20).

are eschatological in nature. The message is that in the end time, there will be a final battle between God and the evil forces in the world. God will defeat and destroy the forces that are antagonistic to His redeemed people. He will triumph over the evil powers in the world. The burial of these forces signifies the ultimate end and disappearance of evil. God's victory will culminate in a celebration, and He will magnify His name throughout His creation. The whole world will come to know that He is the Lord.

A Jewish cemetery on the Mount of Olives. God promised Ezekiel that He would open up graves and give life to the dead (37:1-14).

■ The New Jerusalem (40:1 — 48:35)

These final chapters describe Ezekiel's visions of Israel beyond the days of her restoration and the

---

I Interpretation of Ezekiel 40—48

There is no consensus among Christians on the meaning and interpretation of Ezekiel 40—48. Did these visions already become a reality through the restoration of the exiled Jews back to their homeland and the Temple rebuilding? Some Christians think so. Some think that a literal fulfillment of these visions will take place with the second coming of Jesus Christ and the establishment of His kingdom. Others think that these visions are being fulfilled in a spiritual sense in the life of the Church today. There are many other views on these chapters.

Ezekiel 40—48 presents the prophet's understanding of God's kingdom from the perspective of his religious experience and his former priestly traditions. The Temple, the priesthood and sacrifices, and the inhabitation of the 12 tribes around the city of Jerusalem were all part of the traditional Israelite concept of God's sovereign rule.

When we compare these chapters with Revelation 20—22, we find some parallels and also some key missing elements.[4] In Revelation, we do not find any of the earthly concerns of Ezekiel—the Temple, the priesthood, the sacrifices, and so forth. The visionary of Revelation saw the reality of the kingdom of God and God's ultimate rule from the perspective of his experience and religious traditions of the Early Church. Jesus' coming inaugurated a new era of God's activity in the history of humanity. The kingdom of God was established through the preaching of the gospel. The Church now waits in eager anticipation of the Second Coming and God's dwelling with His people forever.

The New Jerusalem that the Church anticipates is not an earthly city but a heavenly city. This New Jerusalem will be a part of the new heaven and the new earth in which there will be no evil, no tears, no death, and no pain and sorrow (see Revelation 21:1-4). What Ezekiel saw dimly through a mirror, the visionary of Revelation portrays vividly for the Church as the reality awaiting all of God's people.

defeat of her enemies. The first part of the visions contains elaborate details of the Temple, its courts, gates, chambers, and rules and regulations for various offerings and sacrifices. In the second part, Ezekiel deals with the boundaries of the land and the allotment of the land to various tribes of Israel. Significant to this section is the vision of a river that flows from the Temple that would bring productivity and life to the land. The visions end with the description of the city of Jerusalem and its 12 gates, each gate named after a tribe of Israel. The city would receive a new name, "THE LORD IS THERE" *(Yahweh Shamah).*

Summary Statements

- Ezekiel was once a priest and a part of the Jewish people exiled to Babylon in 597 B.C.
- God's call came to Ezekiel in a supernatural vision of God's glory.
- Ezekiel spoke about God's judgment and the destruction of Jerusalem until 586 B.C.
- Ezekiel spoke about God's restoration after the fall of Jerusalem.
- Ezekiel emphasized each individual's responsibility to live a righteous life.
- God promised to come as the Good Shepherd to restore Israel.
- God promised to give new life to the exiled nation, cleanse them, and give them a new heart and a new spirit.
- Ezekiel's end-time teachings include the final defeat of God's enemies and the establishment of Jerusalem as the city of God.

Questions for Reflection

1. Ezekiel described Judah as a stubborn and rebellious nation. What is the spiritual condition of our nation today? What are the areas in our personal lives where we show resistance to God's word?
2. Ezekiel said that God does not desire the death of the wicked. What does this say about God? What hope and challenge do we find in this word for the wicked?
3. Describe God as the Good Shepherd in your personal life.
4. Describe various ways in which we may experience God's life-giving power today.
5. What is the difference between a "heart of stone" and a "heart of flesh"? How would a clean heart make a difference in the way we live today?

Resources for Further Study

Greenberg, Moshe. "The Vision of Jerusalem in Ezekiel 8—11: A Holistic Interpretation," in *The Divine Helmsman: Studies in God's Control of Human Events, Presented to Lou H. Silberman.* New York: KTAV, 1980.
Howie, C. G. "The Date and Composition of Ezekiel." *Journal of Biblical Literature,* Monograph Series IV, 1950.
Taylor, John B. *Ezekiel: An Introduction and Commentary.* Downers Grove, Ill.: InterVarsity Press, 1969.
Weavers, John W. *Ezekiel. The New Century Bible.* Grand Rapids: Eerdmans, 1969.

29 Daniel

bjectives:

Your study of this chapter should help you to:

- Describe the nature of apocalyptic literature and how to approach it.
- Understand the main messages of the Book of Daniel.
- Become familiar with the major events of the Greek period in Judah.

ey Words to Understand

Apocalyptic writings
Daniel
Antiochus Epiphanes IV
Darius
Cyrus
Nebuchadnezzar
Belshazzar
Maccabees
Alexander the Great

Questions to consider as you read:

1. What fears and concerns do believers have about a hostile culture?
2. Where is human history headed?
3. Who really controls the affairs of nations?

Daniel is unique among the books of the Old Testament. Though the book is found among the prophets in the English Old Testament, scholars usually classify it as apocalyptic writing. The Hebrew Bible placed this book in the Writings section, thus separating it from the prophetic literature.

What is apocalyptic writing all about? The term *apocalyptic* comes from the Greek word *apocalypse,* which means "revelation" or "unveiling." **Apocalyptic writing** focused upon revealing the future, especially the end of human history. Typical features of this literature include: (1) symbolic language and surreal images, (2) visions of the future that are guided by angels, (3) strong contrast between the present evil age and the future good age, (4) prediction of a climactic intervention of God in human history, (5) authorship falsely ascribed to a famous person, and (6) history written as if it were prophecy.

In the Old Testament, apocalyptic language is found in Isaiah 24—27, Ezekiel 38—40, and Zechariah 9—14. Scholars label Daniel and Revelation as apocalyptic books in the Bible. Both Jews and Christians produced a number of other apocalyptic writings between the third century B.C. and second century A.D. These books did not become part of canonical Scripture.

Scholars think that apocalyptic writings emerged in the context of intense religious persecution, which produced hopelessness and despair among the believers. The evil in the world seemed to overtake the faithful. These writings aimed to give hope and courage to the oppressed and to convey to them the reality of God's ultimate victory over evil. The emphasis of such literature is clear. Salvation is coming. God remains in charge and will bring an end to evil in this world. He will rescue His saints and create a new kingdom on earth. Apocalyptic writings not only offer hope but also challenge the believers to remain faithful to God during crisis.

Though Daniel shares many characteristics of noncanonical apocalyptic books, some scholars think that Daniel was the real author of the book. They think it would not have been canonized if it were written under a false name. For the same reason, many scholars also believe that Daniel contains true predictive prophecy. How one views these issues depends somewhat on one's understanding of the date of the composition of the book.

Date

Scholars continue to debate the date of the writing of Daniel. Some view it as a product of the sixth century B.C.; others think that the book belongs to the second century B.C.

Those who see it as a second-century document believe it was written around 165 B.C. to encourage the Jews during the Maccabean revolt. They note the increasing focus of the book upon this era and the appropriateness of many of its key themes for people living during that time. Chapter 11 provides great detail on the reign of **Antiochus Epiphanes IV.** By contrast, some details in the Babylonian and Persian periods appear fuzzy or perhaps even inaccurate.

The assumption of this view is

that the Book of Daniel is named after a great hero of the Jewish faith. Those who follow this view describe its content more as historical than predictive. Scholars also think that the writer of this genre of literature stood in the ancient prophetic tradition that viewed God's establishment of His sovereign rule in the world. In the final analysis, the writer preserves and supports the theological convictions of his predecessors, the great prophets of Israel.

Those who support a sixth century B.C. date suggest that either Daniel or some other writer composed the book. In the latter case, the book would have been completed soon after Daniel's death. They affirm that its prophecies are genuine predictions of the Persian and Greek empires and beyond. Any alleged historical inaccuracies in the Babylonian and Persian periods can be accounted for. The themes and messages of the book speak not only to the sixth-century period but also to the Jewish community of the Persian and the Greek period.

Those who support the sixth-century date do not think that a work written under a false name would have been accepted as authoritative Scripture. To the modern mind this feature appears to undermine the trustworthiness of a document. The second century B.C. date also raises questions about the placement of the book in the Hebrew canon. Some scholars think that Judaism would not have accepted a book that did not belong to the period of prophecy in Israel.

Fortunately the outcome of these questions and concerns does not affect the essential message of the book. The primary

theological truths remain unchanged. The issues have more to do with one's concept of predictive prophecy in the Bible.

Daniel the Hero

Daniel (meaning, "God is my judge") was the younger contemporary of Jeremiah and Ezekiel. He was a young man when the Babylonians took control of the region of Judah in 605 B.C. The Babylonians took him along with other promising youth to serve the kingdom of Babylon. They

Historical Difficulties in Daniel

Some scholars have questioned the historical accuracy of Daniel, especially in regard to the Babylonian and Persian empires. Each of these alleged inaccuracies, however, has a viable answer.

Daniel 5:31 mentions **Darius** the Mede as the one who conquered Babylon. Other sources name **Cyrus** the Persian as Babylon's conqueror. Some scholars suggest that the name Darius the Mede is a special throne name for Cyrus. In fact 6:28 could be accurately translated "Daniel prospered during the reign of Darius, that is, the reign of Cyrus the Persian."

Another historical difficulty is **Nebuchadnezzar's** madness in 4:32-33. This seems to fit better with what we know of one of his successors, Nabonidus. However, a period of 30 years is missing from the chronicles of Nebuchadnezzar's reign, so we do not know all the details of his life. It is believed that he suffered a severe illness just before his death.

In the past, many scholars assumed that the mention of **Belshazzar** as ruler of Babylon in chapter 5 was inaccurate. Babylonian records showed that Nabonidus was the last ruler of the empire. But now scholars recognize that Belshazzar was indeed coregent with his father, Nabonidus. Further, Nabonidus absented himself from Babylon for over 10 years and left the kingdom in his son's hands. Belshazzar was the ruler of Babylon at the time of its fall.

Apocalyptic Literature—Principles of Interpretation

Since biblical apocalyptic literature is a unique genre, we add here the following general guidelines for reading and interpreting Daniel:

- Consider the historical context. Ask about the meaning of images, words, and themes for the original audience.
- Consider the literary type. Remember the main features and themes of apocalyptic literature. Look for symbolic, not literal, meanings to numbers and images.
- Consider the literary context. Notice parallel passages and interpret ideas of one passage in light of its corresponding passage. Understand the unknown on the basis of the known.
- Consider the canonical context. Compare ideas and styles of other apocalyptic visions found in Isaiah, Ezekiel, Zechariah, and Revelation.
- Remember your limitations. Focus on clear passages and leave the unclear ones till there is more information available. Some of it we will not likely understand this side of heaven.

gave him the Babylonian name Belteshazzar (meaning "Bel protect his life").

Daniel possessed the gift of interpreting dreams and carried a reputation for exceptional wisdom. He held high-level positions in Babylon, including head of the wise men of Babylon (2:48) and the third highest ruler in the Babylonian Empire (5:29). Later he became one of the top three administrators in the Persian Empire (6:2). That means he witnessed some of the major shifts in the political history of the ancient Near East—the rise and fall of Babylon and the emergence of Persia. The last date given in the book is "the third year of Cyrus king of Persia" or about 535 B.C. (10:1). He would have been well over 70 years old when he served the Persians.

Content

The Book of Daniel consists of the following two parts:

1. Stories of Daniel (1:1—6:28)
2. Visions of Daniel (7:1—12:13)

Both sections progress historically, from the earliest date to the latest. A uniqueness of the books is the Aramaic section in 2:4—7:28. We do not know why the author dropped Hebrew and picked up Aramaic as the language to continue the narrative in this section. The stories of this section reflect a Babylonian historical context. So it is likely that the author used Aramaic, the language of Babylon, to give authenticity to these stories.

■ Stories of Daniel (1:1—6:28)

The first six chapters consist of selected stories from the life of Daniel and his friends. These are hero stories, but their purpose is not to lift up Daniel. Their aim, rather, is to emphasize God's control over the affairs of humanity. The primary message is clear: God is sovereign over the world; therefore, His people can risk remaining faithful to Him.

These stories have a common pattern. Each moves from some

sort of test to a divine deliverance. Three stories (see chaps. 1, 3, and 6) focus on a test of faith. Biblical values and beliefs are confronted by a hostile culture. The other three stories (see chaps. 2, 4, and 5) deal with a test of interpretation. Daniel is challenged to explain what God revealed to him through dreams and signs.

Chapters 1, 3, and 6 give three examples of those who had the courage to maintain their convictions in the midst of major tests to their faith. In these stories, Daniel and his friends were confronted with a threat of severe consequences for holding on to their beliefs. If they did not compromise, the consequence was rejection from the royal court (chap. 1), death in a fiery furnace (chap. 3), or death in a den of lions (chap. 6). In each case they chose to remain faithful and trust God. They refused to defile themselves by eating meat from the king's table, by bowing to an idol, or by ceasing to pray to their God.

Their conviction was rewarded. God rescued His faithful servants and revealed His unique power. The end result was that the most powerful kings on earth acknowledged the sovereignty of Israel's God. The Persian king confessed, "He is the living God, enduring forever. His kingdom shall never be destroyed, and his dominion has no end" (6:26, NRSV).

The truth of this statement is the key theme of chapter 2. Nebuchadnezzar dreamed of a large statue made of four metals. Daniel interpreted the dream by the power of God (2:27-28). Four kingdoms would arise on earth, but none of them would survive. By contrast, God's kingdom "will

Dreams in the Ancient World

People of the ancient world took dreams very seriously. They understood them to be one way the gods communicated with people. Egyptians, Assyrians, Babylonians, and Greeks had specially trained experts in the art of dream interpretation. These experts served, much like Daniel, as professional advisers for kings. Some of their writings included instructions for interpreting dreams, dietary regulations for dreaming, and records of "fulfilled" dreams.[1]

Dreams are mentioned numerous times throughout the Bible. Those who heard God's message while dreaming included Jacob (Genesis 28:12-15), Solomon (1 Kings 3:5-15), prophets (Jeremiah 23:25-28), Joseph (Matthew 1:20; 2:13, 19, 22), the magi at Jesus' birth (Matthew 2:12), Pilate's wife (Matthew 27:19), and Paul (Acts 16:9; 18:9; 23:11; 27:23-24).

The two great interpreters of dreams in the Bible were Joseph and Daniel. Joseph interpreted dreams for his friends in prison and for Pharaoh (Genesis 40:5-22; 41:1-38). Daniel was called upon to interpret two dreams of Nebuchadnezzar (Daniel 2:1-47; 4:1-19). In both cases the interpretations served to bring honor to God.

never be destroyed, nor will it be left to another people" (2:44). The precise identification of these four kingdoms is not the main issue. The point is that human kingdoms will not last, but God's kingdom will. Chapter 7 picks up this imagery and theme again.

Chapters 4 and 5 make the same point as chapter 2. They contain two stories about two prideful kings who are humbled before Israel's God. Both kings received divine messages that needed interpretation. Nebuchadnezzar had a dream (chap. 4), and Belshazzar saw handwriting on a wall (chap. 5). Daniel deciphered both messages, which foretold

Daniel deciphers God's handwriting on the wall.

the humbling of these kings. The final outcome was the fulfillment of the prediction and an affirmation of God's sovereignty. The power of earthly kings ceased when God ordained it.

■ Visions of Daniel (7:1 – 12:13)

The final six chapters of Daniel report four visions of the prophet. They are arranged in chronological order with an increasing focus on the details of the Greek Empire. They tend to stress the same themes as the earlier stories.

Chapter 7 gives a vision that Daniel saw in a dream during the first year of Belshazzar (550 B.C.), the year in which Cyrus the Persian began his revolt against the Median Empire. Daniel saw four beasts rise up out of the sea and the throne of God set up for judgment.

The meaning of the vision was interpreted by a heavenly being. The four beasts represent four earthly kingdoms (v. 17), and the throne of God represents God's dominion over the earth (v. 27). In

Nebuchadnezzar

Nebuchadnezzar was Babylon's most prominent and powerful monarch, reigning from 605 to 562 B.C. He was the son of the founder of the Babylonian Empire, Nabopolassar. He married Amytis, the daughter of the king of the Medes. His successes as a general in the Babylonian army prepared him to ascend the throne at his father's death. He continued to expand the Babylonian Empire over his long reign, pushing its boundaries to modern-day Turkey and Egypt. Such conquests brought great wealth to the city of Babylon and provided for major building projects such as the famed Hanging Gardens. He was a worshiper of Marduk, the patron god of Babylon, as well as other gods and goddesses.

The Bible mentions Nebuchadnezzar by name over 90 times. Daniel's characterization of him as proud and arrogant accords well with what we know of him otherwise.

this context Daniel saw the coming Messiah establishing his rule. He described him as "one like a human being coming with the clouds of heaven" (v. 13, NRSV). All peoples would eventually acknowledge His dominion.

The passage does not identify the kingdoms of earth by name. Modern scholars have suggested several possibilities, but there is no consensus. Whatever the exact identification of these kingdoms, the main point remains undisputed. Though human kingdoms rise and fall, God will have the final victory.

The vision in chapter 8 focuses on two of the four kingdoms mentioned in chapter 7. This vision came about 547 B.C., during Cyrus's conquest and expansion of his empire. In this vision Daniel saw two animals, a ram and a goat. According to the interpretation given to Daniel, the ram rep-

Daniel's visions included a ram with two horns (8:3).

resented the Persian Empire and the goat represented the Greek Empire (vv. 20-21). The vision predicted that the Greeks would conquer the Persians. Then the Greek Empire would split into four and

Identity of the Four Kingdoms

One of the challenges of interpreting Daniel is identifying the four kingdoms mentioned in chapters 2 and 7. The first is clearly identified in 2:38 as Babylon. The other three are open to interpretation. There are two main schools of thought on this matter. One group identifies the four kingdoms as Babylonia, Media, Persia, and Greece. Another sees them as Babylonia, Persia, Greece, and Rome.

Many scholars believe that the kingdom of God will emerge following these kingdoms. If the Roman Empire represents the fourth kingdom, this would accord well with the coming of Jesus during Roman rule. If, however, the fourth kingdom stands for the Greek Empire, then the kingdom of God would be the Hasmonean kingdom, established by the descendants of the **Maccabees.**

The text does not necessarily suggest that the kingdom of God would come after the human kingdoms are destroyed. It may in fact emerge within them. The curious phrase "in the days of those kings" in 2:44 (NRSV) indicates that God's kingdom can arise in the midst of these kingdoms. The point of the text then would be that as human kingdoms rise and fall, God's kingdom continues on. This is truth for all time.

one of these rulers would oppress the people of Israel and desecrate their sanctuary.

All of this did take place. The Greek general **Alexander the Great** conquered Persia in 331 B.C., and his kingdom was divided into four at his death. One of these four kingdoms, the Seleucid Empire, eventually came to control Judah and oppressed its people. One of its kings, Antiochus Epiphanes IV, took over the Jerusalem Temple for pagan worship in 168 B.C. The appendix gives more details of his rule.

Daniel's third vision (see chap. 9) happened about 539 B.C. That year Cyrus conquered Babylon, and the Exile was ended. The Jews were free to return home to Jerusalem. Daniel recognized that Jeremiah's prediction of 70 years of Babylonian dominance (609—539 B.C.) had been fulfilled. So he prayed a prayer of praise and confession.

In response to his prayer Daniel received a vision about the coming of "an anointed prince" (9:25, NRSV). The timing of his coming is marked by "seventy 'sevens'" (v. 24). The precise meaning of this phrase is difficult to determine. Scholars give various interpretations since no arithmetic calculation renders a completely satisfactory solution. What seems clear is that a long period of time would elapse between the decree to restore Jerusalem and the coming of the Messiah. Once the Messiah comes, He would be "cut off" and suffering would follow (v. 26). These predictions found fulfillment in Jesus' death but may await further fulfillment prior to the second coming of Christ.

The final vision of Daniel is recorded in chapters 10—12. It occurred during the third year of Cyrus (536 B.C.). At this time the first group of Jews returned to Jerusalem to begin restoring their land (Ezra 1).

Daniel's vision projects some of the intense struggles the new community would face. It focuses with increasing detail upon oppression of the Jews under the Seleucids in the second century B.C. In 11:21-45 the tyrannical rule of Antiochus Epiphanes IV (175-164 B.C.) is clearly envisioned. His rule would be cruel and distressing. But Daniel also saw the end of this oppression and deliverance coming from heaven. Once again, God's rule wins out.

Some scholars believe that the visions in chapters 7—12 also deal with events at the end of human history. They think that though these visions were once fulfilled in the second century B.C., there will be a final fulfillment yet to come. The text refers to "the time of the end" (8:17, 19; 11:35, 40). The Book of Revelation in the New Testament picks up on several images in Daniel and relates them to the end of human history when Jesus Christ will return (e.g., Revelation 12:3-4; 13:1; 14:14; 16:18). This is the telescoping quality of biblical prophecy that focuses upon the immediate future and the distant future at the same time.

From this perspective, the cruel ruler of chapter 11 reflects not only Antiochus Epiphanes IV but also the Antichrist at the end of time. The suffering and wars are descriptive of the last days as well as the days of the Maccabees. The book thus anticipates the final judgment and victory of God over evil and the establishment of God's ultimate rule in the world.

Summary Statements

- Daniel was a statesman and an interpreter of dreams.
- The Book of Daniel belongs to the literary type known as apocalyptic writings.
- There are two views on the date of the writing of Daniel, the sixth century B.C. and the second century B.C.
- Daniel is a carefully structured book made up of stories and visions.
- The visions of Daniel have an increasing focus upon the Maccabean period.
- The main message of Daniel is that God will win in the end, so His people can risk remaining faithful.

Questions for Reflection

1. What are some of the modern examples of severe tests of faithfulness in the history of the Christian Church?
2. While we wait for God's sovereign rule to become a reality through the Second Coming, what kind of life should believers live (use illustrations from Daniel)?
3. What does the Book of Daniel say about oppressive powers in the world today?

Resources for Further Study

Baldwin, Joyce G. *Daniel: An Introduction and Commentary. Tyndale Old Testament Commentary.* Downers Grove, Ill.: InterVarsity Press, 1978.

Murphy, Frederick J. *Introduction to Apocalyptic Literature.* Vol. 7 of *The New Interpreter's Bible.* Nashville: Abingdon Press, 1995.

Smith-Christopher, Daniel L. *Daniel: Introduction, Commentary, and Reflections.* Vol. 7 of *The New Interpreter's Bible.* Nashville: Abingdon Press, 1995.

Towner, Shelby W. *Interpretation: A Bible Commentary for Teaching and Preaching: Daniel.* Louisville, Ky.: John Knox Press, 1984.

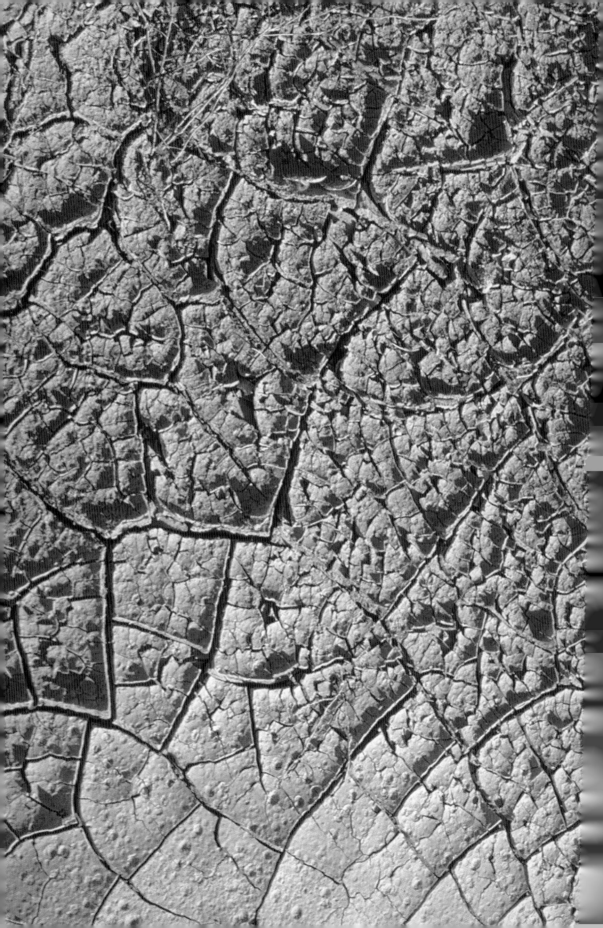

30 Hosea, Joel, Amos, and Obadiah

Objectives:

Your study of this chapter should help you to:

- Summarize the historical settings of the ministries of Hosea, Joel, Amos, and Obadiah.
- Describe the content of the Books of Hosea, Joel, Amos, and Obadiah.
- Describe the key theological teachings of Hosea, Joel, Amos, and Obadiah.

Questions to consider as you read:

1. What is unconditional love?
2. Describe radical obedience.
3. What is the relationship of worship to common life?
4. What is the consequence of harboring hatred?

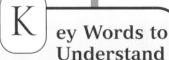

Key Words to Understand

Hosea
Ephraim
Jeroboam II
Baal
Gomer
Jezreel
Lo-Ruhamah
Lo-Ammi
Beth Aven
Joel
The Valley of Jehoshaphat
Amos
Tekoa
Bethel
Gilgal
Justice
Righteousness
Obadiah
Edomites
Sela

Hosea

Hosea's book is well known for its intense and passionate expressions of God's love, anger, agony, and despair. It is profound in theology and daring in approach to Israel's understanding of her covenant God.

Hosea's Personal Background

The book introduces **Hosea** as the son of Beeri. The name in Hebrew *(hoshea)* means "salvation." Scholars think that he was a member of the kingdom of Israel (Northern Kingdom). His oracles were directed to Israel, which he often addressed as **Ephraim**, after the most prominent tribe in the north. The story of Hosea indicates that he was married and had three children to whom he gave symbolic names to convey God's judgment upon Israel.

Setting

The opening verse (1:1) gives the reigns of Uzziah, Jotham, Ahaz and Hezekiah, kings of Judah, and **Jeroboam II**, king of Israel, as the setting for Hosea's ministry. Hosea began his ministry sometime during the days of Jeroboam II (perhaps around 750 B.C.) and continued until 722 B.C. This was a time of extreme political instability, assassination of rulers, and unpredictable foreign policy in Israel.

The social condition of Israel during Hosea's ministry was deplorable. Hosea's book shows evidence of corruption, violence, murder, stealing, lying, and other signs of the breakdown of Israel's social and economic structure (see 4:1-3; 6:7-9; 7:1-7; 10:13; 12:7-8). The prophet described these conditions as the outcome of Israel's total disregard for God's moral and ethical demands.

Israel's religion was corrupted through idolatry and Baal worship. Israel regarded **Baal** as the provider of her agricultural productivity, flocks, and children. The people offered sacrifices and took part in drunken and sexual orgies in order to benefit from Baal's procreative power. Even Israel's priests were guilty of promoting idolatry in the land.

Content

The Book of Hosea can be divided into the following parts:
1. Hosea, Gomer, and the Children (1:1—3:5)
2. Sin, Judgment, and Repentance (4:1—8:14)
3. The Outcome of Judgment (9:1—10:15)
4. Israel—God's Prodigal Son (11:1-11)
5. A Call to Repentance (12:1—13:16)
6. The Promise of Healing and Love (14:1-9)

■ Hosea, Gomer, and the Children (1:1—3:5)

The Book of Hosea begins with God's command to Hosea to marry a woman from a family of harlots. Hosea's marriage to **Gomer** may have been a way for God to speak to Israel through the prophet.[1] Through his radical obedience to God's strange command, the prophet conveyed the message of Israel's unfaithfulness to God, her covenant partner. The names of the children meant serious judgment against Israel. **Jezreel** ("God scatters") stood for the end of the political state of Israel. **Lo-Ruhamah** ("not pitied") meant God

Hosea's Marriage to Gomer

Hosea's marriage to Gomer is a puzzle to us. Often people ask, "Why did a holy God ask Hosea to marry a sinful woman?" Perhaps we should ask, "What should be our response when God comes to us with an unusual and even unorthodox demand?" The God of Hosea acted in an unconventional way and against all traditional expectations. Hosea himself became a fool and a madman for God (9:7). We might say, "A strange God and His strange prophet!" Nonetheless, here we find the Old Testament illustration of one person's radical obedience to God's radical call. Jesus said, "If any want to become my followers, let them deny themselves and take up their cross and follow me" (Mark 8:34, NRSV).

would not show pity to Israel. **Lo-Ammi** ("not my people") symbolized the end of God's covenant relationship with Israel. Though God pronounced His judgment against Israel, He also promised to restore and reestablish the covenant relationship with Israel.

The people of God claimed that Baal was the giver of their prosperity. God would withhold from Israel His blessings and thus punish the nation for going after other gods. However, after the judgment, God would restore His people and be betrothed to them forever (2:1-23).

God's plan to restore Israel is the message underlying Hosea's purchase of his estranged wife (chap. 3). Though she had left him to go after other lovers, he purchased her and brought her to his home. He denied her the freedom to continue her harlotry. In the same way, God would take away from Israel her political and religious freedom.

■ Sin, Judgment, and Repentance (4:1—8:14)

Hosea announced God's legal complaint against Israel because there was no faithfulness, cove-

nant loyalty, and personal knowledge of God in the land. Idolatry and Baal worship were rampant. The prophet announced God's judgment upon the whole nation.

Hosea also said that God would return to His people with compassion and grace if the people would seek God and confess their guilt. This call went unheeded by the nation that was evil through and through. Though the people were sinful, they claimed to know God.

■ The Outcome of Judgment (9:1—10:15)

God's judgment would send Israel to exile in Assyria. The people disregarded the prophetic voice and continued in their idolatry. Hosea mockingly called Bethel ("the house of God") **Beth Aven** ("house of iniquity"). He announced shame and dishonor to its priests and the king of Samaria.

■ Israel—God's Prodigal Son (11:1-11)

Though God brought His son Israel out of bondage and raised him with tenderness and compassion, the son rebelled against his Father's love. The rebellious son deserves death; yet, God's com-

Hosea's God

Hosea described God as the loving and forgiving Husband, the compassionate and gracious Father, and the Healer of His people. These metaphors help us discover the enormity of God's grace and His love for sinful humanity. The Gospel writer John captures the mystery of God's love in the statement, "For God so loved the world that he gave his one and only Son"(John 3:16). Here, then, lies the hope of a world that is estranged from God.

passion would not allow Him to hand Israel over to destruction (see Deuteronomy 21:18-21). He is "God—the Holy One" among His people. Here we find the clearest expression of God's amazing grace to sinners who deserve nothing but death.

■ A Call to Repentance (12:1—13:16)

Hosea challenged the people to return to God and seek His favor, as Jacob their ancestor had sought God at Bethel. The people of God must show love, carry out justice, and always wait for God.

Israel paid no attention to the God who had brought them out of Egypt. They forgot their God who had provided for them. Hosea warned Israel that death and destruction await those who are ungrateful to God. No one can rescue a people destined for doom and destruction.

■ The Promise of Healing and Love (14:1-9)

The oracles of Hosea end with the prophet's plea to Israel to return to God from their sinful ways of life. Hosea prayed a model prayer, in which he acknowledged the guilt of the nation and the mercy of God as the only source

Repentance

Hosea taught that repentance must be a way of life for the people of God. Repentance is evidence of an active faith—faith that operates with consistency in our desire to please God. Where there is no genuine repentance, love for God is "like a morning cloud" (6:4, NRSV) and faith is fraudulent. Genuine repentance, on the other hand, leads us to "offer the fruit of our lips"—a continual "sacrifice of praise" to God through the name of Jesus Christ (Hosea 14:2; Hebrews 13:15).

of the nation's salvation. He anticipated that God would respond to the nation's penitence with His healing and love. Israel would become fruitful and prosperous under God's watchful care.

The final verse of the Book of Hosea is a wisdom statement. It is an exhortation to discern and walk according to God's ways. The righteous will find God's way to be the source of life, whereas it will be a stumbling block to sinners.

Joel

This little book gave the Christian disciples the Old Testament basis for the events that took place on the Day of Pentecost (Joel 2:28-32; Acts 2:17-21). The apostle Paul found in Joel's prophecy the promise of salvation to all who call on the name of the Lord (Joel 2:32; Romans 10:13).

Joel's Personal Background

The book introduces **Joel** as the son of Pethuel (1:1). The name *Joel* is also found a number of times in the Old Testament, but it is difficult to establish the identity of the prophet. The name means "Yahweh is God." We assume that he was a citizen of Judah. His oracles address the population of Judah.

Setting

The book also lacks any specific reference to the time of Joel's ministry. Scholars have proposed various dates for his ministry, ranging from the ninth century to mid-fourth century B.C. Though there are still advocates for a pre-exilic date for Joel, most scholars prefer to place this book in the postexilic period, somewhere between 500 and 350 B.C.

Content

The following is an outline of Joel's book:
1. Lament over Natural Calamities (1:2-20)
2. God's Army Is Coming (2:1-11)
3. Call to Repentance and God's Response (2:12-27)
4. Spiritual Restoration (2:28-32)
5. The Valley of Decision (3:1-21)

Joel's oracles are contained in three chapters in English translations of the Bible. Joel 2:28-32 (English) is 3:1-5 in Hebrew. Joel 3:1-21 (English) is 4:1-21 in Hebrew. Some scholars think that 2:28—3:21 (English) is a later addition to the book by another writer. We regard this section as an essential part of the message of the prophet. This second part describes the reversal of Judah's misfortune and God's continued work on behalf of His people, including the outpouring of His Spirit upon them.

■ Lament over Natural Calamities (1:2-20)

Joel's book opens with an admonition to elders and all the people to preserve for future generations the memory of the locust attack that devastated the land (1:2-3). Verses 19-20 imply that a severe drought also affected the land. Joel summoned the people to weep and wail over the ruin and destruction of crops, fruits, and pasture that the people and their livestock needed to sustain their life.

■ God's Army Is Coming (2:1-11)

A locust plague gave the prophet the language and war imagery to describe the intensity of "the day of the LORD," the day of God's judgment upon those who oppose Him. No one can endure that dreadful day because God will be the commander of His army.

■ Call to Repentance and God's Response (2:12-27)

This section begins with God's summons to Judah to return to Him with their whole heart, with fasting, weeping, and mourning. In order to receive God's graciousness and compassion, repentance must be an act of the human will and not just an external ritual. The prophet called his listeners to consecrate themselves to God. God promised that He would restore the blessings of the land.

■ Spiritual Restoration (2:28-32)

God also promised to pour out His Spirit upon all people. Joel anticipated the Spirit's work in equipping God's people to speak (prophesy) for God. He connected the outpouring of the Spirit to the nearness of the "day of the LORD." Though the day of the Lord will be the day of judgment, Joel said that God would save all who call upon His name from His wrath and judgment.

■ The Valley of Decision (3:1-21)

The final chapter in the Book of Joel contains several oracles of judgment against the nations in **"the Valley of Jehoshaphat"** (vv. 2, 12), also called "the valley of decision" (twice in v. 14). These are symbolic names that refer to the reality of God's final judgment of the wicked. God would sit in judgment against the nations. He would reclaim Jerusalem as His holy dwelling place. God's people would experience His blessings and forgiveness.

Amos

Scholars think that **Amos** was the first canonical prophet of Israel. Amos did not receive much attention in the Jewish and Christian tradition prior to the 19th century.[2] In the last century, this book became a primary biblical resource for the advocates of justice and righteousness in our world. Today, we hear even secular leaders citing Amos's passionate call for social justice: "But let justice roll down like waters, and righteousness like an ever-flowing stream" (Amos 5:24, NRSV).

Amos's Personal Background

The book contains only two brief references about Amos's personal background (1:1; 7:14-15). According to 1:1, Amos was a

---

The Promise of the Spirit

Our repentance with broken and contrite heart is necessary for the experience of spiritual blessings from God. The promise of the Spirit's outpouring is a reality today. The Spirit came upon the early Christians on the Day of Pentecost. The Spirit continues to come to our lives, not only to transform us but also to equip us to become His spokespersons in our day. Joel reminds us to live in newness of life through Christ and in the power of the Holy Spirit as we wait for the Second Coming.

breeder *(noqed)* of sheep from **Tekoa**, a village about 12 miles southeast of Jerusalem. According to 7:14-15, Amos was a herdsman *(boqer),* a breeder of large cattle, and a dresser of sycamore trees. It is thus likely that he was an owner of livestock, perhaps both cattle and sheep. The latter vocation may have entailed the task of artificially ripening the green sycamore fruit to make it sweet and edible. Though he was a citizen of the Southern Kingdom, God called him to be a prophet to Israel, the Northern Kingdom.

Setting

Amos 1:1 indicates that his ministry took place during the reign of Uzziah, king of Judah (783-742 B.C.), and Jeroboam II, king of Israel (786-742 B.C.). The text also refers to a more precise date for Amos, "two years before the earthquake" (1:1; see also Zechariah 14:5). Scholars connect this with a massive earthquake that destroyed Hazor around 760 B.C. Amos's ministry is thus dated to 763/762 B.C. We do not know the length of his ministry. It is possible that his ministry lasted only for a year.[3]

Amos came to the Northern Kingdom when the nation was at the height of its military and economic prosperity under Jeroboam II (2 Kings 14:23-29). Amos's oracles reflect the fact that the economic prosperity did not benefit the poor in the land. The rich who maintained winter and summer houses and houses of ivory lived a hedonistic lifestyle without any concern for the plight of the poor. The poor were traded as commodities—victims of economic exploitation, sexual abuse, legal and judicial corruption, and miscarriage of justice.

Though oppression and violence were rampant in the land, there was also a revival of interest in religious festivals and rituals. **Bethel** and **Gilgal** were centers of idolatry that promoted false worship and false confidence in the presence of God with them. Amos's words were thus addressed to a people who failed to see any relationship between worship and everyday life.

Amos was a shepherd before he became a prophet.

Content

Amos's book can be divided into the following parts:
1. Introduction (1:1-2)
2. Judgment upon Israel's Neighbors (1:3—2:3)
3. Judgment upon Judah and Israel (2:4-16)
4. Judgment Oracles Against Israel (3:1—6:14)
5. The Visions of Amos (7:1—9:10)
6. Rebuilding and Restoration (9:11-15)

▉ Introduction (1:1-2)

The opening oracle announces the theme of Amos's book. Amos saw God as the God of judgment who speaks His word of judgment from His Temple in Jerusalem.

▉ Judgment upon Israel's Neighbors (1:3—2:3)

Amos declared God's judgment upon Israel's neighboring nations

God, the Universal Judge

God is the sovereign Judge of all humanity. Violence against human beings is a sin against God. We learn from Amos that God is involved in our contemporary human affairs. He is intensely concerned with the way we treat others. As in the days of Amos, our world is filled with oppression, slavery, ethnic cleansing, war crimes, and terrorist activities. God will bring His judgment on all who sin against Him, whether or not they recognize His sovereignty.

—Syria, Philistia, Phoenicia, Edom, Ammon, and Moab. These nations would suffer various forms of judgment for their war

Amos described God as a roaring lion (1:2).

crimes and ruthless behavior. In all cases except the oracle addressed to Moab, Israel was the victim of the crime of these nations. Nations that showed no mercy to other nations would receive no mercy from God.

■ Judgment upon Judah and Israel (2:4-16)

Amos identified the sin of Judah as her rejection of the instructions (Torah) of the Lord. The sins of Israel, the Northern Kingdom, included slavery, oppression, gross sexual immorality, injustice, total disregard for the poor, and disregard for Yahweh's past saving actions. They broke all boundaries of proper moral and ethical conduct in the society.

■ Judgment Oracles Against Israel (3:1—6:14)

In this section we have a large number of oracles, mostly short judgment sayings against Israel. Israel failed to live by the principles of her election and covenant with God. Using various proverbial sayings, Amos announced that God seldom did anything without revealing His plan to His prophets. The complacent, idolatrous, and oppressive people of Israel, which included the aristocratic women of Samaria, would be completely destroyed by the divine judgment.

Amos held the view that God's judgment was inevitable because repentance had no place in Israel's religious life. He warned Israel that the sanctuaries of Israel were already destined for destruction and ruin. Amos was convinced that even in this final hour, God would be gracious to His people if they would "seek the LORD" and "seek good, not evil"

T **Justice and Righteousness**

The concern for **justice** (*mishpat*) and **righteousness** (*sedeqa*) is a key theme in the Book of Amos. We do "justice" when we fulfill our covenantal obligations to others. "Justice" is the fruit of our right relationship with others. Amos reminds us that our lives should show evidence of our "hunger and thirst" for justice and righteousness. Jesus was a true friend of the marginal and the outcast people of His day. When justice and righteousness flow like an ever-flowing stream in our community life, then we will have met the preconditions for acceptable worship (5:24; see Matthew 5:6).

(5:6, 14). Amos declared "the day of the LORD" as a day of darkness and gloom. God demanded justice and righteousness more than festivities, music, and offerings.

■ The Visions of Amos (7:1—9:10)

The visions of the plague of locusts, fire, the plumb line, the basket of summer fruit, and the sanctuary continue the theme of the coming judgment. The first two visions (locusts and fire) portrayed the totality of judgment. Amos interceded with God to have mercy on His people. The vision of the plumb line conveyed the message that Israel failed to align herself with the divine standards required of His covenant nation. God would not spare such a nation from His judgment.

Amaziah the priest barred Amos from speaking at the royal sanctuary at Bethel and told him to go back to his home. Amos responded that though he did not belong to a prophetic family, God took him out of his vocation and sent him to speak to Israel. A true prophet cannot be silenced by anyone, not even by the highest ecclesiastical authority!

The vision of the basket of fruit conveyed the message that "the end had come" for Israel. Like the ripe fruit ready for harvest, Israel was ripe for judgment. God's judgment would lead to a complete withdrawal of His word from His people. Furthermore, no place in this universe would be a safe place for sinners.

■ Rebuilding and Restoration (9:11-15)

The book ends with hope for the future. The promise of the book is that beyond judgment, there would be Israel's rebuilding, restoration, and return to the days of prosperity and blessing from God.

Is There a Future for Israel?

Is there a future for Israel? Amos certainly thought so. The nation that was faced with its "end" will have a glorious future. Judgment does not nullify God's plans. God will continue to work out His plans for the salvation of humanity. Amos's word about the "end" pointed to a new beginning in the history of salvation. That beginning is what the Church proclaimed through the coming of Jesus Christ in the world (see Acts 15:15-18).

Obadiah

Obadiah's Personal Background

The Book of Obadiah is the shortest book in the Old Testament. The name *Obadiah* (meaning "the servant of the Lord") and its related forms are found a number of times in the Old Testament. The book gives us no reference to his family or vocational background.

Setting

Lack of clear reference to any historical event makes it difficult to place Obadiah's book in a specific setting. Some scholars have proposed an early date in the ninth century B.C. based on the account of Edom's rebellion against Judah (see 2 Kings 8:20-22). There are others who place the book in the mid-fifth century B.C., during the Edomite occupation of the Negev.[4] Most scholars think that verses 11-14 refer to the Babylonian invasion of Judah and Jerusalem. That would place the book around 587 B.C. or immediately thereafter.

The prophet spoke about the pride and arrogance of the **Edomites** who maintained a long-standing hatred toward the people of Israel. The Edomites were the descendants of Esau, the brother of Jacob. They lived in the area south of the Dead Sea, a region surrounded by deserts and mountains. The hostility between Edom and Israel continued throughout the history of both nations.

Though Obadiah addresses the violent and the oppressive people with the word of judgment, here we also find a word of comfort to the oppressed and those who are in exile, that God would also act on their behalf to deliver and restore them to their land.

Content

Obadiah's oracle against Edom is preserved in one chapter. The author introduces the content of the book as "the vision of Obadiah."

Obadiah announced God's plan to make Edom insignificant in the world because of its pride, arrogance, and false confidence. The capital city **Sela** (means "rock" in Hebrew) was surrounded by mountains, which provided the city the safety and shelter of a fortress. Though the Edomites thought they were unassailable and inaccessible to invading armies, God planned to bring them down and humiliate them with utter destruction.

The primary sin of Edom was its ongoing hatred of Israel. When an enemy invaded Jerusalem, Edom had stood and watched without any pity. Moreover, the Edomites had joined with the enemies to plunder and destroy the city.

Obadiah announced that Edom and the nations would receive from God the same kind of destruction they had inflicted upon Judah. But "the day of the LORD" would be a day of salvation for Judah and Israel. When death and destruction rule against Edom, there would be deliverance on Mount Zion. Obadiah ended his message with the confident hope that the kingdom of the Lord would ultimately be established in the world.

The Nabatean rock city Petra that most scholars identify as the location of Sela, one of the centers of the Edomites (Obadiah 3).

T

How Then Shall We Live?

Edom's mistreatment of Israel stemmed from its unchecked anger and stubborn refusal to forgive the sin of Jacob, Israel's ancestor. Retaliation and revenge became a way of life for the Edomites. Obadiah reminds us of the truth that God will hold us accountable for our inhospitable and unloving attitudes toward others in our social and familial relationships. The kingdom of God is a kingdom of compassionate and gracious living. He will establish that kingdom through His righteous judgment of sinners. Revelation echoes this conviction: "The kingdom of the world has become the kingdom of our Lord and of his Christ, and he will reign for ever and ever" (Revelation 11:15).

Summary Statements

- Hosea compared God to a forgiving and loving husband and father.
- God's judgment was upon Israel for breaking the covenant with God.
- Hosea called the nation to repent and to seek restoration and healing from God.
- Joel used the imagery of a locust attack and drought to convey the intensity of the coming judgment.
- Joel anticipated the spiritual restoration of Israel and the outpouring of God's Spirit on all people.
- Amos described God as the sovereign Judge of all nations.
- Amos called for social justice as the prerequisite for God's acceptance of Israel's worship.
- Amos challenged Israel to seek God as the source of life.
- Obadiah believed that God would ultimately establish His kingdom and bring an end to hatred and pride in the world.

Questions for Reflection

1. Discuss practical ways to show commitment and faithfulness in our relationships to God and to others.
2. Describe God's love, based on Hosea's book.
3. What does "calling upon God's name" mean and what blessings does God bestow on those who call upon His name?
4. Give a list of the major human atrocities in our world in the last 50 years, and discuss what Amos may be saying to us about judgment, justice, and righteousness.
5. What does Obadiah say to us about our unforgiving attitude to others?

Resources for Further Study

Gowan, Donald E. *The Book of Amos: Introduction, Commentary, and Reflections.* Vol. 7 of *The New Interpreter's Bible.* Nashville: Abingdon Press, 1996.

Limburg, James. *Interpretation: A Bible Commentary for Teaching and Preaching: Hosea-Micah.* Louisville, Ky.: John Knox Press, 1988.

Mays, James L. *Amos. The Old Testament Library.* Philadelphia: Westminster Press, 1969.

———. *Hosea. The Old Testament Library.* Philadelphia: Westminster Press, 1969.

31 Jonah, Micah, Nahum, and Habakkuk

Objectives:

Your study of this chapter should help you to:

- Summarize the historical settings of the ministries of Jonah, Micah, Nahum, and Habakkuk.
- Describe the content of the Books of Jonah, Micah, Nahum, and Habakkuk.
- Discuss the major theological teachings of Jonah, Micah, Nahum, and Habakkuk.

Questions to consider as you read:

1. What is your attitude toward those who belong to other races or religious and denominational backgrounds?
2. How do you worship God?
3. How do you handle crises in your life?

Key Words to Understand

Jonah
Gath Hepher
Nineveh
Micah
Moresheth
Theophany
Bethlehem Ephrathah
Nahum
Elkosh
Ashurbanipal
Nabopolassar
Habakkuk
Babylonians

Jonah

Did **Jonah** spent three days and three nights in the belly of the fish? Readers of this unique book often get entangled in the debate over the literalness of Jonah's story. We invite you to hear the message of the book, rather than be concerned with the historicity of certain details in the book that we cannot prove or disprove with certainty.

Jonah's Personal Background

The opening statement (1:1) identifies Jonah as the son of Amittai. According to 2 Kings 14:25, Jonah son of Amittai, a prophet from **Gath Hepher,** prophesied about the restoration of the border of Israel during the reign of Jeroboam II. The village of Gath Hepher was located southwest of the Sea of Galilee. Some scholars think that the writer gave Jonah's name to the main human character of this book. The Gospel of Matthew confirms the authenticity of Jonah as a prophet to **Nineveh** (see 12:41).

Joppa, the port city from which Jonah sailed to Tarshish (1:3).

Setting

The book lacks reference to any event that would help us place Jonah in a particular time in history. Based on 2 Kings 14:25, we may place him in the eighth century, somewhere between 786 and 746 B.C. Scholars have assigned various dates for the writing of the book, ranging from the eighth century to the third century B.C.[1] The book assumes the existence of Nineveh as a great and wicked city. The Babylonians destroyed Nineveh, the capital of Assyria, in 612 B.C. Jonah's ministry seems to have taken place before the rise of Assyria as a powerful empire under Tiglath-pilesar III in the latter part of the eighth century B.C.

Content

The story of Jonah is like a drama with the following scenes:

Scene 1: Jonah Disobeys God (1:1-16)

Scene 2: Jonah in the Belly of the Fish (1:17—2:10)

Scene 3: Jonah Goes to Nineveh (3:1-10)

Scene 4: Jonah's Anger and God's Response (4:1-11)

▉ Jonah Disobeys God (1:1-16)

The book begins with the report of Jonah's disobedience to God's command to go and preach to the city of Nineveh. He traveled to Tarshish by ship, in a direction opposite from Nineveh. The storm at the sea prompted the panic-stricken sailors to cast lots, which identified Jonah as the one responsible for bringing this calamity upon them.

Jonah acknowledged his guilt

and told them that the sea would become calm if they would throw him overboard. With fear and hesitation, they did as Jonah requested. The storm ceased and the sea became calm. The sailors worshiped God.

■ Jonah in the Belly of the Fish (1:17—2:10)

The unexpected happened. A great fish swallowed Jonah. We cannot speculate on the zoological identification of the fish, nor can we discard the narrative as fiction. Jesus described this event as a "sign" to His unbelieving audience (Matthew 12:38-40). In the belly of the fish, Jonah offered a thanksgiving prayer for God's deliverance of his life. He pledged to fulfill the vow he had taken in response to God's salvation. The fish vomited him up after three days and three nights.

■ Jonah Goes to Nineveh (3:1-10)

God's word came to Jonah again with the same command. He went and preached a very short message of judgment. Though it would have taken him three days to travel through the city, he went only a day's journey to deliver his message. Amazingly this pagan city and its citizens responded to his message. The news even reached the palace, and the king issued a decree calling for fasting and prayer throughout the city. God responded to the repentance of the Ninevites with compassion. He canceled His judgment and saved the city from destruction.

■ Jonah's Anger and God's Response (4:1-11)

Nineveh's salvation infuriated Jonah. He admitted that God's

T Jonah's Silence

The story of Jonah ends with God's question to Jonah for which he does not give an answer. Jonah received God's compassionate grace, but he failed to recognize others in the world as deserving the same grace. He was not moved by the marvelous work of God's grace. He was angry and then preoccupied himself with the things that brought comfort to him. When God asked the great question, there was silence—no angry words, no attempt to run away, just a cold silence.

The Book of Jonah invites us to free ourselves from our narrow worldview and prejudicial thinking, and embrace the gospel of Jesus Christ as a gospel for all humanity. "When he [Jesus] saw the crowds, he had compassion on them" (Matthew 9:36). Ministering God's compassionate grace to our sinful world is the only way to break Jonah's silence.

---

compassion and mercy for those who deserve punishment was the reason for his escape to Tarshish. He wished to die, because God changed His mind. Jonah may have been concerned about his reputation as a prophet. The punishment for being a false prophet was death (see Deuteronomy 18:18-22). He went outside the city and waited to see if calamity would come upon it. God provided a vine that gave shade to Jonah from the intense heat. The next day a worm destroyed the vine. Jonah was angry again because of the destruction of the vine.

God responded with a reminder about Jonah's concern over the vine that he did not cultivate or make grow. God asked Jonah if He should not show concern for a people who had no moral discernment. The book ends without an answer from Jonah.

Micah

The prophet **Micah** is well known for his words about God's great requirements of justice, kindness, and a humble walk with God. The Christian tradition is also familiar with Micah's statement about the coming of the Messiah from Bethlehem Ephrathah. In this little book, we also find scathing criticism of injustice and oppression, and the prophetic concern for justice and righteousness in the community of faith.

Micah's Personal Background

Except for the name *Micah* of **Moresheth** (1:1), we know very little about the person of the prophet. His name means "who is like Yahweh?" He came from a town called Moresheth, about 25 miles southwest of Jerusalem. Micah identifies himself as a prophet "filled with power, with the Spirit of the LORD" (3:8) whom God called to declare to Israel her sin and transgression.

There is no consensus on the authorship of the oracles found in the book. The book in its final form is attributed to Micah of Moresheth. However, some scholars think that only some portions of the book belong to Micah. They think that most of chapters 4—7 belong to later times, including late exilic and postexilic period.

Setting

The title statement (1:1) indicates that Micah prophesied during the days of Jotham, Ahaz, and Hezekiah, kings of Judah. We may place his ministry sometime between 742 and 687 B.C. During the trial of Jeremiah, certain elders pointed out that King Hezekiah and Judah sought God's favor when Micah of Moresheth spoke about Zion's destruction (Jeremiah 26:17-19). This text thus confirms the historical setting of his ministry, which includes the reign of King Hezekiah (see 1:1).

Various oracles indicate that Micah prophesied when the society was corrupt and the leadership was guilty of oppression and abuse of power. The powerful in the land not only planned evil but also carried it out. The people held false confidence that God's presence offered them protection and safety. False prophets and corrupt priests misled and caused confusion among people regarding God's requirements. Micah shared the same concerns of other eighth-century prophets (Amos, Hosea, and Isaiah).

Content

Micah's book has the following parts:
1. God's Case Against Samaria and Jerusalem (1:2-16)
2. Judgment on Corrupt Leaders (2:1-13)
3. On True Leadership (3:1-12)
4. Zion's Restoration (4:1—5:4)
5. Defeat of Assyria and Israel's Enemies (5:5-15)
6. God's Lawsuit Against Israel (6:1-16)
7. Micah's Lament and Prayer (7:1-20)

■ God's Case Against Samaria and Jerusalem (1:2-16)

Micah's oracles begin with an announcement that God is the

judge of all humanity. The prophet proclaimed God's appearance **(theophany)**, accompanied by terrible and devastating effect upon the earth. This is the direct consequence of the idolatry of Samaria and Jerusalem. He lamented over the impending destruction and called upon his audience to show signs of grief and sorrow over their loss.

Judgment on Corrupt Leaders (2:1-13)

When disaster comes, the powerful in the land who oppressed and defrauded their powerless victims would be deprived of their wealth. The land was God's gift to His people for them to enjoy as their blessing. Exile would be the consequence for violating their inheritance from God.

False prophets commanded Micah not to prophesy such bad things. They were confident that God would not be angry. The people and their false prophets who prophesied for wine and beer were faced with the punishment of exile from their land.

In the midst of a severe word of judgment, Micah also proclaimed God's plan to save and gather His remnant from their exile. Like a shepherd who gathers his flock, God would bring His people and they would go out under His leadership.

On True Leadership (3:1-12)

The leaders of Israel had perverted justice and committed merciless acts of cruelty against God's people. When the judgment came, though these sinners would call, God would hide His face from them. In the same way, disgrace would come upon the

---

God's Grieving Messenger

Micah was God's grieving messenger. But he refused to give up hope in God's pardon, forgiveness, mercy, and compassion. Micah calls us to have a heart that grieves over the sinfulness of the world. The overwhelming effect of sin may prompt us to withdraw and isolate ourselves from the sinful world. Micah teaches us to bear the burden of sin while detaching ourselves from its power. Jesus "wept over" the city as He approached Jerusalem (Luke 19:41). Judgment is the consequence of sin. But even in judgment, God's grace is at work. Micah invites us to have this hope and confidence.

---

false prophets who preached peace *(shalom)* as a means of livelihood.

The mark of a true prophet is his courage to preach God's word even when his listeners do not want to hear it. Micah was convinced that he was God's prophet, filled with God's Spirit. He was not afraid to declare to the leaders of Israel their sinfulness. On account of their sin, Micah proclaimed that God would destroy Zion and make it a ruined and desolated place.

Zion's Restoration (4:1 — 5:4)

The words of Micah 4:1-3 are also found in Isaiah 2:2-4. Zion would be restored by God, and the nations would come to Zion seeking God's instruction (Torah). Micah said that Judah's exile was God's plan for her salvation. Jerusalem would be under siege and the enemy would remove her king, yet God would restore her former glory. God promised that a ruler would come from a little, insignificant town called **Bethlehem Ephrathah.** This ruler will

A Ruler from Bethlehem

The Gospel writer Matthew understood the birth of Jesus as the fulfillment of Micah 5:2. Micah encouraged the people of his day to face the reality of God's intense and severe punishment without giving up hope in their future salvation. Our sins alienate us from God, the outcome of which is our exile and the withdrawal of God's blessings from our lives. The good news for us is that Christ, the "ruler" from Bethlehem, has come as "our peace"—the source of life and hope for those who live in conflict and hostility, "without hope and without God in the world" (Ephesians 2:1-22).

These ruins of an ancient city in Israel remind us of Micah's words of judgment, "Zion shall be plowed like a field" (3:12).

guide them and will be the source of peace for His people.

Defeat of Assyria and Israel's Enemies (5:5-15)

God's deliverance of the land from the invading army of Assyria is the focus of 5:5-6. Micah saw the rise of various political powers that would bring an end to Assyria. But God would make Israel a blessing and a source of fear in the land of their exile. Verses 10-15 speak of the destruction of the nations that trusted in their own resources and practiced idolatry and divination.

God's Lawsuit Against Israel (6:1-16)

Micah used a lawsuit (legal dispute) genre to convey God's judg-

God's Great Requirement

Our daily walk with God is more important to God than our attempt to make things right with Him through certain religious rituals. Micah invites us to live a life appropriate for God's people. Justice, fairness, equity, covenant loyalty, and faithfulness are important qualities of the Christian life. Life lived in this world should also become a daily walk with God with humility and gratitude. When we live out these qualities, we will find freedom from the nagging questions of our self-worth, the merits of our deeds, and our capacity to save ourselves through our work. The outcome will be trust and reliance on God's forgiving and saving grace.

ment against Israel. The mountains stood as witnesses of this controversy between God and Israel. God wanted to know how and why He had become a burden to His people. He called them to remember their deliverance from Egypt and His guidance in their wilderness journey. Israel responded to God's charges with perplexing and even sarcastic questions about what it would take to please God. Micah responded with a simple answer. What God required from His people was already known to them—live a life showing justice, kindness/covenant loyalty, and humility before God. The prophet announced the utter ruin of Israel because the nation lacked these essential qualities of covenant living.

■ Micah's Lament and Prayer (7:1-20)

The last chapter of the book contains the prophet's expression of grief and sorrow over the sinful condition he witnessed among his people. This chapter also contains the hope of the prophet. The nation was totally corrupt with deceitful neighbors and violence and hatred even within families. Jerusalem, though fallen, would rise again. God would bring her out of her dark days into light to show His justice before the nations. Micah concluded his oracles with a prayer for God to restore Israel as her divine Shepherd. He affirmed his faith in God as an incomparable God, forgiving and compassionate, the God who casts the sins of His people "into the depths of the sea" (7:19). Micah was confident that God would remain true to His covenant with Israel's ancestors.

Nahum

Jonah's book showed God as a compassionate God to the people of Nineveh, who repented when they heard the message about their judgment. In Nahum's book, we see another portrait of Nineveh and God's response to cruelty and violence in the world.

Nahum's Personal Background

We have little knowledge about the person **Nahum.** The name appears in the introduction to the book. This name is also found in Luke's Gospel as the name of an ancestor of Jesus (3:25). The name means "consolation" or "comforter." The prophet is called the Elkoshite. The exact location of **Elkosh** is not known.[2] Some scholars identify Elkosh with the original site of Capernaum (which means "the village of Nahum"), located on the northwest corner of the Sea of Galilee. The message of the book offers comfort to Judah. This has led many scholars to think that Nahum was from Judah.

The ruins of a 4th century A.D. synagogue in Capernaum. Capernaum (known as Kaphar Nahum, meaning the "village of Nahum") may have been the place of Nahum's birth or ministry.

Setting

The message of the book, which is a prediction about the impending doom of Nineveh, leads us to think that Nahum gave his oracle during the Assyrian domination of Judah (3:18). Scholars connect the description of the capture of Thebes [No Amon in Hebrew] (vv. 8-10) with the Assyrian invasion of Thebes, the capital of Egypt, by **Ashurbanipal** in 663 B.C. Assyria's power declined after Ashurbanipal's death (627 B.C.). The Neo-Babylonian Empire emerged as a major player in international politics under **Nabopolassar** (625-605 B.C.). Nineveh, the object of Nahum's judgment speeches, was destroyed by the combined forces of Babylonians, Medes, and Scythians in 612 B.C. Nahum's oracle against Nineveh belongs to this period of sharp turns of events in history. We may date his ministry to sometime between 663 B.C. and 612 B.C.

Content

The Book of Nahum can be divided into the following sections:
  1. God's Wrath and Goodness (1:2-15)
  2. Get Ready for Battle (2:1-13)
  3. Woe to the City of Blood (3:1-19)

■ God's Wrath and Goodness (1:2-15)

The book begins with an announcement about God's vengeance and His power as the Creator to carry out His wrath. Those who plot evil against God cannot hope to succeed in their plan. He will destroy Nineveh without leaving anyone to carry on its name (v. 14). However, the faithful have no reason to fear. They can depend on the faithfulness of God. He would deliver Judah from the oppressor. Nahum summoned Judah to look and see "the feet of one who brings good news, who proclaims peace" to its citizens (v. 15).

■ Get Ready for Battle (2:1-13)

Nahum warned Nineveh to prepare for battle because God was sending an army city to destroy it. Using military language and metaphors, he described the appearance of the invading army (vv. 3-4). The Ninevites may put forth their best effort to stop the invaders, but the invaders would plunder the city and exile the people. The strength of Assyria will be broken and crushed because God is against that nation (vv. 11-13).

God and Nineveh

We find in Nahum a sharp change in God's dealing with Nineveh. The compassionate God of the Book of Jonah is portrayed here as a God of wrath and vengeance. His plan is to wipe out Nineveh from the face of the earth. Nineveh stands for the violent people in the world. God will deal with them according to His ways of judgment. But He will be a refuge to those who suffer violence and evil at the hands of God's enemies. This is the comfort Nahum proclaims to us today.

■ Woe to the City of Blood (3:1-19)

Nahum said that evil and misfortune awaited the Ninevites. The city known for its bloodshed and plunder will be filled with dead bodies. God will reveal its shame and filth. The city will be in ruins, and no one will mourn for it. Nineveh will suffer the fate of Thebes, a city that once thought it was protected and defended by the Nile. The troops of Nineveh will be helpless and powerless to protect the city from the impending siege. The book ends with a message to Assyria's king that he will suffer a fatal injury. Those whom he oppressed without mercy will rejoice at his fall.

Habakkuk

This little book has been a source of inspiration for millions of believers. Many have found in the courageous faith of **Habakkuk** a challenge to go on trusting God in the midst of severe adversities and trials in life (see 3:17-19). The prophet's words, "the righteous will live by his faith" (2:4), became the cornerstone for the apostle Paul's teaching on justification by faith (Romans 1:17; Galatians 3:11).

Habakkuk's Personal Background

The book contains no information on the personal background of Habakkuk. His name appears in 1:1 and 3:1. In both texts he is identified by the title "prophet." His name is also found in the Akkadian language as a word for a garden plant. This has prompted some scholars to think that he was a non-Israelite who had adopted the Jewish faith.[3] Gowan proposes that Habakkuk may have been a Temple prophet who gave oracles and composed songs for worship in the Jerusalem Temple.[4]

Setting

The book lacks specific references to events or persons. The opening verses indicate a widespread growth of wickedness and violence and the total breakdown of law and justice in the land (1:1-4). The phrase "I am raising up the Babylonians" (v. 6) helps us place the book in the seventh century B.C. Most scholars think that the **Babylonians** refer to the powerful Neo-Babylonian Empire, which gained control of the Syria-Palestine region around 605 B.C. Like his contemporary Jeremiah, the prophet Habakkuk saw the Babylonian invasion as God's judgment against Judah.

Content

The Book of Habakkuk can be divided into the following parts:
1. Habakkuk's Complaint (1:1—2:1)
2. The Answer (2:2-4)
3. Woe to the Oppressor (2:5-20)
4. Habakkuk's Prayer (3:1-19)

■ Habakkuk's Complaint (1:1—2:1)

Habakkuk lived during a time of widespread growth of wickedness among the people of God. He saw violence and destruction all around him. Habakkuk complained to God against such atrocities and expressed his frus-

T

"How Long, O LORD?"

Habakkuk's question, "How long, O LORD?" is a legitimate expression of faith because God is a good and just God. Such questions and expressions of our inner agony affirm our faith in God, who alone is the source of strength and help to the poor and the hurting people in the world. He is sovereign, and He will not allow evil to triumph over His kingdom. Habakkuk challenges us to speak to God passionately about the pain, oppression, violence, and injustice in the world today.

The Coming of God

God did not solve Habakkuk's crisis; neither did He give any comforting words. If things are only going to get worse, what good is God in our life? What good is our religious faith? The comfort we find in this book is that God came. God came to Habakkuk in the midst of his complaints and crisis of faith. That coming of God, which happens again and again in this book, was the real divine answer. God's coming is also our comfort in the midst of trouble-filled lives.

A watchtower. Habakkuk said he would stand and watch for God's word to come (2:1).

tration. He thought God permitted such things to take place because he saw no evidence of God's judgment upon the wicked.

God's response to Habakkuk was that He was "raising up the Babylonians" (v. 6), a more ruthless and violent people than the people of Judah. Habakkuk realized that the Babylonians would bring God's judgment against Judah. However, he did not understand why the holy and morally pure God would use a wicked nation to punish Judah, though it deserved judgment. He asked why God remains silent when the wicked destroy the righteous. Habakkuk decided to take his stand like a watchman and wait for God's answer to come.

■ The Answer (2:2-4)

God's answer to Habakkuk contained the instruction to "write down the revelation" ("vision" in NRSV) so that it may be made

> T
>
> ## Habakkuk's Triumphant Faith
>
> Habakkuk was determined to live a triumphant life though evil continued to increase in his world. His resolve was not just to "hang in there somehow" but rather to live an active, meaningful, and productive life. He knew that God would faithfully carry out His plans. Living a faithful life through uncertain and difficult times is a mark of righteousness in relationship with God. Centuries later Paul quoted Habakkuk: "The righteous will live by faith" (Romans 1:17).

public to the people by prophetic messengers (2:2). The "revelation" is God's answer. It has an appointed time for its fulfillment. In the meantime, Habakkuk must model righteousness by waiting for the fulfillment of God's word and by being faithful to God.

■ Woe to the Oppressor (2:5-20)

Habakkuk pronounced a series of "woe" oracles against the Babylonian Empire. The prophet spoke words of judgment against the wicked Babylonians, who built their empire by stealing, extortion, plunder, bloodshed, and violence.

■ Habakkuk's Prayer (3:1-19)

The last chapter is like a psalm, with a title and direction to the director of music (vv. 1, 19). This chapter is for the most part an elaborate description of God's appearance **(theophany)**. Some scholars view this chapter as an apocalyptic hymn added by later editors of the book.[5] We regard this chapter as Habakkuk's own composition that gives the book a fitting conclusion.[6]

The prophet begins with a prayer followed by the description of God's majesty and splendor as a mighty and delivering warrior God. The prophet saw God's own personal visitation to destroy the forces of evil as the answer to his questions about the problem of evil and injustice in the world. The vision of God's coming gave Habakkuk the impetus to go on living his life with patience and hope in the certainty of God's word. More than that, it challenged him to find joy and comfort in his Savior God, though he knew that forces of evil were about to viciously rampage his country and destroy everything in the land.

As far as we know, life continued to be difficult and uncertain for Habakkuk. But God came again, and he experienced God's faithful presence. God's faithful presence with us and in us also enables us to face the difficulties of life with triumph and joy. Such joy is the outcome of a relationship founded on the conviction that "neither death nor life . . . nor anything else in all creation, will be able to separate us from the love of God that is in Christ Jesus our Lord" (Romans 8:38-39).

Summary Statements

- Jonah went to Nineveh after his attempt to escape God's call did not succeed, and he reluctantly fulfilled his mission.
- God showed compassion when the Ninevites repented of their wickedness.
- Micah proclaimed Zion's judgment and restoration, and the coming of a ruler from Bethlehem as the shepherd of God's people.
- Micah summed up worship as doing justice, loving kindness, and walking humbly with God.
- Nahum proclaimed God's judgment upon Nineveh, and salvation to Judah.
- Habakkuk, though he complained to God about the growth of wickedness, believed that God would bring an end to all evil.
- Habakkuk rejoiced in God in the midst of intense calamity that came upon Judah.

Questions for Reflection

1. Discuss meaningful ways to show God's concern for the world under judgment because of sin and wickedness.
2. Compare and contrast worship during Micah's time and our present-day worship. What would Micah say about the contemporary forms of Christian worship?
3. Do we have the right to bring judgment upon those who are God's enemies? Explain your answer.
4. What should a Christian do in a world that seems to be overtaken by the power of violence and wickedness? Illustrate your answer using Habakkuk's life.

Resources for Further Study

Allen, Leslie C. *The Books of Joel, Obadiah, Jonah, and Micah. The New International Commentary on the Old Testament*. Grand Rapids: Eerdmans, 1976.

Gowan, Donald L. *The Triumphant Faith in Habakkuk*. Atlanta: John Knox Press, 1976.

Mays, James L. *Micah: A Commentary. The Old Testament Library*. Philadelphia: Westminster Press, 1976.

Smith, Ralph L. *Micah—Malachi. Word Biblical Commentary*. Waco: Word Books, 1984.

32 | Zephaniah, Haggai, Zechariah, and Malachi

bjectives:

Your study of this chapter should help you to:

- Summarize the historical settings of the ministries of Zephaniah, Haggai, Zechariah, and Malachi.
- Describe the content of the Books of Zephaniah, Haggai, Zechariah, and Malachi.
- Discuss the theological teachings of Zephaniah, Haggai, Zechariah, and Malachi.

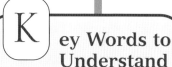ey Words to Understand

Zephaniah
Cushi
Haggai
Darius the Great
Zerubbabel
Joshua
Zechariah
The LORD of Hosts
Apocalyptic
Burden
The Messiah
Holiness
Malachi
Imagined disputation

Questions to consider as you read:

1. Why do we find in the Old Testament a great emphasis on God's universal judgment?

2. Why do people show a great deal of interest in building churches?

3. Does God expect people to contribute to His kingdom work even though they are struggling financially?

4. How does one regain a sense of passion for God when religious activities become boring?

Zephaniah

Zephaniah's Personal Background

The title statement introduces **Zephaniah** as the son of **Cushi**. The genealogy that follows traces his ancestry to Hezekiah. Some scholars identify this individual as King Hezekiah. That would place him as a member of the Davidic royal family and an influential member of the Jerusalem aristocracy. Cushi means "Ethiopian," which also suggests an African heritage for the prophet. The Book of Jeremiah mentions a priest by the name Zephaniah on several occasions (Jeremiah 21:1; 29:25, 29; 37:3; 52:24) as an important person and a messenger of King Zedekiah to Jeremiah. Some scholars identify this priest as Zephaniah the prophet.[1] The name *Zephaniah* means "Yahweh hides/protects."

Setting

The opening verse (1:1) indicates that Zephaniah prophesied during the reign of Josiah king of Judah (640-609 B.C.). The precise date of Zephaniah's prophetic ministry is not known. Some scholars think that he prophesied before 622/621 B.C., while others place him after that date. Zephaniah's oracle against Assyria's capital Nineveh indicates that he prophesied before the fall of Nineveh in 612 B.C. Again, a date before 622 B.C. seems more logical since we find strong words of judgment against those who were worshipers of Baal and other pagan gods (1:4-13).[2] That would mean Zephaniah's ministry coincided with the early days of Jeremiah's ministry, which began in 627 B.C.

Content

The following is an outline of the Book of Zephaniah:

1. The Day of the LORD (1:1—2:3)
2. Oracles Against the Nations (2:4-15)
3. Against Jerusalem (3:1-8)
4. Salvation to All (3:9-20)

■ The Day of the LORD (1:1—2:3)

The introductory oracle focuses on the theme of God's judgment of everything on the entire earth. Everything on earth will be swept away by God's judgment. The language here indicates the reversal of the creative acts of Genesis 1. This is followed by specific charges of idolatry and apostasy against the citizens of Judah.

Zephaniah spoke of the "day of the LORD" as "the day of the LORD's sacrifice," using the language of the ritual of worship. The worshiping community that paid homage to foreign gods and their cult in the Temple will be the sacrificial victim. On the day of judgment, God will come like a warrior. The prophet invited the sinful nation, and particularly the "humble of the land," to seek God. He expressed the hope that seeking God through righteousness and humility would perhaps prompt God to spare them from ruin and destruction.

■ Oracles Against the Nations (2:4-15)

Zephaniah pronounced judgments against Philistia, Moab, Ammon, Cush, and Assyria. These nations would be judged because of their hostility toward God and His people of Judah.

■ Against Jerusalem (3:1-8)

Zephaniah labeled Jerusalem a city of oppression, rebellion, and defilement, a city where there is no evidence of covenant relationship with God. The inhabitants of the city and the leadership failed to recognize God's justice at work among them. Therefore, God would destroy not only Judah but also the nations, because the people of God had become like the people of the world.

■ Salvation to All (3:9-20)

Zephaniah concluded his oracles with the promise that God would "purify the lips of the peoples" (v. 9) and enable them to call upon His name. Here we find the hope that the people who were once the object of God's wrath would find favor and receive salvation. God would restore Jerusalem, and the remnant would experience God's presence and love.

Haggai

What can you do to get people motivated to work for God's kingdom? We hear this question asked often by leaders of our churches. **Haggai** faced this challenge during the early part of the postexilic period. His ministry lasted only for a few months, but he knew how to get people excited about God's work.

Haggai's Personal Background

The book does not give any details on Haggai except his identity as a prophet. Jewish tradition holds that he had lived in exile in Babylon and was an old man when he spoke the words of this book. The name *Haggai* means "my feast." He may have been born during one of Israel's annual

> T **Universality of Salvation**
>
> God's plan of salvation is for all of humanity. Long ago, He promised to Abraham that through his family all the families of the earth would receive a blessing (Genesis 12:3). This universality of salvation is an important theme in all the prophets. The promise of salvation includes the promise of His cleansing us from all defilement that would keep us from worshiping God with all our heart, soul, and strength.

festivals. His interest in the Temple rebuilding suggests that he may have belonged to a priestly family.

Haggai dates his messages specifically to the second year of the reign of **Darius the Great,** king of Persia. According to the modern calendar, he gave the oracles between August 29 and December 18, 520 B.C. Though Haggai's recorded ministry lasted less than four months, we assume that he may have spoken other oracles, in addition to those recorded in the book.

Setting

The conquest of Babylon by the Persian king Cyrus paved the way for the exiled Jews to return home from Babylon (see Ezra 1—6). Those who returned home around 538 B.C. laid the foundation of the Temple amid great celebration and optimism. Soon, however, obstacles arose and discouragement set in. Political opposition and poor economic conditions prompted the Jews to discontinue the Temple rebuilding. The people also became busy with building their own homes. The foundation of the Temple remained untouched for about 18 years.

Rebuilding the Temple was a primary concern of Haggai and Zechariah.

The second year of Darius the Great (520 B.C.) was the beginning of a new era of prosperity and stability in the Persian Empire. Haggai perhaps saw the prospect of this period as a great opportunity for his fellow Jews to complete the Temple rebuilding.

Content

Haggai's messages are royal oracles addressed to **Zerubbabel** the governor and **Joshua** the high priest. They are predominantly motivational and encouragement speeches. His message can be outlined as follows:

1. First Message and Response (1:1-15)
2. Second Message (2:1-9)
3. Third and Fourth Messages (2:10-23)

■ First Message and Response (1:1-15)

Haggai's opening message challenged people to ponder their present situation and reevaluate their priorities. Haggai asserted that the current economic reversal was the result of not putting God first. The ruined Temple was a reminder of the people's lack of priority for God. Haggai summoned the people, therefore, to begin honoring God by rebuilding the Temple.

The response of the leaders and people was immediate. They began to work on the Temple. God responded to the efforts of the people with His gracious words of comfort, "I am with you" (v. 13).

■ Second Message (2:1-9)

Soon after the Temple rebuilding started, discouragement set in again. The task was too overwhelming. Resources for building on the scale of Solomon's Temple were simply not available. Haggai encouraged the people with God's word that the glory of the Temple they were building would someday outstrip the glory of Solomon's Temple. This prediction was fulfilled some 500 years later when Jesus, the long-awaited Messiah, graced this very Temple with His presence.

■ Third and Fourth Messages (2:10-23)

In the third message, Haggai told the people that they had reason to be hopeful about the coming crops. Their obedience in rebuilding the Temple would bring blessing from God. The Temple in ruins had defiled the land, and it remained unproductive. The Second Temple initiative opened a new era of God's blessing for the people.

In the fourth message, addressed to Zerubbabel (vv. 20-23), Haggai affirmed the messianic hopes of Israel. As a descendant of

Natural Disaster

Haggai showed a connection between natural disaster and the judgment of God. In the Old Testament, there is a direct link between material prosperity and spiritual vitality. God withholds rain or sends blight when His people are disobedient. It is one way God judges sin.

The Bible does not, however, indicate that every material reversal in life is an outcome of sin. The Book of Job makes it clear that disaster can strike for other reasons. Just as prosperity does not always indicate spirituality (see Matthew 5:45), so disaster does not always indicate God's judgment. Disaster gives the people of God a context in which to examine their relationship to God.

Zechariah

Early Christians found in **Zechariah** an important source for understanding Jesus and the end of human history. The Gospel writers quoted Zechariah more often than any other prophet in order to explain the events of the final week of Jesus' life. As the apostle John wrote the Book of Revelation, he relied heavily upon Zechariah's word pictures to help describe the scenes of his visions.

View of the Temple Mount and the Dome of the Rock.

David, Zerubbabel stood as a symbol of God's designs for a messiah. One day, God would usher in His kingdom on earth in a new way. The Davidic throne would be restored to its rightful heir.

Yahweh Sebaoth

Haggai, Zechariah, and Malachi show a marked preference for the divine name *Yahweh Sebaoth* **("the Lord of Hosts").** Of the 237 occurrences in the Prophets, these prophets punctuate their prophecies 91 times with the term.

The name emphasizes God's power and sovereignty in the world and His heavenly and earthly resources to accomplish His purpose. The prophets used the appellative to remind their audience that God was able to handle any and all situations. Though the sovereignty of God might be questioned because Israel had been humbled by foreign powers, the prophets declared that God was still in control of His world.

Zechariah's Personal Background

Zechariah was a contemporary of Haggai. While Haggai provided the initial motivation for building the Temple, Zechariah was responsible for follow-up. His messages supplied the encouragement needed to continue the project.

Zechariah's name ("the LORD remembers") is a common name in the Bible. Over 20 different people bore this name, including kings of Israel. The book identifies him as "son of Berekiah, the son of Iddo" (1:1, 7). According to Nehemiah 12:4, a priest named Iddo returned to Jerusalem with Zerubbabel. This person may have been Zechariah's grandfather. Zechariah is listed as the head of Iddo's household in Nehemiah 12:16.

Zechariah's priestly perspectives are obvious throughout the book. Also, his message shows his indebtedness to the prophetic tra-

dition, especially to the interests and images of the Book of Ezekiel.

Based on the dates mentioned in the book (1:1, 7; 7:1) we believe that Zechariah was active during 520-518 B.C., when the Temple rebuilding was resumed by the Jews. We do not know how long he carried out his ministry. The later chapters in the book seem to indicate that his prophetic ministry continued for a number years after the Temple's completion in 515 B.C.

Setting

The messages of Zechariah 1—8 came while the Temple was under construction. Zechariah provided continued affirmation and renewing of vision to the community. He reminded them about two things: first, building the Temple was truly worthwhile, and second, that it could be done.

The historical setting for Zechariah 9—14 cannot be easily determined. There are no dates given, and the historical allusions in this section are open to a variety of interpretations. We assume these messages come from sometime after the completion of the Temple. The people seem to have continued their questions of God's adequacy and His purposes for His people.

Content

Zechariah's message can be outlined as follows:

1. Call to Repentance (1:1-6)
2. Eight Visions (1:7—6:8)
3. A Symbolic Act (6:9-15)
4. Joy of the Messianic Age (7:1—8:23)
5. Triumph of the Messianic Age (9:1—14:21)

Authorship of Zechariah

Many scholars have questioned the unity of the Book of Zechariah. Chapters 9—14 do not contain specific dates for the messages. Their content and vocabulary are markedly different from chapters 1—8. Chapters 9—14 (known as Second Zechariah) also show some resemblance to **apocalyptic** writings. Scholars suggest several different authors and dates for the second part of the book.

There is, in fact, much continuity between chapters 1—8 and 9—14. The points of connection are not only thematic but also structural. The book does stand as a cohesive literary unit. For lack of compelling evidence otherwise, it seems reasonable to treat chapters 9—14 as part of Zechariah's work. Perhaps it comes from late in his lifetime, during the first quarter of the fifth century B.C.

■ Call to Repentance (1:1-6)

The book begins by looking at the past before looking into the future. Zechariah reminded the people of the sins of their forefathers and their punishment. He did this to motivate his audience to turn to God.

■ Eight Visions (1:7—6:8)

Zechariah described the main features of the messianic age in a series of eight visions. These features are: God's control of the world, God's care for His people, defeat of His people's enemies, elimination of wickedness, and empowerment of God's leaders. These visions affirmed the legitimacy of rebuilding the Temple and assured its accomplishment.

In the first vision (1:7-17), Zechariah saw horses that patrolled the earth in order to affirm God's sovereignty over His world. God declared His intentions to rebuild Jerusalem and its Temple. The second and third visions (1:18-21 and 2:1-13) focused on judgment upon enemies of God's people and God's plan to dwell in Zion.

Visions four and five (3:1-10 and 4:1-14) emphasized God's provision and empowerment of leadership. Present leaders (Joshua and Zerubbabel) stood for the ideal agent of salvation, the Messiah. God would raise up His servant, "the Branch." God would accomplish His purpose not through the power and might of human beings but by His Spirit.

The sixth and seventh visions (5:1-4 and 5-11) declared God's war on sin. There would be an end to falsehood, thievery, and wickedness. The eighth vision (6:1-8) affirmed God's sovereign rule over His world by pictures of horses roaming the earth. God's Spirit was at rest in all the lands of His enemies.

■ A Symbolic Act (6:9-15)

Zechariah was instructed to make a crown and place it on the head of the high priest Joshua. In so doing, he affirmed the close connection between the political and spiritual realms in Jerusalem. Joshua represented the merging of these roles in the messiah of another era.

■ Joy of the Messianic Age (7:1—8:23)

Chapters 7—8 are a collection of messages that signal the joy that accompanies the new age. Religious leaders questioned whether or not mourning and fasting for the destruction of the Temple should continue. Zechariah first responded by questioning their motive for the fasts. Had they fasted for God or for themselves? He reminded them that the sufferings of exile had been the results of refusal to apply God's laws to real life.

Zechariah affirmed God's care for His people and His presence with them in Jerusalem. Because of this, the fasts would become a source of joy for God's people. Through a word picture, Zechariah presented the hopes of the new age. Nations would express their desire to be joined with the Jews to worship God in Jerusalem.

■ Triumph of the Messianic Age (9:1—14:21)

Zechariah 9—14 takes us beyond the Temple rebuilding project. These chapters expand upon the picture of God's kingdom designs introduced in the first eight chapters. Through apocalyptic lan-

The Mount of Olives. Zechariah said that when the Lord comes, He would stand on the Mount of Olives (14:4).

guage and imageries, the prophet describes here the painful struggles and ultimate triumph of the messianic kingdom.

These chapters contain two evenly balanced sections of material: chapters 9—11 and chapters 12—14. Each section is introduced as a **"burden"** or "oracle" (in Hebrew, *massa'*). This term indicates the sense of obligation the prophet felt when a message from God must be delivered.

The first "burden" (chap. 12) begins by asserting God's ultimate conquest of Israel's enemies and the preservation of the Temple. Then God's messiah would arrive to establish His kingdom and consolidate the victory. God, the Good Shepherd who will bring unity and other blessing to His people,

The Messiah

Zechariah's portrait of **the Messiah** blends concepts found in other prophets. The Messiah will be a conquering Branch from the Davidic line who also will perform priestly roles as a Servant. He will come humbly and in peace and lead his people as a Good Shepherd. He also will suffer rejection before His ultimate triumph. Such a portrait accords well with the life of Jesus. It is not hard to see why early Christians turned to the Book of Zechariah in order to understand their Savior.

Holiness in Zechariah

Zechariah shows a marked interest in **holiness**. Zechariah is the only book in the Bible that uses the term "holy land" as a reference to the land of Israel (2:12).

Most significant, however, is Zechariah's vision of the holy character of the messianic kingdom. In that day, the center of the kingdom, the Temple Mount in Jerusalem, will be called "the Holy Mountain" (8:3). Then holiness will characterize all of life in the Kingdom. Even common cooking pots and bells on horses will be as sacred as the vessels in the Temple (14:20-21). The messianic kingdom will be a holy kingdom, to fit the character of a holy God.

Olive trees that are hundreds of years old. Zechariah saw in his visions two olive trees (4:3).

I · Difficulty of Interpreting Zechariah's Images

Many of Zechariah's images leave the interpreter uncertain about specific historical settings and meanings. Some of the difficulties include identification of the horsemen, the horns, and the craftsmen (chap. 1), and the seven eyes on a stone (3:9). Also, particularly elusive is the interpretation of the three shepherds and the worthless shepherd in chapter 11.

In chapter 4, in one of the most significant visions of the book, the reader is hard pressed to determine the relationship of the various images. How the two olive trees relate to the seven-channel lampstand is unclear in light of the message of the passage. God is the source of power for His projects (v. 6), yet the olive trees that supply oil to the lamp are Joshua and Zerubbabel (v. 14).

This is the nature of eschatological (end-time) material. Often the authors are not interested in locating each image in time and space. They are painting pictures of realities to come without reference to historical setting. They move freely between present and future without clearly signaling transitions. Present experiences pale in significance to future hopes in such literature. This is clearly the case in Zechariah.

will care for the new kingdom. The people would reject the compassion of the shepherd. As a result, judgment will come upon them.

The focus of the second "burden" (chaps. 13—14) is on the final messianic kingdom of God. In the final days, God would conquer the nations and protect Jerusalem. God promised an outpouring of His spirit of grace for His people as they mourn and receive forgiveness for rejecting Him. This section ends with a vision of God's ultimate rule over all the earth. In the messianic age, everyone and everything will be sacred unto God, and all nations will worship the Lord as King.

Malachi

Malachi is the final book of the writing prophets. It serves as an appropriate conclusion to prophetic literature. It recalls once more, in its own unique way, many of the main themes found in other prophetic books.

Malachi's Personal Background

We know very little about Malachi. No family lineage is given,

The Golden Gate, also known as the East Gate of Jerusalem.

and no historical events or political leaders are identified in the book. He is not mentioned elsewhere in the Old Testament.

The name *Malachi* means "my messenger." It is not a typical Hebrew name. Some have suggested that it is simply a general appellative and not a proper name. They feel it should be understood in the same way as the word in 3:1. There, "my messenger" identifies the person who will prepare the way for the coming of the Lord. Yet, the form of 1:1 is typical of introductions to prophetic books. We consider Malachi the prophet's proper name.

Setting

The setting for the ministry of Malachi appears to be very similar to that of Ezra and Nehemiah, around the middle of the fifth century B.C. Whether Malachi preceded Ezra and Nehemiah, followed them, or worked alongside them is difficult to determine. We think his ministry took place around 460 B.C., just prior to the arrival of Ezra.

Members of the Jewish restoration community had grown lax in their worship and practice. The book suggests that the community was faced with issues such as poor spiritual leadership, marriage and divorce practices, injustice, tithing and Sabbath keeping, among other things. Malachi's audience possessed a feeling of hopelessness. Their efforts at religious practice seemed futile to them.

Content

Malachi employs a rhetorical device that may be called **imagined disputation**. This feature, which was employed at times by other prophets, projects an argumentative dialogue between God and the people. The typical pattern is as follows: (1) God states His issue with the people, (2) the people respond with a question, and (3) God responds with a message of challenge.

The book consists of a series of six imagined disputes dealing with different, yet related, issues in the life of the community. They are:

1. Dispute over the Lord's Love (1:1-5)

2. Dispute over Poor Spiritual Leadership (1:6—2:9)

3. Dispute over Breaking Faith (2:10-16)

4. Dispute over Justice in the Land (2:17—3:5)

5. Dispute over Tithes and Offerings (3:6-12)

6. Dispute over Futile Worship (3:13—4:6)

■ Dispute over the Lord's Love (1:1-5)

Malachi's listeners did not believe that God loved them. God responded with an illustration from Israel's past history. God's election of Jacob was an act of love. Israel was still the object of God's love and care. Edom, the descendants of Jacob's brother Esau, had no future. The future that God promises to Jacob's descendants is a display of God's love.

■ Dispute over Poor Spiritual Leadership (1:6—2:9)

Judah's spiritual leaders were responsible for corrupt and substandard worship practices. They dishonored God and violated the covenant He had made with them. Malachi's remedy for half-hearted religion was a commitment to honor God. He said that God should at least receive the honor due a father, a master, or the governor. Malachi challenged the priests and the Levites to honor God so He would be honored among the nations in the world.

■ Dispute over Breaking Faith (2:10-16)

The people's dysfunctional relationship with God produced problems in their relationships with one another. Men were marrying women who worshiped pagan gods and divorcing their Jewish wives with whom they had made a marriage covenant. Malachi said that God hated such unfaithfulness. Such actions showed a breach of covenant commitment. God's people must be people of integrity and fidelity in their most important relationships of life.

■ Dispute over Justice in the Land (2:17—3:5)

The people did not believe God was fair and just, because the wicked seemed to prosper while the righteous suffered. God's response was to declare that someday He would set things straight.

The Messiah would come and bring justice. He would judge everyone like a "refiner's fire" that separates pollutants from the pure silver.

The New Testament writers understood "the messenger" in 3:1 to refer to John the Baptist (Matthew 11:10; Mark 1:2; Luke 7:27). Thus, Jesus was "the Lord you are seeking" and the refiner of His people (Malachi 3:1).

■ Dispute over Tithes and Offerings (3:6-12)

Malachi called the people to repentance. God assured them that if they returned to Him He would return to them. The giving of tithes and offerings was a tangible means of showing that they had turned to God. The tithe was what one owed God, so to withhold it was like robbing Him. Malachi saw a close relationship between giving to God and bless-

Malachi as the Final Book in the Old Testament

Malachi serves as a fitting conclusion to the Prophets, with its emphasis on the role of the prophet as a messenger of God. He sums up the key emphases of the other prophets.

Malachi and other prophets of the Old Testament still speak to us and remind us of our responsibility to God, who has made a covenant with us through Jesus Christ. God's love for us is an indisputable fact. He is intensely interested in the way we maintain our fidelity to Him, the way we worship Him, the way we honor Him through our devotion to Him. He desires from us integrity in our relationship with others. The restoration of relationship with God, which is a key theme in Malachi and other prophets, is now a possibility for us through our faith in Jesus Christ. This is the "good news" that awaits us in the New Testament.

ing in life. Blessing would follow our attentiveness to God.

■ Dispute over Futile Worship (3:13—4:6)

The final dispute is about the people's sense of hopelessness in serving God. They did not see any advantage to being God's people. God's response was to lift their eyes beyond the present circumstances to a future day when justice would be served. Evildoers would be consumed in God's fire of judgment, while those who fear and honor God would know the protecting power of "the sun of righteousness" rising "with healing in its wings" (4:2).

This day would not come unannounced. God promised to send Elijah to prepare for its coming. The New Testament writers identified this forerunner as John the Baptist (Matthew 11:14; 17:12; Mark 9:11-13; Luke 1:17).

Summary Statements

- Zephaniah announced God's judgment on all who are wicked, but salvation and cleansing to those who seek Him.
- Haggai and Zechariah were contemporaries who challenged people to rebuild the Temple.
- Haggai emphasized that rebuilding the Temple would be a sign of putting God first.
- Zechariah told the people that they were participating in the messianic age by rebuilding the Temple and that God would supply all the resources they needed to do it.
- The messianic age is characterized by holiness, joy, and the ultimate triumph of God over evil.
- Malachi challenged people who questioned God's love and had grown lax in their spiritual lives.
- Malachi's remedy for half-hearted religion was a commitment to honor God.

Questions for Reflection

1. Why does building a Temple for God show we are putting Him first in our lives?
2. How does a vision of the messianic age help us deal with the everyday tasks of life?
3. Why is honoring God so important to our spiritual well-being?

Resources for Further Study

Baldwin, Joyce G. *Haggai, Zechariah, Malachi: An Introduction and Commentary. Tyndale Old Testament Commentaries.* Downers Grove, Ill.: InterVarsity Press, 1972.
Bennett, Robert A. *The Book of Zephaniah: Introduction, Commentary, and Reflections.* Vol. 7 of *The New Interpreter's Bible.* Nashville: Abingdon Press, 1996.
March, Eugene W. *The Book of Haggai: Introduction, Commentary, and Reflections.* Vol. 7 of *The New Interpreter's Bible.* Nashville: Abingdon Press, 1996.
Ollenburger, Ben C. *The Book of Zechariah: Introduction, Commentary, and Reflections.* Vol. 7 of *The New Interpreter's Bible.* Nashville: Abingdon Press, 1996.
Smith, Ralph L. *Micah—Malachi. Word Biblical Commentary.* Waco: Word Books, 1984.

18 * Now this man p
ith the reward of iniqu
eadlong, he burst asunt
nd all his bowels gushe
19   And it was know

Appendix

Jewish History from 331 to 63 B.C.

Scholars usually consider around 400 B.C. as the end of the Old Testament history. The period from 400 B.C. to the birth of Jesus is commonly called the intertestamental period. We will give here a brief outline of this era between the Old and New Testaments to prepare the reader for the stories of the New Testament.

With the final defeat of the Persian armies in 331 B.C., a vast region from the Aegean Sea to the Indus River came under the control of Alexander the Great. As a result the character of the Middle East was changed forever. The goal of Alexander's conquest was to bring both political and cultural unity to his world. A student of Aristotle, he was convinced of the superiority of the Greek culture. Each place he conquered he determined to hellenize, that is, to incorporate Greek ideas and ways into the local culture. One important outcome of Alexander's fervor was that Greek became the international language of the Middle East.

At Alexander's death in 323 B.C., his generals fought for control of the vast empire. After the smoke cleared in 301 B.C., Syria and Mesopotamia came under the rule of Seleucus, while Egypt came under Ptolemy's rule. The land of Judah and Samaria served as a buffer zone between the two

kingdoms and, at first, lay within the Ptolemaic Empire.

The center of the Ptolemaic Empire was Alexandria in Egypt. It was a showcase city of Greek culture in every way. Among its population lived a large group of Jews who undertook a translation of the Old Testament into Greek during the middle of the third century B.C. This translation, the Septuagint, provided ready access to the Old Testament books for Greek-speaking people throughout the Mediterranean world.

Under the Ptolemies, Judah was left to carry on with its own cultural traditions. Several cities and persons did adopt Greek ideas and practices, but the traditional worship of Israel's God at the Temple

Coin of Antiochus Epiphanes IV.

H Antiochus Epiphanes IV

The Seleucids' most tyrannical despot was Antiochus Epiphanes IV, who ruled from 175 to 164 B.C. His title Epiphanes suggested that he thought of himself as "god manifest." The Roman historian Polybius, however, may have been more accurate when he nicknamed him Epimanes, meaning "madman."

His reign was filled with war, suspicion, and intrigue on every front. Having failed to conquer Egypt after several bloody attempts, he determined to strengthen his hold on Palestine. In 168 B.C. he attacked Jerusalem on the Sabbath and slaughtered many of its inhabitants. Then, according to 2 Maccabees 6:1, he ordered the Jews "to depart from the laws of God." He set up an altar in the Temple courts and offered a sacrifice to Jupiter. This was "the abomination that desolates" of which Daniel 9:27 and 11:31 (NRSV) speak.

in Jerusalem was left undisturbed. When the Seleucids successfully incorporated Judah into their kingdom in 198 B.C., the state of affairs changed considerably. The Seleucids were much more intentional in their designs to hellenize their empire. A gymnasium and theater appeared in Jerusalem along with other indicators of increased hellenization. Eventually, in 168 B.C., the Seleucid emperor Antiochus IV outlawed the worship and practices of Judaism and used the Jerusalem Temple for sacrifices to Jupiter.

The Seleucid policy toward Judaism provoked the Maccabean revolt. Mattathias, a priest who had retreated from Jerusalem, lived in a small village about 20 miles northwest of Jerusalem. He attacked and killed a Greek soldier who came into the village and demanded pagan sacrifices. Subsequently, Mattathias and his five

sons (John, Simon, Judas, Eleazer, and Jonathan) escaped into the hills of Judea. Other Jewish rebels soon joined them. From the hills, they began guerilla war against the Greek garrisons. Mattathias died in the battle, and soon Judas became the leader. He became known by the nickname Maccabaeus—"the hammer"—because he hammered away the Greek soldiers. Later the whole family became known as the Maccabees. The Jewish rebels were able to oust the Seleucid troops and gain independence for Jerusalem and its surrounding areas. In 164 B.C. the Maccabean forces recaptured Jerusalem and the Temple. They cleansed and rededicated the Temple to the worship of Israel's God once again. This event is still commemorated annually at the Feast of Lights, or Hanukkah.

In the continuing battle, Eleazer and Judas were killed. Jonathan, who succeeded him, became the high priest and governor of Judea. However, later the Greek army killed him while he was on a mission of diplomacy with Syria. Simon took over the leadership, and he was able to unify the various elements within Judaism. In 140 B.C. he became the high priest and ethnarch of the Jews. This marked the beginning of the Hasmonean dynasty that ruled the Jews until 63 B.C. Different successors gradually expanded the borders of the state, including the regions of Galilee, Idumea, and Moab. Suspicion and intrigue marked the Hasmonean rulers as each in turn sought more power and prestige. This eventually led to the downfall of their fragile kingdom.

Following the death of the Hasmonean ruler Salome Alexandra, factions backing each of her two sons vied for control of the state. Both finally called upon the Romans to intervene and back their side of the dispute. Pompey, who had been consolidating Roman rule in Syria, moved in with his troops, and Judah no longer was free to rule itself. He appointed Hyrcannus II to administer the area under Roman guidance. The real power behind Hyrcannus was an Idumean by the name of Antipater. It was Antipater's son Herod who eventually ruled the land with an iron fist and brought stability to the region just prior to the birth of Jesus Christ.

The Greek period produced some important developments within Judaism. To counteract the negative influences that sometimes accompanied hellenization, a grouped called the Hasidim emerged. They championed the call to return to the standards of Mosaic laws. An outgrowth of the group is met later on in the New Testament in the form of the Pharisees. Another reactionary group was the Essenes. These people moved out to the Judean desert in protest of the corruption in the Jerusalem Temple brought on by the Hasmoneans. One such group located near the Dead Sea at Qumran made copies of Old Testament books and placed them in caves for storage. These scrolls, known as the Dead Sea Scrolls, were discovered in A.D. 1948.

A third development in Judaism during this time was a focus upon apocalyptic literature. This kind of literature saw the hopes of God's people more in the world to come than in the present age. Inspired by books of Old Testament prophets like Ezekiel and Zechariah, these works were especially meaningful during times of national crisis, such as the Maccabean revolt. Interest in this kind of literature continued on into the New Testament era and provided a background for Christians to understand the person of Jesus.

Conclusion

We have traveled with the people of Israel from the beginning of their existence to the decades before the birth of Jesus of Nazareth. In Israel's history and in God's dealings with humanity as a whole, we saw again and again His grace at work. God's gracious purpose of His call of Abraham was to bring a blessing to all humanity through the family of Abraham. But we find the children of Abraham themselves in crisis and turmoil, living with unfulfilled dreams and without any sense of their mission in the world. Judea was once again a province under a foreign power. Different religious factions within Judaism emerged with different perspectives about Israel's destiny in the world. It was into this setting of foreign political domination, conflict and crisis within Judaism, as well as despair and hopelessness among God's people that God sent His Son Jesus. This is the story of the New Testament.

Notes

Chapter 1

1. For further understanding of Israel's understanding of time and history, see G. Von Rad, *Old Testament Theology,* vol. 2, trans. D. M. G. Stalker (New York: Harper and Row Publishers, 1965), 99-112.

2. For a Wesleyan understanding of the inspiration of Scripture, see H. Ray Dunning, *Grace, Faith, and Holiness* (Kansas City: Beacon Hill Press of Kansas City, 1988), 65-73.

Chapter 2

1. See John J. Collins, "Dead Sea Scrolls," vol. 2, *The Anchor Bible Dictionary* (New York: Doubleday, 1992), 85-101. Hereafter abbreviated ABD.

2. For an excellent survey of the history of the transmission of the Old Testament text, see Shemaryahu Talmon, "The Old Testament Text," in *Qumran and the History of the Biblical Text,* ed. Frank M. Cross and Shemaryahu Talmon (Cambridge, Mass.: Harvard University Press, 1975), 1-41.

3. See Harry Y. Gamble, "Canon," vol. 1, ABD, 837-61.

Chapter 3

1. Herbert Danby, *The Mishna: Translated from the Hebrew with Introduction and Brief Explanatory Notes* (London: Oxford University Press, 1933), 103, 112.

2. "The First Epistle of Clement" in *The Apostolic Fathers with Justin Martyr and Irenaeus: An American Edition,* ed. A. Cleveland Coxe (reprint ed., Peabody, Mass.: Hendrickson Publishers, 1995), 8.

3. For a survey, see Edgar Krentz, *The Historical-Critical Method* (Philadelphia: Fortress Press, 1975).

4. "The Epistle of Barnabas" in *Apostolic Fathers,* 142.

5. For a survey, see Norman Habel, *Literary Criticism of the Old Testament* (Philadelphia: Fortress Press, 1971).

6. For a good survey, see Gene M. Tucker, *Form Criticism of the Old Testament* (Philadelphia: Fortress Press, 1971).

7. Hermann Gunkel, *The Psalms: A Form Critical Introduction,* trans. Thomas M. Horner (Philadelphia: Fortress Press, 1967).

8. Martin Dibelius, *From Tradition to Gospel* (New York: Charles Scribner's Sons, 1965). Rudolph Bultmann, *The History of the Synoptic Tradition* (New York: Harper and Row, 1963).

9. See Norman Perrin, *What Is Redaction Criticism?* (Philadelphia: Fortress Press, 1969).

10. See J. A. Sanders, *Canon and Community: A Guide to Canonical Criticism* (Philadelphia: Fortress Press, 1984).

Chapter 4

1. See "Akkadian Myths and Epics," trans. E. A. Speiser, in James B. Pritchard, *Ancient Near Eastern Texts Relating to the Old Testament,* 3rd ed. (Princeton, N.J.: Princeton University Press, 1969), 68. Hereafter abbreviated ANET. Reprinted by permission of Princeton University Press.

Chapter 5

1. For a full text of this epic, see Pritchard, ANET, 60-72.

2. For a survey of the various views on the week of creation, see Henri Blocher, *In the Beginning: The Opening Chapters of Genesis* (Downer's Grove, Ill.: InterVarsity Press, 1984), 39-59.

3. For a theological understanding of the image of God, see Dunning, *Grace, Faith, and Holiness,* 150-61.

4. See the full text of this epic in Pritchard, ANET, 72-99.

Chapter 6

1. See Gerhard Von Rad, *Deuteronomy: A Commentary,* trans. Dorothea Barton (Philadelphia: Westminster Press, 1966), 84.

Chapter 8

1. See Victor Hamilton, *Handbook on the Pentateuch* (Grand Rapids: Baker Book House, 1982), 165-66, for a possible connection between plagues 1, 2, 4, 5, 7, 8, 9, 10, and various gods of Egypt.

2. See Childs, *Exodus,* 232-37 for an excellent summary of the history of interpretation of the Exodus-Crossing of the Sea in the Christian and Jewish writings.

Chapter 9

1. See the Code of Hammurabi in Pritchard, ANET, 163-80. Reprinted by permission of Princeton University Press.

2. Scholars are divided on the issue of the parallels between the Sinai covenant and the ancient Hittite treaties. See D. J. McCarthy, *Treaty and Covenant* (Rome, 1963), for a survey of the debate.

3. See Hamilton, *Handbook,* 213-21, for an analysis of the laws of the covenant code and the nonbiblical legal codes.

Chapter 10

1. Yehezkel Kaufmann, *The Religion of Israel* (Chicago: University of Chicago Press, 1960) and J. Milgrom, *The Anchor Bible: Leviticus 1—16* (New York: Doubleday, 1991) are among the advocates of the early seventh century B.C. origin of the Book of Leviticus.

2. See Baruch Levine's "The Meaning of Dietary Laws" in *The JPS Torah Commentary: Leviticus* (Philadelphia: Jewish Publication Society, 1989), 243-44.

3. Jacob Milgrom presents 26 strong reasons and 23 supportive ones for his assessment that the priestly materials in the book belong to a period much earlier than the postexilic period. See *The JPS Torah Commentary: Numbers* (Philadelphia: Jewish Publication Society, 1989), xxxii-xxxv.

Chapter 11

1. For a detailed discussion in support of a date much earlier than the seventh century B.C., see P. C. Craigie, *The Book of Deuteronomy: The New International Commentary on the Old Testament* (Grand Rapids: Wm. B. Eerdmans Publishing Company, 1976), 24-32.

Chapter 12

1. Martin Noth is responsible for introducing much of the concept of the Deuteronomistic history into the discussion of biblical studies. The suggestion of a preexilic and an exilic edition of the Deuteronomistic history was made by Frank Moore Cross in *Canaanite Myth and Hebrew Epic: Essays in the History of the Religion of Israel* (Cambridge, Mass.: Harvard University, 1973). A briefer overview of the development of the Deuteronomistic history is provided more recently by William J. Doorly, *Obsession with Justice: The Story of the Deuteronomists* (New York: Paulist Press, 1994).

2. See the chronology in Edwin R. Thiele, *The Mysterious Numbers of the Hebrew Kings: A Reconstruction of the Chronology of the Kingdom of Israel and Judah,* Revised edition (Grand Rapids: Eerdmans, 1965), and Albright, William F., *From Stone Age to Christianity* (New York: Doubleday, 1957).

3. See Martin Noth, *The History of Israel* (New York: Harper and Brothers, 1960), 68-84; and M. Weippert, *"Canaan, Conquest and Settlement of,"* supp. vol., *Interpreter's Dictionary of the Bible* (Nashville: Abingdon Press, 1976), 125-30.

4. Norman Gottwald, *The Hebrew Bible: A Socio-Literary Introduction* (Philadelphia: Fortress Press, 1985), 272-76. See also Gottwald's *Tribes of Yahweh: A Sociology of the Religion of Israel, 1250-1050 B.C.E.* (Maryknoll, N.Y.: Orbis Books, 1981).

5. For a full text of this "Hymn of Victory of Mer-ne-Ptah" (also known as the "Israel Stela"), see Pritchard, ANET, 376-78.

Chapter 13

1. See John Day, "Canaan, Religion of" in vol. 1, ABD, 831-37.

Chapter 15

1. See R. W. Corney, "Zadok the Priest," vol. 4, in the *Interpreter's Dictionary of the Bible* (Nashville: Abingdon Press, 1962), 928-29, for various proposals on Zadok's place in Israel's history.

Chapter 16

1. According to 1 Kings 9:16, Pharaoh of Egypt gave Gezer as a wedding gift to his daughter whom he gave as a wife to Solomon. Bright thinks that Pharaoh was attempting to make Solomon an ally by this unusual marriage relation, since Egyptian Pharaohs were not known for giving their daughters in marriage to foreign kings. See John Bright, *A History of Israel,* 4th ed. (Louisville, Ky.: John Knox Press, 2000), 212.

2. See the full text of this Moabite Stone inscription in Pritchard, ANET, 320-21.

3. This chronology is based on John Bright's reconstruction of Israel's history. See Bright's Chronological Charts in his *A History of Israel* cited above. Other chronological schemes present the division of the kingdom at 930 B.C. See Edwin R. Thiele, *The Mysterious Numbers of the Hebrew Kings: A Reconstruction of the Chronology of the Kingdoms of Israel and Judah* (Grand Rapids: Eerdmans, 1965).

Chapter 17

1. For an excellent evaluation of the history of Israel and Judah narrated in 2 Kings, see Bright, 248-339.

2. See Bright's Chronological Charts in the appendix of *A History of Israel.*

3. Pritchard, ANET, 287-88. Reprinted by permission of Princeton University Press.

Chapter 18

1. For a good summary of the situation of the Jews in Judah and in Babylon, see Peter R. Ackroyd, *Exile and Restoration: A Study of Hebrew Thought of the Sixth Century B.C.* (Philadelphia: Westminster Press, 1968), 20-38.

2. Scholars are divided on the date of the final destruction of Jerusalem by the Babylonian army. Some place the event in March of 586 B.C.

3. See Pritchard, ANET, 316. Reprinted by permission of Princeton University Press.

Chapter 19

1. See R. K. Harrison, *Introduction to the Old Testament* (Grand Rapids: Eerdmans, 1969), 1153-57, for a detailed discussion of the authorship and date of Chronicles.

2. For a survey of Old Testament genealogies, see Robert R. Wilson, "Genealogy, Genealogies," in vol. 2, ABD, 929-33.

Chapter 20

1. See Harrison, *Introduction to the Old Testament,* 1145-49, for a detailed study of the date of the ministry of Ezra and Nehemiah.

2. See ibid., 1087-90, for a detailed discussion of the problems of dating and authorship of Esther.

Chapter 21

1. Lowth's lectures on the Sacred Poetry of the Hebrews (1753) showed parallelism as the key feature of Hebrew poetry. Robert Lowth, *Lectures on the Sacred Poetry of the Hebrews,* 2 vols., trans. G. Gregory (1787; reprint, New York: Garland, 1971).

2. See the full text of the *Instructions of Amen-em-Opet* in Pritchard, ANET, 421-24. Reprinted by permission of Princeton University Press.

3. See *The Babylonian Theodicy,* a poem on human suffering in the form of a dialogue between the suffering individual and a friend, in Pritchard, ANET, 601-4.

Chapter 22

1. See the full text of *The Admonitions of Ipuwer* in Pritchard, ANET, 441-44. Reprinted by permission of Princeton University Press.

2. See ANET, 434-37.

3. See ANET, 601-4.

4. See John Hartley's excellent introductory work on literary genre and parallels in his commentary, *The Book of Job: New International Commentary on the Old Testament* (Grand Rapids: Eerdmans, 1988).

5. For a discussion of the date and authorship of Job, see Robert Gordis, *The Book of God and Man: A Study of Job* (Chicago: University of Chicago Press, 1965), 209-18.

Chapter 24

1. Review chapter 21 on wisdom, particularly wisdom in the international context, and Proverbs and the *Instructions of Amen-em-Opet.*

2. See Elizabeth R. Achtemeier, "Righteousness in the OT," vol. 4 of *Interpreter's Dictionary of the Bible* (Nashville: Abingdon Press, 1962), 80-85.

3. See James L. Crenshaw, "Ecclesiastes, Book of," vol. 2, ABD, 271-80.

4. This book represents, according to most scholars, the latest Hebrew in the Bible. Robert Gordis, citing the relationship of the apocryphal book Wisdom of Ben Sirach (Ecclesiasticus) to Qoheleth, proposed a time around 250 B.C. as the date of Qoheleth's composition. Robert Gordis, *Koheleth—The Man and His World* (New York: Schocken Books, 1968), 67.

5. See the Epic of Gilgamesh in Pritchard, ANET, 64. Reprinted by permission of Princeton University Press.

6. For a detailed survey of the history of the interpretation of Song of Songs see Marvin H. Pope, *Song of Songs: A New Translation with Introduction and Commentary,* in *The Anchor Bible* (New York: Doubleday, 1977), 89-229.

7. Ibid., 210.

Chapter 25

1. For a general survey of prophets and prophecy outside of Israel, see J. Lindblom, *Prophecy in Ancient Israel* (Philadelphia: Fortress Press, 1973), 6-46; for a detailed discussion of prophecy in the ancient Near East, see H. B. Huffmon, "Prophecy in the Ancient Near East," supp. vol., *Interpreter's Dictionary of the Bible* (Nashville: Abingdon Press, 1976), 697-700. See James B. Pritchard (ed.), ANET, for translations of the prophetic materials from Egypt and Mesopotamia.

2. This classification is based on the work of Paul D. Hanson, *The Dawn of Apocalyptic* (Philadelphia: Fortress Press, 1975), in which he argues that apocalyptic eschatology in Israel emerged out of prophetic eschatology.

3. For an excellent study of the various forms of prophetic speech, see Claus Westermann, *Basic Forms of Prophetic Speech* (Philadelphia: Westminster Press, 1967).

Chapter 26

1. Christopher R. Seitz gives a good analysis of the theological structure of these chapters in his *Isaiah 1—39: Interpretation* (Louisville: John Knox Press, 1993), 15-18.

2. See Paul D. Hanson, *Isaiah 40—66: Interpretation* (Louisville: John Knox Press, 1995), 1-4, 185-92, for an overview of the possible historical setting and the relation of Isaiah 56—66 to Isaiah 40—55.

3. Hanson maintains the view that the oracles in Isaiah 56—66 reflect inner community struggle; deteriorating social, economic, and religious conditions; and intense polemic against the Zadokite priests who were determined to return to the Temple rituals of the preexilic period. See *Isaiah 40—66,* 185-200.

Chapter 27

1. See the lament texts from ancient Mesopotamia in ANET, 458.

Chapter 28

1. Herbert G. May cites 47 phrases found frequently throughout the book, which indicates that the book comes from a single author. See his commentary, *The Book of Ezekiel,* vol. 6 of *The Interpreter's Bible* (Nashville: Abingdon Press, 1956), 50-51.

2. See various interpretations of these symbolic acts in Ralph H. Alexander, *Ezekiel,* vol. 6, *Expositor's Bible Commentary* (Grand Rapids: Zondervan Publishing House, 1986), 769-71; John B. Taylor, *Ezekiel,* in *Tyndale Old Testament Commentaries* (Downers Grove, Ill.: InterVarsity Press, 1969), 74-85; Walther Eichrodt, *Ezekiel: A Commentary.* Trans. Cosslett Quin (Philadelphia: Westminster Press, 1970), 80-91.

3. For a discussion of the composition of chaps. 8—11, see Eichrodt, *Ezekiel,* 112-19.

4. See a discussion on the various points of contact between Ezekiel 38—48 and Revelation 19—22 and on the interpretation of Ezekiel 40—48 in Alexander, *Ezekiel,* 937-52.

Chapter 29

1. See Leo Oppenheim, *The Interpretation of Dreams in the Ancient Near East* (Philadelphia: American Philosophical Society, 1956) for examples.

Chapter 30

1. See this view expressed by James L. Mays, *Hosea: A Commentary* (Philadelphia: Westminster Press, 1969), 24-25.

2. Donald E. Gowan, *The Book of Amos,* vol. 7 of *The New Interpreter's Bible* (Nashville: Abingdon Press, 1996), 340.

3. See James L. Mays, *Amos: A Commentary* (Philadelphia: Westminster Press, 1974), 2.

4. See Samuel Pagan, *The Book of Obadiah,* vol. 7 of *The New Interpreter's Bible* (Nashville: Abingdon Press, 1996), 436.

Chapter 31

1. See Phyllis Trible, "Jonah," in vol. 7 of *The New Interpreter's Bible* (Nashville: Abingdon Press, 1996), 466, footnote 8 for bibliographic references to various dates for Jonah proposed by scholars.

2. See O. Palmer Robertson, *The Books of Nahum, Habakkuk, and Zephaniah,* in *The New International Commentary on the Old Testament* (Grand Rapids: Wm. B. Eerdmans Publishing Company, 1990), 32, and Ralph L. Smith, *Micah—Malachi,* in *Word Biblical Commentary* (Waco: Word Books, 1984), 63, for various views on the home of Nahum.

3. See Smith, *Micah—Malachi,* 93, for a summary of various legends and views on the identity of Habakkuk.

4. Donald E. Gowan, *The Triumph of Faith in Habakkuk* (Atlanta: John Knox Press, 1976), 14.

5. Theodore Hiebert, *The Book of Habakkuk,* vol. 7 of *The New Interpreter's Bible* (Nashville: Abingdon Press, 1996), 654.

6. See Robertson, *Books of Nahum, Habakkuk, and Zephaniah,* 39.

Chapter 32

1. See Smith, *Micah—Malachi,* 121, for this view proposed by Donald L. Williams in *Journal of Biblical Literature* 82 (1963), 85-88.

2. See Smith, *Micah—Malachi,* 121-23, for an extensive analysis of various proposals for the date of Zephaniah's ministry. He prefers a date around 627 B.C.

Subject Index

Name Index